Thomas Wright

Womankind in Western Europe

From the Earliest Times to the Seventeenth Century

Thomas Wright

Womankind in Western Europe
From the Earliest Times to the Seventeenth Century

ISBN/EAN: 9783337123727

Printed in Europe, USA, Canada, Australia, Japan

Cover: Foto ©Andreas Hilbeck / pixelio.de

More available books at **www.hansebooks.com**

Womankind

In All Ages of Western Europe

by

Thomas Wright

London * Groombridge * & * Sons *

WOMANKIND.

WOMANKIND

IN WESTERN EUROPE

FROM THE EARLIEST TIMES TO THE SEVENTEENTH CENTURY.

By THOMAS WRIGHT, M.A., F.S.A., Hon. M.R.S.L., Etc.,

CORRESPONDING MEMBER OF THE IMPERIAL INSTITUTE OF FRANCE (ACADÉMIE DES INSCRIPTIONS
ET BELLES LETTRES).

LONDON

GROOMBRIDGE AND SONS

PATERNOSTER ROW.

MDCCCLXIX.

F. BENTLEY AND CO., PRINTERS, SHOE LANE, FLEET STREET, LONDON.

THE RIGHT HON. LORD LYTTON,

THE FIRST ENGLISH WRITER OF OUR TIME,

AND THE ONE MOST CAPABLE OF APPRECIATING THESE MATERIALS

FOR THE SOCIAL HISTORY OF OUR FOREFATHERS,

THIS VOLUME

Is Dedicated,

WITH FEELINGS OF SINCERE RESPECT,

BY THE AUTHOR.

PREFACE.

It was not my intention in the following volume to write a philosophical treatise on the character or condition of woman, or to investigate woman's claims or woman's rights. Several attempts have been made to compose a general history of the female sex, but they have too often ended in mere imperfect compilations. I have not ventured upon so wide a field; but I have ventured to believe that a history of the sex in that particular division of mankind to which we ourselves belong would not be unacceptable to the general reader. I have endeavoured, therefore, to trace from sources which are not commonly known, and many of which are not very approachable, the history of Womankind in Western Europe, and to describe the condition, character, and manners of the sex through the various revolutions of Western society. My desire has been to give, as far as possible, a true picture of female life in each particular period, and I have avoided as much as possible all speculative views. In the earlier ages of history, the materials are too scanty to enable us to give more than an imperfect view of the subject, yet they are sufficient to show us the female sex holding a very important position in the world's history, not only in a social point of view, but even in its political agitation and movement. When historical records and literary monuments come to our aid in greater abundance, in the different branches of our race, especially in France and England, we can draw our picture of Woman-kind with far greater accuracy and with far more of detail. When we enter upon the feudal period, this latter class of materials,—literature, and especially the poetry and romances,—presents a vast field for exploration, but one which is little known but to the few who have made it their especial study. I have endeavoured to make as much use of these materials as I could without overloading my book with references and quotations. I am not aware that any writer has previously attempted otherwise than very briefly to give a picture of woman's life in the feudal castle, yet it is that which has contributed probably more than anything else to the formation of her character in modern society.

The period of transition from the old society to the new, from mediæval society to that of modern times, was long and full of troubles, and agitation, and confusion. If we enter into it minutely, the picture revealed to us is by no means so attractive as that of the ages which preceded, and I have therefore treated it more as a sketch; or rather, I may perhaps say, that I have thrown into the picture of feudalism itself as much of it as still remained feudal. Anything like a history of Womankind during the sixteenth century would itself fill a large volume.

I consider that the line of division in Western Europe between the old society and the new, as far as we can make anything like a line, lies through the earlier years of the seventeenth century, the com-mencement of the reign of Louis XIII. in France and that of Charles I. in England. When I entered upon this subject, my idea was to write a complete history of Womankind in the West, and to continue it down to our own time; but I found, as I advanced with it, that I was undertaking a task which, to be carried out properly and completely, would require a much greater extent of research and labour, and a much larger space, than could be given to the present volume. I thought it, therefore, advisable to limit my period, and divide the subject. I have traced as fully as I think the materials would permit, the history of the female sex in Gaul and Britain during the Roman and the Frankish and Anglo-Saxon periods. I have entered at far greater length into the history of the women of the feudal ages, because I believe that, in spite of the richness of the materials, it is but little known to readers in general, and perhaps I may venture to say that it is the period which has been more the subject of my own study than any of the others. I have given, as hinted before, a sketch of the great period of transition, and I have stopped at the line of division I have just laid down, leaving the history of Womankind during modern times to be written at some future period.

The Elizabethan age itself is one of extreme interest in relation to the development of the female character in our own island. With her successor came in the less severe morality of the court of Scotland, which had been much more influenced by French feelings than that of England. Under Charles I. the character of English society became greatly sobered, and the progress of Puritanism was gradually impressing upon it what became its prevailing spirit under the Commonwealth and the Protectorate. The women of this period had far more of plainness and simplicity in their character as well as in their dress than at any of the previous periods, and they displayed a strictness in their lives and manners which passed into a tone of rigidity. French society during this period had gone through none of these changes, though at the heart it had become more sober; but with the second Charles its fashionable vanities and its more objectionable characteristics were largely imported into our island, and influenced very extensively our character. The reign of Charles II. is celebrated in our annals for its vanity and licentiousness. During the seventeenth century the general character of females remained nearly on a level in France, while it was gradually improving in England. In the latter, from time to time, periods occurred in which French influence again prevailed, and we still continued to imitate the costume of France, and to adopt some of her fashionable weaknesses. The terrible revolution which closed the century in France effected a great change in the social character of the period which followed, and exercised an influence even in England, and may be considered as an introduction to the social condition of our own time. In all this there is an abundance of materials for a very important history.

THOMAS WRIGHT.

14, SYDNEY STREET, BROMPTON.

November, 1869.

CONTENTS.

CHAPTER XI.

CHAPTER XII.

CHAPTER XIII.

CHAPTER XIV.

CHAPTER XV.

CHAPTER XVI.

CHAPTER XVII.

CHAPTER XVIII.

CHAPTER XIX.

CHAPTER XX.

CHAPTER XXI.

CHAPTER XXII.

WOMANKIND

IN ALL AGES OF WESTERN EUROPE.

CHAPTER I.

WOMAN IN GAUL AND BRITAIN UNDER THE CELT AND THE ROMAN.

I CONFESS to being one of those who feel a difficulty in believing that intellectual humanity is the mere natural development of an original and
primeval savage. Nor, although there be advocates for such a theory, can
I believe that a savage woman, taking the word "savage" to mean man in
a state, mentally and bodily, which could only fit him to be the companion
of animals, ever gave origin to the gentle and loving qualities, and to those
winning graces, which render dear to us the female portion of the society
among which we live—in other words, that there is any natural affinity
whatever, derived from however remote a period, between Beauty and the
Beast. I believe that the mankind among which we live has no inherent
qualities in possession of which we were not at first created, and that the
greater or less outward display of them, and the form in which they have, at
different periods, shown themselves, have depended entirely upon the circumstances under which man lived. Setting aside the mere question of reproduc-
tion, man and woman were created, I believe, equal—one intended to be the
affectionate and cheering companion to the other, with some peculiarities,
physical rather than mental, which tended to make the one dependent upon

1

and attached to the other. It is in this sense only that we have any right to call Womankind the weaker sex.

But this is a question which I am not now called upon to discuss any farther. Our own modern society has grown out of a gradual amalgamation of different divisions and subdivisions of one great race of mankind, known under their different movements by a variety of names, but especially by those larger denominations of Celts, or of Romans, or of Teutons. My task is to trace, so far as I can, the position and the influence of Womankind through some of these developments. Of course, as we go far back into time, our knowledge on this subject becomes very scant, from want of historical records. The Greeks and Romans, through whom all our knowledge is derived, only knew the different peoples whom we consider as our earlier forefathers, and whom they called barbarians, as men whom they sometimes met as enemies, and they had little opportunity, indeed, for studying their domestic life. The first chapter of a work like this, therefore, must necessarily be imperfect, and can hardly be considered as anything more than an introduction to the story itself.

So far as history throws any light upon the subject, Western, like Central, Europe, appears to have been gradually occupied by successive waves of population, which all spread hitherward from the East. Of the first of these we know very little, and they are of no great importance to our subject. We are ignorant even of the extent to which they had originally occupied Western Europe ; they appear never to have made any great name there, and they seem to have been driven onwards and crushed by the Celts. To the Romans, when they became acquainted with Gaul, the remnant of these peoples was known by the name of Aquitanians, and they are believed to be represented in our time by that very mysterious people, the Basques. Amédée Thierry's idea seems now to be generally adopted, that the Celtic race moved westward in two great successive emigrations. The first of these emigrations belongs to a remote period, of which we cannot fix the date, any more than we can of the second, except that we can be certain that it was at no great distance from what we call, in regard to Western Europe, the historic period. The new Celts drove their predecessors before them still further westward, until they seem to have been represented only, when the Romans came here, by a portion of the inhabitants of the western coast of Gaul and of a part of the British Islands. The subdivisions of the race are of little importance to the present subject. We will consider them all under the general name of Celts.

Under this name, or under that of Gauls (*Galli*), they were well known, in their earlier movements in Eastern and Central Europe, to the Greek and Roman historians. Among other great exploits, they invaded Greece, overran Macedonia and Thessaly, and plundered the temple of Delphi. They entered Asia Minor, exacted tribute from most of the Asiatic states, and actually disposed of the throne of Bithynia, and placed upon it Nicomedes the First. They overran Italy, and burnt Rome. Yet all we know of the domestic condition and manners of this extraordinary people at this early period of their history, for we are going back to the beginning of the third century before Christ, is derived from two or three detached anecdotes, which have been preserved merely because they made a strong impression upon the imaginations of the Greeks and Romans. These will be better understood by one or two preliminary remarks of a general character.

Woman's position, in the earlier ages, was certainly not that given to her by nature, but one which arose out of the primitive forms of society. The earliest form of government was that called patriarchal. When the population was not large, and at the same time scattered over the earth, each head of a family was naturally the ruler over all the other members of the same family; and as he himself acknowledged no superior authority, except in heaven, he possessed absolute power over them, extending to life and death, with the only exception, perhaps, of his wife, for her family had, in disposing of her, reserved a certain right of interference for her protection. Of the males, one only held a marked position as the next successor to the headship; the others were mere dependents upon the head, until, by some arrangement or other, they left the family to form each a family of his own. The females of the family, the daughters of the head, were, if anything, more dependent than the males, because they were looked upon as the weaker sex; they could not create independent families of their own; they were therefore employed in domestic labours, and in supplying the clothes and other necessaries of the whole family. The father sold his daughter in marriage into another family, and disposed of her entirely at his will. Alliances between families were formed, and family hostilities arose, which led to war on a more or less extensive scale; and, to ensure the united action of many families in one cause, a chieftain was necessary, elected, of course, by the whole. This chieftain became a king, and through him kingly power was introduced, and gradually became a permanent institution. Kingly power, in its earlier period, meant war. This great revolution, for it was a great one, affected chiefly the mass, the families in confederation, if we may so express it, and not the members of each family, for the father still preserved the same authority over his sons, and especially over his daughters. Woman, however, did not universally submit to her position. Attempts to form matrimonial alliances according to her own inclinations were continually made, and often with success, and these sometimes led to violent feuds between families or tribes. Moreover, we find her, to judge by individual cases which are the only ones we see in history, constantly aspiring towards a superior position. But of this I have more to say in a subsequent chapter.

When, as the population of the earth increased in numbers, the necessity of expansion compelled races to migrate in search of new homes, and when the migratory parties must of course act under kingly power or chieftainship, the patriarchal authority became, probably, more and more diminished. When we first obtain any knowledge of the different branches of the Gallic race, they had either passed through their great migrations, or were in the midst of them.

The natural effects of migration would be to modify, in some degree, the character of the Celtic women, as they must have had to pass through continual hardships and dangers, which would impress upon them the more masculine characteristics of endurance and courage. According to Strabo (lib. iii. c. 4), the Celtic women, in common with the Scythians and Thracians, were remarkable for their courage. In the Cimbric wars of Marius, about a century before Christ, we find both Teutons and Gauls accompanied to battle by their wives and families. In the great defeat of the Cimbri and Ambrones by that general in the neighbourhood of Aquæ Sextiæ (Aix in Provence), their women, who had been left with the chariots, threw themselves among the fugitives, and, reproaching their husbands with their cowardice, attacked the victors, and saved the confederate Gauls and Teutons from destruction by their valour; and in the second great victory of that war, gained, in the year following, over the Gallic invaders of Italy in the Raudian plain, near Vercelli in Piedmont, the women of the vanquished stoutly defended their chariots long after the flight of their husbands, and, when they saw that further resistance would be in vain, and Marius had refused their petition to be allotted as slaves to the priestesses of the Italian temples, which would have saved their chastity from the outrages of the Roman soldiers, they put their children to death and then slew themselves. At a later period, during the wars of Cæsar in Gaul, at the siege of Avaricum, the Gaulish women prevented their husbands from abandoning the defence of the town, and the assistance and encouragement they gave to them contributed greatly to the defeat of the Romans. Down to the latest period of Gaulish independence, it was the custom of the women to accompany the men in their warlike expeditions.* In the insurrection of Civilis and the momentary empire of the Gauls in the latter half of the first century of the Christian era, we are told by Tacitus that that chieftain, when he marched at the head of his Gauls against the Roman legions, placed in position behind his line of battle his mother and his sisters, and the wives and children of all his soldiers, that they might be an incitement to victory and a shame to those who gave way.†

These qualities of courage and ferocity could only belong to women who were living in the midst of war and strife ; the women, in fact, of tribes in a state of migration, though perhaps we might, from a comparison of other facts, think they were characteristic of the Gallic race more than of any other. They were those traits of character which first struck the minds of the people of a higher degree of civilization with whom they came in temporary contact in their movements, and whose writers have chronicled them rather than their domestic virtues, of which therefore we know little. Yet, if the Celtic women held such a position in presence of the other sex in the battlefield, they can hardly have been the slaves of their husbands at home. The two sexes must have marched in their migrations and in their wars almost, if not quite, on a footing of equality. We learn from the Greek writer Athenæus, that the Celtic women were celebrated for their personal beauty. They had no less a reputation for their chastity; and the philosophic Plutarch, who has left us a treatise in Greek, "On the Virtues of Women," has recorded more than one touching anecdote on this subject. One of these belongs to the beginning of the second century before Christ. When the Gauls moved upon Greece and into Asia Minor at this early period, they as usual carried with them their women, and a great multitude of these remained the captives of the Romans in the great victory gained over the Tectosagi and their confederates, at Mount Olympus, by the consul Cneius Manlius, B.C. 189. The guard of these captives was entrusted by the consul to a centurion, who possessed, in a more than ordinary degree, the vice of debauchery as well as that of covetousness, which then entered into the character of the soldier. Among the captives was the beautiful Chiamara, the wife of the chief of the Tectosages, who appears to have exercised the

---

* It is curious that during the Middle Ages the Welsh, in their hostile excursions upon the English border, appear to have been usually accompanied by their women, who, however, were less distinguished on these occasions by their courage than by their ferocity towards the wounded enemies, and by their aptitude at plunder. These were qualities derived perhaps from their Gaulish ancestors.

† Matrem suam sororesque simul omnium conjuges parvosque liberos consistere a tergo jubet, hortamenta victoriæ vel pulsis pudorem.—*Tacitus, Hist.*, lib. iv., c. 18.

supreme command over the Gauls in this expedition. With this lady the Roman centurion became enamoured, and, after in vain attempting to prevail over her virtue by persuasions, he had recourse to violence. The centurion had acted contrary to his duty, and would have incurred punishment at the command of his own general ; and, to calm the indignation of his victim, he promised to give her her liberty, but required a sum of gold amounting to the value of a talent by way of ransom. A place was appointed to which the money was to be brought, and Chiamara was allowed to choose one from the other captives to be sent to acquaint her relatives with the terms on which she was to be liberated. She chose an old slave of her husband's who chanced to be there, and the night following she was secretly conducted to the appointed place, where the money was brought in ingots of gold by two Gauls. The centurion began eagerly to weigh it, in order to assure himself that it was the full sum. While he was thus employed, Chiamara, in her own tongue, which was unknown to the centurion, ordered the two Gauls to draw their swords and slay him. She then took his head, wrapped it up in the skirts of her robe, and proceeded to join her husband ; but when he approached to embrace her, Chiamara stopped, threw down the head of the Roman before him, and then informed him what had happened. "Oh, wife," he said, in his exultation, "what a beautiful thing is fidelity !" His wife replied, "It is a still more beautiful thing to be able to say, 'No two men living will boast of having possessed me.'" This story is told by several of the Roman historians ; Polybius, according to Plutarch, related, in a part of his history now lost, that he himself had an interview with this Gaulish lady at Sardis, and that he was astonished with her elevation of mind and understanding.

These examples, and many others we might quote, seem to show that chastity was one of the earliest virtues of Womankind, and that, even in the primitive ages, it was prized and insisted upon by the other sex. Some of the old writers, it is true, speak of tribes in a very low state of barbarism who lived in the utmost licence ; but the old writers of this class were always on the look out for the marvellous, and those they speak of as living in this condition were people in remote parts who were only known to them by vague report. The advocates of the theory of the "savage" origin of mankind represent that, among many of the lower tribes of savages, female virtue is looked upon with a very indifferent eye, and seem to consider it as one of the developments of the human race, so that it is satisfactory to find from history that the contrary feeling becomes stronger, instead of weaker, in proportion as we go back. In fact, licence in this respect seems to have been hitherto one of the developments which accompany civilization, rather than one of the vices which it extinguishes.

When the Gauls, three centuries before the birth of Christ, marched into Italy and burnt Rome, they found there a people not far superior to themselves in civilization, and boasting of the same class of heroic virtues, modified only by the circumstance that they were a people stationary in their own country, making wars to extend their power, and not a people wandering over the earth in search of war and consequent plunder. The Roman women of the earlier period possessed most of the nobler qualities of their sex in a very high degree. They were not accustomed to follow their husbands and fathers to battle, and therefore they possessed none of that fierce courage displayed by the Gauls of their sex; but they often showed, under sudden misfortune, a constancy of mind which was truly noble. We need only appeal to such examples as that of Lucretia as evidence of the purity of their minds. They were educated with care, for we know that the beautiful Virginia, the heroine of one of the most touching stories of Roman history, went to school. The Roman women of the times of the kings and of the republic appear to have possessed in a special degree the good qualities which render domestic life happy; they are represented as faithful wives and excellent mothers, gentle, modest, and sober. They were forbidden by law to drink wine. Athenæus, in speaking of this fact, with the very ungallant reflection that "it is a well-known fact that all the race of women is fond of drinking," adds a piece of information which further illustrates some traits in the domestic life of the early Roman ladies—"It is impossible," he says, "for a woman to drink wine without being detected: for, first of all, she has not the key of the cellar; and, in the next place, she is bound to kiss her relations, and those of her husband, down to cousins, and to do this every day when she first sees them; and besides this she is forced to be on her best behaviour, as it is quite uncertain whom she may chance to meet; for if she has merely tasted wine, it needs no informer, but is sure to betray itself." * In proof of the excellent domestic character of the Roman women of this early period it is only necessary to state that, although the Roman husbands had almost unlimited power of divorce, the first occasion on which it was exercised is said to have occurred no less than five hundred and twenty years after the foundation of Rome.

In course of time, the character of the Roman women became depraved, and the change, when it began, was rapid and fearful. While, on one hand, they became proud and haughty, vain and cruel, on the other they too

* *Athenæi Deipnosophistæ*, lib. x., c. 58.

generally lost all their old respect for chastity and sobriety, and became remarkable for their excess of licentiousness and debauchery. This is the character which they bore when their example began to exercise an influence over the inhabitants of Western Europe, the people of Gaul and Britain. But it will be sufficient here to state this circumstance; it is not necessary to enter into particulars. That which now more especially interests us is their dress, because it no doubt influenced the costumes of the conquered races and that of the Middle Ages.

The ever-varying change in the forms and character of female dress which constitutes the fashion in modern times, was unknown to the ancients. The different articles which composed the female costume in ancient Rome, hardly varied from the earliest period of its history till it became mediæval. It consisted generally of three garments, very simple in form. The first was the tunic (*tunica*), which was what we call in modern times a shift, it was made of thin (sometimes almost transparent) material, fitted rather closely to the body, and had no sleeves. Over this was drawn another garment called the *stola*, differing only in shape from the *tunica*, in having short sleeves, covering only the upper part of the arm. This was usually fastened in front by means of fibulæ and brooches, the number and richness of which were regulated by the wealth of the individual. The tunic reached a little below the knees; the *stola*, on the contrary, was very long, while it was girded so as to make a quantity of broad folds under the breast, still, however, reaching so low that it half covered the feet. It was the characteristic dress of the Roman matrons, and was forbidden by law to all who were not free women and of pure life. The tunica and stola constituted the ordinary dress of the Roman lady indoors; * when she went out she wore over the stola the third article of dress, the *palla*, or mantle. The palla resembled the toga of the male attire, and was put on in

A ROMAN LADY PUTTING ON THE PALLA.

---

* It would seem, from paintings found at Pompeii and elsewhere, that, in the privacy of home, the Roman ladies frequently retained the tunic as their only garment, and they sometimes appear in a very extreme state of *négligé*.

the same manner   It consisted of a rather long piece of cloth cut somewhat in the form of a half circle, though the curve was not exactly the segment of a circle.   The wearer, in dressing with it, began by placing one end on her breast; it was then drawn over her left shoulder, round her back, under her right arm, across her breast, over her left shoulder and arm again, and the end was fastened behind. The left arm and shoulder were thus doubly covered, while the right arm was left bare. The cut on the last page, taken from one of the wall-paintings in Pompeii, represents a lady dressing herself with the palla, and will sufficiently explain itself.   When on the body, it sometimes reached to the feet, but more frequently it extended only a little below the middle or to the knees. This, however, was regulated entirely by the taste of the wearer, who was extremely particular in the manner in which it was adjusted, and bestowed more care and ornament upon it than upon any other article of her dress, except, perhaps, upon her *coiffure.*

The Roman lady, no doubt, paid great attention to the latter. There is a beautiful picture among the wall-paintings found in Pompeii, representing ladies at their toilette, attended by servants, or slaves. At the time of which we are speaking, that when Roman manners were beginning to influence the people of Gaul and Britain, the slaves of both

A ROMAN LADY AT HER TOILETTE.

sexes in a Roman family of any respectability in life were very numerous ; and, as in India in modern times, each was considered to have only one sort of work to attend to.   In the Pompeian picture alluded to, one of the

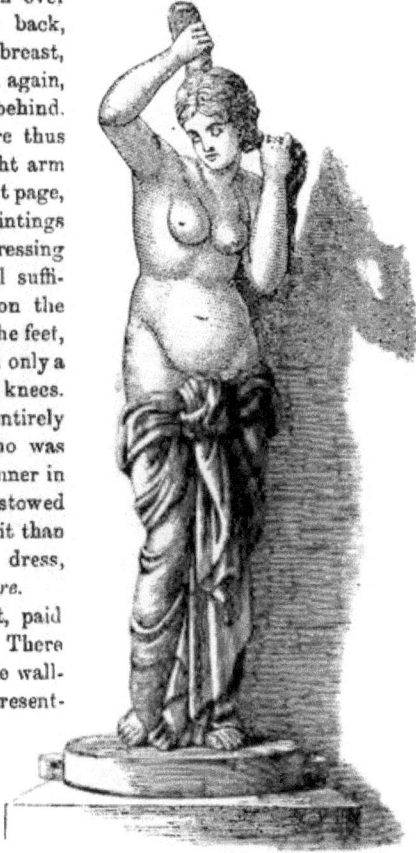

2

ladies is under the hands of the hair-dresser, who proceeds just in the same manner as the female arranges her own hair in the cut we give here. It is, no doubt, their especial province, and both she and her companion, who is adorning the lady's arm, seem to be attending to their duty with zeal. The form of *coiffure* most prevalent among the Roman ladies seems to have been the separation of the hair on each side from the top of the forehead; it was combed out, and formed into a large knot behind, which was held together by a hair-pin, on which latter was often bestowed very considerable ornamentation. A portion of the hair appears in many cases to be twisted, and

A ROMAN LADY'S HEAD-COVERING.

carried over the top of the head; or this was sometimes replaced by an ornamental band of other material. The lady in the scene just described is seated in her simplest dress, the tunica alone, which is thrown down so as to leave the greater part of her body bare. The female represented in our second cut is in much the same costume, but she is dressing her hair with her own hands. This subject is also taken from a painting in Pompeii, as well as the cut on the present page. As far as we can judge from the monuments which remain, the Roman women went commonly abroad without any covering on their heads; for, to say the least, anything like a hat or bonnet is rarely met with. There are, however, several figures among the paintings found in Pompeii in which the palla seems to be thrown over the head so as to form a cover for it, or some separate cloth is used for that purpose. An example of this is given in our third cut. It is interesting as being a part of the Roman costume which seems to have been adopted by the people of Gaul and Britain, and was continued into the Middle Ages, forming, in fact, the model of the mediæval *couvrechef.*

That which is especially worthy of remark in the Pompeian painting alluded to is the uniformity in the colour of the hair—all, ladies and servants, have hair of the same shade of yellow. Yellow hair, we know, was the favourite colour among the Romans. Pyrrha, the admired of Horace, was yellow-haired—

> Cui flavam religas comam,
> Simplex munditiis?
> *Horat. Carm.*, i. 6.

The verb *religas* is explained in the old gloss by *nodo colligis, i.e.,* bind up in a knot, which is just what the maid is doing in this picture, and which was the usual *coiffure* of the Roman ladies. Catullus (*Carm.* lxvi., line 62) speaks of the *flavus vertex,* or yellow crown, of his Berenice. Propertius, among the beauties of his Cynthia, says that her hair was yellow and her hands long—

> Fulva coma est, longæque manus.
> *Propert. Eleg.*, lib. ii. 2.

And Tibullus, when protesting against the supposition that his affections had been gained by magical incantations, says that his mistress fascinated him, not by the operation of such charms, but by the beauty of her face, the elegance of her limbs, and by her yellow hair—

> Non facit hoc verbis; facie tenerisque lacertis
> Devovet et flavis nostra puella comis.
> *Tibull. Eleg.*, i. 5, line 43.

So in Virgil, the hair of Dido was yellow; *flaventesque abscissa comias* (*Æn.,* iv. 590), and

> Nondum illi flavum Proserpina vertice crinem
> Abstulerat.
> *Æn.* iv. 698.

As well as that of Lavinia—

> Filia prima manu flavos Lavinia crines
> Et roseas laniata genas.
> *Æn.* xii. 605.

Of course to produce this uniformity of colour, as seen in the Pompeian painting, artificial means must have been employed, either dye or powder, and we know that among the wealthy and extravagant it was not unusual to powder the hair with gold-dust. We shall not proceed far in the history of Womankind before we meet again with this practice of artificially colouring the hair, which, indeed, appears to have existed among most peoples from a very early period.

The fresco paintings on the walls of Pompeii and Herculaneum are so much taken up with subjects chosen from mythology or from the heroic history of Greece and Rome, that we find comparatively few illustrations of contemporary life, especially so far as it might make us acquainted with the outward appearance of contemporary society. We are not very fully acquainted with the difference in this respect between the wife of the Roman citizen, the women of the ordinary class in Rome, and those of the rural population.

With regard to the latter, we have one rather curious and interesting picture. The walls of a court in what has been called the House of the Tragic Poet in Pompeii are painted with scenes from country life, one of which represents the interior of the yard of a country villa, with some of the people of the household and apparently of the farm assembled in it. We give a portion of this picture in our coloured plate. The yard is filled with domestic animals, chiefly goats, and on a bench on one side are two carved figures, no doubt the patron gods of the establishment. Beyond this, leaning against the wall, is the yoke for oxen. A group of both sexes, in the centre of the picture, appear to be so much excited that some occurrence of interest has evidently taken place, and, as one of them appears to have just brought in a naked infant, it has been conjectured by some that this picture represents the discovery and adoption of Œdipus by the shepherd of Polybus. This is only a conjecture; but the group is interesting as giving no doubt a faithful picture of the appearance of the population of the country in Roman Italy.

We know very little of the dress of our Celtic forefathers, whether Gauls or Britons. If we believe some of the ancient writers, the British costume, as well as that of the Gauls—we cannot correctly call it dress—was simply nakedness painted blue, and by way of further ornament they had recourse to the practice of tattooing. Cæsar is the first writer from whom we derive this information, and he adds that the substance with which they painted, or rather dyed, their bodies, was derived from the plant woad. It is repeated by other Roman writers, and was so generally believed, that when the poet

Martial speaks of a lady of British descent, he talks of her ancestors as
" azure-coloured Britons " :—

> Claudia cœruleis cum sit Rufina Britannis
> Edita, quam Latiæ pectora plebis habet!
> *Martial. Ep.*, lib. xi. ep. 53.

This story has been so generally credited, that that worthy old historian,
John Speed, in his folio " History of Britaine," has treated us with a care-
fully-executed picture of a British lady, in all her nudity, covered with
tattooing of the most pictorial character. Yet I would venture to doubt if
it were ever more than a fable. Cæsar, in all that he tells from his own
knowledge, is correct and trustworthy, but here he probably repeated stories
relating to people in the interior of the island, with whom he had no
acquaintance, and the truth of which he had not the power of testing.

Others of these hearsay stories of the manners and condition of people
in distant countries have been handed down to us by the ancient writers,
most of them probably no more worthy of credit than the one just told.
Cæsar informs us that, among the Britons in the interior of the island, by
whom we are to understand the original Celtic population, the sentiment of
domesticity was so imperfect, that ten or twelve men, generally belonging to
the same family, had their wives in common, the children being considered
as belonging severally to the man who first married their mother. The
well-known stories of two British queens, Boadicea of the Iceni, and Cartis-
mandua of the Brigantes, seem hardly consistent with a state of society
such as indicated by these tales, either in the maritime states or in the
interior of the island. However, at the time of Cæsar's invasion, social life
among the Gauls was in a very low state of development, and had still
hardly emerged from its patriarchal condition. He tells us that the
husbands had the power of life and death over their wives and children, and
it seems to have been generally assumed that the wife had no great love for
her lord. When a man of importance happened to die suddenly, or in an
extraordinary manner, it was taken for granted that his wife or wives were
the cause of his death, and she or they were immediately seized and subjected
to torture. If there appeared the slightest ground for suspicion, the unfortunate victims were committed to still greater torments, and finally burnt to
death. An anecdote of Gaulish life is preserved in an epigram in the
Greek Anthology,* which would seem to show that, at least in some parts
of Gaul, it was taken as a general principle that a woman's fidelity to

* *Anthologia*, lib. i. c. 43, ep. 1.

her husband was always to be suspected. Among the Belgic tribes the deity of the Rhine (for in those times every river had its god), was believed to pay especial attention to the conduct of the Belgian wives. In this belief the father took his new-born child to the river, placed it upon his spacious buckler of wood, and launched it on the water. If it swam on the surface, the father was satisfied of the legitimacy of his paternity; if it sank, he was equally convinced of the illegitimacy of the child, abandoned it to its fate, and no doubt wreaked his vengeance upon the mother. Cæsar informs us of a custom which prevailed in Gaul in his time, the earlier half of the first century before Christ, which shows a marked advance towards the equality of the sexes. On a man's marriage, whatever sum he received with his wife under the name of dower, he added to it the same sum from his own property, and the whole was kept along with the fruits (*fructus*) as a reserved fund, which belonged to the survivor of the two. The mother, also, had the entire care of the children, until the boys had reached the age at which it was customary to instruct them in the use of arms, and, till that period, a father looked upon it as disgraceful to appear publicly in company with his son.

No circumstance in ancient history is more remarkable than the readiness with which the peoples who came under the influence of Rome abandoned their own nationality, and became Romans. Roman laws, Roman manners, and, more observable than all, Roman costume, gradually superseded those of the conquered. The two remarkable characteristics of the male costume of the Gauls were the wearing of trousers, or breeches, on the legs, and the practice of carrying their hair long. The first portion of Gaul which was formed into a Roman province was that within the Alps, and therefore nearest to Rome, which, on that account, was usually spoken of as Gallia Cisalpina; but from its early adoption of the Roman dress, it soon received the name of Gallia Togata, or Gaul where the toga was worn. When a second province was established, consisting of the portion of Gaul on the other side of the Alps, and bordering upon the Mediterranean, the inhabitants kept for some time their native costume, and on that account it was called Gallia Braccata, or Gaul where trousers were worn. The Gauls themselves knew this article of dress by a name Latinized into *braccæ*, or *bracæ;* it is remarkable that the same word, with the same meaning, is found also in the Teutonic languages—in Anglo-Saxon it is *bréc*, or *bræc*, the origin, of course, of our English word breeches. As the province became more Roman, the braccæ were abandoned, and it received the new name of Gallia Narbonensis, from its chief town Narbona (*Narbonne*).

In the same manner, the next Roman province received the title of Gallia Comata, or hairy Gaul, so long as its inhabitants retained their old fashion of wearing their hair long.

It would appear that the trousers were a garment worn equally by the Gauls and the Teutons, and the name was probably one of the words common to both languages from their earliest formation. The Teutons, when they become known to us, also wore their hair long, and probably the costume varied little in the two races. But we are very imperfectly acquainted with that of the men, and we have still less knowledge of that of the female sex. The men, we are told, were very fond of dress, and prided themselves in a great display of personal ornaments, such as collars, bracelets, and rings. They dyed their hair of a bright red colour with a sort of pomatum, which Pliny says was made of tallow and cinders.* How far the Gaulish women imitated their husbands in these fashions we are not informed, but they probably adopted the red hair, and covered themselves with jewels, as far as lay in their power. We find, however, that in the state of society which the Romans included under the title of barbarian, the men are generally more given to display in dress and personal ornaments even than the other sex.

After the establishment of the Roman power in Gaul and Britain, the costume of the Romans in Italy was everywhere adopted. The Romano-Gaulish, as well as the Romano-British, lady, wore the tunic, the stola, and the palla, just as the Roman ladies of Pompeii wore them ; and the personal ornaments of females found so plentifully in excavations on Roman sites in Britain and Gaul are all entirely Roman. But our materials for the history of Womankind during this period are very scanty, and are hardly to be looked for among the ancient writers ; though we have a few interesting materials of another class, which are undoubtedly truthful, and which enable us to contemplate the features and costume of the inhabitants of Gaul and Britain in the earlier part of the Roman period. These are the sculptured monumental stones, which were no doubt intended by the sculptor to present portraits of the individuals he commemorated. Unfortunately, but a small number of them are preserved ; and for this reason, and on account of their extreme interest, it seems desirable to give all which relate to our subject. Their importance is increased by the circumstance that, in most of them, the inscription enables us to give the names of the persons delineated, and tell who they were. I may add that the greater part of them have been published

* Galliarum hoc inventum rutilandis capillis fit ex sebo et cinere.—*Plin. Hist. Nat.*, lib. xxviii. c. 12.

by our distinguished antiquary, my friend Mr. Roach Smith, in his most valuable publication, the "Collectanea Antiqua."

The first of these monuments, which was found at Mayence, represents a family of citizens of the Roman city of Moguntiacum. The head of the family, as we learn by the inscription on the stone, was Blussus, the son of Atusirus, and his profession was that of a navigator (*nauta*)—he was probably engaged in the commerce of the Rhine. His wife, the lady we see, was Menimane, the daughter of Brigio, and behind them stands their son

A FAMILY OF MOGUNTIACUM (*Mayence*).

Primus, who raised the monument to their memory, as a token of filial piety. Blussus died at the advanced age of seventy-five, but the lady appears to have been much younger, and probably outlived him many years, for the blank left in the inscription for the insertion of her age when she died has never been filled up. She was evidently a lady possessed of personal attractions, and was fully aware of it, if we may judge by the richness of her dress and personal ornaments. She wears first the tunic, which differs from the ordinary Roman tunic in fitting closely to the arms and bust, and in being furnished with long sleeves, which turn back in cuffs, resembling the modern gauntlet cuffs. It is gathered at the neck to a sort of frill, which is inclosed by a torques. The tunic reaches to the feet. Over it Menimane wears the stola, which reaches only a little below the knees, and hangs loosely and gracefully over the breast. As Mr. Roach Smith

A MAIDEN OF BORDEAUX (*Burdigala*).   THE POTTER'S DAUGHTER OF BURDIGALA.

observes, her jewelry is of no common description, nor niggardly bestowed. Upon her breast, below the torques, is a large rose-shaped ornament or brooch, and beneath it a couple of fibulæ; two more, of a similar pattern, fasten the stola near the right shoulder, and upon the left arm just above the elbow; an armlet encircles the right arm, and bracelets the wrists; and two

3

of the fingers of the left hand have rings. Her hair is raised up into what was probably the fashionable *coiffure* of the day. This profusion of jewelry, and the money-bag which Blussus holds in his hand, bespeak a family of no inconsiderable wealth. The boy behind holds what is probably intended for a ball; and the mother, in spite of her brilliant attire, grasps in her hand the implements of weaving, to typify her attention to her household duties, and has on her lap her pet little dog. The couple sit in one chair, which casts a pleasing air of domesticity over the whole picture.

Our next cut represents a young maiden of the Roman town of Burdigala, the modern Bordeaux, where the monument was found. Her name has been lost by an accidental erasure of part of the inscription, and we only know the name of the father who raised this monument to her memory, which was Lætus. She also wears the tunic, and the outer garment (answering to the stola of the Romans), which here reaches lower than in the former instance. Her hair is dressed somewhat in the same style as that of the navigator's wife, and like her, also, she has her pet animals, in this instance, a kitten and a cock. There is a special interest attached to the former, as the domesticated cat is not mentioned in the ancient writers, and it has been recently asserted by one of our distinguished men of science that the cat was never domesticated by the Romans. The love of the Roman ladies, and sometimes of the gentlemen also, for domesticated animals is well known. Every reader of the classic poets is acquainted

A LADY OF NÎMES (*Nemausum*).

with Lesbia's sparrow (*passer*) and Corinna's parrot. Martial has commemorated, in a graceful epigram, the qualities of Issa, the favourite little dog of the painter Publius.

Issa est blandior omnibus puellis;
Issa est carior Indicis lapillis;
Issa est deliciæ catella Publi.

Martial, Epig., i., 110.

And in another epigram he has furnished us with a list of the favourite pet animals of his time. The archæological discoveries at Bordeaux have furnished us with another monumental figure of a young damsel of Burdigala, which is represented in the cut on the right of the same page. Her name is given in the inscription, as will be seen, as "*Axula, Cintugeni fi[guli] filia,*" Axula, the daughter of Cintugenus the potter. It is the first sepulchral monument with the name of a potter which has been discovered; and Cintugenus must have been a man of wealth and distinction in his profession, for Mr.

A LADY OF LINCOLN (*Lindum*).

Roach Smith, to whom we owe the publication of this interesting monument, has not only traced the name of the family in other Roman monuments in the Museum at Bordeaux, but he has met with it stamped as the name of the maker on Roman pottery found in London. Axula has rather a short dress, which exposes to view a well-defined pair of shoes; she holds in her left hand a basket of fruit, and in the right a mirror of the well-known Roman form, perhaps as one of the first implements which the Romano-Gaulish damsel was taught to use.

The only other Romano Gaulish female I have to show is a lady of Nemaustum—now represented by the town of Nîmes—which was engraved by the Comte de Caylus, in the third volume of his " Recueil d'Antiquités." It is a head sculptured in relief, and is interesting as giving an example belonging to the Roman period of the head-covering of the females. We will pass from it into our own island of Britain, where we are again indebted to the indefatigable labours of Mr. Roach Smith. Our next cut represents a piece of a broken monument belonging to the Roman town of Lindum, in Britain, which was dug up some years ago in the immediate neighbourhood of its modern representative, Lincoln, and is now preserved in the cloisters of the cathedral. It is, no doubt, intended for the portrait of a lady who lived in the ancient Roman town, and is interesting as an illustration of the costume of a British female of her age, which Mr. Roach Smith places under the reign of Severus, or very soon after it—that is, in the earlier part of the third century of the Christian era. She wears, evidently, the tunic and the stola, the former terminating in what bears some resemblance, like that of Menimane, to a frill, the latter open in front; but the object of most interest is her necklace, which is evidently formed of jet beads, resembling those which are found not unfrequently on ancient sites, and especially in sepulchral interments in Britain. They are flat on one side, and ribbed on the other, and were no doubt of native manufacture.

A ROMANO-BRITISH FAMILY OF OLICANA *(Ilkley).*

A very interesting Roman sepulchral monument was discovered at Ilkley, in Yorkshire, generally considered to be the *Olicana* of the Romans, in the October of the year 1867. It commemorates a Romano-British family of Olicana, but the inscription on the tablet below the sculpture, which no doubt gave us the names of the individual and of his wife and son figured above it, has unfortunately been entirely erased. The lady's head-dress points to the age of Severus, or a little later, as the date at which this family lived. She wears a necklace of pendants, and holds in her right hand a little basket of fruit, or flowers, but the object she has in her left hand is so much worn that it cannot easily be defined. The boy holds a box and a wreath. It is worthy of notice that, among the inscriptions found at Ilkley, there was one commemorating the rebuilding of some public building here by Virius Lupus, who was pro-prætor of Britain in the reign of Severus.

Our last cut is that of a statue found at Chesters, in Northumberland, the site of the Roman station of Cilur-

DRESS OF A NORTHUMBRIAN MATRON
UNDER THE ROMANS.

num. The tunic, reaching to the feet, and the stola, descending only a little below the knees, are well and distinctly pictured, and may probably be considered as representing those articles of dress as worn by a lady of rank in the country to the north of the Humber. The character of the waist-band, or girdle, is especially remarkable. The statue appears to have been intended for that of a goddess—supposed to be Cybele, who is worthily represented in the well-known garb of a matron. It is to be regretted, however, that our Romano-British matron has lost her head.

In these few sculptured monuments, we have seen something of the appearance of the ladies of Gaul and Britain during the time these remained Roman provinces. The same class of monuments furnishes us with some curious illustrations of the domestic sentiments as they prevailed—or, at all events, existed—during the same period. It was the practice of the Romans to make of their tombstones affectionate memorials to the departed on the part of the survivor, and the inscriptions often contain traits of personal character which, if not always strictly true, tell us at least what were the qualities which the people of those days valued most in the female sex. It is thus among the abodes of the dead that we must seek for the last traces of the virtues of Womankind in Roman Gaul and Britain. We find these memorials of affectionate feelings at the very extremity of our British province. At Chesters, in Northumberland (*Cilurnum*), a station on the

line of the Wall of Hadrian, an altar monument was found, dedicated by
Fabius Honoratius and his wife, Aurelia Egliciane, to the memory of their
"most sweet daughter" (*filiæ dulcissimæ*), who was named after her father
Fabia Honorata.   They were a family of Vangiones—a people of Belgic
Gaul.   At Carvoran, another Roman site on the line of the Wall, a monument was inscribed by a centurion, named Aurelius Marcus, as a testimony
of his affection for " his most holy wife, who lived thirty-three years without
a single stain."

> OBSEQVIO CON
> IVGIS SANCTIS
> SIMAE QVAE VI
> XIT ANNIS XXXIII
> SINE VLLA MACVLA.

The lady in this case was a native of Salona.*

If we go over to Gaul we shall find these affectionate memorials in greater
numbers.   Many of them have been collected by Orellius, in his valuable
work on " Latin Inscriptions," and in the supplementary volume by Henzen.
Some of the more common epithets applied by husbands to their wives in
these early inscriptions are " most dutiful wife" (*uxor piissima*), " most
dear spouse and wife" (*sponsa ac marita karissima*), " most innocent woman"
(*innocentissima femina*), " incomparable woman" (*incomparabilis femina*).
Many of these monuments have been found at Lyons, on the Rhone, the
Lugdunum of the Romans.   One of them was dedicated by Silenius Reginus
to his most dear sister, Camilla Augustila, " who lived thirty years and five
days, and for whom none of her kin ever grieved except at her death." †
Two of these ladies of Lyons, most remarkable for their virtues, were Greeks
by birth.   One, Lanina Galatia, had lived, according to her husband's
testimony, thirty years without any sin. ‡   Arelatum, also, the modern
Arles, appears to have furnished some good examples of Womankind.   A
young married woman named Julia Lucia, who died at the age of twenty years
and eight months, is declared by her husband and father-in-law, who erected
the monument, to have been, " in morals as well as in accomplishments an
example for the rest of Womankind." §   The wife of a citizen of Narbonne
was " dutiful and thrifty."   A lady of Avignon, or, at least of the neighbour-

---

* These inscriptions are published by Dr. Bruce, in his great work on "The Roman Wall."
† De qua nemo suorum unquam doluit nisi mortem.—*Orellius*, vol. ii., No. 4464.
‡ Quæ vixit annos xxx sine ulla animi læsione.—*Orellius*, vol. ii., No. 4465.
§ Quæ moribus pariter et disciplina ceteris feminis exemplo fuit.—*Orellius*, vol. ii.,
No. 4638.

hood, was "dutiful and chaste," and her husband, in his regard for her, dedicated to her "the best memorial his poverty would permit." *

The ladies, be it said to their credit, were not in arrear with their husbands in these testimonials of affectionate feeling. A townswoman of the Roman Lugdunum of the Batavi, now Leyden, named Nævia Fortunia, speaks of her deceased spouse as "an incomparable husband, with whom she had lived nineteen years." † A monument raised, on the other hand, by a husband to his wife, but found in Italy instead of Gaul, gives us rather an interesting enumeration of what were considered to be the domestic virtues of an excellent woman. The literal translation of this memorial, which was inscribed on a sarcophagus, is, "Here has been laid Amymone, the daughter of Marcus, in character most excellent, in person most beautiful, a diligent plyer of the distaff, affectionate, modest, thrifty, chaste, *and a keeper at home.*" ‡

---

* Conjugi piæ et castæ .... maritus qualem paupertas potuit memoriam dedi.—*Orellius*, vol. ii , p. 220, No. 4648.

† Conjugi incomparabili cum quo vixit annos xix.—*Orellius*, vol. i., No. 171.

‡ Hic sita est Amymone Marci, optima et pulcherrima, lanifica, pia, pudica, frugi, casta, domiseda.—*Crellius*, vol. ii., No. 4639.

CHAPTER II.

THE WOMEN OF TEUTONIC MYTHOLOGY AND ROMANCE.

AT the close of our last chapter, we left Western Europe on the eve of a mighty revolution. We must not suppose that its dominant population belonged any longer to the old Celtic races, but, on the contrary, it was a mixture—we may fairly say an amalgamation of different races from many parts of the Roman empire. In the few instances I have already given, we have Vangiones from Belgium, in one of the towns in the north of Britain, and people from Salona in another, and we have seen people of Greek origin at Lyons, on the Rhone. It was the policy of the Romans to colonize permanently the territories they had conquered in more distant and less civilized parts, and the first towns in these parts were Roman military colonies, and the inhabitants soldiers, with their relatives, and people who accompanied them. In most places, each town, or station, appears to have been occupied by a uniform population from the same country, and to have been generally recruited from that same country; but in course of time the circumstances altered, and the soldiers, or, in other words, the townsmen, were recruited from any part of the Roman empire most convenient. The population became thus very mixed in its ethnological character; but this was probably not outwardly observable from the circumstance that it had all become in manners and dress, and perhaps to some degree in spirit, Roman. This was, no doubt, still more the case in Britain than in Gaul, in some parts of which the original Celtic population had possessed towns before the Roman conquests. The great source from which the population was thus recruited in Northern Gaul and Britain during the later Roman period appears to have been Germany, and many facts lead us to believe there was in these countries a very considerable population of Teutonic blood long before the time when the authority of Rome was withdrawn. Our second chapter thus introduces us to that great Teutonic race, from which we ourselves claim to be descended.

Fortunately, too, with our German forefathers, the materials of history begin to be clearer and more copious, and we shall soon be able to treat our subject much more satisfactorily. But before we consider the primitive Teutons as they lived upon this earth, we will pay a visit to them in their heaven above, for it should be in their mythology and mythic romance that we shall be able to learn the true Teutonic *idea* of Womankind. The outline of the primitive mythology of our Teutonic race has been preserved to us in the two Eddas, the first of which consists of a series of the early Scandinavian mythic poems collected in the latter part of the eleventh century by a priest named Sæmund; the other, which is known as the Prose Edda, formed, about half a century later, chiefly from the songs of the elder Edda, by another priest named Snorro.[*]

According to this Scandinavian mythology, there were three principal worlds, or, as they called them, gards, *i.e.*, yards, or inclosed residences. Towards the south was Asagard, the residence of the Asas, or gods; to the north was Utgard, or the outer residence, otherwise called Jotunheim, or the home of the Jotuns (in Anglo-Saxons cotens), or giants; and between them lay Midgard, or the middle residence, which was the earth, inhabited by men. The giants, or evil beings, had existed before the gods, and therefore, through longer experience, possessed greater knowledge of things. The oldest and highest of the gods was Odin, as he was called by the Scandinavians, or Woden, as the name was pronounced in the German dialects, including our Anglo-Saxon. Odin had many names and epithets, but he was most commonly spoken of as Allfadur, or the Father of All things. His wife was the goddess Frigga, who was spoken of as the Mother of All; and from them were descended the other gods and goddesses. Odin was in possession of the precious liquor, the drinking of which produced poetry, and which he had stolen from the dwarfs in a rather dishonest manner. It was the etiquette among the gods to talk in verse, and the language of poetry, whether we find it in the primæval dialects of Scandinavia, or in Anglo-Saxon, is full of metaphor and imagery, which, though often extravagant, is sometimes remarkable for its beauty. Several of its metaphorical phrases have relation to Womankind. Thus Odin himself is called *Friggiar faþmbygguir, i.e.*, the inhabitant of the bosom of Frigga, meaning her husband; and similarly Loki, the least worthy of the gods, is

* The edition I use of the Poetic Edda, or Sæmund's Edda, is that of Copenhagen, in 3 vols. 4to.

spoken of in another of the Edda songs, as *Farmr Signyiar arma*, the
burthen of the arms of Signyia, his wife.   Still more elegant was the
metaphor usually employed in Anglo-Saxon poetry for a woman—*freðɗu-
webbe*, a weaver of peace.   In Beowulf, it is said of the hero's aunt Hygd,
the wife of Hygelac, whom she was accused of having murdered—

ne bið swylc cwénlíc þeáw,	such is no womanly custom,
* * *	* * *
þætte freðɗu-webbe	that a peace-weaver
fnores onsæce,	plot against the life,
æfter lig-torne,	after burning anger,
leófne mannan.	of a dear man.

Beowulf, l. 3884.

And at the opening of the fragment called the Gleeman's Tale, we are told
that Widsith travelled in company with his wife to visit the Hreth-king's
court—

he mid Ealhhilde,	he with Ealhhild,
fælre freðɗu-webban,	faithful peace-weaver,

that is, faithful woman.   The beauty of the metaphor will be still better
appreciated if we bear in mind that the chief domestic occupation of
Womankind among the different branches of the Teutonic race, was weaving.
It is an assertion of one of the most precious attributes of the sex.   The
principal building in Asagard was Walhalla, the Hall of Slaughter, in which
the souls of men who fell bravely in battle lived and feasted.   Odin had a
high seat or throne, from which, when seated upon it, he overlooked the
universe, and on which none of the Asas was permitted to sit, except Odin
and Frigga.

  Once, in the morning of time, to use still the metaphorical language of
this primeval poetry, the Allfather was sitting upon his seat, and the Mother of
All sat by his side.   The god, like a good husband, said to his spouse, "Give
me thy counsel now, Frigga, for I have an earnest desire to visit Vafthrudnis,
and to dispute with that all-knowing giant on points of ancient knowledge."
Frigga, who knew that it was a long journey beset with dangers, and that
Vafthrudnis was the strongest, as well as the most learned, of the giants,
would have persuaded Odin to remain at home; but she found him resolutely bent upon the adventure,—like some husbands of more earthly
character, he had evidently made up his mind what to do before he asked
his wife's advice upon it; and, seeing this, the goddess gave him affectionately her parting wishes for his safety.   For those who may wish to

know what was the language spoken by the Mother of All, I repeat her words as they are given in the opening of the Edda. Frigga said to Odin —

heill þu farir !	safe be thou in going !
heill þu aptr komor !	safe be thou in coming back !
heill þu Asynnom ser !	safe be thou for the goddesses !
öþi þer dugi	may thy talent be sufficient
hvars þu scalt, or alldafauþr,	wherever thou shalt have need, our allfather,
orþom mæla Jotun.	to address the giant with words.

Odin seems to have had two objects in view—first, to obtain knowledge from the all-knowing giant, which he proposed to do by going in the disguise of a poor traveller, and drawing out from him information which he would not otherwise give; and, secondly, to spy the country, or, as he expresses it, to see what sort of halls Vafthrudnis lived in. Accordingly, Allfather presents himself in disguise under the name of Gangrad, the traveller, and the rest of the poem is a continuous conversation between the Asa and the giant, so arranged as to give an elementary outline of the primitive mythology. Here and there, among these obscure songs of a remote age, we gain a hint of the position of Womankind among the gods. In the För Skirnis, or Journey of Skirner, who went to gain for Thor's son, Njörd, the love of Gerda, the daughter of a Jotun, the damsel acts quite independently of her father. In the Harbarz Lioth, or Song of Harbard the ferryman, in which Thor, Odin's eldest son, and the first of the gods under him, and Harbard tell each other their adventures, to the question, "What wert thou doing, Thor ?" the god replies, "I was beating the wives of the giants in Hlesey, for the wickedness they had perpetrated towards mankind." Harbard then remarks, "It was a disgraceful act that thou committedst, Thor, when thou gavest blows to women." Thor felt the reproach, and excused himself by urging that these were wolves rather than women. Facts like these show us woman, according to the primitive ideas of our race, in a position of dignity far different from that of savages.

In the songs of the Edda, the goddesses are not only represented as sitting in the hall on an equality with the gods, but they also meet in council together on the same footing, and give their opinions, which are listened to with respect. At the opening of the Vegtams-Quida, we find the Asas of both sexes thus assembled in council to debate on the danger with which the young Baldur had been threatened in a dream. In Thryms-Quida, likewise, the gods and goddesses sit and act together in the council held to consult on the proposal to disguise Thor in the dress of a bride. In the Ægis-Drecka, or Æger's banquet, the social position of the goddesses is quite equal to that of their husbands, they take the same share in the conversation, and come in for the same share of the insults of the base Loki, the most wicked of the gods. According to this story, Æger gave a great feast to the Asas, to which came Odin and his wife Frigga. Thor came not, as he was absent in another part of the universe, but his wife, Sifia, attended alone. Among others present at this entertainment were Bragi, and his wife Idunna; Njörd, and his wife Skadi; and Freyja, the goddess of Love. Loki, who was one of the party, showed his natural perversity by slaying one of Æger's attendants, in consequence of which he was expelled from the hall, and forbidden to return. Nevertheless, he soon presents himself again, and demands his horn of mead. He is received in silence, with the exception of a gentle rebuke from Bragi; but a seat is granted him, and he takes his place, and drinks to the assembled Asas, excepting Bragi, whom he accuses of cowardice. Bragi replies, and his wife interferes to prevent an unseemly brawl; but Loki insults Idunna, and charges her with disgraceful licentiousness. The goddess Gefion, who was celebrated for her chastity, is subjected to a similar charge, nor is Frigga herself, or Freyja, the goddess of love, or Skadi, or any of the other goddesses, spared from the same or even worse imputations, until Thor makes his appearance, and drives away the turbulent intruder. If we judge by the imputations thus freely scattered among the goddesses by Loki, we might be led to form a rather low estimate of their characters; but the old writers intimate that the greater part, at least, of his charges were no better than a mere unfounded libel. Yet we learn from other parts of the Eddas that neither goddesses nor gods were totally unacquainted with intrigues, and in this respect, indeed, they seem to have resembled, to some degree, the deities of classic fable. Most of the gods of the Teutonic mythology had several wives—the number of Odin's wives was rather considerable—so that polygamy was certainly countenanced in Asagard.

A list of the goddesses of our primitive mythology, with their characters, is given in the prose "Edda," or "Snorro's Edda." Eir was the goddess of medicine. Gefion was the maiden goddess, and all females who died maids became her handmaidens. The fifth in the Edda list was Fulla, who was likewise a maid, and who went with her hair flowing over her shoulders, and her head adorned with a gold ribbon. She was entrusted with the toilette and slippers of Frigga, and was the confidential repository of her secrets. The next of the goddesses in rank after Frigga, the Mother of All, was Freyja, who possessed the celebrated necklace Brising, answering to the cestus of Venus, who holds in classical mythology nearly the same position as Freyja in that of the North. The goddesses of Asagard are almost all gentle and affectionate in temper. The husband of Freyja is described as leaving his wife in order to travel into very remote countries; the goddess, after wandering through many lands in vain search for him, returned home, and she passes her time in continually weeping for his absence. She weeps tears of gold. The "Edda" song, "Fiöl-Svinns Mal," concludes with a passage describing, in simple but touching terms, the joy of two lovers of the Asa race on their re-union after a long separation. Several of the goddesses presided over the affections of men and women, and over affairs of love. There were different classes of goddesses of inferior rank, such as the Valkyrier, who were present at battles, and selected those who were to be slain, and the Norni, or fates. Even these seem to be gentle and affectionate, when not engaged in their sanguinary duties, which, too, were looked upon as beneficent acts, as it was considered the greatest of God's bounties to take a man direct to Walhalla. The Valkyrier waited upon the heroes in the hall of Walhalla. It was, indeed, one of the great duties of the high Teutonic dame, to serve the mead or other drink to her husband's guests in the hall.

Our information on the costume of the fair goddesses of Asagard is unfortunately very scant. They were evidently proud of adorning their persons with a profusion of jewelry. Freyja had rings of gold on her hands, and a necklace of gold round the neck. The latter seems to have been a usual ornament; one of the heroines of the "Edda," Menglad, took her name from the brilliance of her necklace. The goddesses appear to have been especially proud of the whiteness of their arms, which they washed diligently. In the "Ægis-Drecka," Loki compliments Idunna on her arms being "excellently washed" (*arma þína ítr-þvegna*). From this we may assume that the dress had no sleeves, but that the arms were left bare. The material appears to have been usually linen, which they wove at home. In the "Thryms-Quida," Freyja is recommended to put on her "bridal linen" (*brudar líni*). In this particular case, we have, at all events, some account of the manner in which a goddess dressed for her marriage. Thor had lost his famous hammer, which was in the power of Thrym, one of the Jotuns, or giants. Thrym refuses to give it up on any other condition than that Freyja shall be given to him for a wife. Loki persuades Thor to go with him to the court of the Jotun disguised in the garb of Freyja, and act the part of the bride. Accordingly they bound round Thor the bridal linen, placed round his neck "the great glittering necklace," made the keys ring under it, and the female vest (*kvendþir*) to flow about his knees. The keys were hung to the girdle as symbolical of the duties and cares of the new bride. They placed broad gems on his breast, and a band round the top of his head. It appears to have been the custom to cover the bride with a thick veil on these occasions, and Thor's disguise proved safe except in as far as he nearly betrayed himself by his own indiscretion; for the god, who was renowned for his appetite, was no sooner seated at the table in Thrym's hall, than he eat without halting an entire ox, eight salmons, and all the dainties which are usually served to ladies under such circumstances, and with these he drank three hogsheads of mead. Thrym, giant as he was, felt somewhat surprised at the appetite of his betrothed, and said, "I never saw a bride eat more at a meal, or a maiden drink a larger quantity of mead." Loki excused her by stating that so anxious had she been for the time when she was to go to Jotunheim, that she had eaten nothing for eight days and eight nights. Thrym next sought to obtain a glance at the face of his bride by lifting up the corner of her linen, but he drew back in terror, with a remark on the fierceness of her eyes. This is explained by the assertion that she had not slept during eight days and eight nights. At length the hammer is produced, and, the moment Thor feels it in his hand, he assumes his true character, and destroys Thrym and all his household.

From Asagard and Walhalla, we come down to Odin's more distant descendants, who have not yet passed under the judgment of the Valkyries; and whose sphere of action lies within the limits of Midgard, or this earth. Their legends, some of which occupy a part of the Edda songs, bring us out of the region of pure mythology into that of romance, and to the very bounds of history itself. In them, Womankind oft takes a more boldly-defined position than in the mythology. The great qualities of woman often influence, either for good or for evil, the whole course of events more power-fully than those of man. In fact, in these mythic romances, woman begins to appear as the great moving force of the history. There is one important cycle which runs through a number of the later songs of the Edda, and which may be taken as an example of the earlier class of these romances. It will be remarked how it rises out of the merely mythic and poetical into something like the real. The great family of the Volsungs, descended im-mediately from Odin, was represented at the time when this story begins by a prince named Sigurd, who had obtained the power of understanding the language of birds. This notion of the secrets of mankind being known to the birds, and of that knowledge being obtained by certain individuals who have obtained a mysterious acquaintance with their language and listened to their talk, often makes its appearance in the literature of the Middle Ages. One day Sigurd heard the birds talking of a beautiful maiden whose name was Brunhild, and who waited for a liberator of the other sex. She was a Valkyrie, who had offended Odin, and in return had been condemned to abandon her condition of Valkyrie, to submit to marriage, and to be subject to death. She had been thrown, clad as she was in her armour, into a magic sleep, and placed on the top of a mountain surrounded by a barrier of flames; the hero who should pass the fiery barrier and rescue her, was destined to be her husband. Sigurd resolves to undertake the adventure, and succeeds, but he leaves Brunhild, with a promise upon oath to return and take her away as his wife. Sigurd then proceeds to the country of the Niflungs, and forms a friendship with their three kings, the brothers Gunar, Hogni, and Guttorm. Their sister Gudruna becomes enamoured of him, and, through a magic potion administered to him by her mother, he forgets his vows to Brunhild, and marries Gudruna. Some time afterwards, Gunar, the eldest of the three brothers, hears the story of Brunhild, and determines to obtain possession of her. He secures the assistance of Sigurd, who alone has the power of passing through the flames, and by this means Brunhild is brought away and married to Gunar. But the Valkyrie retains her passion for Sigurd, and has forgotten nothing that had passed, and she now only seeks to punish him for his desertion. She excites her husband Gunar and her brothers against him, and in the sequel Sigurd is slain by them. Brunhild immediately repents of her deed, laments the fate of Sigurd, slays herself, and is burnt on the same funeral pile, leaving her curse upon Gunar and his brothers. The Edda songs go on to tell the vengeance which fell severally upon the three princes of the Niflungs. Subsequently their sister Gudruna makes her appearance again as the wife of Attila, whom she slays at a feast; and the story continues through a new series of feuds and slaughters.

These Edda songs, which present the earliest form of what was afterwards expanded into the grand German mediæval romance of the Nibelungen-Lied, or song of the Nibelungs, picture Womankind not in her most pleasing colours. We have in our Anglo-Saxon literature only one representative of these mythic romances, the poem of Beowulf; but we cannot but feel that in this venerable relic left to us by our forefathers, the other sex appears to us more domestic in character, and in more amiable colours, than in the story of Brunhild. The name of Beowulf figures as one of the early links in the Anglo-Saxon mythic genealogy of the race of the Anglo-Saxon kings.

Hrothgar was a king in Denmark, who had built for himself a princely residence, to which he gave the name of Heorot; but it was visited by a fiendish being named Grendel, who carried off Hrothgar's nobles to devour them in his retreat, and none had the power to resist. At this time Beowulf reigned over the Geats, or Goths of West Gothland, and, hearing by fame of the distress of Hrothgar's court, he proceeded thither with a party of his warriors, in the true character of the mythic hero, in order to combat the monsters. Beowulf is joyfully received in Hrothgar's hall, and the scene of feasting, the story-telling, the minstrel's song, the boisterous mirth, are all graphically described. Then, in due time, Hrothgar's queen, the noble Wealtheow, the "gold-adorned" (*gold-hroden*), advanced from her seat, to bear the cup to the warriors. First she offered it to the king her husband, greetingly "bade him be blithe at the beer-drinking, he who was dear to his people." Then she went round the hall, offering the cup, and distributing gifts to each. At length "the ring-adorned queen, exalted in mind," bore the mead-cup to Beowulf himself, and "sagacious in words" (*wisfæst wordum*), addressed the hero in flattering terms. Beowulf replied that he intended to destroy the Grendel or die in the attempt. There and then:—

eóde gold-hroden	went gold-adorned
freólicu folc-cwén	the joyful people's-queen
to hire freán sittan.	to sit by her lord.

Beowulf, l. 1285.

The "joy in hall" was then renewed, until Wealtheow retired to her bed, and Hrothgar soon followed. I will not enter into the details of the combat in which Beowulf gave the Grendel its mortal wound: other feasts in the hall followed, in which the queen, to whom the poet applies the epithet of "peaceful tie of peoples" (*friðu-sibb folca*), rewarded the hero with princely gifts, while Hrothgar's daughter carried round the cup.

We see that there is not much scope in "Beowulf" for bringing forward the character of the female sex; and unfortunately we have no other Anglo-Saxon romance of the same class left in anything like its original state. There is one other early romance, however, which is worthy of attention. It is that of Walthere, Latinized into Waltharius, and preserved only in a Latin metrical version, supposed to have been made in the tenth century.*

It was the age when Attila with his Huns was ravaging the centre of Europe, and he was already directing his march against the kingdom of the

---

* The *Waltharius* has been printed several times. The editions I use are those by Jacob Grimm and Ands. Schmeller, in their *Lateinische Gedichte des x. und xi. jh.*, Gottingen, 1838, and by M. Edélestand du Méril, given in his *Poésies Populaires Latines*, Paris, 1843.

Franks, when Gibico, who was then their king, took counsel of his nobles, and resolved to save his people from the horrors of invasion, by making his peace with Attila, and paying him a tribute. The offer was accepted, and a young Frankish noble, named Hagano, was delivered as a hostage, accompanied with a large mass of treasure. Attila now turned his arms against Burgundy, where Herric was king, who had an only daughter named Hildegund, remarkable for her beauty. Herric followed the example of the king of the Franks, made his peace with Attila, and his daughter Hildegund became the hostage. The Aquitanians submitted to the same conditions, and their king, Alphere, gave as hostage his son Walthere, a young prince of great promise. Now Herric and Alphere had already entered into a treaty for the marriage of Walthere and Hildegund, so that the couple, ignorant of the engagement made by their fathers, went into exile together. It is an example of the authority of a father over his children. So Attila returned with his hostages into Pannonia, where they were treated at his court with great kindness, as though they had been his own children, and the maiden was given in charge to the queen. The two young princes were trained to arms, and became distinguished among the warriors of Attila's army ; while the maiden rose rapidly in the favour of his queen, whom she pleased by her noble manners, and by her industry in her domestic duties, until she was at length made keeper of the royal treasures, and her influence was almost equal to that of the queen herself.

> Moribus eximiis operumque industria abundans;
> Postremum custos thesauris provida cunctis
> Efficitur, modicumque deest quin regnet et ipsa.
> *Waltharius*, l. 112.

We have seen in "Beowulf" that it was the lady of the household who distributed the gifts of her husband's treasures to his guests in the hall, and she appears also to have had them in her keeping. During this time the king of the Franks died, and was succeeded by Gunthere, who immediately threw up his dependence upon Attila, and refused his tribute; and the Frankish hostage, Hagano, made his escape from Attila's court, and fled back to his home. But Walthere remained one of the most distinguished leaders in the army of the Huns, and the king, at the suggestion of his queen, sought to retain him by pressing upon him a Hunnish wife. Walthere found, or pretended to find, an excuse for declining this proposal in the plea that the attractions of a female companion might withdraw him from, or make him less eager in, his path of glory. At length, on his

5

return from a great victory he had gained for the Huns, Walthere, in a private interview with Hildegund, becomes enamoured of her while she is offering him the festive cup, still ignorant of the treaty of alliance which their fathers had formed for them. The result is, they agree to fly together, and make their way to the land of the Burgundians. As the opportunity for their escape, they choose a great feast-day, at which Walthere contrives that the whole royal household shall be made more drunk than usual, and, when they are all stretched helpless on the floor, he selects a swift horse from the stables, arms himself, and carries with him part of the king's most valuable treasures, and with his lady-love makes for the forest.

The fugitives hasten towards their native land, travelling by night, and concealing themselves in the woods or mountain caverns by day; and while Walthere rode armed and prepared to repel any hostile attack, the Princess Hildegund took charge of the horse which carried their treasure, and of the fishing-rod with which they procured part of their provisions. Thus the noble pair wandered laboriously until, on the evening of the fortieth day of their flight, they reached the banks of the Rhine, near Worms, then the seat of the Frankish kings, and Walthere gave some of his recently-caught fishes to the boatmen who conveyed him across the river; and then, with the fair Hildegund, made for the forest of Vosagus, now called the Vosges. The boatman carried the fish to the palace, and sold them to the royal cook.

Next day, Gunthere (*Guntharius*), who was then king of the Franks, was seated at his table at dinner in his palace, when these fish delicately cooked were set before him. The king declared that he had never seen such fish in France before, and demanded whence they had been obtained. The boatman was brought, and from his description Hagano, who was now the favourite thane of king Gunthere, recognized Walthere in the fugitive, and knew that he had escaped from the court of Attila; and from the description of the boatman it was evident that he carried with him a certain amount of treasure. The king rose proudly from his table, called for his horse, and summoned twelve of his bravest warriors to accompany him, and declared his intention of pursuing Waltharius, and taking from him his treasure and his damsel before he escaped from his territory. He led Hagano with him, in spite of the earnest efforts of the latter to turn him from his inhospitable design.

Meanwhile the two fugitives had reached a spot where a cave in the mountain, approached by a narrow pass, offered them a safe and pleasant asylum. Walthere resolved to take advantage of it, and it was arranged that he should first sleep and Hildegund keep watch, and that afterwards he should be the watchman while the princess took her repose. As, since they left the court of the Huns, Walthere had never slept except in his arms and on his shield, he resolved now, trusting to the security of the spot, to disarm, and, while he laid himself on the ground, he enjoined Hildegund to keep a careful look out, and arouse him on the appearance of the slightest cause of alarm. He had slept for some time, when Gunthere and his companions, who had traced the fugitives by the footmarks of their horses, were seen approaching. The lady Hildegund gently roused her lover, and, terrified at the thought that they were the Huns, begged him to slay her with his sword rather than let her fall into their hands. But Walthere had confidence in himself, and he lost no time in arming to receive them. On the other side, Hagano had made another effort to pacify the king of the Franks, but still in vain, and he determined to stand aside and take no part in the combat; and Gunthere sent his warriors one after another, for only one could advance at a time, to attack the Aquitanian prince, and each in his turn fell under the strength of his victorious arm, until king Gunthere stood alone. He now, in rage and despair, addressed himself to Hagano, who stood at a distance looking on, and demanded his assistance, that they two should attack Walthere together. Hagano again urged the king to give up the feud, but Gunthere was still obstinate; and Hagano, with the feeling which in feudal times would be called faithfulness to his sovereign, agreed to assist his king, and proposed that he and Gunthere should withdraw, and watch till Walthere and his fair companion should quit their place of defence, then follow them in their retreat, and attack them at their disadvantage. Accordingly they withdrew to a place where they could put their horses to grass, where they would be themselves concealed from observation, and whence they would overlook the road which Walthere must take.

Soon afterwards the shades of night spread themselves over the scene, or, to use the words of our poet—

> Interea occiduas vergebat Phœbus in oras,
> Ultima per notam siguans vestigia Thilen, etc.

Walthere, seeing no more enemies, prepared to pursue his journey. He appears to have procured more horses, and he now placed all his luggage on four, mounted Hildegund on the fifth, and took the sixth for himself. On the latter he placed his more valuable treasures. They had ridden a short distance, when the alarm of Hildegund was excited, as she threw a glance behind, by seeing two men stealthily descending a hill, and she immediately warned her lover. Walthere at once recognized the pursuers. The fugitives, also, were mounting a hill, and Walthere directed Hildegund to hurry forward with their treasures, and seek in a neighbouring wood a place of shelter, while he remained to face the pursuers. He tried to reason with them, appealed to the old friendship of Hagano, and pleaded the inhospitable character of their attack, but without effect; and the king and Hagano rushed upon him at the same time. The result of the combat was that all three heroes were seriously wounded and disabled, and, at the call of Walthere, the Princess Hildegund hurried to the spot, attended to their wounds, and bandaged and treated them as the women of those days knew how to treat wounds. Then she performed another lady's duty. "Now, pour out the wine," said Walthere, "and offer it first to Hagano, who is a good champion if he were but faithful to his engagements; and then serve it to me, who have borne more than the others; and last let Gunthere drink, as the least courageous among the heroes of the fight."

> Jam misceto merum, Haganoni et porrige primum,
> Est athleta bonus, fidei si jura reservet;
> Tum præbeto mihi, reliquis qui plus toleravi;
> Postremum volo Guntharius bibat, utpote segnis
> Inter magnanimûm qui paruit arma virorum,
> Et qui Martis opus tepide atque enerviter egit.

Hildegund obeyed—it was the lady's duty to serve the wine or mead. With the wine they all became friends, and praised one another. King Gunthere, badly wounded, was placed upon his horse, and, with Hagano, returned, not in triumph, to Worms. Walthere and Hildegund pursued their way, without further interruption, into Aquitaine, where they were received with great honours, and their marriage was celebrated amid much rejoicing. After his father's death, Walthere succeeded to the throne of Aquitaine, and ruled happily over his people for many years.

CHAPTER III.

THE FRANKS IN GAUL.

It was the beginning of the fifth century of our era, when the different branches of the great Teutonic race were making their grand and final movement upon the Western Empire. The name of Germans was known to the Romans at a rather early period, as embracing the numerous cognate tribes who occupied the centre of Europe, and who, no doubt pressed forward by the movements of other peoples from behind, were continually seeking to advance towards the west. Cæsar, when he entered upon the conquest of Gaul, encountered the Germans on the borders of that country, and drove them back. It continued to be the policy of the Romans to repress and conquer these peoples through the whole period of their supremacy in the west. Tacitus, before the close of the first century after Christ, describes their manners and condition, which appear to have borne a sufficiently close resemblance to those of the Gauls before they were Romanised. As with the ancient Gauls, the Germans were accompanied in war by their wives and families—it was, in fact, a necessary consequence of the migratory state in which they lived—and their women cheered and encouraged them in battle, and attended to the wounded. Like the Gauls, in regard to their Druidesses, the Germans looked upon Womankind as possessing something divine in its character, and as communicating with the gods more easily than men; and Tacitus mentions as instances of the veneration thus paid to the sex, the examples of Velleda, and Aurinia, "and many others" (*et complureis alias*). Like the Gauls, as I have said on a former occasion, the men wore the *braccæ*, or breeches. They wore also a dress which fitted close to the body, and over it a *sagum*, or mantle. Tacitus tells us that the women adopted much the same clothing as the men, except that they were more usually clad in linen garments dyed purple, and that they did not extend the upper part of the dress into sleeves, but went with the whole arm naked, as well as the upper part of the breast.* This, as it will be remembered, was the costume of the goddesses in the Eddas, and it explains a provision, in that part of the early Frankish laws which was made for the protection of the female person. By the Salic law, if a free man squeezed a free woman's arm below the elbow, he was liable to a penalty of twelve hundred denarii; if it were above the elbow, the fine was raised to fourteen hundred denarii; and if he touched her breast, he was punished by a fine of eighteen hundred denarii. Women who required this protection evidently went with bare arms and bare breasts. We learn from the same laws that the Frankish women of this early period had their hair bound up on the head by a sort of cap or coif called an *obbo*, for one law provides that, "if any one derange a woman's hair, so that her obbo fall to the ground, he shall be condemned to a fine of fifteen solidi."†

Tacitus praises highly the chastity of the German women, and assures us that the Germans were almost the only people among the barbarians who lived satisfied each with one wife, "except a very small number, who, not through licentiousness, but as a mark of nobility, seek to have many wives."‡ Polygamy we have seen, in the preceding chapter, allowed among the Teutonic gods, and we shall soon find it prevailing among the Teutons who obtained possession of Gaul. Tacitus goes on to say that, among the Germans of his time, it was not the wife who brought a dower to the husband, but the husband who gave it to the wife. This was of course the *morgane-ghibu*, or morning-gift, the *morgan-gifu* of our Anglo-Saxon forefathers, a sort of marriage settlement, which was arranged on the eve of the marriage, but was given by the husband to the wife on the morning after the marriage was completed. It was, in itself, a sort of acknowledgment of woman's position. The historian adds that the parents and kindred were present to see that the terms of the gift were duly performed, and that it consisted not of objects intended for feminine indulgence, or for the gratification of female vanity, but of oxen, and a horse with its bridle, and a shield with spear and sword. These were the symbolical gifts—for symbolism prevails largely in the childhood of peoples—by which the wife was to

* Nec alius feminis quam viris habitus, eosque purpura variant, partemque vestitus superioris in manicas non extendunt, nudæ brachia ac lacertos, sed et proxima pars pectoris patet.—*Tacitus, Germania,* c. 17.

† Si quis mulierem excapillaverit ut ei obbonis ad terra cadat, solidos xv. culpabilis judicetur.—*Lex Salica,* c. 75.

‡ Nam prope soli barbarorum singulis uxoribus contenti sunt exceptis admodum paucis, qui non libidine sed ob nobilitatem plurimis nuptiis ambiuntur.—*Tacitus, Germania,* c. 18.

understand that she was henceforth to consider herself the companion of her husband in his labours and dangers, to share with him his fortunes in peace and in war.

The Romans sought to conquer these Germans, and, during the flourishing period of the empire, they were successful, and drove them far back from the borders of Gaul; but as the Roman power in the west fell more and more into decline, the imperial government was first obliged to conciliate those whom it had formerly defied, and afterwards to rest upon their support. Captives taken in war were always treated as slaves, and at an early period Gaul began to receive large accessions of Teutonic servile population. Then the Romans adopted the policy of encouraging the German tribes to place colonies in the northern parts of Gaul, where the population was very thin, and, in return for the protection they received, they formed on this side the guard of the Roman province. They thus constituted an extensive military colony, and the Romans knew them by the name of *læti*, in which we can hardly avoid recognizing the same word as the modern German *leute*, people. More than this, the Romans found that the Germans made better soldiers than any of their other barbarians, and they enlisted them into their armies and disciplined them. It was the impetuous charge of the German cohorts which decided the victory at Pharsalia. From this time it was the pride of successive emperors to possess German troops, and they made their body guards of German soldiers. After a while these formed the main force of the empire, and they were everywhere introduced into the offices of state, and even reached the imperial throne in the person of the Goth Maximinus, in the first half of the third century. In the fourth century the great officers of the imperial court and army, and those who occupied the novel charges of counts of the domestics, dukes of the frontiers (*limites*), and masters of the soldiery (*magistri militiæ*), were almost all Franks, or Alemanni, or Goths, or Burgundians. Such a state of things could not constitute a permanent strength, and accordingly, the Western Empire presented a scene of continual turbulence, which encouraged the Teutonic peoples outside to seek their fortunes in it, while they began towards the fourth century to be pushed forward by the advance of masses of peoples of other races from behind. The Salian Franks, driven by the Saxons from their primitive establishment in the interior of Germany, established themselves in the country to the extreme north of Gaul, between the Scheldt and the Meuse, in the middle of the fourth century. But it was at the beginning of the century following that the great invasion of the Teutons began, and within a few years the whole of Gaul was divided into three great independent kingdoms, between the Franks, the Visigoths, and the Burgundians. In the first years of the sixth century, as the result of a long series of intrigues and wars, nearly the whole of Gaul fell under the domination of the Franks.

We can trace little of the social condition of the Teutonic conquerors of Gaul during the long period of the wars of invasion, and can only suppose that, as far at least as concerned the Franks, it differed not considerably from that described by Tacitus. No doubt the invaders were accompanied in their expeditions by their women and families, for we have a remarkable story in confirmation. One of the most formidable of the Frankish chieftains in the invasions of the earlier half of the fifth century was named Chlodio. His head quarters lay between Brussels and Louvaine. Having sent explorers to report upon the attractions of the country to the southward, he assembled the leaders of his people, caused himself to be elected their military leader, and plunged with the whole tribe into the forest of Charbonnière (*Carbonaria*), a part of the Ardennes. Issuing from the depths of the forest, these Franks suddenly made their appearance on the banks of the Scheldt, and after taking and destroying Tournai and Cambrai, and massacring their inhabitants, they overrun the country as far as the banks of the Somme. It was at the time when the great Aetius was commanding the Roman armies, and victoriously protecting the empire against the new invasions of the barbarians, and he hurried from Brittany, crossed the Somme, and found the Franks encamped at a place named by the Latin historians Helena, but supposed to be Lens in Artois. They were so far from anticipating the probability of an attack, that they were busy celebrating, with barbaric grandeur, the marriage of one of their chieftains. A poet of Gaul, Sidonius Apollinaris, who wrote at this time, has left us a poem commemorating the event. He describes how, while the legions of Aetius and Majorianus were silently crossing the river, the hill beyond resounded with the noise of the nuptial festivities.

> Fors ripæ colle propinquo
> Barbaricus resonabat hymen, Scythicisque choreis
> Nubebat flavo similis nova nupta marito.
> *Sidon. Apollinar. Panegyr. Majoriani*, l. 219.

Suddenly the heads of the Roman legions appeared on the ground, and the Franks were taken by surprise, and, after a short but vigorous resistance, they were defeated with great slaughter. They had made an attempt to carry off the provisions of the festival in their chariots, but both the bride and the feast fell into the hands of the victors. There, as the poet tells us, might be seen glittering on the waggons the scattered preparations for the feast of the barbaric nuptials, and the dishes thrown together pell-mell, and the dainties captured, and the great cauldrons crowned with sweet smelling garlands.

> Plaustris rutilare videres
> Barbarici vaga festa tori, convictaque passim
> Fercula, captivasque dapes, cirroque madente
> Ferre coronatos redolentia serta lebetes.

Thus was Chlodio driven back in temporary disgrace upon his old hiding place in the forest of the Ardennes. The son of this Chlodio is called by the Latin chroniclers Meroveus, and by the French Mérovée, and he was the father of Clovis, who established the monarchy of the Franks, and from whom, as a Meroving, or son of Mérovée (it is the well-known Teutonic patronymic), the Frankish kings of the first race took the name of Merovingians.

The annals of the earlier period of Frankish history throw little light on the domestic character and condition of the people, and especially on that of female society. The Franks appear to have been distinguished from most of the other branches of the Teutonic race by their great ferocity and cruelty, and the story of their establishment in Gaul presents one continual and wearisome series of massacres and murders. We feel this painfully in reading through the narrative of Gregory of Tours, who seems as if he had only occupied himself with recording the crimes and vices of his countrymen and countrywomen. Females like Fredegond, and Brunehild, and many others whose names are recorded in these annals, all of whom were women of high and lofty minds, appear as if born only to exercise a fatal influence on human society. Perhaps we must blame history itself, which at this period has delighted in recording that which is wicked, because it carried with it more thrilling interest, and while all these queens of evil influence are arresting our attention, we must not forget that it was a woman, Clotild, the queen of Clovis, who led the Franks in the way to the truths of Christianity, and that it was another Frankish lady, Bertha, the daughter of king Charibert, who brought the truth of the Gospel from the land of the Franks into that of the Anglo-Saxons.

To use the phraseology of the modern French historical writers, the Franks, on their establishment in Gaul, came in face of two elements of civilization, the Roman element and the Christian element. They were barbarians in one of these points of view, and pagans in the other. The

Roman offered all the refinements of luxury, displayed splendid garments in rich materials, and dazzled with precious metals and jewels; the Christian urged the worthiness of poverty, the virtues of coarse apparel, and proscribed jewelry and ornament, except when used in the ceremonies or ornamentations of the church. The barbarians had soon begun to show a taste for Roman luxury, and, as they became acquainted with that people, they adopted more and more their manners and mode of life. The female sex, at least, adopted the Roman costume, and no longer appeared with naked arms and bosoms. The Roman ladies had themselves adopted some new fashions in dress, especially the *camisia*, from which word is derived the modern French word *chemise*, and which was introduced in the fourth century. It appears to have been an inner tunic, worn by women, and not laid aside at night; for Isidore gives the word, and tells us that it was derived from *cama*, a low Latin word for a bed, and that it was so called, "because we sleep in them in beds."* It was adopted by the Franks, and the name occurs in the Salic law. The camisia of queen Radegond (the saint) was embroidered with gold. The women, about the same time, brought into use a sort of buskins, or boots. The form of the tunic was modified by rounding it, and plaiting it in front.

The object of most importance to a woman was her hair, which in both sexes had in earlier times a political signification. A free man, or a free woman, always wore it long, and it was a grave offence to cut a woman's hair. By the law of the Burgundians, a free man who cut off the hair even of a woman who was a slave, was subject to a penalty, and a slave who cut off the hair of a free woman was punished by death. Unmarried girls were obliged to carry their hair loose without ornament, so that if a damsel was long unmarried, it was usual to say, "She remains in her hair," *remanet in capillo*. Married women might plait their hair, and adorn it with garlands, and with little fillets, called by the Franks *stapiones*, or *scapiones*—it is doubtful whether we ought to read the second letter as a *t* or a *c*.

With the Carlovingian period, the forms of society were becoming more firmly settled, but they underwent no radical change. The Roman type still prevailed in the female costume, and some further borrowings were made from the south, while whatever remained of the primitive dress of the Franks was rapidly disappearing. The usual dress of the women consisted of two tunics, of which the one underneath was longer and fitted closer than the other, and had close sleeves plaited at the wrist. The outer tunic was shorter and sat looser, with wide sleeves which reached only to the elbow.

* Camisias vocamus, quod in his dormimus in camis, id est, in stratis nostris.—*Isidore.*

Bands of different colours adorned the extremities of this vestment, which appears always of a different colour from the under tunic. A band, or girdle, encircled the hips, and a head-cloth, which was often richly embroidered, covered the head and enveloped the shoulders, and sometimes descended almost to the ground. The hair was thus entirely concealed. This part of the dress was richly adorned, and often of very brilliant colours. Among new articles of dress introduced during the Carlovingian

THE VISITATION.

period, was one common to both sexes, called a cape (*capa*), a sort of mantle or cloak, which is said by the old writers to have been a revival of the Roman caracalla. It appears to have been susceptible of great display of ornament, for it was forbidden by the council of Metz in 888 on account of its extravagance.

The Franks were slow in receiving a taste for literature, and appear to have written few books during the earliest period of their history, so that they have left us no pictorial representations of the female costume during

the Merovingian period, and very little until rather late in that of the
Carlovingian dynasty; and the illuminated manuscripts even of the latter
period are all Bibles, or service books, or lives of saints, which contain only
figures of sacred personages. Fortunately, however, these mediæval artists
drew every body in the exact character and costume of their own time.
The cut in the last page is a copy of an illuminated initial letter in a manuscript of the Latin Bible of the eighth century, in which it forms one
of the letters of the first word of the
Gospel of St. Luke. It was intended
to represent the Visitation, and the
two nimbuses show that the women
are sacred personages, but they may
be taken with equal truth for two
Frankish ladies of the age of Charlemagne, saluting each other. They
are charming figures, dressed in the
upper and under tunic as just described. The head-dresses are peculiar, and appear to be detached from
the mantle or (perhaps) cape. In the
figure to the left, the forepart of the
hair is seen, divided in the middle,
under the head-covering.

Our coloured plate is also taken
from a manuscript of the Latin Bible,
written in the ninth century, and
represents St. Jerome explaining the
Holy Scriptures to the noble mother
and daughter, Paula and Eustochia.
They were two Roman ladies in whose
house Jerome lived while he performed
the duties of secretary to Pope Da-
masus. The lady nearest to Jerome
is, by the richness of her costume,
evidently Paula, and the next her
daughter Eustochia, who had made a
vow of virginity. The difference in

FRANKISH LADIES.

dress was intentional on the part of the illuminator, for we know that the
dresses of married women were allowed to be much more rich, in material

GREEK SCHOOL OF THE NINTH CENTURY.

and ornament, than those of maidens. It may be well to remark that the parts here coloured yellow are gold in the original.

The next cut, also taken from a manuscript of the ninth century, represents two females, drest in the same costume. They wear, over the tunic, with the sleeves fitting tight to the wrist, a long robe which entirely covers the body, and has wide hanging sleeves.

There is a simplicity of character in the forms of this womanly costume, which gives a sort of imposing grace to the wearers. In this respect, they seem to have undergone no perceptible change during the whole Frankish period, but in richness of material and of jewelry they differed greatly. We hear the old writers speaking continually of the costly embroidery of the dresses of the Frankish ladies, which was usually of gold. Silks had been introduced among them from an early period of their settlement in Gaul, and other costly materials are mentioned. Silk and fringes of gold are often mentioned by Gregory of Tours. The clergy exceeded even the laity in this extravagance, and the ladies of the convents (as well as the ecclesiastics of the other sex), prided themselves on the richness of their dresses, and on the quantity of jewels with which they covered their persons. The great jeweller of the Franks—the patron of the jeweller's craft—was St. Eligius (or St. Eloi, as he is called in French). Yet these same ecclesiastics are always complaining of the extravagance and vanity of the laity. A preacher of Marseilles, in the fifteenth century, named Claudius Marius Victor, made a violent attack upon the vanities of Womankind in that city, in which he accused them of painting their faces; and it is spoken of as the practice among these Frankish ladies, at least at one period, to have their hair curled by means of curling irons. The extravagance in dress and in the toilette during the Carlovingian period appears to have been excessive.

The cut in the next page is given by Willemin, in his "Monumens Inedits," from a manuscript now preserved in the Imperial Library in Paris, which is understood to have been written and illuminated at Treves about the year 989. It represents two persons, evidently of rank, engaged in conversation. The lady is richly dressed, and is remarkable for the large handsome fibulæ, or brooches, which adorn her breast, and which remind us to some extent of the large brooches, of somewhat similar character, found in the Teutonic graves of the earlier pagan period, whether Frankish, or Anglo-Saxon, or Alemannic. It would seem as though this taste for the large fibulæ were especially Germanic, and, to judge from some of the figures given in our first chapter, that it showed itself in our western lands rather early. Our

Gallo-Roman lady Menimane, given in our first chapter (p. 16 of the present volume), might rival in this respect the Frankish lady of the close of the tenth century, represented in the present cut.

Before the Germans came into Gaul, women had already been employed, on a tolerably large scale, in productive labour. Among the Germans themselves, in their primitive period, the women of the household were constantly engaged in weaving the materials and in making garments for their husbands and families. It was the case also among the Romans in Italy, where a name derived from the Greek, gynæceum, was given to the room set apart for the females, in which they assembled to their work. In course of time, public establishments were formed, for the manufacture of the same products, in which women were similarly employed, and to which they gave the same name of gynæcea. They were placed under the direction of matrons, but a considerable proportion of the workwomen were slaves. They were early introduced into Gaul, where they formed the nuclei of the staple manufactures of particular localities, the materials being confined in some of them to flax, and in others to wool. Thus the Attrebates monopolised the manufacture of serge, and the same article still continues to be one of the staple manufactures of Amiens, which represents one of their principal cities. St. Jerome speaks of the fine texture of the stuffs made in his time at the civitas Atrebatum, or Arras. After the settlement of the Franks, the native industry revived in Gaul, and the gynæcea were re-established, apparently on an extensive scale, for they soon became very numerous. The historian Gregory of Tours (lib. ix.) tells us how a lady of the court of Theodebert, charged with plotting against the king's life, had her face branded, and was in that condition sent to the village of Marlheim, to be there employed in turning the mill, and in preparing the meal necessary for the nourishment of the women who dwelt in the gynæceum which existed in that place. The great fairs of Gaul, such as that of St. Denis, were sup-

FRANKISH NOBLES IN CONVERSATION.

plied with merchandise from these gynæcea, and Italy and other countries sought their products. A capitular of Dagobert, of the date of A.D. 630, fixes the punishment of a man who violated the person of one of the women of the gynæceum at a fine of six solidi of gold. Under the Carlovingians, the gynæcea remained in full activity. That at Stephanswert, belonging to Charlemagne's own domain, contained twenty-four women employed in fabricating vestments of woollen and linen, and of fillets for the legs. Charlemagne published several enactments relating to these establishments. In the celebrated capitular of the year 800, he enumerates the various implements and other things which were to be supplied to the workwomen. The great emperor was so anxious that Womankind should be employed in productive labour, that he made his own daughters work in the domestic gynæceum as diligently as the other females.

After the age of Charlemagne, the character of the women of the gynæcea began to fall into discredit. The old laws for the protection of their virtue were apparently no longer carried into effect, and corruption found its way among them. It became customary to speak of the inmates of the gynæcum as mere courtezans, until at length this was the only sense in which the word was used.

In the primeval ages, manual work alone had occupied the female part of the population, and literature, except the song in the hall, was unknown. Their conversion to Christianity, and its introduction under the forms in which it was then known, brought a new element of development among the Teutonic race. In the comparative solitude of the cloister, Womankind became acquainted with letters, and her mind gradually became enlarged and elevated, and embraced a new kind of refinement. Even in these early times, life in the convent was not quite of that ascetic character, bodily or mentally, as people are accustomed to suppose. The language of the new literature, which had been thus introduced, it is hardly necessary to say was Latin; and the books which were brought within the scope of monastic reading were not merely the Scriptures and works of a religious character, but they included the old Roman writers; and the more intelligent of the nuns, as well as monks, made themselves familiar, as far as they understood them, with Virgil, and Horace, and Terence, and Plautus. Nuns became learned as well as literary.

Literature did not flourish to any great extent among the Franks, and it would be a very unsatisfactory task to attempt a list of names of Frankish literary ladies, but among kindred Germanic blood we can point out examples of woman's talent and fitness for these higher studies which are

quite worthy of remark. The Benedictine abbey of Gandersheim, or
Gandesheim, in Saxony, was founded in 852 by Ludolf duke of Saxony,
at the instigation of his wife Oda, a Frankish princess, who became its
first abbess. Three daughters of the duchess Oda ruled after her in succession. On the death of the last of Oda's daughters, in 903, a successor
was chosen among the community of the nuns, and she appears to have
been selected for her literary accomplishments, for it is told of the abbess
Hrotswith that she excelled in various sciences, and especially in logic and
rhetoric, and she is said to have written a treatise on the former, though it
is not preserved. The name of Hrotswith appears to have been propitious
to literary aspirations, for another lady of the name in the latter half of
the tenth century gave celebrity to the abbey of Gandersheim by her talents.
This second Hrotswith was a poetess and a dramatist, and her writings
in both characters are preserved. Among these are eight poems in Latin
hexameter verses on sacred subjects, chiefly legends of saints. Hrotswith has also left two historical poems, one a panegyric of the family of
Odda, the ducal house of Saxony; the other, a history of the foundation of
Gandersheim. But, without any doubt, the most interesting and the most
characteristic of her works are her dramatic writings, or, as they are termed
by their author, her comedies.

The comedies of the Saxon nun of Gandersheim are six in number; they
are simple enough in plot, and are conducted with ease and grace, though,
as may be supposed, the language is not entirely pure in its Latinity.
But they show a cultivated mind, far superior to what we are accustomed to
suppose was to be found in that age, and above all they display a wonderful
knowledge of the world, when we consider that the writer was a lady, the
inmate of a convent, and, it is believed, not much more than twenty-five
years of age. She informs us that it was her intention to write in imitation
of Terence, whose works enjoyed great popularity, and were much read
among her contemporaries.* Hrotswith's object in all these plays is to
extol the virtue and celebrate the triumph of chastity, and it leads to scenes
that it required a very skilful hand to depict. Yet the Saxon maiden has
been singularly successful, and there is a degree of tenderness and delicacy
in her pictures, and these combined with a knowledge of human nature and
an intimacy with human life, which we should hardly expect. Her subjects
are sometimes calculated to alarm our feelings of modesty, but they are

---

* The best edition of the comedies of Hrotswith is that by Charles Magnin, "Théatre de
Hrotsvitha, Religieuse Allemande du x_e siècle," containing the text with a French translation.
8vo. Paris, 1845.

always treated with great tact and delicacy, and without any of the pretentious modesty which we might look for from the pious recluse. The first of these dramas has for its subject the history of a Roman general, of consular rank, named Gallicanus, who seeks, as the reward of his great military services, the hand of the beautiful princess Constantia, the daughter of the emperor Constantine. Constantia is a Christian convert, and has made a vow of chastity, and devoted herself to the service of God; and it is natural, therefore, that she should refuse to listen to the proposal of Gallicanus. But the general was on the eve of an important expedition against the Scythians, and it was resolved to give him an encouraging answer. He is therefore led to expect that his petition will be granted; and he marches with his forces against the enemy. The campaign, however, proves much more arduous and difficult than was expected; for the Scythians were brave and able soldiers, and they had also in their favour a great superiority of numbers. The Roman soldiers themselves became discouraged, and seemed to have lost their old prestige. In the midst of the battle, the general, in danger of being overcome, embraces, at the exhortation of two of Constantine's Christian officers, the faith of Christ, and by God's favour gains the victory. He determines, in consequence, to devote himself to a monastic life, and thus the virtue of Constantia is preserved through the interference of heaven. The subject of Dulcitius, the next, and perhaps the most remarkable, of Hrotswith's plays is somewhat different in character. Though the subject itself be sufficiently tragic, the plot of this piece is characterized by so much genuine humour, that it may not only be allowed the title it claims of a comedy, but we might even give it that of a farce. The scene is laid at Thessalonica, in the reign of Diocletian. Three beautiful Christian virgins, Irene, Agape, and Chionia, refuse to submit to the tyrant's command in returning to Paganism and marrying three of his officers, and the emperor commands them to be delivered to his governor Dulcitius, who has orders to throw them into prison preparatory to delivering them to martyrdom. Dulcitius, whose impure desires have been excited by the beauty of his prisoners, orders them, as more convenient for his own designs, to be inclosed in an apartment in the vestibule of which the kitchen utensils were kept. In the middle of the night he visits them, leaving his guards with their torches outside the door; but a spell has been thrown over him, and instead of enfolding the maidens in his arms, he unconsciously embraces in their stead the pots and kettles, until, all besmeared with soot and grime, he has more the appearance of a demon than of a human being. The scene is described to her two companions by Irene, who witnesses it through

7

a crack in the door.* When Dulcitius returns to his guards they know him no longer, but, taking him in fact for some demon, they fly in terror. He repairs to the palace to seek an interview with the emperor, but the doorkeepers (*ostiarii*) refuse to let him enter. Astonished at the manner in which he is treated by everybody, Dulcitius now proceeds to his own house, and presents himself before his wife; and becoming through her representations aware of the delusion to which he has been exposed, he orders the three holy maidens to be stripped and exposed publicly to the last outrages. They are, however, protected by the divine power. The subject of the next drama, Callimachus, is a horrible story, which occurs more than once in mediæval legend.

The fourth of Hrotswith's "comedies" is entitled Abraham, from the name of its hero. Abraham is a pious hermit, who has persuaded a young and beautiful niece named Mary to abandon the world, consecrate her virginity to Christ, and retire to a cell attached to his own hermitage. There she lives twenty years in great sanctity; but at the end of that period she allows herself to be seduced by a monk, flies from her cell, and takes up her abode in a house of prostitution. There, after an abandoned life of two years, she is found by her pious uncle, who penetrates to her in the garb of a lover, and succeeds in restoring her to her better sentiments, and carries her back a penitent to her hermitage. The truthfulness with which the Saxon recluse pictures scenes belonging to a life to which she must have been a stranger, is not the least remarkable part of this singular composition. The next of these pieces, Paphnutius, has a somewhat similar plot to that of Abraham. Paphnutius, like him, is a hermit who is seized with the desire to recall from her vicious ways an abandoned courtezan named Thais. The drama opens with a scene in which Paphnutius is

---

* The following passage from the scene in which Irene describes to her companious the proceeding of Dulcitius among the kitchen utensils may serve as a specimen of Hrotswith's Latin:—

Chionia. Quid sibi vult collisio ollarum, caccaborum, et sartaginum?

Irene. Lustrabo.—Accedite, quæso, par rimulas perspicite.

Agape. Quid est?

Irene. Ecce, isto stultus mente alienatus æstimat se nostris uti amplexibus.

Agape. Quid facit?

Irene. Nunc ollas molli fovet gremio, nunc sartagines et caccabos amplectitur mitia libans oscula.

Chionia. Ridiculum!

Irene. Nam facies, manus, ac vestimenta, adeo sordidata, adeo coinquinata, ut nigredo quæ inhæsit similitudinem Æthiopis exprimat.

Agape. Decet, ut talis appareat corpore qualis a diabolo possidetur in mente.

introduced giving a philosophical lecture to his disciples, very singular as coming from the pen of a female. Paphnutius has heard of Thais, visits her in the disguise of a lover, and converts her to better sentiments in his own character. She burns all the riches she has collected by her evil life, and is led by her convertor to a nunnery. The last of these curious dramas is entitled Sapientia (wisdom), and has for its heroines three holy virgins, named Faith, Hope, and Charity, who are represented as suffering martyrdom under the emperor Hadrian. Sapientia is a Greek princess, and the three virgins are her daughters. It is simply an old religious legend, in which there is, perhaps, a certain shade of allegory.

Such is the earliest known dramatic authoress of Western Europe. Hrotswith was evidently possessed, at so young an age, of a mind which was singularly cultivated and refined.

CHAPTER IV.

THE ANGLO-SAXON WOMEN.

WE have no authentic history of what took place in our island during the period between the time when the Roman government was withdrawn from it, and that in which the Anglo-Saxon power became established in Britain; that is, during the first half of the fifth century. The towns seem to have lived in separate independence. Their populations, as I have remarked before, appear to have been recruited in later times chiefly from Teutonic blood; but they had adopted Roman manners, had embraced the Roman civilization, no doubt with most of its vices as well as its virtues, and spoke the Latin language. They were, in fact, looked upon by the invaders as Romans and as enemies, and, as the Teutons were themselves unacquainted with the advantages of living in towns, when these fell under their power they were plundered and destroyed. But the townsmen were protected by strong walls, and knew how to defend them; and the Anglo-Saxon chieftains, as they assumed regal power, soon saw the advantage of compounding with and conciliating the towns, and securing to themselves a revenue by taking a tax just as the townsmen had before paid their tax to the imperial government. Thus there came into existence throughout the country two forms of society, the patriarchal clanship, if we may so call it, of the Teutonic peoples, in alliance with the Roman civilization of the towns. In their slow, imperfect amalgamation, the former gave the force, the latter the polish, to the whole. The Saxon freemen who had conquered the land shared it among them in lots, and each thus became a landholder and the head of a family. In this manner the inhabitants of the towns formed so many little governments, republican in character, while the broad lands outside were in the possession of a strong aristocracy, which acknowledged a superior chieftain who claimed the title of king. Thus arose that distinction, we might almost say antagonism, in character and spirit between town and country which has continued, more or less, down to the present time.

When the Anglo-Saxons settled in our island, the patriarchal spirit existed among them in its full force. The father was absolute master in his own family, and could dispose of his children at his will. He sold his daughters into wedlock, and he not unfrequently sold his sons into slavery. An Anglo-Saxon poem of Gnomic Verses, preserved among the contents of the well-known Exeter Book, tells us somewhat quaintly that "a maid is the delight of the eyes" (*mægð egsan wyn*), and that "a lover requires a physician" (*lefmon læces behofað*); though the idea intended to be conveyed in the latter saying is not very clear. It is certain that the maiden was entirely in her father's power, and absolutely at his disposal, and that she had no will or choice of her own. In fact, at the time when St. Augustine brought Christianity among our Anglo-Saxon forefathers, maid or wife was regarded absolutely as an article of property, in the one case of her father, in the other of her husband; and the laws of Ethelbert, our first Christian Anglo-Saxon king, contain distinct provisions to meet the crime of stealing them. The words of the first are, "If a man carry off a maid by force, let him pay fifty shillings to her owner, and afterwards buy her from him;" the terms of the other law are, "If a man carry off a freeman's wife, let him procure him another with his own money, and deliver her to him." It appears that the former was the primitive method of procuring a wife; the lover, who certainly ran the risk in this state of things of being in want of a physician, after he had fixed his eye upon a maiden to his taste belonging to some other family than his own, and, perhaps with her secret consent, went with some of his friends and carried her off. This was the form of proceeding of a man who prided himself on his bravery. The girl's relatives took up the feud and pursued him, and the quarrel was only appeased by the lover paying the value fixed upon her by her father, and so retaining possession. My friend Mr. Thrupp, in his excellent and interesting volume, "The Anglo-Saxon Home," has traced the progress of the transition from this rather lawless practice of stealing first and paying the price afterwards, to the more legal and reasonable proceeding of buying in the first place for a stipulated price.

The price of a maiden was generally fixed at so many head of cattle. A passage in the Gnomic Verses of the Exeter Book, which I have already referred to, shows us how universally this practice of buying the wife prevailed. It is as follows :—

Cyning sceal mid ceape
cwene gebicgan;
bunum and beagum
bu sceolon ærest
geofum gód wesan.

A king shall with cattle
buy a queen;
with cups and bracelets
both shall at first
in gifts be bounteous.

Thorpe's edit. of the Codex Exoniensis, p. 338.

At a later period, when the peoples began to enter more extensively into diplomatic relations with each other, the king gave away his daughters for political purposes; but their own feelings were never consulted. So, after the introduction of Christianity and monasticism, the father dedicated his daughter to a monastic life, if he willed it, long before she was capable of forming a judgment for herself. In the middle of the seventh century, when Oswy, king of the Northumbrians, had defeated and slain Penda, the pagan king of the Mercians, he gave his daughter to Christ, who thus, according to the views of the church, became her spiritual husband, and she was consecrated to Him in perpetual virginity. Bede, who was nearly a contemporary, tells us that the princess was at that time scarcely a year old. The clergy laboured to weaken and break down the power of the father or husband, and especially the former, over the daughter or wife, and they were in the end successful. The change was going on gradually for three or four centuries, and it was not till after the middle of the tenth century that woman obtained the right of insisting upon her own objection to any husband proposed to her by her father, and thus became so far her own mistress. It may be remarked, that the memory of the old principle of the father's right over his daughter is still preserved in the marriage ceremony, in our modern form of a father giving the bride.

The primitive marriage ceremony among our forefathers was very simple, consisting, in fact, of a bargain and a sale; its principal form was hand-fasting (*hand-fæstnung*), or pledging each other's hand. The contracting parties took each other by the hand, proclaimed themselves man and wife, and made certain promises of love and affection on the part of the bride, and of good treatment and protection on that of the husband. The lady's friends were present, and her father or guardian received the purchase-money, which had been agreed upon, and delivered her to the bridegroom. In a bargain like this, it is evident that a good amount of deception might be practised on the part of the father in misrepresenting his daughter's qualities or attractions, and this was evidently not uncommonly the case, for one of our earliest codes of Anglo-Saxon laws, that of Ethelbert, Augustine's convert, contains a provision against it. It was, no doubt, a very early law

of the Anglo-Saxon people, for, though written in the code of laws as prose,
it seems, by its rhythm and the natural division of the lines, to have been
originally composed in alliterative verse, to be more easily carried in memory
by the primitive dispensers of justice, and I will therefore give it here
arranged in verse, as a singular monument of primeval manners :—

Gif man mægð gebigeð	If a man buy a maiden
ceapi, geceapod ay,	with cattle, let the bargain stand,
gif hit unfacne is;	if it be without guile;
gif hit þonne facne is,	but if there be deceit,
ef[t] þær æt ham gebrenge,	let him bring her home again,
and him man his sca:t afere.	and let man give him back his money.

Ancient Laws and Institutes of England, vol. i. p. 22.

We have no direct information as to the limit of time after marriage, in the
earlier ages, within which the husband was required to send back his wife
to her father if dissatisfied with her. In course of time the father sought to
conceal the mercantile character of this transaction, by representing it as a
compensation for the expense for the young lady's feeding and education;
and the money paid was then called a *foster-lean*, or payment for
nourishing.

The custom of espousals also prevailed among the Anglo-Saxons at an
early period, that is, the father entered into an engagement for the future
marriage of his daughter at any period before she had reached a marriage-
able age. After the introduction of Christianity, the clergy gradually
reduced this engagement to a regular and stable system, by applying to it
the Roman law of espousals; and the lover was required to give at that
time a *wed*, or security, for the due performance of his part of the contract.
Hence the ceremony of marriage has been called in English, down to the
present time, a *wedding*.

At first the foster-lean was expected to be paid at the time of the
espousals, which was a sort of selling beforehand, and led to other abuses.
By the law of espousals, by which the ecclesiastics sought to establish more
and more their influence over the female sex by emancipating them from
the paternal power, the contracted bride, up to a certain age, had the right
of refusing to perform the contract; if she did this at ten years of age, the
contract was void, and neither father nor daughter were liable to any
punishment; if she did it at any time between her tenth and twelfth years, the
father was liable to a fine; after that age, both were punishable. It is
evident how this law might be abused by the father of an attractive daughter,
who might espouse her and obtain the foster-lean, and then espouse her to a

second lover, and obtain a second payment, and so on to the third, and all
this without parting with the girl, yet retaining the money. It will be seen
that in these primitive times, lovers were liable to be imposed upon in more
ways than one. And we may be sure that this last-mentioned mode of
deception was not of very unfrequent occurrence, for, though not provided
against in the secular laws (for the practice of such matrimonial pre-
contracts was an ecclesiastical institution), it was condemned in the laws of
the church; and in the Pœnitentiale of Theodore of Canterbury, and the
Confessionale and Pœnitentiale of Ecgbert of York, there are severe enactments against it. The latter orders that if any woman be espoused
(beweddod) to a man, and another take her from him, she shall be excom-
municated; and in the two former codes it is ordered that "it is not permitted to her parents to give to another man a girl who is espoused, unless
she declare that she is altogether resolute not to have him."[*] This ecclesiastical law appears not to have been popular among the people, and
instead of allowing the espoused girl, when she refused the first husband
provided for her, to be given to another, Theodore and Egbert's ecclesiastical
law ordered her to retire to a convent. Still this proved unsatisfactory, and
it was finally arranged that the foster-lean should be paid, not at the
espousals, but on the completion of the marriage.

The clergy had laboured to introduce more formalities into the ceremonial of marriage, and to add to it more that was typical and figurative.
At the espousals, after the taking of hands, the couple who were thus engaged,
made an exchange of presents. Among those given by the bridegroom was
a ring, which was placed on the maiden's right hand, and which was to be
worn so until the time of her marriage. They also exchanged a solemn
kiss, which was looked upon as having a spiritual meaning. At the
marriage, if espousals had previously taken place (for they were not
necessary), the ring was removed by the bridegroom to the bride's left hand,
and was placed on the first finger—if there had been no espousals, he then
gave it her, and placed it on the first finger of the left hand. The father
then transferred to the husband his authority over his daughter, which is
called in Anglo-Saxon the mund (from mundian, to protect), but for this also
he required payment. This transfer was made by another typical gift; the
father delivered the bride's shoe to the bridegroom, and the latter touched
her on the head with it, whereby he was considered to assume the marital

* Puellam desponsatam non licet parentibus suis dare alteri viro, nisi illa omnino declarat
se cum nolle; tunc, si velit, licebit ei id derelinquere, et vitam monasticam sibi eligere, si velit.—
Confes. Ecgberti, 20. Compare Theodori Liber Pœnitent., vi. 29.

authority. This early ceremony, too, is still preserved in memory in the popular custom of throwing a shoe after the newly-married couple when they are starting on their wedding excursion.* After these mere ceremonies were over, came the more substantial considerations on both sides, which had been arranged beforehand, but which had now to be completed. Among these, the most remarkable was the gift made to the wife by the husband the morning after the marriage, and called from this circumstance the *morgen-gifu*, or morning-gift. It was originally a mere voluntary gift, made on the morning after the wedding, to testify the degree of satisfaction of the husband with his wife, and depended upon his natural generosity and upon his approval of her. Afterwards it was considered as one of the most indispensable articles of the marriage-contract, and the amount was stipulated before the ceremony, partly because it was an acknowledgment that the husband was satisfied, and, after he had given the morning-gift, he had no longer the right of returning his bride. It was at first a comparatively trivial present, but it afterwards became, among wealthy families, a large amount of property, and sometimes consisted of considerable estates, which became the absolute property of the wife, and she had the full power of disposing of them if she became a widow. Thus, at the close of the tenth century, the lady Wynflæd, by her will, leaves to one of her relatives the estate at Faccancumb, which had been given to her as her morning-gift; and, near the same date, Elfhelm makes an entry in his will, " And I make known what I gave my wife for a morning-gift ; that is Baddow, and Burstead, and Stratford, and the three hides at Heanhall; and I gave to her, when we first came together, the two hides at Wilbraham, and at Rayne, and what is thereto adjacent."† The practice of the morning-gift was established throughout the Teutonic race. When King Athelstan's sister, Eadgith, was married to Otho, Emperor of Germany, her imperial bridegroom gave her for her morning-gift the city of Magdeburg.

* It has been supposed that this custom of the gift of the shoe had its origin in that of placing the foot on the neck of a prisoner or slave, and that it was typical of the state of subjection in which the bride was placed towards her husband. When the married pair retired to rest, it seems that the shoe was placed at the head of the bed on the husband's side; and that, by way of practical joke, when the lady was accused of being rather tyrannical in temper, some facetious individual sometimes stole into the room, and slyly transferred the shoe to the wife's side. See Mr. Thrupp's *Anglo-Saxon Home*, already referred to, for a longer and more detailed account of the customs and ceremonies of the Anglo-Saxon marriages than I can give here.

† See the original wills in Thorpe's *Diplomatarium Anglicum Ævi Saxonici*, pp. 533 and 596.

In all these stipulations of inferiority and subjection of the wife to the husband, there was far more of theory than of practice. The natural influence of Womankind soon overruled and suppressed them, at least practically, which was of greatest importance. If she was bound to an apparent subservience, he was bound to cherish and protect her ; and he had, as far as his means went, to endow her with property. The position of the wife, and indeed of woman generally, went on improving during the whole Anglo-Saxon period. By the time of Cnut, it had become usual, if not compulsory, on a man of any property, to make at his marriage a substantial settlement upon his wife, and she had a legal right, upon his death, to a certain portion of his wealth. But, if the widow married within a year after the death of her husband, she forfeited everything she had received from him. This is, no doubt, the origin of our feeling that a widow ought to remain a year after her husband's death before marrying again. Singularly enough, the Danes, who are usually looked upon as mere sanguinary savages, appear to have been instrumental in finally raising the position of Womankind in England, and the sex appears as enjoying most consideration and protection, legally at least, in the laws of King Cnut. One of woman's domestic privileges among the Northmen was curious enough ; she had a right to the custody of her husband's keys, and, if he refused, she had a remedy at law, by which she could compel him to give them up to her. Cnut introduced this provision into the Anglo-Saxon laws, and he did so with the object of abolishing a part of the older Anglo-Saxon law, which was very cruel towards the wife and family. By the earlier laws, if a husband committed theft, his wife and all his family, even the child in the cradle, as well as himself, were liable to be sold into slavery, and this continued to be the case for a long period, until Cnut abolished it. He enacted that in regard to the object stolen, "unless it has been brought under his wife's key-lockers (*cæg-locan*), let her be clear ; for it is her duty to keep the keys of them, namely, her *hord-ern*, and her chest, and her *tege*. If it be brought under either of these, then she is guilty." * These three depositories are to be explained as her store-room, her chest, and her cupboard, and they are apparently those parts of the house only which were locked.

The interior of the house, indeed, was the wife's special province, and, as with the Roman lady whose epitaph has been given in a former chapter,† one of her most estimable virtues was being "a keeper at home." In the

---

* *Ancient Laws and Institutes of England*, vol. i., p. 419.
† See p. 23 of the present volume.

poem of Gnomic Verses, quoted before from the Exeter Book, we are told :—

<table>
<tr><td>
Fœmne æt hyre bordan gerisc[ð] ;
wid-gongel wif word gespringe[ð],
oft hy mon womnaum bilih[ð],
hæle[ð] hy hospe mænu[ð],
oft hyre hleor abreote[ð].
</td><td>
A damsel it beseems to be at her table ;
a rambling woman scatters words,
she is often charged with faults,
a man thinks of her with contempt,
oft smites her cheek.
Thorpe's Codex Exon., p. 337.
</td></tr>
</table>

The females of the Anglo-Saxon household were not idle in their bower, but, as with the Franks also, worked industriously, both in producing the materials of the dresses, and other objects used by their husbands and themselves, and in making them. We have from time to time, in early writers, allusions to this domestic industry. In the Pœnitentiale of Theodore of Canterbury, which dates from soon after the middle of the seventh century, women are forbidden to employ themselves on Sunday, either in weaving or in cleaning the vestments, or in sewing them, or in carding wool, or in beating flax, or in washing garments, or in shearing the sheep, or in any such occupations.[*] Here we see, at that early period, the whole process of the construction of clothing entirely in the hands of the women of the household. Boniface, in one of his letters (Epist. 20), tells of a damsel who was grinding in a mill, and who saw lying near her another woman's new spindle, which was ornamented with carving (*novam colum sculptura variatam*), which seemed to her so beautiful that she stole it. The distaff was so generally the distinguishing implement of the lady of the family, that the word distaff, or spindle, was used for her in distinction from the spear, as distinctive of the man. King Alfred, in his will, made soon after the year 880, says, in his directions for the distribution of his property, that his grandfather had bequeathed his lands "to the spear-side (*on þa spere-healfe*) and not on the spindle-side (*on þa spinl-healfe*), and that, therefore, he wished it to go by preference to his male descendants.[†] These occupations were considered equally fitting to queens and princesses as to ladies of ordinary rank. William of Malmesbury tells us that the daughters of King Edward, Alfred's son and successor, employed themselves from their childhood in the labours of the distaff and the needle. Long before this, in the seventh century, Aldhelm, who wrote especially for the ladies,

---

[*] Item feminæ opera textilia non faciant, nec abluant vestimenta, nec consuant; nec lanam carpere, nec linum batere, nec vestimenta lavare, nec verveces tondere, nec aliquid hujusmodi habeant licitum.—*Theodor. Pœnitent.*, p. 45, in the *Ancient Laws and Institutes,* vol. ii.

[†] See Alfred's will in Thorpe's *Diplomatarium*, p. 491.

had made the distaff (*fusum*) the playful subject of one of his riddles. Before the Norman period, the English ladies had become celebrated even on the Continent, for their skill in spinning, weaving, and embroidering; and one of the Norman writers on the history of the Norman conquest of England, whose name is not known, tells us how the French and Normans admired the beautiful dresses of the English nobility, and adds that the English women "excell all others in needlework, and in the art of embroidering with gold." * Another Norman writer of the same period, William of Poitiers, assures us that the Anglo-Saxon ladies were so celebrated for their superior skill in embroidery, that the finest productions of the needle were called by way of distinction "English work" (*Anglicum opus*).†

The Anglo-Saxon ladies of rank were especially skilful in embroidery, and that from a very early period. English girls are spoken of in the life of St. Augustine as employed in skilfully ornamenting the ensigns of the priesthood and of royalty with gold, and pearls, and precious stones. St. Etheldreda, the first Abbess of Ely, a lady of royal rank, presented to St. Cuthbert a stole and maniple which she had thus embroidered with gold and gems with her own hands. At a later period, Algiva or Emma, the queen of King Cnut, worked with her own hands a stuff bordered in its whole extent with gold work, and ornamented in places with gold and precious stones arranged in pictures, executed with such skill and richness that its equal might be sought through all England in vain.‡ Dunstan is said to have designed patterns for the ladies in this artistic work. The early historian of Ely tells a story of an Anglo-Saxon lady who, having retired to lead a religious life in that monastic establishment, the nuns assigned to her a place near the abbey, where she might occupy herself more privately with young damsels in embroidery and weaving, in which they excelled. We trace in early records the mention of women who appear to have exercised these arts as a profession. We find, for instance, in the Domesday book, a damsel named Alwid holding lands at Ashley in Buckinghamshire, which had been given to her by Earl Godwin for teaching his daughter orfrey, or embroidery in gold,§ and a woman named Leviet or

---

* *Anonymi Gesta Gulielmi ducis, op. Duchesn.*, p. 211.

† *Gulielmi Pictavens.*, ib.

‡ Ut nulla alia in Anglorum regione talis operis et protii inveniatur.—*Hist., Eliens. in Gal.*, p. 502.

§ Do his tenuit Aluuid puella ii. hidas . . . . et de dominica firma regis Edwardi habuit ipsa dimidiam hidam, quam Godricus vicecomes ei concessit quamdiu vicecomes esset, ut illa doceret filiam ejus aurifrisium operari.—*Domesday Book*, fol. 149.

Leviede is mentioned in Dorsetshire as employed in making orfrey for the king and queen.*

Aldhelm, in the seventh century, speaks of the passion for wearing cloths of various colours and ornamentation, and says that they would not satisfy the eye if they were of a uniform colour.† A fine illuminated Psalter, of the earlier part of the Norman period, preserved in the library of Trinity College, Cambridge, furnishes the accompanying cut, which repre-

LADIES AT THEIR WEAVING.

sents the females of an English household engaged in the occupation of weaving. The lady seated in the chair is probably the mistress. The implements used for cutting are of the form common to the Romans and to the Saxons, and were called, in the language of the latter, a *scear*, a word still preserved in the name of the *shears* of our modern clothiers.

With such skill in working the materials, we are not surprised at hearing the old writers more than hinting at the love of the Anglo-Saxon women for dress and ornament. Thus Aldhelm, in the latter part of the seventh century, comparing the women of the cloister with the women of the world, describes the latter as yearning to adorn their necks with necklaces, and their arms with bracelets, and to be decked with rings on their fingers, set

---

* Hæc Leviede fecit et facit aurifrisium regis et reginæ.—*Domesday Book,* fol. 74.

† The words of Aldhelm are rather a curious illustration of the subject. They are, Siquidem cortinarum sive stragularum textura, nisi panniculæ purpureis immo diversis colorum varietatibus fucato inter densa filorum stamina ultro citroque decurrant, et arte plumaria omne textrinum opus diversis imaginum toraciclis peroruent, sed uniformi coloris fuco sigillatim confecta fuerit. —*Aldhelmi de Laud. Virginit.,* cap. xv., ed. Giles.

with gems. . . . . They sought to arrange delicately their waving locks, curled artificially by the curling-iron, with their cheeks dyed red with stibium.* And in another part of the same book, his treatise of the Praises of Virginity, he complains of their changing the natural colour of the fleeces, for woollen was very extensively used in their garments, in order to dye them red, and purple, and various other colours, looking forward to the time when all this vanity will come to an end, and when the wool will cease learning to counterfeit other colours than its own.

Nec varios discet mentiri lana colores.†

We might suppose from the words of Aldhelm that the material used for

THREE OF THE VIRTUES IN ANGLO-SAXON COSTUME.

the dress in his time was chiefly woollen, but we know that linen was also in general use; and at this time silk (*seolc*), and other valuable materials of foreign manufacture, had been introduced.

It is to be lamented that the Anglo-Saxon writers who have left us their

---

* Ista tortis ciucinnorum crinibus calamistro crispantibus delicate componi et rubro coloris stibio genas ac mandibulas suatim fucare satagit.—*Aldhelm de Laudibus Virginitatis*, cap. xvii., ed. Giles.

† *Aldhelm de Laud. Virginit.*, cap. lvi.

protest against the richness of the materials, the variety of colours, and the love of jewelry displayed by the Anglo-Saxon ladies, have given us no description of their dress, or of the different articles of which it consisted; and it is only at a comparatively late date that the Anglo-Saxon artists enable us, by the illuminations in their manuscripts, to form a notion of its outward appearance. We have every reason, however, to believe that the Anglo-Saxon costume, which seems to have resembled pretty closely that of the Frank, hardly underwent any change through several centuries, except so far as regarded its richness of material and ornamentation. A few groups from the illuminations just mentioned will convey to our readers the best

AN ANGLO-SAXON CONVERSATION.

idea of this costume, and of the general appearance of Womankind among our forefathers at this remote period. Our first cut is taken from a manuscript of the Psychomachia of Prudentius, which is, perhaps, of the latter part of the tenth century (MS. Cotton. Cleopatra, C. VIII. fol. 4, v°.). The original represents the lady Wisdom addressing the Virtues, three of whom are here given as good examples, not only of the costume, but of the gesture, and action, and characteristic appearance, of Anglo-Saxon ladies at this date.

The garb of these Anglo-Saxon ladies is extremely modest; very different from the older dresses of the Roman and Romano-Gallic period, and from what is understood to have been the costume of the older Germans; nothing is here uncovered but the face and hands. In the second cut, which represents a conversation between two persons of different sexes, and is taken from the same manuscript (fol. 31, r°), the lady presents exactly the same characteristics of costume and the same style of character; she is intended here to represent Faith, and in the original she is preaching to a crowd of people, of whom only one is introduced here that we may contrast the costume of the two sexes.

It has been stated in the preceding chapter, how the *camisia* (the French *chemise*) was added to the older Roman costume at the close of the western empire. It was no doubt adopted from the Franks by the Anglo-Saxons, for in the Anglo-Saxon glosses it is explained by the same word in an Anglo-Saxon form, *cemes* or *cemis*, and it appears to have held the place of the modern shift; that is, it was the garment next to the skin, and it was probably of linen, but, as may be supposed, it is never visible in the drawings. Over this was thrown the tunic, which also was derived, no doubt, from the Romans, and had preserved its Roman name in that of *tuneca*. It was a long full dress, almost concealing the feet, and had close sleeves reaching in rolls to the wrists, where they appear to have been usually confined by a bracelet. As the Anglo-Saxons had, in some cases, more than one word for the same article of dress, we often find a difficulty in identifying them. Such is the case with the word *cyrtel*, our modern *kirtle*. It is used in the old glosses to explain the Latin *tunica*, so that it seems to have been another name for the garment just described, or perhaps for an outer garment of the same kind, answering to the outer tunic of the Roman ladies. We certainly see on the ladies of the Anglo-Saxon illuminations two robes, one over the other; the outer of which is raised, and shows that they differ in colour and apparently in materials, while the inner dress can hardly be the *camisia*. This part of the dress was tightened round the waist by the girdle, which is often very broad, but sometimes so narrow as to be little more than a belt. Over all these was thrown a mantle, answering to the Roman *palla*, and derived apparently from it. The Anglo-Saxon name for it was, perhaps, a *wæfels*; at least that word is given in the Anglo-Saxon glosses as synonymous with the Latin *palla*. The mantle of the Anglo-Saxon ladies appears to have been formed exactly like the *palla*, and to have been put on and worn in the same manner. The Anglo-Saxon ladies, like the Franks, seem to have always worn a covering to the head; at least they are always represented thus covered in the engravings, and it will be best understood by our cuts. It appears to have been usually called simply a head-rail (*heafod-hrægel*), or head-garment, for we are not aware of any special name given to it among the Anglo-Saxons. It appears sometimes as covering the head closely, and reaching no lower than the neck; at others, and in fact usually among the Anglo-Saxons, it sits looser and flows over the shoulders, and even beyond them, so as to form a kind of hood. Sometimes the lower part appears to be separate from that which covers the head, and the former may then be what the Anglo-Saxons called the *winpel*, or wimple.

We will now pay a visit to the Anglo-Saxon ladies in two other illuminated manuscripts of the period, and, if we learn not much more of their dress, we shall at least see them in other situations and characters. The works of the Anglo-Saxon artists of this period are singularly characterized by their spirited sketchy style of drawing, which is quite peculiar to them, and executed with a skill we could hardly expect, and of which the two manuscripts just mentioned are excellent examples. The first is a fine manuscript in the Harleian library in the British Museum (MS. Harl., No. 603), containing a copy of the Book of Psalms in Latin, profusely illustrated with these sketches. I

A GROUP OF ANGLO-SAXON WOMEN.

give, in the accompanying cut, as an example of its style, a small group of Anglo-Saxon women, evidently all in a state of excitement; the two foremost seem especially agitated, while the one behind appears to be possessed with a degree of quiet dignity which is not easily ruffled. The second of our manuscripts is an equally fine and valuable volume (MS. Cotton. Claudius, B. IV.), containing a copy of the Anglo-Saxon translation of the Pentateuch by one of our most celebrated Anglo-Saxon prelates, Alfric of Canterbury. It is, like the other manuscript I am now using, largely illustrated, in a different style of art, but still the drawings are often as full of spirit as they are truthful. I give, in the next cut, an example from this manuscript (fol. 46, v°). It is intended in the original to represent the patriarch Jacob and his wife Leah, and his two sons by her handmaid Zilpah, Gad and Asher. It was a peculiar characteristic of the draughtsman of the Middle Ages, and especially in the illuminated manuscripts, that, whatever might be the subject, he invariably drew it in the costume and

9

manners of his own time. The scene before us may be described in entire correctness as an Anglo-Saxon family group—the head of the family and his wife seated on their settle, or double seat, and accompanied by their two boys. The father is dressed in his in-door costume; their mother in the full dress of the Anglo-Saxon dame, as just described; the eldest of the boys has reached the age at which he is allowed to have at least a mimic sword.

AN ANGLO-SAXON FAMILY.

Our last cut on the present occasion is taken from the previously-described manuscript of the Psalms (MS. Harl., No. 603, fol. 15, v°). It represents a man, with a woman and child, at the entrance to what is, perhaps, intended to be a temple. It is the same style of costume, with the exception of the child, which is perfectly naked. Perhaps this is characteristic of a lower class of society.

Our coloured plate is another scriptural subject from the manuscript of Alfric's version of the Pentateuch (MS. Cotton. Claudius, B. IV., fol. 51, v°), and it may be taken as a very good example of the Anglo-Saxon idea of a patriarchal family. It is true that it represents the children of Jacob with

PATRIARCHAL FAMILY.

their mothers, Leah and Rachel, and their handmaids, Zilpah and Bilhah. To the left we see Rachel and her single son, and Leah with her six—her daughter is not counted; to the right, Bilhah and Zilpah have respectively their two sons (Gen. xxix., xxx.). The costume of Anglo-Saxon ladies and Anglo-Saxon boys is here very well shown; but there is one peculiarity which is deserving of special notice, the colour of the hair—sky blue. Blue hair is certainly not natural, and can only have been given, as apparently a favourite colour, by artificial means—by powder, or by the process of dyeing. It seems to have been equally a favourite colour with both sexes. Unfortunately, the Anglo-Saxon ladies are invariably represented in the illuminations of the manuscripts with the head covered with the head-rail. There is one exception: when Eve appears in Paradise with no covering of any kind for any other part of her

PARENTS AND CHILD.

body, it is not to be expected that she would have a covering for her head, and accordingly we find her in her hair. Her hair is blue. We trace in other pictorial manuscripts this taste of the Anglo-Saxons for blue hair. It must, of course, have been coloured artificially, either by a dye or by powder.

It is curious that Aldhelm and the other writers of his class say nothing of this practice of dyeing the hair, though they accuse the ladies of curling it and of painting their cheeks. Perhaps, however, these Anglo-Saxon Latin writers were only applying to their countrymen and countrywomen the denunciations of the southern ecclesiastics of Gaul and Italy. They seem to have overlooked a little what was going on at home, and they may have thought only worthy of condemnation that which they found condemned by authorities nearer Rome; or, perhaps, they had a taste for blue hair. At all events, the existence of blue hair is not alluded to by the Anglo-Saxon writers, whether in their own vernacular tongue or in Latin. But, among the Anglo-Saxons, as among the Franks, the hair was an object of great importance. In earlier times, the cutting of the hair in either sex indicated slavery, or crime which merited the severest punishment. Even down to the present day, the condemned criminal has the head shaved. Among the Anglo-Saxons, long and loose hair in the female sex was typical of freedom and of pure virginity. Hence, in earlier Anglo-Saxon times, an unmarried girl was obliged to wear her hair in this condition. The only indulgence was, that, after a certain age, she was allowed to plait it. On her wedding-day she unplaited it, and threw it loose and scattered over her shoulders, because this indicated her nobleness of birth as well as her virginity. After the marriage, however, the woman's hair was cut short, to show that she had accepted a position of servitude towards her husband; but, as civilization developed itself, this degrading part of the marriage ceremony was dispensed with, and brides were only required after the ceremony to bind their hair in folds round the head. Loose hair continued to be the distinction of an unmarried girl, while a married woman was known by her hair being bound up. Even this distinction seems to have been kept up in practice till a very recent period.

There is a part of the costume to which I have not yet alluded, the shoe. There appears to have been among the Anglo-Saxons no difference between the shoe (*sceo*) of the two sexes; both are usually represented black, though at times various colours are introduced; and both are represented as rising to the ankle, as having an opening down the instep, and as fastened at the top by a thong (*sceo-þwang*). This form of shoe was, in all probability, derived from the Romans, as it is exactly that of the Roman shoes procured by Mr. Roach Smith from excavations in London.* With princes and nobles, and especially with the higher ecclesiastics, the upper leather appears, among the Franks and among the Anglo-Saxons, to have been often stamped or punched with elegant patterns similar to those of the shoes described by Mr. Smith. Perhaps, also, the soles of the shoes were studded with nails like those of the Romans, for we find in the Anglo-Saxon glosses the word *sceo-nægel*, a shoe-nail.

The men among the Anglo-Saxons certainly wore stockings, and there can be little doubt that they were worn by the women also; we know nothing of the material of which they were made; but that of the men appears from the illuminations of the time to have been of different colours. The Anglo-Saxons also wore gloves, for the word (*glóf* in Anglo-Saxon, and *glófi* in Old Norse) belongs to the Anglo-Saxon and Northern languages. We trace them on the hands of ladies in one or two instances in the

---

* Descriptions, with engravings, of these Roman shoes, which are now in the British Museum, will be found in Roach Smith's *Illustrations of Roman London.*

drawings of Anglo-Saxon manuscripts, but the word itself cannot have been of very common use, for we find, especially in the older writers, that, instead of using the correct name, they speak of the glove by the rather singular name of a hand-shoe (*hand-sceo*).* It has been remarked by some of our writers on costume, that the Anglo-Saxons never went without shoes; that even labourers, though generally represented as bare-legged, are not represented bare-footed. This, however, is not strictly correct; at least as applied to the female sex. The party of gossips in the accompanying cut, taken from the Harleian Manuscript, No. 603, already described (fol. 12, r'), are bare-footed as well as bare-legged,

ANGLO-SAXON GOSSIPS.

and the infants they carry in their arms are entirely naked. No doubt they belong to the lower classes of society. In our last cut (page 67), we have seen a woman leading by the hand a child of a more advanced age, who is similarly naked. These examples would seem to show that, among the lower orders of Anglo-Saxon society, the children were allowed to go naked until the age when they could be left to walk about by themselves.

As stated before, the wife, though above all the rest of the family, was inferior to and dependent upon her husband. He was the sole possessor, and everything in the house originated from him. If he made war, the spoils taken from the enemy, as far as his followers were concerned, belonged to him, and he distributed them among his warriors. The duty of distributing his gifts appears to have been considered to belong to his wife, and was performed at the great feasts. Then the chieftain's wife, the lady of the household, from time to time, rose from her seat and crossed the hall, and not only served the ale or mead to the guests, but delivered to them the presents destined for them by her husband; and in this she was assisted by her daughters, or by some other noble females attached to her person. In the poem of Beowulf, Hrothgar's queen is represented as performing this office :—

* The first gloves among the Germans and Scandinavians appear to have been warlike implements, things fitted upon the hands with which you could scratch and tear in a very destructive manner.

Hwílum mæru cwén,   At times the great queen,
friðu-sibb folca,   the peace-tie of peoples,
flet eall geond-hwearf,   all traversed the hall,
bædde byras geonge;   her young sons addressed;
oft hió beáh-wriðau   often sbe a ringed wreath
secge sealde,   gave to the warrior,
ær hfe to setle geng.   before she returned to her seat.
Hwílum for duguðe   At times before the nobles
dóhtor Hróðgáres   Hrothgar's daughter
eorlum on ende   to the earls in order
ealu-wæge bær,   bore the ale-cup,
þa ic Freáware   whom I Freáware
flet-sittende   the court residents
nemnan hyrde,   heard name,
þær hió gled-sinc   where she bright treasure
hroleþum sealde.   gave to the warriors.

Beowulf, l. 4038.

On reading this, we more fully understand the force of the passage of the Gnomic Poem in the Exeter Book, which tells how an earl's wife—earl was the title assumed by the head of the family—was usually beloved of her people:—

And wif gebeon,   And his wife (shall) flourish,
lof mid hyre leodum,   beloved with her people,
leoht-mod wesan.   be of cheerful mind.

Thorpe's Codex Exoniensis, p. 338.

If the head of the family had store of bread, it showed that he possessed broad lands, and that he cultivated them. There were three words in the Anglo-Saxon language which indicated, almost poetically, the position of the different parts of the family towards each other. The chieftain himself was called the *hlaf-ord*, the origin or source of the bread, he to whom it belonged; his wife was the *hlaf-dig*, the distributor of the bread; his retainers and his servants, and all who lived at his table, were called *hlaf-œtas*, eaters of the bread. The two former words, *hlaford* and *hlafdig* gradually took a nobler place in our language, and are now represented by the well-known words *lord* and *lady*.

It has been supposed that it was only towards the tenth century that the women of the household gained the right of sitting at table with the men, and that this is evidence of a great advance in their social position. This, however, may be an assumption founded too hastily upon our mere want of knowledge. We must bear in mind that the dinners described by the poets and other early writers are usually great feasts, more or less of a ceremonial character. The guests seem not generally to have taken their ladies with them, and the ladies of the household who were worthy to accompany their chief and his lady were few in number; and it is not stated by the writers who describe these scenes that they were not in the hall. I have shown, in a previous chapter, that, according to the ideas of the Scandinavian mythology, the gods and goddesses sate together in hall, without any distinction. We find several pictures of table scenes in the later Anglo-Saxon manuscripts, of which we give one in the accompanying cut. It is taken from the manuscript of Alfric's translation of Genesis (MS. Cotton., Claudius, B. IV., fol. 36, v°), where it is intended to represent the feast given by Abraham on the occasion of the birth of his child. The guests are seated at a long table, and are in the act of drinking from the ale-cups, and pledging each other. It will be seen that men and women are here mixed together without any order, the latter distinguished by having their heads always covered with the head-rail.

ANGLO-SAXON LADIES AT TABLE.

It may be doubted, indeed, whether this picture of the two sexes sitting together indiscriminately at table be a proof of an improvement in woman's position in society; but there can be no doubt, that for this improvement she was indebted in a great measure to the interference of the Christian clergy. They laboured to destroy, or at least to diminish, the old patriarchal spirit, and to emancipate the female sex from the too great authority of fathers and husbands. Some old customs were abolished at an early period after the introduction of Christianity. Among these was polygamy, which certainly existed among some branches of the German race, and which we have seen was practised among the gods of Scandinavian fable. There can hardly be a doubt of its existence among the Anglo-Saxons, at least in their earlier times, because at a later period we find it forbidden by law. One of these, the code of laws of the Northumbrian priests, prohibits, "with God's prohibitions, that any man have more wives than one." * This prohibition, it will be remarked, belongs to the ecclesiastical law; it is not found in the secular laws. It appears to have been the usual custom throughout the Germanic race, when a head of a family died, leaving a wife by a second marriage, that the son and heir married his step-mother. Perhaps she was considered as a part of the father's property, and therefore of the son's heritage. This practice was proscribed by the Church. Ethelbert, King of Kent, the first Anglo-Saxon king who embraced Christianity, took a second wife after the death of his first queen, the Frankish princess, Bertha. His son, Eadbald, was in his heart opposed to the new faith. When Ethelbert died, in 616, and Eadbald succeeded to the throne, the latter at once rejected Christianity, and, returning to the customs of his ancestors, married his father's widow. The well-known miracle by which King Eadbald was converted and reformed is related by Bede, who tells that he "abjured the worship of idols, and renounced his unlawful marriage"—unlawful, of course, only under the ecclesiastical laws. At a later date, Ethelwulf, King of Wessex, the father of Alfred, in his old age took for his second wife Judith, the daughter of Charles the Bald, of France. On his death, in the year following (857), his son Ethelbald, who succeeded him, married his widow, Judith. The clergy were indignant, and Swithun, Bishop of Winchester, persuaded him to separate himself from her.

When the clergy laboured to emancipate the female sex, they were certainly looking to their own interests. They had seen how the gentleness and pious spirit of the sex had assisted more than anything else in the early progress of Christianity in the West. It was to Bertha, the Queen of Kent, that they owed the conversion of King Ethelbert, and to Ethelburga, that of Edwin, King of Northumbria. They sought, therefore, to substitute their own influence over Womankind for that of the family. The women were drawn away from earthly marriages to be, as they expressed it, married to Christ; that is, to enter the monasteries, and become nuns. The religious houses were thus filled with women who had either separated from their husbands, or refused to accept the husbands designed for them by their fathers, usually under the protection, if not under the encouragement, of the

* Ancient Laws and Institutes of England, vol. ii., p. 301.

ecclesiastics. In the pagan Saxon period it appears that a man could divorce himself almost at pleasure; and if he and his wife agreed to separate, each was at liberty to marry again, without publicly assigning any cause for their separation. After the establishment of Christianity, the bishops assumed the right, not only of giving their sanction to such divorce or separation, but of annulling a marriage at their own will for any cause they chose to assign. It appears that, even during the seventh century, a very small cause of dissatisfaction on the part of the husband was considered a sufficient reason for putting away his wife. The primitive Anglo-Saxon notion of divorce, as it will be seen, was simply repudiation, and the practice of this was gradually wearing out during the seventh century, and in its place the clergy permitted these separations by mutual consent.

There are sufficient reasons for believing that these assumptions of the clergy to interfere in the domestic relations of the family were never liked by the Anglo-Saxon laity, and that those who had the power frequently set them at defiance. They were, indeed, carried to a degree which made them often extremely burthensome, and in some cases quite unbearable. The clergy had introduced a scale of consanguinity—within which marriage was not permitted—so ridiculously wide, that it was not easy to be sure whether you were within its limits or not, and thus provided themselves with an excuse for interfering almost whenever they liked. According to the Anglo-Saxon ecclesiastical laws, it was unlawful to marry within the fifth degree of consanguinity. How the power thus acquired by the clergy could be abused is shown in the treatment of Elfgiva, the beautiful queen of Edwy, by his ministers, Archbishop Odo and the imperious Dunstan. Elfgiva is said to have been related to her husband within the prohibited degrees, but it is not clear how. At the feast which followed the coronation, several days, as was the custom, were devoted to feasting and drinking, and on one of these the king, weary of the revelling, absented himself from the drinking hall, and repaired to the chamber of his bride. When his absence was discovered, it was taken as an insult to the company, and Dunstan, then abbot of Glastonbury, with Kinsey, bishop of Lichfield, were sent in search of him. Bursting rudely into the queen's chamber, they found the king fondling with his wife, in the presence of her mother. They insulted both mother and daughter with the grossest imputations, and, seizing the young king, they dragged him violently along the passage back into the hall. Elfgiva, in her resentment, joined the party of the nobles, and of the old and more national clergy, who were resisting the encroachments of the ecclesiastical power, and by whose

10

temporary influence Dunstan was soon afterwards sent into banishment. The
queen thus became an object of hatred to the monastic party, and Archbishop
Odo, who was now their leader, avenged them by persecuting the queen.
Two years after the occurrences just related, Odo, having obtained the
approval of the Pope, pronounced that the marriage of Edwy and Elfgiva
was unlawful, because within the prohibited degrees of kindred, and annulled
it. The king might have resisted this act of tyranny, and he would, no
doubt, have been supported by his people. So Archbishop Odo sent a strong
party of his retainers unexpectedly, who carried off the queen, seared her
face and lips with red-hot irons, in the hope of destroying her beauty, in
which they supposed that her influence over the king resided, and then sent
her to Ireland, probably as a slave. She remained in Ireland a short time,
until the scars on her face were so far healed that she had recovered much of
her beauty, and then she made her escape, and crossed over to Gloucester.
But she was discovered there by Odo's agents, who caused her to be
disabled from wandering further by severing the sinews of her legs,
and committed such injuries on her person that she died a few days
afterwards.

It is difficult to estimate the exact result of the influence of the establishment of monasticism upon the character and position of Womankind in
Saxon England. The Anglo-Saxon clergy of the older schools shared in the
domestic sentiments of the laity, and it was not considered to be inconsistent
with their profession, any more than in Protestant England, to have wives
and children. In the earlier monasteries the two sexes lived together in the
same building, though they were bound to strict continence and chastity.
Corruption, however, soon introduced itself, and the character of the inmates
of the religious houses became more and more secular. With the latter part
of the eighth century the Anglo-Saxon nuns became proverbially dissolute
in their character, and from this time forward the Anglo-Saxon kings
sometimes took their wives, and very frequently their mistresses, from the
convent. The monastery certainly did not improve the moral character of
Womankind. It became the practice for men of wealth to found a
monastery, and endow it with their broad lands, and to introduce into it a
number of their retainers and friends, in the garb (but with no other
qualifications) of monks, in order to live luxuriously and at their ease, and
escape the duties and troubles of secular life. The great ecclesiastics, both
here and on the continent, while they inveighed loudly against the love of
the laity for finery, displayed an extravagant passion for dress themselves.
To illustrate this fact, I need only give the description of the costume of the

lady abbess of one convent in the words of Mr. Thrupp.* "She appeared," he tells us, "in a scarlet tunic, with full skirts and wide sleeves and hood, over an under vest of fine linen of a violet colour, with shoes of red leather. Her face was rouged, and her hair curled with irons over the forehead and temples; ornaments of gold encircled her neck; heavy bracelets adorned her arms; and jewelled rings were upon her fingers. Her nails were worn long, and cut to a sharp point, to resemble the talons of a hawk." Odo and Dunstan represented the new ecclesiastical party, who were labouring to reform monachism in England, by introducing the Benedictine order and stricter Romanism.

There appears to have been more of gentleness and of the domestic spirit in the Anglo-Saxon race than in that of the Franks. The women of the former appear in a brighter light, and seldom as the authors of frightful crimes, such as those perpetrated by a Fredegonde or a Brunehild. We can gather only two such examples as standing prominent in our history—that of Eadburga, daughter of the great Offa, king of the Mercians; and that of Elfthrida, the wife of King Edgar; the latter celebrated in the Anglo-Saxon annals as the heartless murderess of her stepson, Edward the Martyr. The daughter of Offa was married to Bertric, king of the West Saxons; and, contrary to what appears to have been the usual custom of the Anglo-Saxons, she was enthroned by his side and crowned. According to the national feelings, she would be considered only as the king's wife, just like the consort of any other chieftain. This distinction arose probably from the extraordinary influence she had gained over Bertric's mind, which was seldom exercised for good. According to William of Malmesbury, it was her custom to rid herself by poison of all persons at court who rose independently into the king's favour, or who stood in her way. A young noble, named Worr, high in birth and character, and popular on account of his good qualities, had become a great favourite with King Bertric, and, therefore, an object of hatred to his queen. Eadburga, according to her usual practice, prepared a poisoned cup, of which, by accident, the king as well as his favourite partook, and both perished. The West-Saxons, in their indignation, drove the murdress into banishment, and resolved that in future no wife of a king should be enthroned beside her husband, or bear the title of queen. After this the king's wife bore the simple title of "The Lady." Eadburga, with her treasures, fled to the land of the Franks, and presented herself at the court of Charlemagne, who, knowing she wanted a husband, and being at that moment desirous of providing an excuse for carrying out designs he

* *The Anglo-Saxon Home*, p. 231.

had of aggrandisement in England, offered her the choice of himself or his son. Eadburga replied that she preferred youth to age. The great emperor, disgusted with her levity, replied that she should have neither; and, as he knew she was a wicked woman, he made her the abbess of a rich monastery. It appears that, at this period, the morality of monastic life was at as low an ebb among the Franks as among the Anglo-Saxons. Eadburga exercised her duties of abbess for a short time, until her low amours became so notorious that the emperor ordered her to be expelled from the convent. She went into Italy, accompanied by one slave; and the daughter of one great monarch, and wife of another king, died in beggary in the city of Pavia. To these we may perhaps add Cynedreda, the wife of King Offa, and mother of Eadburga, who was accused—it may be unjustly—of the murder of Ethelbert, king of the East Angles, over whose bones was raised the stately cathedral of Hereford; and one or two others, whose crimes seem equally doubtful.

Against these we may place a far larger number of names which appear in history in a light honourable to Womankind. Such was Ethelburga, the queen of Ina, of Wessex; and that other Ethelburga, through whose gentle influence over her husband the Northumbrians were converted to the Gospel. Such, as far as we can understand her character, was the noble Sexburga, of Wessex—the only Anglo-Saxon lady who has left us the example of a reigning queen. Such, too, was Elfgiva, the mother of King Edgar, who was made a saint for her virtues. Such, truly, was the noble Ethelfleda, who was known to her admiring countrymen as "The Lady of the Mercians." Such was Edith, the daughter of Earl Godwin, and the wife of King Edward the Confessor—distinguished equally for her beauty, her piety, and her learning—for learning was looked upon as an accomplishment in Anglo-Saxon ladies. The account of his interview with her in his boyhood, given by the monk Ingulf, presents an agreeable picture of the homely and gentle character of the Anglo-Saxon queen. "I saw her often," he says, "when still a boy, I visited my father, who was dwelling in the king's court; and very often when I met her as I was coming from school, she questioned me in my grammar and verses, and, most readily passing from the solidity of grammar to the lightness of logic, in which she was skilful, she would confute me with the subtle threads of her arguments; always, after counting out to me by her handmaid three or four coins, she sent me to the royal larder, and dismissed me after I had taken refreshment."* I

* Vidi ego illam multotiens, cum patrem meum in regis curia morantem adhuc puer inviserem, et sæpius mihi de scholis venienti de literis ac versu meo apponebat cum occurrerem,

am a disbeliever in the authenticity of the History which goes under the name of Ingulf; but it may have been partly founded upon traditions and records which were preserved at Croyland as late as the beginning of the fourteenth century, and I confess that the story of Ingulf's boyish intercourse with Queen Edith sounds more like an Anglo-Saxon truth than an Anglo-Norman invention. We might add to the names given above, that of Godiva, another lady of Mercia—the heroine of Coventry legend; and a multitude of other equally bright examples of Anglo-Saxon Womankind.

It may be remarked, further, that the names given to girls at their baptism almost all marked the appreciation of the Anglo-Saxons for gentleness and goodness in the female sex, for they were all founded upon the expectations or hopes of the parents as to the future character of their offspring. Thus, of the names I have just introduced to the reader, Eadburga means the citadel or mansion of happiness; Ethelburga, the citadel of nobility; Ethelfleda, the flood or stream of nobility; Edith, (Eadgythe) the gift of happiness, or the happy gift; Elfgiva, the gift of the elves, or fairies, or the spiritual gift ; Elfthrida, the strength of the elves, or spiritual strength; Godiva (Godgifu) the gift of God, or the divine gift. It was very common among our forefathers of this period to give to their daughters names compounded of the word elf, or fairy, both to indicate the great qualities they hoped that they would possess, and perhaps also with the feeling of placing them under the protection of the spiritual world.

It is among the illuminations of the Anglo-Saxon manuscripts that we first see woman on horseback. Riding appears never to have been a favourite practice with either sex among our Anglo-Saxon forefathers. It was long the opinion of our writers on costume and domestic manners, founded on a statement of an old writer not deserving of much credit, that until the closing years of the fourteenth century (the reign of Richard II.), women invariably rode astride, like men, and our first example might seem to favour this belief. It is taken from a finely-illuminated manuscript of the "Psychomachia" of Prudentius (MS. Cotton., Cleopatra C. VIII. fol. 10, v°). The equestrian, in this case, is the Lady Pride. She is represented in the poem of Prudentius as engaged in combat with her enemy Humility, and dashing through the routed troops of her foes on an unbridled horse, its back and shoulders covered with the skin of a lion. Seated on this, she

---

et libentissime de grammatica soliditate ad logicam levitatem qua callebat declinans, cum argumentorum subtili ligamine me conclusisset, semper tribus aut quatuor nummis per ancillulam numeratis ad regium penu transmisit et refectum dimisit.—*Ingulfi Historia, in Gale's Rerum Anglic. Scriptores,* vol. i., p. 62.

looks down with scorn on the hostile troops. She has collected her plaited locks on her head in the form of a lofty tower, so that together they might increase the building of curls, and the forehead support the lofty peak. A mantle (*palla*) of fine linen from the shoulders is joined at the top of the bosom, fastened over the breast by an elegant knot. A veil, surrounded by

PRIDE ON HORSEBACK.

a delicate fringe, flowing from the head, receives the breeze thrown into it with swelling folds.

Forte per effusas inflata Superbia turmas
Effræni volitabat equo, quem pelle leonis
Texerat, et validos villis oneraverat armos.
Quo se fulta jubis jactantius illa ferinis
Inferret, tumido despectans agmina fastu.
Turritum tortis caput accumularat in altum
Crinibus, exstructos augeret ut addita cirros
Congeries, celsumque apicem frons ardua ferret,
Carbasea ex humeris summo collecta coibat
Palla sinu, teretem nectens a pectore nodum.
A cervice fluens tenui velamine limbus
Concipit ingestas textis turgentibus auras.
Nec minus instabili sonipes feritate superbit,
Impatiens madidis frenarier ora lupatis.

Prudentii Psychomachia, l. 170.

The Anglo-Saxon artist has attempted, in the above figure, to give a pictorial explanation of the above lines, not, I fear, very successfully in its details. The Lady Pride (*Superbia* in Prudentius—in the Anglo-Saxon gloss, *seo Ofermodnes*, literally, high-mindedness) is so in temper, but not in garb. She is bare-legged and bare-footed. The draughtsman was so used to depicting ladies with the head-rail, that he has not attempted the head-dress as described in the original. The *palla*, or mantle, is spreading itself out to the winds in a very wild manner.

We can trace, in the remainder of the dress, two articles, either the chemise and the tunic, or the outer and inner tunic.

The position of Lady Pride on her horse is certainly an exceptional one, and is not in accordance with other Anglo-Saxon monuments. In our next cut, taken from Archbishop Alfric's translation of the Pentateuch (MS. Cotton, Claudius, B. IV.), the manner of sitting on horseback of either sex is clearly defined, though the lady sits, according to our modern notions, on the wrong side of the horse, so that she has her left hand to the bridle, while in her

A GENTLEMAN AND LADY ON HORSEBACK.

right hand she holds a whip of rather remarkable character. It may well be described, in the words of the Dictionary, as "a whip, or *scourge*." The book of Genesis (chap. xxxi., verse 17) tells us how Jacob, when he removed into the land of Canaan, "rose up, and set his sons and his wives upon camels." The illuminator of the Cottonian manuscript of Alfric's translation (MS. Cotton, Claudius, B. IV., fol. 47, r°) has endeavoured to represent this scene in a group, some figures of which are given in the cut on our next page. The knowledge of the camel displayed by the Anglo-Saxon artist is not great. His women are riding exactly in the same position as in the foregoing cut of the lady on horseback, and sit in the same manner on the wrong side of the beast. How his ladies held their seats it would not be easy to explain. The manuscript of Prudentius, from which we have borrowed so many of our illustrations (MS. Cotton, Cleopatra, C. VIII.), gives a representation of a lady driving in a chariot, which we reproduce in our last cut. It is drawn by two horses, and the lady is armed with the same formidable description of whip which we have met with before. The Anglo-Saxons had two names for a chariot,

JACOB'S FAMILY RIDING ON CAMELS.

both which rather intimate the homeliness of its character. One was *wægn*, or *wæn*, the modern word waggon; the other *cræt*, or *crat*, which

A LADY CHARIOTEER.

is our modern word cart. The chariot here represented is not unlike a market-cart.

CHAPTER V.

WHEN the Anglo-Saxons came in contact with the Roman civilization and literature, the eagerness with which they attached themselves to the latter is quite remarkable. The earlier Anglo-Saxon converts to Christianity became almost at once Latin scholars, grammarians, poets, and philosophers. The zeal with which the female sex entered into this pursuit was at least equal to that of the men, and we hear of Anglo-Saxon nuns writing with a certain ease Latin both in prose and verse, perfecting themselves in science (as perfection in science was then understood), and even becoming accomplished logicians. With these accomplishments we find combined none of the harshness and stiffness which belong to asceticism, but an affectionate gentleness of temper which appears very pleasing, and this displayed in a manner which shows that the tenderness between the sexes which monachism was supposed to quench, continued to exist in all its force. The Anglo-Saxon female character, indeed, is beautifully displayed in the sentiments of the Anglo-Saxon nuns, which we trace, in their newly acquired Latin, in some of their familiar letters which have been fortunately preserved.

About the year 680, a child of the West Saxons was born at Crediton, in Devonshire, of a noble, if not royal race. With that hopeful foresight to the future character or fortunes of the child with which the Anglo-Saxons selected his name, they gave to him that of Wyn-frith, which means, in Anglo-Saxon, the peace of joy; but at a later period, when he had grown up, and those great qualities had become known throughout the western church which have perpetuated his fame, that church changed his Anglo-Saxon name to that of Boniface, which appeared more noble to the ecclesiastics of continental Europe. This was the usual practice with Anglo-Saxons who rose high in the church. The young Wynfrith, or Winfred (as the name is

11

more popularly spelt), the future Boniface, began to display these qualities at a very tender age; for we are told that he was his father's favourite child, who looked forward to him, as the heir to his worldly possessions, to be the worthy supporter of the family name, but that before he had reached even his fourth year, he displayed in an unmistakable manner an aspiration after piety and study which threw him into the hands of the ecclesiastics. The father, at first unwillingly, placed him at the age of seven years in the monastery at Exeter, and there and at the monastic house named Nhuts-celle, in Hampshire, he distinguished himself in scholastic studies and teaching, until he reached the age of thirty, when he was ordained to the priesthood. This was about the year 710, when King Ine ruled over the West-Saxons, and soon after this Winfred was chosen by the Anglo-Saxon clergy to proceed to Rome, and act there as their agent to the Pope, in a dispute which had arisen among the clergy at home. In consequence of knowledge which he had gathered on this journey, he first entertained the ambition of converting the various tribes of pagan Germans who occupied the interior of Europe. He embraced this design, which became the labour of his life, with the reso-lution and energy which insured success, and which has given him the great and well acknowledged title of the Apostle of the Germans. It was in 723, in the midst of his labours, that the Pope formally conferred upon him the new name of Boniface. At length, in one of his missionary excursions, early in the June of the year 755, Boniface and his companions were slain by a party of pagan Frieslanders, and he was acknowledged by the church as entitled to take a place in the list of its martyrs; at a later period the Church of Rome placed Boniface among its saints. Boniface, though strong and even fiery in his religious zeal, appear to have possessed a gentle spirit, which drew to him the affections of the female part of the religious com-munity of his native country, his relations with whom appear to have been especially tender, and their correspondence forms by no means the least remarkable part of his letters which have been preserved. They are worth our attention as evidence of the mental character and qualities of the Anglo-Saxon women.

Among the first of Boniface's correspondents of this class, and the oldest of his female friends, was a lady named Eadburg, or, as we usually give it in modern writing, Eadburga, who is said to have been a princess, and had, in her earlier days, been an abbess in England, but afterwards she relinquished the exercise of her monastic duties and took up her residence in Rome. According to the custom which prevailed among the Anglo-Saxons, they gave to this lady a second name, which was simply in our modern phraseology, a nickname, though it was accepted as belonging to the individual to whom it was attached. In this case the new name was Bugga, which is believed to mean a bug, but how she became entitled to so disrespectful a qualification we have no information; though she was known ever afterwards by either name, and Boniface himself, in his correspondence, addresses her affectionately in both, and she writes to him under that of Bugga.* She was evidently one of those Anglo-Saxon ladies who had applied herself with some zeal to the new learning and literature brought in by the Roman missionaries, and she, as well as the others of her sex of whose epistolary writings we have here any remains, wrote Latin as well, and apparently with as much ease, as Boniface himself and his fellow ecclesiastics of the other sex. The characteristic of their style, at least of that of the ladies, is an ambition of using rather poetical and inflated language, but this was peculiar to the poetry of the great Teutonic race. Our Anglo-Saxon nuns, moreover, learnt to write Latin in metre as well as in prose. A nun named Leobgitha, writing to Boniface about the year 725, begs him to remember the old friendship which had existed between him and her father, named Tinne, "in the western regions" (that is, of course, in Boniface's native district); who, she says, had then been dead eight years, and also of her mother Ebbe, who was still alive, though very infirm. She tells him that she was the only child of either parent, and that her great desire was to be received by him, in whom beyond all other men of her race lay her trust and hope, on the footing of a sister. She seconds her petition by a little present (*hoc parvum munusculum*) the nature of which is not told in the letter ; but she begs him to excuse the rudeness of her composition, and to correct her language and encourage her by a letter in return. And she concludes by sending him some verses which she had "tried to compose according to the teaching of poetical tradition (*secundum poeticæ traditionis disciplinam*)." This art, poetry, she tells him, she had learned in the school of Eadburga, who thus appears in the character of a teacher. Leobgitha's verses consist only of the four lines which follow, and are only curious as an example of the erudition of an Anglo-Saxon maiden of the earlier part of the eighth century after Christ :—

> Arbiter omnipotens, solus qui cuncta creavit,
> In regno patris semper qui lumine fulget,
> Qua jugiter flagrans, sic regnet gloria Christi,
> Illæsum servet semper te jure perenni.

* These bye-names, or nick-names, were common among the Anglo-Saxons, and people were not only more commonly addressed by them than by their proper names, but they sometimes used them even in signing charters.

Another Anglo-Saxon lady, a nun of course, but whose name is not preserved, ends a letter to a monk named Baldhard, by announcing a present of a fillet or cap (vitta) she had made for him, accompanied also with some Latin verses of her own composition. These are not hexameters, but written in the metre used in the hymns of the Church. I may add that Boniface, in writing to Leobgitha, acknowledges her appeals to him in favour of "a learned damsel" of her acquaintance (ut puellæ cuidam ductæ laborem).

We may suppose, from the letter of Leobgitha, that Boniface's friend, the abbess Eadburga, or Bugga, was the superior of some monastic house in his own native district of Devonshire. Another of Boniface's female correspondents, named Cangitha, also an abbess, speaks of herself as the mother of Eadburga, "surnamed Bugga" (et unica filia ejus Eadburga, cognomento Bugga), in writing to consult him about her own troubles and sorrows.

In a letter written about the year 720, when Boniface was actively employed in his missionary labours among the Germans, Bugga writes a letter to congratulate him on his success. She professes towards him the tenderest affection, expresses her regret at not being able yet to obtain for him a book he wanted (The Passions of the Martyrs), and reminds him of his promise to send her a book of selections from Scripture. There is a tenderness in these letters which tells much more of the sentiments and affections of humanity than we might expect from the lips of a pious recluse. Bugga concludes her letter by announcing as presents fifty shillings in money and a pallium for the altar, which, excusing herself for the smallness of their value, she begs him to accept as tokens of her affection (cum maxima charitate). This interchange of presents is constantly going on in these letters. In one written by Boniface to Bugga, and ascribed to the year 733, he addresses her as "his dearest lady and in Christ's love to be preferred to all others of the female sex;" and after giving her his advice in some questions on which she had consulted him, he thanks her for the presents she had sent him, which consisted of vestments, we may suppose of her own workmanship. An ecclesiastic writing to Eadburga, in 725, perhaps Boniface himself, expresses the pleasure which her presents had given him, and sends her in return a silver stylus for writing (unum graphium argenteum) and some valuable spices, storax, and cinnamon. In this same year, A.D. 733, two disciples and companions of Boniface, the initials of whose names only are given, write from Germany to the abbess Kanebada, who is stated to be of royal blood, intimating the intention of revisiting Britain, expressing warmly their affection and reverence for the abbess, to whom they excuse the rudeness of their diction, and sending her as presents small parcels of frankincense, pepper, and cinnamon.

In this eventful year of 733, when Boniface was so actively engaged among the Teutons of the Continent, planting the Gospel amid the wilds of Germany, another Anglo-Saxon nun, Egburga, writes to him under his more English name of Winfrith, in terms of the warmest affection. "I confess," she says at the opening, "that while I tasted through the inner man the bond of thy love, like something of honied sweetness, the savour of it became settled within me. And although immediately I had obtained it, I was defrauded of the bodily view, yet I shall always cling to thy neck with a sister's embraces. Wherefore, my beloved brother before, but now thou art called both equally in the Lord of lords abba and brother, because since bitter and cruel death has separated from me him whom above all others I used to love, my brother Oshere, I prefer thee almost to all others of the masculine sex in affectionate love. And, not to weary with variety of words, not a day is turned over, or a night passes by, without a remembrance of your mastership." She goes on to remind him of their former friendships, and dwells on the memories of some of her friends who were departed, and on the grief which their loss has caused to her. Again, here is a letter from a nun named Cene:—"Unworthy Cene salutes her revered lover in Christ, Bishop Boniface. Now I confess to thee, dearest, since it is permitted me rarely to look upon thee with my bodily eyes, that nevertheless I cease not to regard thee continually with the spiritual eyes of the heart. And the small presents sent herewith are rather intended as tokens of love, than as being worthy of thy holiness. And this I make known to thee, that until the end of my life I always remember thee in my prayers. And I beseech thee by our pledged (*creditam*) friendship, that thou be faithful to my littleness, for my trust is in thee; and that thou help me in thy prayers, that God Almighty may dispose of my life according to his will. And I beg, that if ever any one of yours come to this province, that he may call upon my poverty; and if in anything either of carnal utility or of spiritual aid I can be of assistance either to thee or to any of thine, that he inform me of it; and that I, to the great health of my soul, I believe, may according to my power fulfil thy command and order. Farewell, ever in the Lord."

We cannot but take the tone of these letters of Boniface's correspondents as more or less illustrative of the character of Womankind among the Anglo-Saxons. They are not the letters of recluses, nor was this the general character of the Anglo-Saxon nuns, who while they embraced a life of purity and holiness peculiar to themselves, did not separate themselves from the world. In our earlier monasteries, monks and nuns lived together in the same building, in social intercourse, without any separation, except that the dormitories of the two sexes were placed on different sides of the building. No restrictions were placed upon the ordinary intercourse and relations of the nuns with the outer world. In course of time this freedom appears to have been abused, and towards the end of the seventh century, and still more in the eighth, it appears to have led to many irregularities, which induced the Church to make an effort to abolish these double monastic establishments for both sexes. But the attempt seems to have been only partially successful. The Anglo-Saxon missionaries appear to have drawn away from the island much of the fervent religious zeal which had marked the earlier period of Anglo-Saxon Christianity, and to have carried it into Germany.

The nuns, moreover, were useful members of society. Each nunnery was a school for the female children of the laity, even of the higher ranks. They were taught to read and write, and they were instructed in the Latin language and even in Roman literature, sometimes in rhetoric and even in logic, and in what we might now call popular science. It is evident that, in general, an Anglo-Saxon lady was not at all illiterate or without instruction. The nuns, as a body, passed a great part of their time in work, and even excelled the women of the laity in their skill in weaving rich stuffs, in embroidery, and in making splendid dresses. From the statements of the Anglo-Saxon writers, we are led to believe that the Anglo-Saxon nuns had no objection to finery themselves, and they are accused of wearing white and violet chemises, tunics and veils of delicate tissue, richly embroidered with silver and gold, and scarlet shoes. In fact, the religious element in the convents became gradually weaker, until they degenerated into societies of ladies of rank, and even of royal blood, who lived together in greater independence and in greater ease than they would have lived elsewhere. After the eighth century, the character of the Anglo-Saxon nun had sunk very low. The female correspondence of Boniface is, however, as I have already remarked, chiefly to be looked upon as a curious monument of the history of Womankind among the Anglo-Saxons.

CHAPTER VI.

TRANSITION TO THE FEUDAL PERIOD—DOMESTIC LIFE IN THE CASTLE— THE ANGLO-NORMANS.

DURING the long period of which we have been treating in our last two chapters, a great revolution had taken place in the condition, social and political, of the dominions of the Franks. The dynasty of the Merovings, by its own discordant character and weakness, had fallen, and given way to another race of kings. Charlemagne gave to the royalty of the Franks a new character; he possessed in a high degree the Roman spirit, and for a while he brought back into existence the Roman empire, with all its powerful centralization. But Charlemagne's influence and power of government belonged to himself, and disappeared after his death, and thus this event was followed very quickly by utter disorganization throughout his vast dominions. Under the terrible invasions of the Northmen, which soon followed, not only all central power, but in some sort all power whatever disappeared.

Out of this great and painful confusion arose an entirely new state of society, which we know as the *feudal system*. It was a state of things to which the old society had been gradually converging; but its immediate cause must be sought in the fearful state of desolation and anarchy which followed the invasions and ravages of the Northmen. All central power, that of the monarchic institutions, had become paralysed, and the great chieftains, with their vast territories, had by the existing system no armed force to defend them. Under these circumstances they introduced a new method of distributing their lands, which was by granting it hereditarily on the conditions that the tenant was bound not only to cultivate the portion of land he held, but to perform certain military services according to its extent; or, in other words, he was bound to lead to the standard of his superior lord in time of war so many armed men for so many acres. This new sort of tenure was called in mediæval Latin *feudum* or *feodum*, and sometimes *feofum*, from which latter form it derives its more modern name of a *fief*. As this plan was found to answer its purpose sufficiently well, the whole landed property of France passed in the course of the tenth century into this sort of tenure, which, from the word just mentioned, was termed *feudal*. It brought with it new institutions and new forms of life. Under this new system, the landed aristocracy assumed and exercised, each within his own domains, sovereign power, both legislative, judicial, and military, and thus the state was transformed into a number of little sovereignties. The new lords of the land formed alliances among themselves, or made war upon each other, at their own will, and their whole aim was to keep themselves in a permanent state of defence. The old residences, which had consisted of a confused mass of buildings, with little or no capability of defence, inhabited in great part by men attached to the cultivation of the land, by artizans of various kinds, and by slaves, were now abandoned, and their places were supplied by almost impregnable fortresses. The castle, indeed, is become, in a manner, the symbol or image of feudalism. In this fortress, placed at a distance from all social life without, the lord and his lady lived in a complete state of isolation. Without occupation in this solitary abode, life at home must have been so wearisome that the great desire of the male part of the household would be to be absent from it; and hence we find the possessors of fiefs passing their time on the high road, in adventures of every kind, courses, wars, plunderings, and anything which promised violent activity. The coarseness and ferocity which arose out of this life threw a new impediment in the way of social and intellectual improvement, and these early ages of feudalism were, indeed, ages of darkness. Yet, as one of the ablest of our modern historians has observed, "at the same time that castles opposed so strong a barrier to civilization, while it had so much difficulty in penetrating into them, they were in a certain respect a principle of civilization; they protected the development of sentiments and manners which have acted a powerful and salutary part in modern society; everybody knows that domestic life, the spirit of family, and particularly the condition of woman, are developed in modern Europe much more completely, and with more happiness, than anywhere else. Among the causes which have contributed to this development, we must reckon life in the castle, the situation of the possessor of the fief in his domains, as one of the principal. Never, in any other form of society, has a family, reduced to its most simple expression, husband, wife, and children, been found so closely drawn together, pressed one against the other, separated from all other powerful and rival relations. In the different states of society of previous periods, the head of the family had, without absenting himself, a multitude of occupations and diversions which drew him from the interior of his dwelling, and at least hindered it from being the centre of his life. The contrary happened in feudal society. As often as he remained in his castle, the feudal possessor lived there with his wife and children, almost his only equals, his only intimate and permanent companions. Without doubt, he often left it, and led abroad the brutal and adventurous life just described ; but he was obliged to return to his home, where he shut himself up in times of danger. Now, whenever man is placed in a certain position, the part of his moral nature which corresponds to that position is favourably developed in him. Is he obliged to live habitually in the bosom of his family, with his wife and children, the ideas and sentiments in harmony with this fact cannot fail to obtain a great empire over him. So it happened in feudal society. When, moreover, the feudal possessor left his castle to go in search of war and adventures, his wife remained there, and in a situation very different from that which women almost always held in previous times. She remained there as mistress, or lady, of the castle, as representative of her husband, charged in his absence with the defence and honour of the fief. This situation of rank, and almost of sovereignty, in the very bosom of domestic life, often gave to women of the feudal epoch a dignity, courage, virtues, and a splendour, which they had not displayed under other circumstances, and contributed powerfully, no doubt, to their moral development, and to the general progress of their condition. This is not all. The importance of the children, of the eldest son among the others, was greater in the feudal household than anywhere else. There was displayed not only natural affection, and the desire of transmitting his goods to his children, but also the desire of transmitting to them that power, that superior situation, that sovereignty inherent to the domain. The eldest son of the lord was, in the eyes of his father and of all his followers, a prince, a presumptive heir, the depository of the glory of a dynasty. Thus, the weaknesses as well as the good sentiments, domestic pride as well as affection, joined in giving to the spirit of family much energy and power. Add to this the empire of Christian ideas, to which I only here point passingly, and you will easily understand how this castle life, this solitary, sombre, and hard position, was nevertheless favourable to the development of domestic life, and to that elevation of the condition of woman, which holds so great a place in the history of our civilization. This great and salutary revolution took place between the ninth and twelfth centuries. We cannot follow it step by step ;

we can only trace very imperfectly the particular facts which assisted its progress, for the want of documents. But that in the eleventh century it was about completed, that the condition of woman had changed, that the spirit of family, domestic life, and the ideas and sentiments which belonged to it, had acquired a development and empire previously unknown, is a general fact which it is impossible to overlook."*

Thus has Guizot told well and concisely the change which had taken place in the character of society in Western Europe (on the continent), between the ninth century and the eleventh. Unfortunately, the records of this period are very barren of materials which would enable us to form any more detailed picture of the state of society, and especially of the position of Womankind at this time. The little information we obtain shows the Frankish women of that time violent, cruel, and rapacious, while they have evidently obtained a greater degree of independence and power. This they owed, no doubt, in a considerable degree to the clergy, who laboured always to break down the old authority of fathers and husbands. The power of the church had been fully established under the influence of Charlemagne, and the clergy interfered in everything, and especially in the questions of marriage, repudiation, and divorce. Although the Franks had lost the greater part of their old Teutonic sentiments and traditions under Charlemagne's empire, yet they still seemed to submit to this interference of the church with reluctance, and often, when they had the power, they resisted it. Frequently the matrimonial relations of kings and great chieftains were, in the eye of the church, remarkably scandalous, and the history of them throws a rather singular light on the character of the Frankish women. Thus, King Robert of France, the second Frankish monarch of that name, married, in 997, Bertha, daughter of the king of Burgundy, and widow of Eudes, count of Chartres. It was a marriage of affection, but the lady was his cousin in the fourth degree, which was within the forbidden limits of consanguinity, and, what was still worse in the eyes of the church, Robert had been godfather to one of her children by her first husband, and had thus contracted what the church considered to be a spiritual relationship far more important than any earthly consanguinity. The Archbishop of Tours, with the agreement of others of the leading French prelates, had granted a dispensation for the marriage, and given the nuptial blessing; but the Pope, who was at this time hostile to the Gallic church, and was glad of an opportunity of showing it, declared the marriage to be incestuous and illegal, and dissolved it. King Robert, who loved his wife affectionately,

* Guizot, *Histoire de la Civilisation en France,* tom. iii., pp. 343—346.

although in character pious and gentle to weakness, refused to submit, and resisted for some years, under what were then the dreadful effects of a Papal excommunication. But at length, under the threat of placing his whole kingdom under an interdict, he yielded, and separated himself from the object of his affections. Robert remained three or four years unmarried, and then took for his queen, Constance, the daughter of the count of Toulouse, a lady of great beauty, although his first marriage had not been annulled. With Constance, what were considered the vain and fantastic fashions of the south were brought into France; but it is rather curious that at this time vanity in dress was characteristic of the male sex, and not of the ladies. The gentlemen of the period, who adopted these new fashions, were affected in their manners, and are accused by the contemporary, or almost contemporary, chroniclers, of being "immodest" in their dress. Not only were their arms and the caparison of their harness extremely fantastic in appearance, but, in their own persons, they cut their hair short, shaved their beards, "like stage performers," wore coats so short, that they descended only to the knees, and were slit before and behind, with small tight shoes terminating in a beak turned up—in fact, to use the words of the monastic censurer, they wore "the livery of the demon." It is again to be remarked that it was the male sex who offended pious feeling and good taste by the extravagant vanity of their dress, while the ladies are not mentioned.

The chroniclers tell strange stories of the manner in which Queen Constance tyrannized over her husband. Once, during her absence on a visit to Aquitaine, Robert's favourite minister, Hugues of Beauvais, urged the king to shake off his domestic yoke, and return to his first wife Bertha. The queen heard of this, and obtained from her uncle six knights who were capable of any atrocity, who by her orders murdered Hugues in the king's presence, while he was hunting. At a later period, a priest named Stephen, who had been the queen's confessor, was condemned, with others, for heresy, and burnt at Orleans. It was at this time the fashion among the ladies, borrowed from the other sex, to carry in the hand a stick with a chased head. Constance, who had placed herself in the church porch to see the heretics pass, walked up to her old confessor, and thrust out his eye with the head of her stick, which was in the form of a bird's head.

Another instance of the loose ideas of the age in regard to marriage is furnished by the history of King Philippe I. Philippe already possessed a queen named Bertha, to whom he had been married in 1071; when, during a visit to Tours in 1092, he fell in love with the beautiful Bertrade, countess of Anjou, who was persuaded to desert her own husband in order to marry the king, and he put Queen Bertha away. A bishop was with some difficulty found, who performed the ceremony of marriage; and Ivo, bishop of Chartres, who opposed it, was seized and thrown into prison. Upon this the Pope, Urban II., interfered, and threatened the king with excommunication, unless he put away Bertrade, and set the bishop at liberty; but he refused to desert his adulterous wife. Two years after the marriage, Urban delivered the sentence of excommunication, which, however, was not very rigidly enforced, and Philippe continued to hold Bertrade as his wife. Philippe had

a son named Louis, destined to be his successor on the throne, who, on that account, was an object of hatred to Queen Bertrade, and she made several attempts on his life, in order to clear the way to the throne for one of her own sons. On one occasion she employed poisoners against him, and he escaped with great difficulty from the effects of their drugs. Bertrade herself had been the third wife of the count of Anjou, all the three being alive. Such are the examples of Frankish Womankind, in the third dynasty, as furnished by the chroniclers.

It has just been remarked that, during these earlier ages of feudalism, the men, not the women, incur blame for the vanity and extravagance of their manners and costume. The costume of the Frankish ladies seems not to have undergone any change until late in the eleventh century; but our materials for the social history of this period are very few.* The dress of a Frankish matron of this period consisted of three principal pieces:—First, a close-fitting robe, with sleeves buttoned at the wrist; over this a second and wider robe; and over these a mantle, which descended behind nearly to

ADELAIDE OF VERMANDOIS.

the feet. A *guimple* (wimple), or stomacher, surrounded the neck, and covered the upper part of the breast. To the head-dress was attached a rather short

---

* M. Louandre, in his fine work, "Les Arts Somptuaires," has made great confusion in the history of this latter period, through taking his chief authority, John de Garlande, for a writer of the eleventh century, instead of the thirteenth.

veil, which formed a great pad over each ear. This description will be better understood by our cut, which represents Adelaide of Vermandois, countess of Anjou, who died at the beginning of the eleventh century. It is taken from the effigy on her tomb, formerly in the church of St. Aubin (of which church she was the foundress), which was made soon after her death, and restored in 1103. In the original the sleeves were red, the cloak blue, and the head-dress and shoes amber-coloured. Our coloured plate of Queen Radegunde, the wife of Clotaire I., taken from an illumination of the eleventh century, represents nearly the same costume, with the exception of the head-dress and the guimple. The queen is seated in her chair of state, and holds in her right hand the stylus, with which she is writing on the tablets of wax which she holds in her left hand. The queen's dress is most remarkable for its richness, for new materials were now being introduced through Italy from the East. Among its most characteristic ornaments are the circular plates of gold, adorned with jewels —probably pearls. It was the fashion at this time to wear fillets, also ornamented with precious stones, round the forehead and head.

The invasions of the Normans in France had, as I have already remarked, been one of the great causes which contributed to give birth to feudalism. Within a short period they had made themselves masters of a considerable part of the territory of the Franks, and established in it an independent sovereignty. As the Normans became settled, they abandoned their old northern manners and language, and adopted the French costume, the French tongue, the feudal form of government, and the Christian religion; and with so much zeal, that, in the eleventh century, Norman was the purest dialect of the *langue-d'oïl*, or northern French; feudalism existed in Normandy in its purest form, and the Norman clergy bore the highest character of any in Europe. We have hardly any information on the condition of the Norman women; but a few anecdotes which have been recorded display no great refinement in female society, nor do the ladies appear to have been treated with much delicacy by the other sex. The second Duke William, afterwards William the Conqueror, who was illegitimate, married Matilda, daughter of Baudouin, count of Flanders. It is related that, when this match was proposed to the lady, she refused indignantly to be married to a bastard; whereupon William, in great fury, waited at the door of the church which she had entered to perform her devotions, attacked her with brutal violence as she came out, threw her down, and continued beating her till she consented to become his wife. Matilda, in after life, when her husband had become king of England as well as duke of Normandy, acted on several occasions in opposition to his will. Ordericus Vitalis blames greatly the Norman women, who, while the barons and knights, their husbands, were engaged in the conquest of England, and remained there longer than pleased them, not only refused to go thither to join them, but sent messengers to tell them that their absence was becoming so irksome that, unless they returned immediately, they would substitute other men in their places. The Normans also appear to have submitted reluctantly to the ecclesiastical regulations in regard to marriages, for we may judge, by the provisions of Norman synods in the eleventh century, that the practice of divorce and repudiation without the license of a bishop, and marriages contrary to the ecclesiastical canons, prevailed widely. According to the Norman historian, William of Jumièges, the first duke Rollo married his wife Popa "in the Danish manner"; and the same writer tells us that his son and successor, the first duke William, was united to Sprota in the same manner.

The Normans brought their language and manners, along with feudalism, into England, and our island was soon covered with castles. Feudalism itself contributed greatly to the assimilation of manners among the aristocracy in different countries; and, during a considerable period, costume, and the forms, at least, of domestic life in England, in Normandy, and in France, were no doubt nearly identical. During this period, in fact, Englishmen were Anglo-Normans.

The costume of the Anglo-Norman ladies resembled, no doubt, that of the Franks, which we have described; and during the reign of William the Conqueror, it probably underwent little or no change. It was in that of his successor, William Rufus, that new and fantastic fashions began to make their appearance in Normandy and England; and in these countries, as among the Franks at an earlier date, the example was set, not by the ladies, but by the other sex. The Norman youth, set free from the firm rule of the first William, seem, under the second, to have run into all sorts of wild extravagance. The historian Ordericus Vitalis, who lived at the time, declaims with great bitterness against the effeminacy and viciousness of the young Normans and Anglo-Normans in the latter years of the eleventh century. "They parted their hair," he says, "from the crown of the head on each side of the forehead, and let their locks grow long like women, and wore long shirts, and tunics, closely tied with points. . . . . They insert their toes in things like serpents' tails, which present to view the shape of scorpions. Sweeping the dusty ground with the prodigious trains of their robes and mantles, they cover their hands with gloves too long and wide for doing anything useful; and, encumbered with these superfluities, lose the free use of their limbs for active employment. The forepart of their heads is bare, after the manner of thieves, while behind they nourish long hair, like harlots. . . . . . Their locks are curled with hot irons, and, instead of wearing caps, they bind their heads with fillets." Ordericus had already told us that "a debauched fellow, named Robert, was the first about the court of William Rufus who introduced the practice of filling the long points of the shoes with tow, and of turning them up like a ram's horn;" and that from this circumstance he became known as Robert Cornard. William of Malmesbury, who lived about the same time, or a little later, also

ANGLO-NORMAN LADIES IN THE HEIGHT OF THE FASHION.

speaks of the dissolute character of the men of the reign of William Rufus, of their "flowing hair and extravagant dress," and of their shoes with curved points.

The ladies no doubt soon caught the madness of the other sex for extravagant fashions in costume; but, oddly enough, they seem to have escaped the censure of the ecclesiastics, and the old chroniclers pass them over in silence. We have, however, some pictorial records of the freaks of Womankind in regard to dress during the reign of William Rufus. In the British Museum there is a MS. volume (MS. Cotton. Nero, C. IV.) which contains two books bound together; the second an Anglo-Norman version of the Psalms, which may possibly be not older than the middle of the twelfth century; but the first, which may have been executed in Normandy, though I think it is Anglo-Norman, is certainly of an early date—probably of the beginning of the same century. It is a very interesting series of drawings of scriptural subjects—in fact, illustrations of the Bible. They throw a singularly-interesting light on the costume of that period. Three of them are copied in the cut on my last page, selected from different pictures and different parts of the book. The first is taken from a picture representing the Slaughter of the Innocents (fol. 14) ; the second is from the folio next following ; and the third, to the right, is from folio 24. The dresses appear

LADIES OF THE SOUTH.

to be much the same as those of the Frankish female costume—the under tunic or robe, the outer robe, and the mantle ; but one of the most distinguishing peculiarities of the costume is the extraordinary form of the sleeves of the outer robe, which had now received in France the name of *gone,* or *gonele* (our modern word *gown*). The sleeve terminates in a long pendent, which will be best understood by the pictures—sometimes so long that it reached to the feet. The gown itself, too, was often so long that it trailed upon the ground. It will be remarked, also, that the waists of these ladies are very slender, and closely fitted with the dress—it was at this time that

stays were first introduced. We see now the women appearing usually without the coverchief, and when exposed to view, the hair is always parted on
the forehead, and turned on either side upon the shoulders. The hair on
each side was often bound with fillets, or ribands, so as to hang backwards
like two long tails. This is represented in the lady to the right in our cut,
where the hair looks as though fitted into a case. It may be remarked that,
although the nimbus shows that two of the figures of our group are saints,
they are all dressed in the height of the fashion; but this was not at all
contrary to ecclesiastical custom.

We have, curiously enough, the means of tracing the direction from
which this new fashion in dress came to Normandy and England. There is

AN ANGLO-NORMAN LADY IN FULL DRESS.

a manuscript in the British Museum (MS. Harl., No. 2821) which contains
a fine copy of the Gospels in Latin, accompanied with elaborate illuminations.
It is considered to be Italian, and to belong to the tenth century. Among
the illuminations are found examples of this curious pendent to the sleeves,
which was introduced among the Anglo-Normans towards the close of the
century following; so that the fashion had evidently travelled hither from
the south. Two figures of females from this manuscript are given in the
opposite cut.* It thus appears that, following the old tradition that everything new came from Rome, the fashions in France and England at this

* The first of these figures is taken from fol. 101, r° of the MS.; the second, the one on the
right, from fol. 22, r°.

time came from Italy and Provence. The lady to the right, in our cut, has a head-covering which descends behind almost to the bottom of her dress. It is equally worthy of remark that the outer dress of the lady on the right is ornamented with plates of gold set with pearls or precious stones, exactly like those of Queen Radegunde in our Coloured Plate; and in this same manuscript (fol. 100, vº), we have a picture of St. Luke in a dress similarly ornamented; so that it appears not to have been confined to the female sex. It is another example of a fashion brought from Italy to the North-West.

In our next cut (p. 97) we have a figure of a Norman lady, taken from a

A FASHIONABLE INDIVIDUAL.

manuscript in the Douce collection at Oxford, apparently of the early part of the twelfth century. Her robe appears trailing largely on the ground, and the pendent to the sleeve has so increased in length, that it requires to be tied up in a knot to prevent its interfering with the movements of the wearer as she walks. The mantle is here more capacious, and the plaited tail of hair is divided at the end into two parts. We have seen, at a rather earlier period, an ecclesiastic condemning the new fashions in dress as so many liveries of the demon. The illuminator who drew the scriptural illustrations in the Cottonian MS. (Nero, C. IV., fol. 18) evidently possessed a satirical spirit; in the picture of the Temptation, he has introduced Satan himself dressed in his own livery—a lady's gown so extravagant in its dimensions that it was necessary to shorten with a knot not only the sleeve but the dress also, to prevent its trailing. The demon, in his new costume, is represented in our last cut. The stays, or the laced body of the gown are here shown very distinctly.

CHAPTER VII.

CONDITION AND COSTUME OF WOMEN IN THE TWELFTH CENTURY.

THE twelfth century was a turbulent period of transition, both in France and in England, from an old state of society to a new one. It witnessed in both countries the great struggle between kingly government and feudal power, and, at the end of it, the advantage remained with the crown, though the victory was but imperfect. Our materials for the history of Womankind during this period are very scanty.

Tho position of women had been, in some degree, raised during this period, especially among the aristocracy. Our kings of the Norman line granted the hereditary right of succession to such titles of nobility as earls, barons, etc., without exception of sex; so that, on failure of male heirs, the title should devolve and be confirmed to the women, and they could convey it by marriage into other families. Thus ladies became nobles in their own right. On the other hand, the authority of the father over his daughters, in regard to giving in marriage, had been transferred to the feudal lord, or at least was placed under his control; and his right to the disposal of wards was more strictly enforced than ever, and was made a means of profit and extortion. Some of the old writers complain of the inconvenience of this practice, by which, as one of them says, "Wards were bought and sold as commonly as were beasts." In the letter or charter of Henry I., prefixed to the laws of that monarch, and written in the first year of his reign, A.D. 1100, or 1101, he promises to act in regard to his authority over his barons in this regard, with the utmost disinterestedness. "And if," he says, "any one of my barons or men wish to give in marriage his daughter, or sister, or grand-daughter, or kinswoman, let him talk to me about it. But I will neither take anything from him for this licence, nor will I forbid him to give her, unless he should intend to unite her with my enemy. And if, my baron or other man being dead, his daughter remain his heir, I will give her with her land by the advice of my barons. And if, the husband being dead, his wife survive, and be without children, she shall have her dower and marriage (*maritationem*), and I will not give her to a husband, except according to her will. But if the wife survive with children, she shall have her dower and marriage, as long as she shall keep her body lawfully, and I will not give her, except according to her will; and either the wife or some other near of kin shall be the guardian of the land and children. And I order that my barons shall forbear similarly towards the sons or daughters or wives of their men." Such was woman's position under feudalism; forbearance was proclaimed nominally, but was far from being the practice, as appears by the writers just quoted.

The innovations introduced into the marriage ceremonies, by the Normans, were few, and not of much importance, with one exception. Two persons, desirous of contracting matrimony, were required to be asked publicly three times in church, unless they obtained a dispensation from the bishop of the diocese. This was, as will be seen at once, the origin of our modern practice; but it was a new step on the part of the church to secure the occasion for interference in marriages. A law was also made under Henry I., by which no contract between a man and woman concerning marriage, without witnesses, should stand good if either of them denied it.

During this same twelfth century, the interference of the church in marriages and divorces was continually exercised, and in a manner which made it almost insupportable, the more so as it became a mere instrument of political intrigue. We know not to what extent it was carried among the middle classes, where the church gained less by its interference, but it enters largely, and rather scandalously, into the history of the kings and great feudal chieftains. Louis VII., of France, had married Alianor, duchess of Aquitaine; but, after a time, great disagreement arose between them. It was said that Henry Plantagenet, duke of Normandy and count of Anjou, persuaded her to apply for a divorce, in order to marry her himself, and thus obtain with her the duchy of Aquitaine. The case was laid before an ecclesiastical council held at Beaujenci in 1152, at which the marriage with King Louis was annulled on the plea that it was unlawful and incestuous by reason of the near relationship between them. This "near relationship" had to be traced back to Hugues Capet, who was the great-grandfather of the grandfather of Louis VII., and who had married a sister of Guilhem Fier-à-bras, the great-great-grandfather of Alianor. But the bishops were satisfied, and granted the divorce. The marriages of Philippe-Auguste were equally a cause of serious difficulties. Through political motives Philippe married Ingeburge, sister of the king of Denmark, on the 24th of August, 1193, and she was crowned by the Archbishop of Rheims next day. Before the ceremonies of the marriage were ended, Philippe was seized with an invincible antipathy to his wife; and three months later, the bishops, assembled in a council at Compiégne, over which the same Archbishop of Rheims presided, pronounced the marriage null on the usual plea of affinity of blood. Ingeburge appealed to the pope, Celestine III., who, in the March of the year 1196, annulled the decision of the council, and enjoined the king to take back his wife. But, instead of obeying, Philippe, within three months, married again, taking for his queen the Princess Marie of Meranie, to whom he was tenderly attached. Some eighteen months after this, Innocent III. succeeded to the papacy, a man exceedingly proud and overbearing, and one of his earliest acts was to address a bull to the king of France, ordering him to put away his "concubine" and to return to his lawful wife. As Philippe remained disobedient, the pope proceeded, after a year spent in attempts to appease him, to place his kingdom under an interdict. The evil resulting from this measure was so great that the king was obliged to yield, and Queen Marie was separated from her husband, and Ingeburge restored. The real cause of the pope's hostility arose from his jealousy of the Gallic bishops, in whom he refused to acknowledge the power of granting the divorce; and, on Philippe's submission to him, he obtained a divorce from Rome, but Queen Marie had died in childbirth during her separation. At the council of Rheims in 1119, Hildegarde, countess of Poitiers, presented herself and complained that her husband, who had been separated from a first wife before marrying her, had repudiated her, and taken to his bed Malberge, the wife of the Viscount of Châtellerault. At the council of Clermont, a few years earlier, one of the principal subjects of complaint was, that it had become a common practice for persons to put away their lawful wives, procure divorces, and take the wives of other men. Thus the church having taken into its own hands the power of marriage, repudiation, and divorce, this power was abused in all possible ways.

There is another subject to which we shall have to revert in a subsequent chapter. The Anglo-Saxon clergy, and no doubt the Frankish clergy also, had wives, to whom we have every reason to believe they were duly married. The new party in the church—perhaps we may call it the high church party —set their faces against the marriages of the clergy—they sought to separate as widely as possible the clergy from the laity in interests and in feelings, thinking, no doubt, that a priest with a wife and family could not fail to sympathize in some degree with common humanity, to unite, in fact, in the cause of the laity around them with whom they had contracted a worldly relationship. Hence the canons passed at the various ecclesiastical councils held in France and England during the eleventh and twelfth centuries are filled with injunctions against the marriage of the clergy, and, in fact, against all intercourse between them and the other sex. It is evident from a multitude of facts, that the clergy in general were very little inclined to yield this point, but by the middle of the thirteenth century the marriage of the clergy appears to have been generally abolished.

Extravagance in the display of jewelry and of rich materials in the dress had increased greatly towards the end of the twelfth century, and were still on the increase. Among the new substances, derived like so many of the others from the East, was one common enough now, but then greatly prized—*cotton*, which appears to have been introduced into France in the twelfth century. The name cotton, which was brought from the East, was given to it by the French. The Germans gave it a name taken from its nature, *baum-wolle*, *i.e.*, tree wool. It was called in mediæval Latin *bombax*. Jacques de Vitry, who wrote in the thirteenth century, describes it as "a mean between wool and linen," and says that it was used for making stuffs of very fine texture.* Cotton appears to have been in general use during the thirteenth century.

The use of silk, at this time, among the higher classes, was very considerable, and it was mixed perhaps with other substances, and received various colours, so as to form a variety of silken stuffs known under different names. The principal of these was what was called *cendal*. It is supposed to answer nearly to the modern taffetas, and was of various and rich colours. Another silken stuff, much in use, was called *siglaton*, which is spoken of in the romance of Partenopex de Blois, an early work of the thirteenth century, as an importation from the East ; for one of the personages of the story "looking towards the sun-rise," a list of the various objects which came from that quarter is given, and among them are the hairs from Alexandria, and "the good siglaton."

> S'esgarde vers soleil levant . . .
> Par là li poile Alixandrin
> Vienent, et li bon *siglaton.*

Another rich silken stuff, usually embroidered with gold, was called *samit*, and appears to have been usually employed in the making of robes for the

---

* "Sunt ibi præterea arbusta quædam, ex quibus colligunt bombacem, quæ Francigenæ *cotonem* seu *coton* appellant ; est quasi medium inter lanam et linum, ex quo subtilia vestimenta contexunter."—*Jacobus de Vitriaco,* lib. i., c. 84.

bishops; we learn in the life of St. Louis, that that monarch kept in reserve such robes "of samit and other valuable stuffs made of silk" (*de samit et d'autres dras de soie precieus*). Velvet was also now in use, called in the Latin of the time *pannus villosus*, or downy cloth.

I might enumerate other names of cloths and stuffs in use as early as the

NOBLE LADIES AND CHAMBER-MAIDEN.

twelfth and thirteenth centuries, for there appears to have been a great variety of them, but some of them are seldom mentioned, and were probably not much in use, while others were employed only in dresses for men. *Saie*, in mediæval Latin *sagum* or *sagus*, was a cloth of very fine texture made of wool. It appears to have been often employed to evade the ecclesiastical rule which enjoined by way of penance the wearing of a woollen garment, intended of course to be rough, next to the skin. *Camelot*, or *camelin*, which also came from the East, is said to have been made of the hair of camels. Some of these cloths were dyed of very rich colours. In the latter part of the twelfth century, and in the thirteenth, embroidery of various kinds was employed in these stuffs, and in the dresses made from them, to a very extravagant degree. It was not unusual to have the crests and armorial bearings of the family embroidered upon the outer dress ; and it was often covered with large figures, not only of plants and flowers, but of animals also. At the council of Montpelier, early in the latter half of the twelfth century, among other complaints against extravagance in costume, it was stated that the ladies of that time wore dresses covered with such fantastic figures that they rather resembled monsters or demons than human beings.

The cut in the preceding page, taken from an illuminated manuscript of the twelfth century in the Imperial Library in Paris, is here copied from one of the plates to the important work of M. Louandre, *Les Artes Somptuaires*—it represents two noble ladies, with a chamber-maiden serving one of the ladies with water to wash. The lady to the left, who wears a curiously shaped hat or coronet, has a grey gown or outer-tunic, and over it a red mantle with a white border. The lady to the right wears a grey outer-tunic, with a yellow border, and an under-tunic of very light brown. Her head is enveloped in a grey couvrechief, or hood. She carries a book in her hand. The *chambrière* wears a white tunic, with grey and green stripes. Their shoes are similar in shape, of brown colour, spotted, the spots being in the first lady white, in the chamber-damsel red, and in the second lady mixed white and brown.

The second cut, a selection from another illuminated manuscript preserved in the Imperial Library in Paris, presents a group of figures of men and women, belonging also, probably, to this same period, the latter part of the twelfth century. They furnish a good example of the varieties of costume then prevailing among both sexes. The lady to the right wears a white dress, with a hood similarly of white material. The hood of the other female is black with white stripes. Her outer dress, as seen here, is salmon-coloured, with red spots, and dark-red lining. Her tunic is yellow. They have both the hanging sleeves, but, at the date to which these figures belong, they were evidently beginning to be worn shorter. In the dresses of the men the prevailing colours are blue and red. The shoes are all of a dark colour with white spots.

11

The hair was still considered as an object of great importance, and was preserved and dressed with a sort of superstitious reverence.   The manner

COSTUMES OF THE LATTER PART OF THE TWELFTH CENTURY.

in which it is arranged in the two principal figures in our first cut is concealed by the position in which they are placed, and by the coverchief of one of them; but in the case of the chamber-maiden, it is plaited, or twisted, very long behind, and apparently enclosed in a case, like that of some of the ladies in our last chapter.   The importance attached to the hair was, as we have seen, of old date, and was shown in many acts of ordinary life.   It was usual with persons of either sex, to give a lock of the hair as a pledge of faithfulness to an agreement or to a contract of friendship, whence we derive our modern practice of preserving a lock of hair as a memorial of affection.   We still find the matron generally wearing the coverchief, as in the three figures given in our third cut, which are enameled in Limoges work on the back of a copper figure of the Virgin seated in a chair. It is

A GROUP OF LADIES OF THE TWELFTH CENTURY.

related of the Cotteriaux, or freebooters, who at this time overrun the country in large troops, that they robbed the churches of their corporales to make vails of them for the loose women who wandered about with them.

CHAPTER VIII.

THE WOMEN OF FEUDAL ROMANCE.—BERTHA AND PARISE.

THE pride of family was very great throughout the Teutonic race, and, indeed, it was much the same among the Celts. The two objects of domestic worship were the gods and the ancestors, the remote founders of the family, who were themselves looked upon as divine. The rehearsal of their names, and actions, and qualities, formed the first poetry; and it was the office of the bard or minstrel to chant this poetry to the assembled household. The more accomplished minstrel was a composer also, a *scóp*, who sang his histories to the accompaniment of the harp. All this singing of the ancient deeds of the race in the hall entered so much into the spirit of our Anglo-Saxon forefathers, that they called it joy or pleasure, *gleó*, from which word we derive our modern word glee, and *dreám*, from which latter word the harper, or musician, was called *dreámere*. The "joy in hall" is often spoken of in Beowulf. Thus we are told of one of the heroes—

þæt he dogora gewham	that he every day
dreám gehyrde	heard joy
hludne in healle :	loud in hall :
þær wæs hearpan swég,	there was the noise of the harp,
swútol sang scopes.	the clear song of the poet.
Beowulf, l. 175.	

And, in another place—

scóp hwilum sang	meanwhile the poet sang
hádor on Heorote;	serene in Heorot (Hrothgar's hall);
þær wæs hæleða dreám.	there was joy of heroes.
Beowulf, l. 987.	

And again—

þær wæs gidd and gleó.	there was song and joy.
Beowulf, l. 4213.	

The same manners and sentiments prevailed among the Franks in Gaul,

who, however, had adopted the language of the Romans in place of their
own Teutonic dialect. They also called this chanting of the deeds of their
forefathers, joy, which they appear to have expressed by the Latin word
jocus; from which was made the word *joculator,* the name given to the poet
or minstrel, answering to the Anglo-Saxon *dreámere,* and moulded down
into the later French *jougleur.* The French called their new language
Roman, and it was first by foreigners, and not by themselves till a much
later period, called Frankish, or French. A song or a book composed in
French was thus called *cantio Romana* (*chanson Romane*), or *liber Romanus*
(*livre Romans*), or simply a *Romans,* the word *livre,* or book, being understood. Hence *Romans* in French became almost synonymous with book,
and as these historical songs of the chieftain's hall formed the mass of the
early literary compositions in French, that word became identified with
them, and was eventually employed, as it is still in French, in the same
sense as its modern English representative *romance.*

These great poems were, through the earlier ages, not written, but only
preserved in memory; and it must be understood that they were called
chansons, as sung in the hall, and only at a later period *romans,* as written
in books. They had already, in passing through different changes in
society, undergone considerable alterations in form and character. They
were at first more divine in their character, as we have seen them in
our second chapter; their heroes were demi-gods, from whom the early
great Teutonic chieftains claimed their family descent. Then, under
Christianity, they descended to the heroic, and the founders of the
great families were still considered by their descendants as something
more than ordinary mortals. In the feudal period they had descended
a few steps nearer to humanity, and as the great feudal families prided
themselves generally as belonging to the age of Charlemagne, their plots
are mostly laid among the great events of that period. Hence they
have been called Carlovingian romances. But all who heard them still
believed in their strictly historical character, and, when they began to
be committed to writing in the twelfth century, to distinguish them from
other works of a literary character, people called them *gesta* or *gestes,* deeds
or histories; and *chansons de geste* or *romans de geste,* songs or books of
history, names which are still retained by the historical writers on mediæval
literature. I here use in treating of them the general and equally correct
term of Feudal Romance because they belong especially to feudalism. They
mark the transition between the earlier and later Middle Ages, and form the
division line between the ruder and more stately poetry of the Northmen

and Teutons, and the more elegant and varied literature of the thirteenth and fourteenth centuries.

These romances, although a well-known date is given to them, represent a half-mythic period of social history. Fairies are active in them, and supernatural agency is largely introduced, and the heroes are endowed with marvellous qualities of physical strength, and with powers of communication with the spiritual world. We may expect, therefore, to find here, in their highest colouring, the feudal ideas with regard to the character of Womankind, and it will be worth while, in many bearings, to take a review of them. They cannot but have exercised a great influence on the actual tone of contemporary society.

The women of feudal romance are represented to us as extremely impressionable, and remarkable for their susceptibility. It is almost invariably the lady who falls in love, and makes the first advances, and who, indeed, conducts the courtship; and this is carried to a degree which is quite startling. It seems to have been the notion that the business of the man was entirely fighting and performing heroic actions, and that his natural reward was the love of the other sex, which was offered to him and not sought. One of the earliest, in its style and general character, of the feudal romances now preserved, is that of Elias (*Elie*) of Saint Giles. The fair Rosemonde was a Saracenic princess in the town of Sorbrie, the daughter of the "amiral," or emir, Macabre. Now, it must be understood that, in these western romances, Saracenic ladies resembled in all respects, except in their religious faith, the same sex among the Christians; possessed the same sentiments, the same manners, and generally the same qualities; and lived in the same style. Elias, the noble Christian knight, was carried grievously wounded into the town of Sorbrie, and the princess took him under her care, for she, like the rest of her sex in those times, was the good physician. She caused him to be carried into her chamber, where she applied successfully to his wounds a precious herb she possessed, which had been gathered at the foot of the cross on which Christ was crucified. When his strength was thus sufficiently restored, the princess prepared a bath for him, and furnished him with a bathing dress; and, in the course of all these proceedings, she let him know by her caresses the sentiments she entertained towards him, and he submitted to them, but somewhat coldly. Elias remained thus in the care of Rosemonde more than fifteen days. Now, Rosemonde, though a Saracen, was a Christian in her heart, and she listened unwillingly to the numerous Saracenic kings who made offers for her hand, until one, named Lubien, who was too powerful to be contradicted, threw down his glove to challenge whoever dared to resist him. Rosemonde, of course, calls upon Elias to protect her, but he accepted the task almost as coldly as he had previously accepted her caresses. However, he took up the glove, and defeated the Saracenic king. Rosemonde's brother, Caïfas, had meanwhile espoused the cause of Lubien, and had accused his sister openly of disgracing herself with the Christian knight. In her anger, she seized him by the hair of the head, and tore off a portion of it. "By my head, sir traitor, what you say there is false; I was never unchaste, nor has any one attempted me; but of a truth, if I had yielded, he would have been well worthy, for he is a good knight, courageous and bold, and you are a coward, and bad and false." She ceased speaking, seized him by the temples, and tore off the hair as much as she held. Caïfas turns, strikes her in the teeth so as to cut her lip, and makes the blood fly from it.

> Par mon chief, dan traitre, vous i avês menti;
> Onques ne fu-je pute, ne on ne l' me requist;
> Mais je le fuisse certes, se il très bien vausist,
> Qu'il est bons chevaliers, corajous et hardis,
> Et vous estes couars et malvais et faillis.
> Elle laist le parler, par les temples le prist,
> Des cheveus a sachiés quanques la bele tient.
> Caïfas se retourne, ens ès dens le refiert,
> Que la levre lui trenche, le sanc en fait saillir.

As soon as Elias had overcome Lubien, he, at the request of the princess, raised his sword and cut off her brother's head. More fighting followed, the Christians were everywhere victorious, Rosemonde was baptized, and, as a matter of course, her marriage with Elias was to follow immediately. But the latter had incautiously acted as godfather at the christening, and when he applied for the emperor's sanction to the marriage, the archbishop interposed, and forbade it on the ground of this spiritual relationship. Elias yielded without difficulty, and in reward received from the emperor the hand of the sister of the latter, the Princess Avise, with the fiefs of Orleans and Bourges. But Rosemonde was not so easily consoled, and refused the hands of some of the highest barons of France. In the romance of *Raoul de Cambrai*, the fair daughter of the noble Gerin falls in love with another of the heroes of the history, Bernier, and is made to say to herself rather naively that, if she can succeed, she will hold him in her arms before night—

> Puis dit en bas, s'ele puet exploitier,
> Que le tenra encor ains l'anuitier.

She causes her chamber to be arranged with elegance, sends her chamberlain to Bernier to invite him to go and play at chess with her; and, when he arrives, she confesses her love for him in the most unequivocal terms, and asks him to make her his wife. Bernier acknowledges his appreciation of the compliment, but explains to her that he labours under the stain of illegitimacy, which would render him, according to feudal notions, unworthy of so great an honour. She, however, persists in her demand, and Bernier agrees to the match. The scene between the damsel and her father, when she asks him for his consent to the marriage, is curiously characteristic. "My daughter," he says, "I love nothing in the world so much as you." "That is what we shall see," she replied; "it is now the custom with many wealthy burghers to caress their children when they are small, but as soon as they are grown up, they care for them no more. My father, I am come to ask you to marry me." "What!" exclaimed Gerin; "is there anything changeable like the minds of women? Did you not, only a week ago, refuse the marriages which were offered you?" "Because," she said, "they were not to my liking; but now I want to take a husband." "Never," said Gerin, with some appearance of reason, "has a young girl talked in that manner. A husband is not a thing which you can buy in the fair or market. Let one come who is to your liking, and, whoever he may be, be he but a poor palmer from beyond sea, I will give him to you." "That is fair speaking, my father; but give me the handsome and brave Bernier." Gerin consents immediately, and the marriage follows.

The romance of *Aiol* presents characteristics of great antiquity. The young hero, who belongs to a noble family, is thrown upon the world, and passes through a number of wild adventures, until, at length, arrived at Orleans, he is sheltered by the Countess Isabelle, his mother's sister, totally unaware of their relationship. The young and beautiful daughter of the countess, the fair Luciane, falls in love with the stranger, and as the charge of his entertainment is entrusted to her, she has full opportunity of declaring her sentiments. She makes his bed, and the description of it is a curious picture of a bed of the feudal as well as of the mythic ages. "Then she made Aiol's bed with great pleasure; the bed ·was of straw, which she placed underneath, and the sheet was of silk, there was no linen; the coverlet was of marten, large and full, and the pillow was made of purple" (purple was the name of a rich cloth)—

> Là fist le lit d'Aiol par grant delit;
> Les kieutes sont de paile que desous mist;
> Et li linceul de soie, n'i ot pas lin;
> Li covertor de martre grant et furni;
> Et l'oreiller fu fait d'un osterin.

The noble maiden took the youth to his bed, undressed him, and put him into it, while a valet served him with wine; and she gave him sufficient marks of her love. The marriage, which would have followed was, however, prevented by the discovery of the near relationship of Aiol and the fair Luciane. I might easily multiply examples of this practice of the heroines of the romances of making love to the heroes, and of the reserve often shown by the latter in meeting their advances. Such was the case with Horn and the Princess Rimel, in the romance of Horn; such was the case with Amile and the daughter of Charlemagne, Belissent, in the romance of *Amis et Amile;* such, again, was the case with the young Duchess of Burgundy and Girart, in the romance of *Girart de Viane.* In the romance of *Auberi,* the Queen Guibour and her young daughter, Seneheut, fall in love at the same time with the hero Auberi, and enter into fierce rivalry. The same sentiments on the part of the wife and daughter of Anséis, king of Cologne, towards Girbert, the son of Garin, enters into the romance of *Girbert de Metz.*

This tendency to fall in love appears to have been peculiar to the ladies of the Chansons de Geste of feudal romance, while, on the contrary, the young heroes were in general more or less reserved towards the other sex, nor were they always very gentle towards them. It would appear from the romance of *Amis and Amile,* that the former was accustomed to beat his wife, Lubias, when she offended him. But Lubias was the perverse woman. When, in the romance of *Raoul de Cambrai,* Raoul's mother, Alaïs, labours to persuade her son from undertaking an unjust war, he insults his mother for her interference, and curses the man who takes counsel of a woman. "Go you into your chambers to take your own ease, drink a draught to fatten your paunches, and occupy yourselves with thoughts of eating and drinking, for it is no business of yours to interfere in anything else."

> Dedens vos chambres vos alés aaisier
> Beveiz puison por vos pance encrassier,
> Et si pensez de boivre et de mengier,
> Car d' autre chose ne devez mais plaidier.

In fact woman's occupations in the romances were much the same as in ordinary life in the age in which they were committed to writing. In the romance of *Renaud de Montauban,* the proud Duke Beuve, when his duchess tries to turn him from mad hostility, uses language to her much the same as that of Raoul of Cambrai to his mother Alaïs. "Lady," said the duke, "go, and seek shade there in your chambers, and dress you well; go in there and give advice to your maids; think of twisting silk, that is your

15

business. My business is with a sword of steel, to strike and joust against a knight. Ill-luck fall on the beard of a noble baron who goes to seek counsel in a lady's chamber."

> 'Dame,' ce dist li dus, 'ulés vous ombroier
> Là dedans en vos chambres, et bien appareillier;
> Laienz û vos puceles prenês à chastoier;
> Pensés de soie tordre, ce est vostre mestier.
> Li miens mestiers si est à l'espée d'acier
> Et ferir et joster encoutre un chevalier.
> Mal dahé nit la barbe à nobile princier,
> Qui en chambre de dame vait pour lui conseillier!

Nor was Womankind very sufficiently protected, for ladies even of the highest rank were exposed to dangers of all kinds. This will be well illustrated by an incident in the romance of *Hervis de Metz*, one of the great cycle of romances of the family of Lorraine. The Princess Beatrix, daughter of the Emperor of Constantinople, was in her garden, with no other companion but her damoiselles, who were making chaplets of flowers, when ten squires, passing by on horseback, seized her and carried her away. When they were beyond any fear of pursuit, they quarrelled as to which should have first possession of their prey, and finished by agreeing to keep her uninjured, and seek an opportunity of selling her for a slave, for their common benefit; and accordingly, they determined to carry her to the fair, which was held at Paris after Christmas. On their way, at Lagni-sur-Marne, they met with the "damoisel" Hervi, who took a liking to the princess and bought her, and they were subsequently married, and Beatrix became the mother of the great hero of this cycle of romance, Garin le Loherain.

The ladies of the romances appear usually to act with great independence. They even give themselves away in marriage. We have seen the daughter of Guerin choosing her own husband. This was a little modified by the feudal feelings, because, when the damsel inherited a fief, the feudal lord claimed the right of giving that, and the damsel rather naturally went with it. In the romance of *Aye d' Avignon*, the fair Aye, with her fief of Avignon, had been given and affianced by her father to Berenger; but after the father's death, Charlemagne, to whom, as the feudal suzerain, the right of disposing of them would fall, gave them to a chieftain who was in his favour, Garnier, the son of the traitor Ganelon. Berenger resents the injury, and the result is a series of desolating wars. The disposal of heiresses is thus the frequent cause of wars in the feudal romances.

The greater proportion of the heroines of feudal romance are noble

women in every sense of the word, and display qualities which justly
entitle them to admiration. In spite of the contempt expressed by chieftains like Raoul de Cambrai, and the Duke Beuve, for woman's counsels, we
find some of the greatest of the heroes of romance guided to their advantage by the wise and good counsels of their wives. This was the case with
one of the heroes of the romance of *Aspremont*, the famous Girart de
Roussillon, the fierce and formidable enemy successively of most of the Carlovingian kings, whose wise and devoted consort, called sometimes Bertha,
and at others, Ermengarde, or Emmeline, had for her mission to heal the
wounds and calm the furies of her haughty lord, and restore him to sentiments of loyalty and justice. There is something touching in the manner
in which the fierce old chieftain bends before her exhortations. A lady of
the same fine character is the fair Aude, the affianced of Roland, in the
romance of *Girart de Viane;* and other examples might be given from these
romances. The beautiful Ludie, the daughter of the treacherous Froment, and
sister of Fromondin, in the great romance of the Lorraine family, presents
a noble picture of female greatness of character. She refuses to accept from
her father the hand of the noble Hernant, when she sees that the marriage
was only intended to draw the latter into a snare; but she becomes his wife
after she has saved him from her father's evil   . The marriage
becomes the signal for a reconciliation between   owerful and hostile
families; but the peace is not long lasting, and a year afterwards, as the
result of a new treason, Ludie is the captive of her brother Fromondin.
New wars follow between the two great families of Lorraine and Bordeaux,
in which the fair Ludie, still the prisoner of her brother Fromondin, uses
her efforts in vain to appease the latter and restore peace. Instead of listening to her, Fromondin, in anger, dashes out the brains of her two children
who are with her, throws them out of the castle window into the foss,
and threatens to treat Lubie in the same manner if she repeats her expostulations. In the sequel, Fromondin experiences defeat after defeat, until he
is deprived of all his territories, and is obliged to fly into Spain, where he
repents and becomes a hermit. Afterwards, by a strange course of events,
Ludie becomes the fierce avenger of her brother Fromondin's murder.
For, as the composer of this romance says, "We must not pay much
attention to woman's anger; but when once she hates in earnest, her fury is
more to be feared than the most violent poison, and her mind invents crimes
which would have made Cain recoil." Ludie renounces her husband Hernant, causes his cousin Girbert to be murdered by two of his and her sons,
and takes shelter with her followers in the castle of Gironville. Hernant

captures the two sons, and causes both to be hanged in revenge for the murder; and thus one crime leads to another through this terrible history. Lubias, the wife of Amis, in the romance of *Amis and Amile*, is an example of the bad woman of these romances.

We sometimes see the great women of the romances exposed to misfortune, which they bear with the utmost magnanimity. The wife of Savari, duke of Aquitaine, we are told, was the beautiful Flore, who was accused falsely by her enemies in the court of plotting to poison her husband. Savari banishes her from his territory, and takes, as a second wife, a woman who had been an accomplice in the treason against her. Flore finds shelter in a peasant's cottage, where she gives birth to a child, which becomes the celebrated romance-hero, Garin de Montglane. When Garin is laid in his cradle, he is visited by three fairies, who bestow upon him such gifts as fairies were in the habit of giving. Mother and child remain in concealment with the peasant until Garin has reached his fifteenth year, when he begins to make himself known in the world.

Women of rank are not unfrequently subjected to such great acts of treason and persecution in these feudal romances, and two of the stories which form the subject of entire romances, deserve to be told at greater length, as admirable examples of the history of Womankind during this heroic age of feudalism. The first of these is the history of Queen Bertha, the wife of Pepin, king of France. It must be premised that this story, which forms the plot of what is entitled in the original, *li romans de Berte aux grans piés*, belongs to the mythology of the northern people, and not to sober history, for Pepin had no queen of this name, or to whom such adventures happened. It is, like the rest of these romances, entirely mythic. Let us now proceed to the story of QUEEN BERTHA.

It was soon after the middle of the eighth century that King Pepin, according to ancient story, at length enjoyed the crown of France in that peace and tranquillity of which, during the earlier part of his reign, the turbulence of his barons had effectually deprived him. His first queen had died childless, and he was anxious to provide an heir to his kingdom. Under these circumstances, he called together his council in haste, in order to consult them on the choice of a queen. Their voices were unanimous in favour of the beautiful and virtuous Bertha, only daughter of the king of Hungary.

The king and queen of Hungary at this time were Floire and Blancheflor, personages no less celebrated in mediæval romance than Pepin himself, and both they and their court, according to the story, were as well acquainted

with the manners and language of France as if it had been their native
land. When the Frankish messengers sent to demand the hand of their
princess, after traversing the numerous petty states into which Germany
was then divided, reached at length the Hungarian court, their embassy
was received in the most favourable manner, and Bertha was entrusted to
their care to be escorted to the kingdom of her future husband. She was
accompanied only by a female serf belonging to her father's court named
Margiste, Margiste's daughter Aliste, and their kinsman Tybert. Margiste
had been taken into the special favour of the king and queen of Hungary,
and had been charged by them with the care of their daughter; and Aliste,
who bore a striking personal resemblance to the princess Bertha, had been
educated rather as her companion than as her servant. Great was the
rejoicing when the princess Bertha entered Paris, and grand the display for
her reception; the wedding festival was magnificent, and King Pepin's
palace resounded with the strains of the most skilful minstrels that could
be gathered together from all parts. Everything seemed to denote lasting
prosperity and happiness.

But, if we accept the teaching of mediæval romance, a mind of servile
origin, however high the individual might be raised in honour and dignities,
always betrayed in the sequel its original baseness, and so it was in the
present case. Amid the rejoicings and festivities which welcomed the
arrival of Bertha in Paris, her confidential attendants, aware that they
formed almost her sole credentials, were plotting treason and murder in
order to substitute Aliste for the princess in Pepin's household. It has
just been stated that Bertha and Aliste bore a close resemblance to each
other. By a stratagem which was in accordance with the manners of
former days, but which will hardly bear relating at present, the princess
was induced to permit Aliste to take her place in the royal bed on the night
of her nuptials, while she herself slept with Margiste in an adjoining
chamber. Before daybreak, Bertha entered the chamber of Pepin silently
to resume her place, as had been agreed, when the slave who had been
personating her rose suddenly from the bed, and, having stabbed herself
unperceived sufficiently to draw blood, and placed the knife in the hand
of her unsuspecting mistress, awoke the king with her screams, and told
him that Aliste, the companion of her youth, had penetrated into the
nuptial apartment, and sought to murder her. At the same time Margiste
rushed into the room, burst into imprecations against her pretended
daughter for the meditated crime, and, with the assistance of Tybert, who
was at hand, and accessory to the plot, dragged Bertha, speechless with

astonishment and confusion, from the royal presence, and bound and gagged her, so as to deprive her of the power of speaking.

The treacherous Aliste was now master of the king, who had not known them long enough to distinguish the slave from the princess, for the nuptials had been celebrated on the day of their arrival. At her instigation, Pepin gave orders that the pretended murderess should be immediately put to death; and, under the pretext of avoiding scandal, it was further resolved that the whole transaction should be kept in profound secrecy, and that the unfortunate princess should be delivered to three of the king's servants, in whom he could place the greatest trust. These, under the direction of Tybert, were to carry her privately to the vast wilds of the forest of Maine, and there put her to death, and leave her body exposed to birds and beasts of prey. Placed on a swift palfrey, Bertha, bound hand and mouth, and her person concealed under a capacious mantle, was carried farther and farther into the forest during five days. On the sixth day they reached one of its wildest solitudes, and there they halted, and, taking the princess from her seat, drew away the mantle, and the cruel Tybert prepared to strike off her head with his sword. But her beauty and dignity excited to such a degree the compassion of the three attendants, that they not only pleaded for her life, but, while one of them kept Tybert at bay, the two others unbound the lady, and she disappeared from their sight amid the thickets of the forest. As it would have been a vain labour to seek to recover their victim, Tybert and his three companions invented a story, by which they convinced Margiste and her daughter, the false queen, that they had duly performed their errand.

The cries of the night-birds and the distant howl of the wolves struck terror into the mind of Bertha, as she fled through the leafy wilderness, not knowing whither. The weather, too, seemed to conspire against her, and the storm broke over her, rain and hail, and thunder and lightning. Onward Bertha fled, and if she thought of anything, it was of the happy court of Hungary, and of her kind mother Blancheflor, until, cold, and wet, and weary, her feet bleeding, and her clothes and skin torn with thorns and brambles, she fainted and dropped on the ground. When she recovered, she fell on her knees and prayed to heaven for protection, and heaven heard and protected her. She then continued her flight, still ignorant as before of the route she was taking, until nightfall came, and then, shivering with cold and hunger, she made herself a bed of leaves under a bush, her only protection against the inclemency of the weather, and lay down to rest. Here a new danger threatened the unfortunate princess. Two robbers of the forest came suddenly and found her, and seized her for their prey; but a dispute for priority of possession led to a sanguinary fight, in which both were mortally wounded, and Bertha again took to flight, till at length she was arrested by a stream, which she could not pass, and she laid her down under a thick thorn-bush on its banks, and wept till she fell asleep. She awoke at midnight. The weather had then cleared, and the moon shone so bright, that she thought it was day, and, after praying devoutly, she continued her flight. She found a well, drank at it, and felt refreshed. Soon afterwards, she met with faint traces of a path, which brought her to a lonely hermitage, and she knocked at the door and asked for shelter; but the holy hermit, astonished to see a beautiful woman in the forest at that hour, concluded that it was the evil one, who had come in disguise to tempt him to unchastity, so he made the sign of the cross, and refused her admittance. Her entreaties, however, so far prevailed upon him, that he gave her a portion of his coarse black bread, and showed her a path which led to the house of the good farmer Symon and his wife Constance.

Symon, whose house was in the forest, happened to be out early that morning, and was not a little astonished to meet in his way a beautiful damsel, whose delicate features and rich garment bespoke rank and wealth, while the state in which she appeared told of the great sufferings she had undergone. He stopped, and asked her who she was, and whence she came. She chose to conceal the truth, and told him a plausible story, how she was the daughter of a gentleman of Alsace, which was then suffering under the ravages of war to such a degree that they had been obliged to seek safety in exile, and that she was herself flying from the cruelty of a stepmother; and she added that she had been recommended by the hermit to the favour of Symon the farmer. Symon immediately took her to his house, and presented her to his wife.

This excellent household consisted of Symon himself, his wife Constance, and two young and fair daughters, named Isabel and Aiglente, all honest and worthy people, under whose hospitable care Bertha soon recovered her usual cheerfulness. Constance took her into her own chamber, placed her before a blazing fire, rubbed her benumbed limbs, and served her with food. The princess confessed that her name was Bertha, and rather shrank from the remark which followed, that it was the same as that of their new queen, the daughter of the king of Hungary. Constance and her two daughters became greatly attached to her, and attended upon her with affectionate care. A new circumstance soon increased this friendship. Symon's two daughters passed their time in working on embroidery; and one day soon after her arrival, Bertha saw them at work, and offered to teach them something which they had not learnt. In those days it was, as already stated in former chapters, a special portion of the education of a princess to excel in embroidery, and in other work of a similar description, and the two damsels were astonished at excellence such as they had never seen before. From that time Bertha was a greater favourite than ever, for she had become a valuable as well as an agreeable companion, and her work and her example were worth more than her board. Thus she remained with her friendly hosts nine years and a half, advancing ever in their esteem and love.

During this time, how went things in the fair city of Paris? The slave Aliste was believed by everybody to be the Queen Bertha, and no inquiry was made as to what had become of Aliste herself. She had two sons by the king, Rainfrois and Heudri, whose conduct in life betrayed the baseness of the blood from which, on one side, they were derived. The false queen, who never went to church, and occupied herself chiefly with the care of amassing treasure, soon made herself hateful by her tyranny and extortion.

Meanwhile changes had taken place at the court of Hungary. A sister and brother of Bertha died a few months after she left her home, and she and her descendants remained the only heirs of King Floire. The latter had no suspicion of Margiste and Aliste, and supposed that the personage known as Pepin's queen was his daughter Bertha. He held counsel one night with his queen Blancheflor, and it was resolved to send a messenger to Paris to ask that Heudri, the youngest of Pepin's sons by Bertha, should be sent to Hungary, to be brought up there as the heir to the Hungarian throne. Under the influence of Aliste and Margiste this demand was refused. The trouble of mind which this refusal caused to Floire and Blancheflor was increased by an ominous dream of the latter, and Floire consented that his queen should proceed to France to see her daughter, and that she should endeavour to bring back with her one of her grandsons, either Heudri or Rainfrois. Blancheflor proceeded on her journey with great pomp; the king accompanied her part of the way, and she carried with her to Paris an escort of a hundred of the best knights in Hungary. When she entered France she found no welcome from the populace, and she heard nothing but words of hatred against the queen her daughter. All this was strange news to the queen of Hungary, who knew that her child had been nourished in high and noble sentiments, and could not believe that she had degenerated from the blood which ran in her veins. Yet everywhere, as she continued her route, she heard nothing but complaints of Queen

Bertha's tyranny and injustice. These complaints increased as she approached king Pepin's capital, and she wondered more and more how a princess so good and so fair as Bertha had been could have been changed into an object of universal hatred.

But the approach of Blancheflor raised another sort of agitation in the royal palace. In those days news travelled slowly, and the queen of Hungary was already near Paris when Pepin received intelligence of her visit, and he immediately announced it to his queen. Aliste—the false Bertha—knew well that Blancheflor could not, like Pepin, be deceived in her identity, and in secret terror she hurried to her mother, and they held counsel with Tybert. Various plans were suggested, one of which was to murder Blancheflor by means of poisoned fruit, but it was finally resolved that Aliste, under pretence of sudden and dangerous illness, should take to her bed, that her room should be darkened, and that it should be insisted that her life would be endangered by the agitation of an interview with her supposed mother. Thus it was hoped that Blancheflor might depart without seeing her, and the danger would be averted.

Meanwhile Blancheflor arrived at Montmartre, where Pepin with his two sons met her, and she was conducted into Paris in state. When she inquired for her daughter, she was informed of her dangerous illness, of which none had heard before, and when the king presented his two sons to her, she experienced an aversion to them which she could not explain, and felt unwilling even to embrace them. Sadness took possession of her heart. Her first desire was to visit her daughter, but Margiste appeared, and did all she could to prevent her. Margiste had formerly enjoyed her confidence, and she suspected no deceit in her. When she inquired for Aliste, Margiste informed her that her daughter had died suddenly, soon after the royal marriage. Blancheflor now insisted on an interview with her daughter, and she was conducted into the chamber of Pepin's queen, in profound darkness, and, at her bed side, had a short conversation that was so little satisfactory that her suspicions were excited. At last, in great agitation, she called in her own attendants, tore away curtains and shutters, and let in the light, and saw that Pepin's queen was not her daughter Bertha, but Aliste, the daughter of the slave Margiste. It is unnecessary to describe the astonishment of Pepin and his court when this unexpected discovery was announced. Margiste and Tybert were immediately seized and thrown into prison. The former, under the pressure of torture, first confessed, and Tybert told all, with the further revelation that Bertha had not, as Margiste believed, been put to death, but that she had escaped into the forest. Margiste was burnt,

16

and Tybert hanged. Aliste, who had been to some extent a tool in the hands of her wicked mother, and had borne children to Pepin, was spared to repent, and became a nun of Montmartre. Blancheflor, believing that her daughter was dead, returned disconsolate to Hungary.

But all this time, where is the true Queen Bertha herself? We left her at work on her embroidery in the humble household of the farmer Symon, where she seemed to have become contented with her lot, resolved on passing the rest of her life in this humble retirement. Symon heard of the strange occurrences just described, and of the supposed fate of the beautiful queen, and, comparing one thing with another, he had his suspicions, and communicated them to his wife Constance; but when they questioned Bertha, she denied that she was the queen. The three men who had set her at liberty from Tybert came before the king, told him all they knew, and he sent them to the forest of Maine to seek information on the fate of their victim. Fifteen days they wandered about the forest, making fruitless inquiries, and then all hope of obtaining further information was abandoned.

One day King Pepin was with his court at Mans; it was Whitsuntide when kings and their courts always sought recreation, and Pepin and his barons went into the forest to hunt. In the heat of the chase, Pepin became separated from his companions, and lost himself in the intricacies of the wood. At length he came to a little chapel, where he found a beautiful maiden occupied in prayer. He addressed her courteously, told her he was one of the king's attendants who had lost his way, and begged her to show him to the nearest house. She replied with the courtesy of a lady, and was conducting him to the house of Symon the farmer, when the king, struck by her beauty and manners, took her in his arms, and prayed her to grant him her love. She resisted, but in vain, and it is hard to say to what length he might have gone, had she not exclaimed, to protect herself against his violence, "I am Queen Bertha, the daughter of Floire and Blancheflor!" It was, indeed, Bertha herself, and the chapel was a little cell where Symon's family, whose house was distant only four or five bow-shots, were accustomed to attend mass, and that day she had been accidentally left there alone. Who was ever astonished like King Pepin, when he thus unexpectedly found his long lost wife? He called Symon before him, questioned him on all the circumstances of his first meeting with the lady, and his answers, compared with the information previously given by the three companions of Tybert, left room for no further doubt of the truth. It is enough to add that the lost queen was carried to Paris in pomp and triumph, that the courts of France and Hungary were filled with joy, and that, according to the story, Queen Bertha lived long and happily with her royal husband, and became the mother of Charles Martel.

The second of the stories to which I have alluded is the romance of *Parise la Duchesse*, and, for more reasons than one, it is believed to be one of the latest of its class; but its character is equally mythic with the others. History, I believe, knows no Raymond, duke of Vauvenice, who answers to the hero of our story, which was, no doubt, composed in the thirteenth century. With this introductory remark, I proceed to relate the adventures of PARISE THE DUCHESS.

Among the great barons of the time of the glorious Charlemagne, who was more noble or more powerful than Raymond, Duke of Saint Gilles? for in his obedience were Vauvenice, Beaucaire, Tarascon, and Valence, and all the countries around, and he had married the beautiful lady Parise, the daughter of the high duke, Garnier de Nanteuil. But there was a great moral sore in Duke Raymond's court at Vauvenice—his douze pairs were twelve unprincipled traitors of the "lineage" of Ganelon, of him who had betrayed Charlemagne's army in Spain, who had been the cause of the disaster of Roncevaux and of the death of Roland. They had murdered Garnier de Nanteuil, the father of the fair Duchess Parise, and their rightful lord.

Once, when Duke Raymond held a full court, as usual, on Ascension Day, the twelve traitors met in council together to consider their particular interests; and their chief, Berenger, who addressed them as their leader, spoke to the following purpose:—"We have slain Garnier, but his daughter remains, and as long as she lives we are not safe—one of these days she will revenge his death by causing us all to be hanged or burnt. I propose that we provide against this danger by poisoning her; and I have a fair daughter whom we will marry to Duke Raymond, then we shall all be his peers and masters in the land." Berenger added that when he was a student he had learnt how to mix a very subtle poison, and with this he offered to prepare poisoned apples and send them to the duchess. All the "traitors" agreed to Berenger's plan, but it failed in its direct aim through an unforeseen accident. Thirty tempting apples are imbued with the deadly poison, and sent as a present to Parise by a messenger, who was instructed not to say by whom they were sent, and who, on his return from his errand of evil, was murdered, in order that there might remain no witness of the crime. Meanwhile, the duchess has taken one of the apples to eat it; but she is prevented by the sudden arrival of Duke Raymond's brother, a young and handsome knight, named Beuve, who is received gracefully, and invited to partake of the fruit. He took the apple in his hand, and in an instant dropped dead. Parise was, as might be expected, shocked and disconcerted; but other feelings soon gave way to the sense of her own danger: and, fearing to be accused of murder, she contrived with the assistance of a faithful maid, to carry away the body unobserved and throw it into an adjoining river; but it had not been carried far by the stream when it was dragged out by fishermen, and the news spread abroad that the duke's brother, Beuve, was dead. The apple still remained tightly grasped in his fingers, and when it was taken from them and thrown into a corner, a swine picked it up to eat and died instantly. The manner of Beuve's death was thus discovered. Duke Raymond had just inquired for his brother, and when he heard what had happened, he made a vow that he would inflict upon the murderer a terrible punishment.

The traitors also were informed of these events, and they held council again. Another cause hastened their resolutions: the duchess was *enceinte*, and if she were not soon put to death, a child would be born, who might some day avenge the murder of his grandfather, Garnier. One of the conspirators, Aumauguin, stepped forward to offer his services. He disguised himself as a pilgrim returning from Rome, and in this manner presented himself before the duke, and declared that he had become acquainted, through confession, of a great crime, which he wished to reveal to him. He told him that the duchess had poisoned his brother; because, as she had no child herself, she feared lest, in the event of her husband's death, young Beuve should inherit his dominions, and lest she should then be driven from her high position into private life and poverty. To reveal a confession was a great crime against ecclesiastic propriety; but the next step of the conspirators was a still greater breach of knightly honour and integrity. The only trial to which the duchess could submit her cause was that of private duel or combat, and if she denied the crime, the accuser was obliged to prove it by force of arms against whoever might offer himself as her champion. It was arranged that one of the "traitors," Milo, who held the office of chamberlain to the duchess, and whom she had loaded with benefits, should present himself as her champion; but that, after a slight show of resistance, he should allow himself to be vanquished, and thus betray her to her destruction. To add to the baseness of this treason, Milo breaks his lance and his sword, and joins the pieces together in such a manner that the two weapons would look perfectly whole and sound, and yet, at the first blow, they would break. As the result of these treacherous contrivances, Milo is vanquished, and Parise, condemned to be burnt, is dragged to the stake. To complete the treason, a hoary bishop, who also was one of the family of the traitors, offers himself to the duchess as her confessor, and immediately proclaims that she had avowed her guilt. But a bold clerk, more honest than the rest, here interfered, and, at his instigation, the bishop, accused of the crime of betraying a confession, was burnt at the stake which had been made for the duchess.

The shock of all these events was almost too much for Duke Raymond, who tenderly loved his duchess, and the sternness which he had first shown soon gave way to more compassionate feelings. He changed the sentence of death into exile, and Parise was driven from her country; but the rigorous sentence forbade anybody, on pain of death, to give her shelter or show charity towards her. There was, however, an old noble, named Clarembaut, honest, and bold, and wise, who had already expostulated with the duke on the ease with which he listened to accusations against his duchess; but, finding his counsels treated with contempt, he retired from the court. He had been greatly in favour with the old duke, Garnier, and was the father of fourteen good knights. To Clarembaut's mansion Parise first directs her steps, and the old man comforts and encourages her, and, for the love of her father, he orders ten of his sons to accompany her in her exile, for her support and protection, and makes them swear never to leave her for fifteen years.

Parise and her ten attendants depart from Vauvenice in the middle of the night. They wander long, until at last they arrive in the great forest of Hungary, where the lady was taken with the pains of labour. All alone, and without the necessary aid, under the shade of a lofty pine, she was delivered of a male child, which bore on its right shoulder the mark of a royal cross. The duchess swathed her infant with rich cloth, as was then the custom, and called her knights to look at it. They found her so weak and feeble that it was impossible to proceed any further, and they broke down boughs from the trees, made her a lodge with them, and laid her on a bed inside. Now, the Hungarians of this period were looked upon as inheriting the predatory habits of their forefathers, the Huns, who laid waste so large a portion of the Roman Empire, and among them robbery was regarded as a very honourable profession. A party of three Hungarian robbers were prowling about the forest near where Parise and her knights had taken their lodging. They watched them, but found them too much on their defence to allow of an attack, but one, approaching in the darkness the place where the lady lay, felt with his hand the swathed infant, and, believing it to be a parcel of valuable articles, carried it away. Next morning, when at daybreak the loss was discovered, Parise was overcome with grief; but the brothers searched the forest in vain, and in sorrow they turned their steps backwards until they reached the city of Cologne, and presented themselves before its lord, the Count Thierry. Parise told him that she was a lady of rank flying from her country, where her father had been slaughtered, that her newly-born infant had just been stolen from her, and that she sought an asylum in some great man's family as nurse or governess to his child. The Count Thierry took compassion on her, received her into his household as governess to his young son, and took her ten knights into his service.

Meanwhile, greatly disappointed were the three robbers when, at day-light, they discovered the nature of their treasure. Nevertheless, they carried it with them to the "master" city of Hungary, where they entered the palace and presented themselves before their king. "On our faith, sire, we have been unfortunate in our expedition ; we have been seven weeks, and have stolen nothing except this small child you see here, which is only a day old. Cause him, sire king, to be washed and baptized, and we will have him nourished and taught, and so, as he grows up, with God's blessing, he will learn to steal." The king gave his consent, caused the child to be carried by the minister to the font, and was so charmed with its beauty that he stood as its godfather, gave it his own name, and called it Hugh. Fifteen years passed by, and young Hugh had become a noble youth, well taught in all princely accomplishments. First, he was instructed in letters till he was proficient in learning ; next he learnt tables and chess, till there was not a player in the world who could mate him ; and then he learned to manage his horse and handle his spear, till few knights could pretend to equal him ; we hear nothing of the progress he made in the art of stealing, for he appears to have regarded this accomplishment with little admiration, though he rose higher and higher in the king's love.

One day King Hugh sat in his hall at his high table, amid his barons and knights, and when they had all eaten well and drunk plentifully, and the napkins were withdrawn from the tables, he called his principal advisers, and addressed them as follows :—" Lords," he said, " listen to me. I am aged and hoary, for I have passed my hundredth year, and it is time to withdraw from the bustle of life. I have a noble daughter, and an adopted son whom I love. I intend to marry my daughter to Hugh, and leave him the kingdom, and he shall reign after me when I am dead."

Among the nobles was a traitor of the kindred of Ganelon, his name was Gontagles de Losane. He, of course, was an alien himself ; he had visited Hungary, and been retained at King Hugh's court, where he became one of his nobles. Gontagles replied to the king : " I, sire, cannot approve your design ; have you not enough of dukes and counts of high parentage at your court who are worthy of your daughter's hand, rather than give her to a mere foundling, of whose origin we are ignorant." But the king loved Hugh, and believed in the nobility of his blood, and he was not easily turned from his purpose. It was finally resolved to put the young Hugh upon the trial of his character. "Sire," said Gontagles, "send for the three robbers, and let Hugh go and lodge with them. At night they shall take him into the royal treasury to rob it, and if he be really of noble blood, he will prove it by stealing none of the money." "Let it be so," said the king.

So Hugh went home with the three robbers, and they passed the evening in jollity; and at night they proposed to their young guest to go together, and make a great prey. Hugh gave a ready consent, for, as stated above, robbery was not considered a dishonourable way of obtaining wealth; he urged only that he was too young to be able to perform any great exploit. But when he learnt that it was the king's treasure they proposed to rob, he refused in an outburst of indignation. He was informed that he had already consented to the robbery and had associated himself with them, and that it was now too late to withdraw; and, under fear of violence, he went with them to the royal treasury. They made a hole in the wall, thrust Hugh through it, and told him, on pain of their vengeance, to examine well the treasure within, and bring away as much as he could. Hugh looked at the treasure which lay amassed before him, and admired it, but touched none; and then, seeing three beautiful ivory dice lying on a casket, he took them and put them in his bosom, and then returned to the three robbers, who were appeased by an evasive statement; and, in fact, when they knew the truth, they had no cause for dissatisfaction, as they had performed their task of subjecting Hugh to a trial. But the "traitor," Gontagles, persisted in his spiteful hostility, and accused him before the king of robbing the treasury; but Hugh refuted the charge so triumphantly, producing the three dice as his evidence, that the king felt more convinced than ever that he was of princely blood, and announced openly his intention of giving him his daughter and kingdom.

Young Hugh had now fallen under the influence of a new sentiment—an irresistible desire to discover who were his parents; and he resolved within himself that he would not marry the king's daughter until he had fathomed this mysterious secret. The hostility and reproaches of the Hungarian youths of his own age, sons of barons and peers, made him feel the irksomeness of his position. "Accursed be the day," they said, when they met together, "when this low fellow was first brought here. We know neither the father who begat him or the mother who bore him. If he were slain it would be for our advantage—we should then be truly the lords of the land, and we should soon be reconciled with the king."

"Yes," said the son of the traitor Gontagles, who resembled his father in wickedness; " let us challenge him to a game at chess in the deep cellar of the palace, where nobody will hear what takes place. We will call him bastard and foundling; he is sure to take up the quarrel; let each be provided with a good sharp knife, and we will all fall upon him and put him to death."

This plot was immediately carried into effect; and Hugh accepted the challenge, and went to the place of rendezvous in the cellar totally unarmed. As might be supposed from his superior skill, he soon checkmated his opponents, but he showed no feeling of exultation. It was his four antagonists who began the quarrel; and, while they all drew their knives from their girdles, the son of Gontagles stepped forward, and insulted him with his doubtful birth. Hugh was a youth of great strength, and a blow of his fist laid him lifeless on the ground; on which the others attacked him all at once with their knives, but he had seized upon the chess-board, and with that as a weapon, after receiving four knife-wounds, he brained his assailants. Hugh had thus slain the sons of four of the great barons of Hungary, and, with some fear of the consequences, he quickly mounted the steps which led up from the cellar, locked the doors which gave the only access to it, and threw the keys through a window where they were not likely to be found, hurried to the stables and saddled the best horse in them, buckled a trusty sword by his side, and rode forth to seek his fortune in some other land. On his way out of the palace, he met the princess, his betrothed, who had fallen deeply in love with him, and, when he told her what had taken place, she fell to the ground in a swoon. But Hugh continued his flight, while the attendants carried the princess to her father, who, when he heard her story, swore that he did not care if his intended son-in-law had killed four hundred of his young barons instead of four, and ordered some of his men to mount and hasten in pursuit, in the hope of persuading him to return; but in vain.

Forward rides Hugh, through wood and over stream, totally ignorant of the direction which he is taking. Soon he enters a vast forest, and in one of its most retired glades he dismounts for the first time to rest himself. Here he feels unusual emotions, and bursts into involuntary tears, wondering at this unwonted agitation in a spot which, to his knowledge, he had never seen before—but Providence has led him to take his first repose on the very spot on which he was born. A step further, and he washes his face and

hands in the same stream in which he was first washed after he was introduced to the world. Then he rides on, and soon arrives at the castle in
which the Duchess Parise had received hospitality when she issued from the
forest, and where he experiences the same attention: and when he leaves, his
host, so far from accepting any remuneration for his hospitality, offers to
give his guest a hundred shillings, for the love, as he said, of a noble lady
who had passed that way fifteen years before, who had there first communicated in his chapel after the birth of a son in the forest, who had been stolen
from her, and to whom, he added, young Hugh bore a striking resemblance.
Here Hugh has his wounds dressed, and starts on his journey refreshed and
strengthened. At length he arrives at a spot where four king's high roads
branched off in different directions, and, totally unable to make a choice, he
commits himself to the guidance of heaven, and gives his horse the rein.
The latter takes the road for Cologne, where they arrive in due time, cross
the bridge, proceed direct to the palace, and find Count Thierry seated under
a noble pine, and attended by the ten sons of Clarembaut. Hugh dismounts,
salutes the count courteously, informs him that he is on his way from Hungary to France, and asks him for his hospitality. "Willingly," replied
Count Thierry, "no man asking hospitality here was ever denied." His
horse is delivered to a squire to be taken to the stable, while the count mounts
into the hall, where the governess, Parise, is seated at the high table, and
young Hugh is appointed to the honourable duty of assisting to serve the
wine at the table.

The feelings of Parise are strangely moved by the appearance of this young
stranger, and she thinks in herself how much he resembles the noble duke,
her husband. The ten brothers also fix their eyes upon him, and remark to
each other his likeness to Raymond of Vauvenice. After dinner, they lead
him with them to a vaulted chamber, their place of assembly, and there
treat him with every mark of regard. Parise, meanwhile, is more and
more agitated by strange feelings and presentiments, and obtains a private
interview with the stranger, during which she obtains from him a truthful
statement of what he knew of his own history.

"I never saw," said he, "my father or my mother. When an infant,
three robbers stole me in the forest, and carried me straight into Hungary,
where I was taken and nurtured by King Hugh, who caused me to be baptized and gave me his name." Hugh went on to recount all his subsequent
history, and told the cause of his flight. There could be no longer a doubt
—the duchess had recovered her long-lost child; and in the strength of her
emotions, she fainted four times before she could muster strength to tell

17

him that she was his mother. Hugh eagerly demanded who she was, and who was his father, and whether he was bastard or of legitimate birth; " For," he said, in the true spirit of that time, "it is better any day to be a good bastard than a bad man, however legitimate." In answer to his pressing questions, Parise told him whose son he was, and repeated to him the history of her misfortunes. Who could be more joyful than the Duchess Parise and her child, and their joy was shared by Thierry and his countess, and by the whole household, as soon as these events were known. Thierry's son, Antoine, who had been brought up under the care of Parise, and stood somewhat in the position of a foster-brother to him, was introduced to young Hugh, and they soon became affectionate friends. But a new solicitude took possession of the heart of the latter—he had found his mother, but he was still a stranger to his father, and he resolved to go in search of him.

Meanwhile, great events had taken place at Vauvenice. Berenger and his kinsmen, strong in the success of their plot, and believing that the Duchess Parise must be dead, resolved to effect the marriage of his daughter with Duke Raymond, and persuaded him to give her the tower of Vauvenice and the fairest part of Parise's personal estate. The aged Clarembaut heard of these proceedings when already the marriage ceremonies were preparing in the minster, and he hurried thither, attended by his four remaining sons, and, addressing himself to the king, " Sir," he said, "I forbid your marriage with the daughter of Berenger; I forbid you giving her a foot of this land, for it belongs to Parise, your wife, whom you have unjustly driven away. She was then big with child, she has now no doubt a son, who will return and destroy all these traitors. And you, sir bishop, I forbid you to celebrate the marriage; if you do, I will skin alive every clerk or priest I meet." The threats of Clarembaut were disregarded, and the marriage solemnized; and then Clarembaut assembled all his vassals, and leaving his residence in Vauvenice, went to a spot not far off and built there a strong castle, in which he established himself to make mortal war upon the duke.

In the midst of this war, the young Hugh and his friend Antoine, with the ten sons of Clarembaut, and six hundred men who had been furnished by Thierry, count of Cologne, arrive and learn the state of affairs. Hugh sends the ten sons of Clarembaut to their father in his new castle of Neuve-Ferté, to offer him his services, with a strict injunction not to tell him who they are. The offer is gladly accepted, and Hugh and Antoine enter the Neuve-Ferté, and receive knighthood from the hands of Clarembaut. An attack upon the castle follows, in which Clarembant's army, led by Hugh and Antoine, inflict a great defeat upon the ducal troops. The citizens of Vauvenice, also, take arms against Duke Raymond, and drive his men out of the town. Another battle follows, in which Hugh encounters his father, and throws him from his horse. But we will not enter further into the details of this obstinate war, which is characterized by all the romantic vicissitudes and traits of feudal hostilities. At length a truce is agreed to, and in the course of the negociations which follow, Duke Raymond learns that young Hugh is his son by Parise. Everything is now made clear : the traitors are all thrown into prison, and the duke and his son proceed to Cologne to visit Parise. In an affecting interview, Duke Raymond acknowledges the wrongs his wife has received from him, and a complete reconciliation takes place, after which they return together to Vauvenice, where the Duchess is reinstated in all her former rights. The King of Hungary, after in vain sending messengers in all directions to seek any traces of young Hugh, at length discovers who he is, and proceeds in person to Vauvenice, and finds his intended son-in-law. There is nothing more to prevent the happiness of young Hugh—all the traitors are put to death ignominiously; the daughter of the King of Hungary, the Princess Sorplante, is brought from Hungary to be married at Aix in Provence, to Hugh, who at the same time is crowned King of Hungary.

CHAPTER IX.

PROVENCE, ITS POETRY AND THE COURTS OF LOVE.

THUS far we have been tracing the influence of the northern and Teutonic element on mediæval society as far as it bore upon Womankind. We have now arrived at the time when another influence began to make itself felt in Western Europe, which was destined greatly to modify the tone of domestic life in the castle and in the court. This came from the south, from Provence and Aquitaine, from the borders of Italy and Spain, and contained much which was derived from ancient Greece and Rome, and from the Arabs; and it is singular that an influence which was thus derived from peoples among whom woman's relative position was not high, and among some of them absolutely degraded, should end in placing her, theoretically at least, on the highest and proudest level she had ever held.

Provence was full of old national customs and national sentiments, bred and cherished under a bright and voluptuous climate, and far more related to those of Italy than to those of the rest of Gaul. Poetry flourished there, but a poetry of a lighter and gentler character than that of the north, the prevailing subject of which was love. Its religion was that of the Christian, but a religion influenced and modified by the doctrines of the later platonism and gnosticism, and many heresies of that description, which found a shelter in it. Among these had arisen mystical doctrines on love and on the relationship between the sexes, which had ripened into sentiments of a peculiar respect for Womankind. Christianity itself had been made to centre, in a great degree, in the worship of the Virgin, who was identified in this poetry with the queen of love and beauty, and who thus received a reverence not differing much from that paid to the goddess Venus. Provence was the country of lyric poetry, no doubt derived in a great measure from Rome and Italy, and it was introduced thence into the western literature of the Middle Ages. The influence through which it reached those distant lands had begun to be felt at an early period. At the beginning of the eleventh century, Robert, king of France, married a daughter of the count of Provence, Constance, who had been educated in the two courts of Arles and Toulouse. The Frankish historian of the day, a zealous monk, gives us a curious description of the men of Provence and Aquitaine who formed her escort. The men of the south did not then stand very high in the good will of the church. He describes them as excessively vain and fickle, affected in their dress, and in their arms and the trappings of their horses, cutting their hair and shaving their beards, and as singular in their appearance as they were corrupt in their morals, and devoid of probity and good faith. "These," he exclaims, "were the men who have to such a degree seduced the nation of the Burgundians and that of the Franks, previously the most orderly of them all, that they have become since that entirely similar to them in perversity and wickedness; and if any pious soul sought to oppose the corruptors who gave such examples, he was treated as a fool." The elegance and comparative refinement of the nobles of the south did not please the Frankish monk.

Provence and Aquitaine had, indeed, little sympathy with the Franks. Conquered by the earlier Teutonic invaders, they had recovered their freedom under the weakness of the Merovingian dynasty, and during their independence they had preferred the alliance of the Spanish Arabs, or Moors, to that of the Franks, until reduced again by the arms of the Carlovingians. These terrible wars and these romantic alliances had tended to cherish rather than enlarge the poetic spirit of the southerns, and to fit them especially for embracing the chivalry which accompanied the introduction of feudalism. The earlier Provencal poetry is lost, but we gather its character from some traces of it in the oldest now known, which belongs to the beginning of the twelfth century. Its subject is universally love and Womankind, and a reverence for the latter, which, though not of a religious character, has still something in it of the mystic worship of the Virgin. But the existence of the pure poetry of Provence was not of very long duration; it died among the terrible wars of the persecutions of the Albigeois, though it had already spread its influence over the literature of surrounding and distant countries. It reached England with our chivalrous king, Richard Cœur-de-Lion. Richard's mother was a princess of Aquitaine. The flourishing period of Provencal poetry, as it is known to us, was the latter half of the twelfth century and the commencement of the thirteenth.

As I have stated, the great object of the Provencal poetry is love and the service of the ladies. The language and tone is delicate and becoming, but not always. Most of the poems of one of their earliest great poets now known, Guillaume count of Poitiers, are coarsely licentious; but two other love songs by the same author are unexceptionable in their character. We can only assume from this contrast, that, whatever may have been the outward elegance and refinement of society at that period, it was under the surface to a great degree coarse and immoral. This remark will enable us better to understand much which I have now to describe. The love which presents itself to us in the mass of the Provencal poetry is, in form and theory at least, a sentiment full of enthusiasm, delicate and respectful, seeking to elevate its object. It is exactly that sentiment upon which rests woman's position in the true spirit of chivalry.

Love, according to the system of the Provencal poets—the *trobadors*— was the ground of all goodness, of all excellence in the world. The man without love, says one of them, Pierre d'Auvergne, is no more worth than an ear of corn without grain. Love, too, made the poet, and, indeed, according to the principles of the Provencal school, poetry and love were almost identical. Giraud le Roux was the son of a poor knight of Toulouse, and, while very young, entered the service of Alphonse Jourdain, count of Toulouse. An old biographer of the *trobadors* informs us that he fell in love with the countess, daughter of his lord, and that the love he had for her taught him to *trobar*, to write poetry.* The daughter was an illegitimate daughter, and, as Fauriel remarks, this fact furnishes one example in evidence that the loves of the trobadors were realities, and not poetical dreams. The history of this family is romantic, like so much of the history of those ages. The count of Toulouse, Alphonse Jourdain, joined the second crusade, in 1147, and took with him his daughter. The count never returned, for he was slain in one of the battles with the infidels; but his daughter, first a prisoner in the harem of Noureddeen, prince of Aleppo, became afterwards his wife, and after his death governed his kingdom as guardian of a son she had by him, who succeeded his father. Few of the trobadors equalled Bernard de Ventadour in the grace and tenderness of

---

* The names given to the art of poetry and to the poet in Western Europe are curious. In Provencal, or the *langue d'oc*, to write verse was called *trobar*, to find or invent; in the *langue d'oil*, or French of the north, *trouver;* and the poet was in one a *trobador*, in the other a *trouvere*, an inventor. In Anglo-Saxon, the poet was a *scop*, from *scypan* or *sceopan*, to make or create; and in later English he was called a *makar*, the old Scots called him a *makker*. Perhaps we may consider the Teutonic notion of the poet somewhat more elevated than that of the peoples speaking dialects derived from the Latin.

his poetry. He chose for his love the viscountess, the wife of his feudal lord and patron, Ebles III., and daughter of the lord of Montpellier, and was accepted by her. Her name was Azalaïs, or Adelaide, but secrecy was a duty enjoined on all lovers; and, as it was the custom for every one to give his mistress a name, the object of which was known only to themselves, Bernard called her in his verses *Bel-vezer*, *i.e.*, fair-to-behold. Arnaud de Marveil also loved a viscountess, Azalaïs, the daughter of Raymond, count of Toulouse, and wife of the viscount of Beziers, whose court he had visited in search of fortune. Arnaud appears to have been somewhat timid of character, and he long celebrated the lady of his choice before he ventured to declare his love; but when at length he took this step, he was accepted, "put into harness," as his early biographer describes it, and long continued to celebrate her beauty. Bernard, like the other poets of the south, appears to have had a great taste for rural beauties. He begins one of his love songs with the following stanza :—

Quant erba vertz e fuelha par,	When the green grass and the leaf sprout,
E'l flor brotonon per verjan,	And the flowers blossom in the meadows,
E'l rossinhols autel a clar	And the nightingale loud and clear
Leva sa votz e mov son chan.	Raises his voice and sends forth his song.
Joy ai de lui, e joy ay de la flor;	I have joy of him, and I have joy of the flowers:
Joy ai de me, e de mi dona maior.	I have joy of myself, and I have greater of my lady :
Vas totas partz sui de joy clans o seinhs,	I am wrapped up in joy on all sides;
Mas ilh es joys que totz los autres vens.	But it is joy which excels all others.

It must be stated, that, in the language of the trobadors, the word *joy* was used to express that state of mental ecstasy which was felt by the happy lover. Arnaud de Marveil commences one of his songs with the words—

Si cum li peis an en l'aigua lor vida,	Just as the fish have their life in the water,
L'ai jeu en joy e totz temps la i aurai,	I have mine in joy, and always shall have it so,
Qu'amors m'a fait en tal domna chauzir	Which love has caused me to choose in such a lady,
Don viu jauzens sol del respieit qu'ieu n'ai.	Through whom I live joyous only in the expectation. .

While Arnaud de Marveil was thus happy in his "joy," Alphonse, king of Aragon, visited the court of Beziers, and fell in love with the fair viscountess; and, under his influence, she withdrew her affections from Arnaud, and forbade him writing any more verses in her praise, in consequence of which he is said to have died broken-hearted. In speaking of this trobador, M. Fauriel has remarked that he was one of the very small number who, during his whole life, had only loved and sung one lady.

Bernard de Ventadour was also unfortunate in his love. The viscount, his lord, became jealous of him, and banished him from his court, and the lady was placed in confinement, and closely watched. Bernard's grief on this occasion is the subject of several of his poems. Towards the year 1160, he abandoned the Limousin, and proceeded to the north, to the court of our Henry II., who was then only duke of Normandy, and who, a few years before, had married Eleanor of Guienne, the granddaughter of William, count of Poitiers, who is looked upon as the most ancient of the trobadors now known. The court of Normandy, under her influence, had become the home of poetry and love, and there Bernard was sure of a good reception. Eleanor was still young and possessed beauty, and Bernard became enamoured of her, his homage was received with equal warmth, and she was the object of his subsequent songs. After Henry had succeeded to the throne of England, Bernard de Ventadour frequently accompanied him or his queen into this country, and his name interests us as the earliest who brought among our forefathers a knowledge of the poetry and chivalrous feelings of Provence and the south.

But to return to the subject of the system of love taught by the trobadors, or, as they called it, the science of love, *sabar de drudaria* (*le savoir de druerie*), it was full of rules and nice distinctions, and quibbles. Thus we are told that there are four degrees in love :—

Quater escalos a en amor:	There are four degrees in love :
Lo premier es de fegnedor,	The first is that of hesitating,
E l' segons es de preiador,	And the second that of supplicating,
E lo ters es d' enteridedor,	And the third that of being listened to,
E lo quart es drut apelatz.	And the fourth is called that of accepted lover.

The anonymous trobador who wrote this, goes on to explain : "He who has a desire to love a lady, and goes often to pay his court to her, but without venturing to speak of his love, is a timid hesitater. But if the lady honours him so much, and encourages him, that he ventures to tell her his pains, then he is justly called a supplicator. And if, through talking and supplicating, he does so well that she retains him, and gives him bands, gloves, or girdle, then he is raised to the degree of one listened to. If, finally, the lady is pleased to grant by a kiss her love to him, she has made of him her lover." It must not be supposed that all these directions were mere playful theory and poetical talk, but we have plenty of evidence that they were carried strictly into practice. A formal ceremony was prescribed for the acceptance of a lover, in which was imitated exactly that by which, in feudalism, the vassal acknowledged his suzerain, and the knight or squire who had gone through it, had contracted similar obligations towards his lady. He placed himself on his knees before her, with his two hands joined between her hands, before witnesses, and he, by words, devoted himself entirely to her, swore to serve her faithfully to his death, and to defend her against all assailants to the utmost of his power. The lady, on her side, declared that she accepted his services, engaged to him her tenderest affections, and, in sign of the union now established between them, she usually gave him a ring, and then she kissed him, and raised him on his feet. This ceremony was termed, on the part of the lady, retaining her lover; on his part, making himself her man, or her servant.

Thus Bernard de Ventadour, addressing his lady, says :—

Domna, vostr' om sui e serai,	Lady, your man I am and shall be,
A vostre servizi guarnitz ;	Bound to your service ;
Vostr' om sui juratz e plevitz,	Your man I am sworn and pledged,
E vostres m'er adesenans ;	And yours I shall be henceforth ;
E vos etz lo meus jois premiers,	And you are my first joy (love),
E si serotz vos lo derriers,	And you shall be the last,
Tan quant la vida m'er durans.	As long as my life shall endure.

This act was looked upon not lightly, but as an affair of great importance, one of the most serious events of a man's or woman's life. Both, of course, had contracted various duties and obligations, and had assumed new qualities in face of the world. The poets of Provence, the trobadors, speak frequently enough of love's law, the *droit d'Amour*, or the *coutume d' Amour*, and of course this law was liable to be broken ; and there must have been frequent cases in which it was called in question. The decision was always referred to ladies, and we know the names of several whose decisions on love questions were greatly celebrated. Among these were especially distinguished in the latter half of the twelfth century, the countess of Champagne, Ermengarde viscountess of Narbonne, and Queen Eleanor of England. Here is a judgment given by the last-mentioned lady, to explain which, it must be stated that, according to this law, love was considered to be incompatible with marriage, which, under feudalism, was a mere affair of political or personal interest. A knight fell in love with a lady, who, having fallen in love on her side with another knight, could not return his affection, inasmuch as it was part of the law that you could only have one love at a time. But in this case, the lady, not wishing to deprive him of all hope, had promised to take him for her knight in case she lost the other knight whom she loved. A little later she was married to the latter, and then the other knight demanded the fulfilment of her promise.

The lady denied all obligation, and replied that, so far from losing the
knight she loved, she now had him for her husband. The case was referred
to Queen Eleanor, who gave judgment that the lady was obliged to keep
her promise to the second knight, because, having taken the other for her
husband, she had lost him as her lover. Again, a knight loved a lady whom
he had few opportunities of seeing, and they agreed to hold their communi-
cations through his secretary. The latter, violating the confidence thus
reposed in him, addressed the lady on his own behalf, and obtained her
favour. The knight laid his complaint before the countess of Champagne,
who gave judgment that the treacherous secretary and the lady were worthy
of each other, and should be left to themselves, but that both should be
excluded for ever from the love of all other persons, and deprived of all
right to the law of love in any case affecting themselves. In fact, they were
proclaimed outlaws to love. Here is another judgment of Queen Eleanor. A
knight sought the love of a lady without success; yet she accepted his
presents, and apparently with an ardour which gave him full encouragement
to hope. Eleanor decided that a woman must either refuse presents offered
her in the name of love, or reward them, or be degraded in her rank among
Womankind.

There are preserved several codes of this feudal love-law, one of the most
curious of which, written in Latin, is pretended to have been drawn up by a
chaplain named Andrew (*Andreas capellanus*). Andrew's code gives thirty-one
articles, two or three of which will serve as a sufficient specimen of the whole.
The first asserts that " Marriage is not a legitimate excuse against love."*
By the third, no one can be bound by two loves at the same time.† According to the fifteenth and sixteenth, which are rather definitions than laws,
" Every lover is accustomed to turn pale at the sight of his lover; and
when this vision is sudden, his heart trembles.‡ The twenty-fourth article
states that " Every act of a lover ends in thinking of his fellow-lover ;"§ and
by the last, or thirty-first, it is provided that nothing prevents one woman
from being loved by two men, or one man by two women."‖ This seems
rather in contradiction to the third of the laws already quoted.

As we learn from the early writers on this subject, the lady-judges who
were appealed to on these questions, called around them a court composed

* Causa conjugii ab amore non est excusatio recta.
† Nemo duplici potest amore ligari.
‡ XV. Omnis consuevit amans in coamantis aspectu pallescere.
   XVI. In repentina coamantis visione cor tremescit amantis.
§ Quilibet amantis actus in coamantis cogitatione finitur.
   Unam feminam nichil prohibet a duabus amari et a duabus mulieribus unum.

of persons of their own sex, to assist them with their counsels. This arrangement appears at first to have been merely voluntary on the part of the lady
who was called upon to judge, but it soon led to a regular and well-acknow-
ledged institution, known as the Courts of Love, each of which consisted of
a certain number of persons, with a president, to which court all questions of
the nature of those we are speaking of were referred, as a matter of course.

A COURT OF LOVE.

The history of these courts, as might naturally be expected, is rather
obscure; and a German professor, Frederic Diez of Bonn, published a book
in 1842, in which he attempted, with much research and ingenuity, to show
that these courts, and the laws by which they are supposed to have been
governed, are mere works of the imagination, allegories, or that, at best,
they were mere occasional games indulged in by the fancy of individuals.

For myself, I am by no means satisfied with the professor's arguments, and I am still contented to believe in the existence of institutions which were not only talked of in contemporary literature, but which have been pictured by contemporary art. MM. Paul Lacroix and Ferdinand Seré, in their great work, *Le Moyen Age et la Renaissance*, have published two pictorial representations of these Courts of Love. The first, given in our last page, is taken from the ivory cover of a lady's circular mirror, as mirrors were made in those days, and may perhaps belong to the thirteenth century. In the upper compartment, Cupid, somewhat oddly represented, is evidently presiding, and receiving the homage of his worshippers. Below, there are vows and caresses, and gifts of rings, which speak of the cases which might be brought before such a court.

A PROVENÇAL COURT OF LOVE.

This picture belongs to an age when the Courts of Love had become known over all Western Europe, and were no longer a new idea. The idea, certainly, had existed from an early period. A game of love was probably the earlier form of a Court of Love, and the oldest of the known Trohadors, William, comte of Poitiers, who flourished in the year 1100, exclaims in one of his songs :—

E si m partetz un juec d' amor,	And if you propose me a game of love,
No suy tan fatz	I am not such a fool
Non sapcha triar lo melhor	That I know not how to choose the best
Entr' els malvatz.	Among the bad ones.

In the earlier times, these courts seem to have consisted almost entirely of ladies, but men were afterwards admitted into them, and held office, and even in some of them presided, when their title was the Prince of Love. It is said that our Richard Cœur-de-Lion held that office. At this time the Court of Love of Provence, according to the old writers, was held annually in the month of May, in an open meadow under an elm, in consequence of which these meetings were called *Gieux sous l'ormel*, the games under the elm. The second picture of a Court of Love given by Lacroix and Seré, which is copied in our accompanying cut, is taken from a manuscript belonging to the Imperial Library at Paris, containing the poems of Gillaume de Machaut, and stated to be of the fourteenth century. We have here, evidently, the Prince or King of Love, as well as the queen, to whom one of the council appears to be expounding the law. This court is held in a field under a tree.

We have many allusions to courts of this description, in the lighter French poets of the thirteenth and fourteenth centuries, and we might point to several small poems of an allegorical character, in which love is introduced holding his court. Among them we must not overlook our own Chaucer's "Court of Love." Amid the dissipation of the French court, at the close of the fourteenth and beginning of the fifteenth centuries, the notion of Courts of Love was brought up again, and carried out on a large scale. In the reign of Charles VI., about the year 1410, there was established in France what was called a *Court amoureuse*, or Love Court, a long list of the officers of which was preserved in a contemporary document which was printed by the Academie des Inscriptions in 1773. Among these names are not a few which belonged to the ranks of the clergy.

CHAPTER X.

THE ROMANCE OF THE ROSE.

THE doctrines and systems of love spread themselves into the north, but there they took rather a different form, less refined, and we may, perhaps, say more substantial, than in the songs of the trobadors. In the course of the twelfth century, a sudden blaze of light seems to have burst upon the mind in Western Europe, a yearning for intelligence, and a longing for something different from that which actually existed. New philosophical notions appear to have taken hold of the world, which originated perhaps partly in the relations with the Saracens of the south. There was a wonderful eagerness for learning, which showed itself in the establishment of universities; a popular desire for religious liberty, for relief from the weight of feudal tyranny; and a great feeling of resistance to ecclesiastical and especially to monkish despotism. Many new and strange religious heresies were advocated, and, among other things, new doctrines and systems were formed in regard to love, and to the relations between the sexes. One of the books which sprung out of these had a great effect on the literature, and perhaps also on the moral feelings, of the later Middle Ages. This was the celebrated Romance of the Rose, which, in accordance with what I have said at the beginning of the eighth chapter, would, perhaps, be more accurately translated in English by, the Book of the Rose.

In the earlier part of the thirteenth century, there lived in the beautiful countries on the banks of the Loire a trouvère, or poet of the langue d'oil, named Guillaume de Lorris, of whose history we literally know nothing, but who wrote during the reign of Philippe-Auguste, and appears to have died about the year 1240.* All further that we know of Guillaume de Lorris is

* M. Paulin Paris, one of the best authorities on such a subject, appears to have given good reasons for adopting this date in an excellent paper on the *Roman de la Rose*, in the twenty-third volume of the *Histoire Littéraire de la France*.

that he conceived the plan, and wrote the earlier part, of the poem which has gained so great a celebrity in the literature of the subsequent ages.

The Romance of the Rose is a somewhat elaborate allegory. Its author tells us that he was in the twentieth year of his age when Love commended this work to him. It was in the month of May, when earth always presented its richest clothing, and Love was most active. The author, in the character of *l'Amant*, the Lover, represents himself to us in a dream, and supposes himself to have reached, on the banks of a fair river, a vast garden surrounded by lofty walls. This is the palace of Deduit, or Pleasure, whose wife is Liesse, or Joy; and his ordinary companions, Youth, Love, Beauty, Nobleness-of-Heart, Liberality, and Courtesy. On the outside of the walls are sculptured the images of the vices most contrary to Love, such as Hatred, Treason, *Felonie* (Despite), *Vilanie* (Baseness), Covetousness, Avarice, Envy, Old Age, Hypocrisy, Poverty. Within the walls all is happiness, and Love is lord over all. It is a curious trait of the spirit of feudal chivalry, that, according to the doctrines inculcated by Guillaume de Lorris, Love was a stranger to ungentle society, to the cottage or the hamlet. It belonged to the palace and the castle, and its two faithful and necessary companions, according to him, were Leisure and Riches. At length l'Amant finds a small wicket (*guichet*), or entrance, through which he obtains admittance by the kindness of the lady Idleness (dame Oyseuse), who tells him the character of the place, and that Deduit was at this time holding a grand festival with his companions, who were singing and carolling. As he approaches, Courtesy called upon l'Amant, and invited him to join in the carole. Then he saw that the god of Love, l'Amour, had two bows, which were held by dame Regard (Sweet-looing), and five arrows belonging to each. The first bow was straight and beautiful, and its arrows were Beauty, Simplicity (or Candour), Sincerity, Company, and Beau-Semblant; the other crooked and ugly, with its five arrows, Pride, Baseness, Despair, and New-thought, the effect of the wounds of which was hatred.

When l'Amant has been thus admitted into the abode of Deduit, he is enchanted with the beauty of the flowers in his garden, and he is especially fascinated by one rose-bud, which is fresher and sweeter than all the others. As he approaches the bud, l'Amour discharges into his heart the five arrows from the beautiful bow. This bud, of course, is the allegory of the woman he loves, and whose love he now seeks to obtain. But the rose in question is surrounded by a thick hedge, which defies all near approach. He is relieved from this difficulty by the courtesy of a bachelor named Bel-Acceuil (Fair-

Reception), who gave him admission into the garden of roses. Meanwhile, after l'Amant had received into his bosom the five arrows of the handsome bow, he acknowledges himself vanquished, swears allegiance to l'Amour, and listens to a long rehearsal of the laws of love, and to an explanation of the obedience he is to give to them. L'Amour had then left him to his own reflections.

But the result of Bel-Accueil's kindness was not so satisfactory as was expected. Guillaume was not yet contented, but, like other lovers, wanted more, and sought permission, not only to touch the rose, but to pluck it. But at this instant a churlish and powerful fellow named Danger, accompanied by three equally rough-looking companions, named Shame, Fear, and Jealousy, suddenly make their appearance, and drive away, not only l'Amant, but Bel-Accueil himself. This Danger was the overlooker and keeper of all the rose-trees, and he had been on the watch.

Now there was a lady who had a lofty tower in the garden—her name was the lady Reason—and she had watched the whole of these proceedings, and came down and addressed herself to l'Amant. She blamed him for all he had been doing, for allowing himself to be seduced into the garden, and, above all, for having given his allegiance to l'Amour, from which she urges him to withdraw at once, telling him that it was still not too late. But he refuses to listen to her, and turns for advice to his friend l'Ami, a faithful companion, who advises him not to be cast down, tells him that he had once known Danger well, that he was a great blusterer, and always opposed love at first, but that he might be gained over. L'Amant found unexpected allies, too, in the fair ladies, Pitié and Franchise, through whose persuasions Danger is appeased, and the lady who is the object of l'Amant's passion consents to see him again, but not at first to admit him within the hedge which inclosed and protected the roses. But while, on one hand, Bel-Accueil has returned, and again given his assistance to l'Amant, Malebouche is absent, Shame is silent, and even Danger shuts his mouth, L'Amant thus passes the hedge, and again approaches the rose, which has increased in beauty since he last saw it. Thus encouraged, he now again claims a kiss. This excites new alarm, and even Bel-Accueil expostulates, and says that this liberty would be taken ill by lady Chastity. At this moment, another high lady in the history, the lady Venus, approaches and speaks to the lady in favour of l'Amant, and obtains for him the long-wished-for kiss. Malebouche, Shame, and Jealousy again interfere, and they awake Danger, and l'Amant is a second time driven from the rose-garden. A strong fortress is now raised against l'Amant; Jealousy causes the rose-trees to be surrounded with deep ditches and lofty walls, forming a vast square fortress, each side strengthened with turrets, and terminated by castles of four towers, one of the castles being entrusted to Jealousy, the second to Danger, another to Shame, and the fourth to Malebouche. In the midst there was a principal tower, or donjon, in which Bel-Accueil was committed to prison, under the guard of an old hag.

In the midst of these events, the imprisonment of Bel-Accueil and the erection of the fortress, one of the metrical headings of the poem informs us that Guillaume de Lorris had ceased to exist, and that the rest of the poem was the work of a continuator, Jean de Meun—

Cy endroit trespassa Guillaume	Here in this place died Guillaume
De Lorris, et non fist plus pseaume :	De Lorris, and made not a line more of it ;
Mais, après plus de quarante ans,	But, after more than forty years,
Maistre Jehan de Meugn ce rommans	Maister Jean de Meun this romance
Parfist, ainsi comme je treuve ;	Completed, as I find ;
Et ici commence son oeuvre.	And here begins his work.

It would appear from this statement, that the work of Guillaume de Lorris had remained unknown, or at least only known very locally, during no less than forty years after his death, when at last it was dragged into publicity by Jean de Meun. Of this new writer little more is known than of his predecessor beyond what he tells us himself, that he was born at Meun, on the Loire, and that his surname was Clopinel.

The object of Guillaume de Lorris, in his plan of this singular production, was to picture, in an allegorical form, the pleasures and pains of love as he understood them, or, as some one has observed, to treat of the physiology of the passion. Jean de Meun was an inferior writer in many respects to his predecessor, and he took up his work evidently in a different spirit. The object he had in view was more a philosophical satire on his times, a declaration of his own free and even licentious opinions on most of the subjects which agitated peoples' minds. In his continuation of the story, Reason again descends from her tower, repeats her lessons to l'Amant, and her exhortations to withdraw his allegiance from l'Amour. Her discourse becomes long. She enters into bitter attacks upon love and upon the female sex, and recommends friendship in place of the former; and goes on to describe in satirical language the various pursuits of life, supporting her lessons with stories taken chiefly from the ancient writers. Reason ends her long discourse by asking three things of l'Amant :—

C'est que tu me vuilla amer,	It is that thou wilt love me,
Et que le dieu d'Amors despises,	And that thou despise the god of love,
Et que Fortune rien ne prises.	And that thou set no value upon Fortune.

19

L'Amant, however, is by no means moved by Reason's discourse, and disputes with him, and in this discussion he attempts to assert the opinion, held by the old Stoics, that no words are really obscene, and that we are free to use them all. The licentiousness which not unfrequently presents itself in the work of Jean de Meun is a stranger to that of Guillaume de Lorris.

L'Amant, now giving up Reason, returns for advice to l'Ami, who had been already introduced on the scene by Guillaume de Lorris, though the particular character he was intended to hold is not very clear.

Jean de Meun seems to take sometimes to himself the character of l'Ami; and, in fact, in l'Ami's advice on this occasion there is far less of the respect for the character of the female sex, very far less of that chivalrous gallantry, and far less of the delicacy of sentiment, which we still feel in Guillaume de Lorris. It is a "jalouz" introduced by this friend, who uses the famous lines which are said to have given so much offence to the ladies of the fourteenth century :—

Preude femme, par Saint Denis!	Of honest women, by St. Denis!
Il en est mains que de fenis.	There are fewer than of phœnixes.

And the two others, still more famous :—

Toutes estes, serés, ou futes,	You all are, will be, or have been
De fait ou de volunté putes.	Unchaste in fact or in will.

These form part of a violent satire against marriage, introduced by l'Ami, who laments the fortunate age when everything was common, and when man possessed no property, before marriage had been instituted, and when every man took the companion he liked. The feelings just described were those which Jean de Meun held in regard to Womankind, and there must have been many who shared in them during the fourteenth and fifteenth centuries. It is unnecessary here to dwell upon the subject any longer, though it occupies many pages of the poem.

L'Amant now prepares to make another attempt to gain Bel-Accueil's prison, and seeks to employ Folle-Largesse, but finds he is not rich enough for this, and sees Poverty in the distance. The god of Love, l'Amour, now returns to his aid, and assembles his barons to lay siege to the castle in which Bel-Accueil is held a prisoner. Among l'Amour's leaders are two, named Constrained-Abstinence and Faux-Semblant, who at first are not well received by the others; but they are admitted under the plea that, to please the ladies, you must often employ the assistance of deception. Under the character of the latter of these two personages, Jean de Meun introduces

THE LADY VENUS

RECEIVING THE MESSENGER OF L'AMOUR.

Digitized by Microsoft®

a vigorous picture of monkish deceit and religious hypocrisy, and he was evidently a warm partizan of Guillaume de Saint-Amour, the champion of the University of Paris against the monks.

I pass rapidly over the incidents of the siege of the castle. We have further lectures on the coquetry and other exceptionable qualities of Womankind. The siege itself is, in some particulars, mismanaged, and the god of Love, almost despairing of success, obtains a truce of several days that he may send his messengers to Citeron (Cythera) to consult his mother, the lady Venus. Now Citeron, the favourite residence of Venus, was a castle built on a mountain, out of reach of any warlike missile, surrounded by an extensive plain covered by a thick wood, in which the goddess was accustomed to follow the chase with her favourite Adonis. They were thus engaged when the messengers arrived, and delivered their credentials. There is in the Harleian Collection of Manuscripts in the British Museum, a fine and well-known manuscript of the Roman de la Rose with beautiful illuminations, which gives at this chapter as curious a picture of the goddess Venus, according to mediæval notions, as we have already had of the castle of Citheron, and I have chosen it here as one of our coloured plates. Venus is listening to the account given by Love's messengers, and declares she will proceed immediately to his assistance, and that she will leave no chastity among Womankind, and orders her doves to be harnessed to her char, for the char of Venus is drawn by a team of eight doves. She finds that l'Amour, who was always an ill keeper of conventions, has broken the truce and is again engaged in combat. He is again unsuccessful.

Here follows another long, philosophical dissertation, in which we are introduced to Nature's forge, and shown in a sort of allegorical picture how that personage is continually engaged in renewing the human race; and this discourse runs into another dissertation upon the doctrine of alchemy. Nature, at her work, nourishes grief in her breast, and she at length makes her confession to Genius, her priest. This confession is preceded by a declamation on the part of Nature against the instability and indiscretion of the female sex. Nature's confession is a grand dissertation on the system of the universe, and her grief arises from the circumstance that throughout, creation man alone is in constant opposition to her laws. Then comes a new scientific discourse, after which Nature proceeds to state the nature of true *gentillesce*, or nobility, which she says is a quality of the mind, and not derived from blood, and speaks disparagingly of that pretended nobility which is shown in frequenting tournaments and running over the country in search of adventures. The peasant may, according to this doctrine, be quite as

noble as the gentleman of family, and the clergy, who are always occupied
in mental studies, would be more noble than all.   It is another assertion of
the natural equality of man, against the pretensions of feudalism.   Nature
sends her high priest, Genius, to the army of l'Amour, to encourage them in
their siege, and their chieftain grants him the investiture of the ring and
pastoral staff.   Genius then excommunicates all who resist the dictates of
natural love, and this is followed by a sermon on those dictates, the licentiousness of which is hardly anywhere concealed.

When Genius has thus performed his office, before his departure he
throws the torch, which l'Amour had entrusted to him, into the castle, and
its flame penetrates into Bel-Accueil's prison, and has the effect of softening
the hearts of those charged with its defence.   Venus puts to flight Shame
and Fear, and as the final result Bel-Accueil is liberated, and l'Amant
plucks the Rose.   And thus this strange allegory ends.

This singular work must have had a very considerable influence on
social sentiment in Western Europe during the fourteenth century.   It had
certainly a wide reputation, and was extensively read.   Our own poet
Chaucer began to translate it in the course of the latter half of that century.
Its effect can hardly have been otherwise than to lower the level of Womankind, both in her own estimate and in that of the other sex, and this, as
well as the bold political and other sentiments contained in it, could not fail
to raise a great outcry against it, while it is equally certain that it found
many advocates and defenders.   Yet it was not till the close of the fourteenth century, as far as we know, that it was made the subject of any serious
attack, and that attack came from the pen of a woman.   Of Christine de
Pisan, and her literary character, we shall have to speak on a future occasion.
In 1399, appeared her Epistle to the god of Love (*Epitre au dieu d'Amour*),
in defence of the honour of the female sex against the attacks of our author,
Jean de Menn.   Three years after the appearance of this defence, one of
the other sex, and no less a personage than Jean Gerson, chancellor of the
church of Paris, made a still more formal attack upon the *Romance of the
Rose*.   Gerson's *Traité contre le roumant de la Rose* was itself composed in
the form of an allegory.   On awaking one morning, the author supposes
himself to be carried to the Court of Christianity, where the lady Canonical-
Justice presides over the court, with Mercy and Truth for her assistants.
Chastity here presents her complaint against the Fol-Amoureux, under
which name we are to understand the author of the second part of the
Romance.   Among the charges against the Fol-Amoureux are those of
seeking to banish from the world Chastity, and her natural guardians, Shame,

Fear, and Danger, to proscribe marriages, and to introduce every kind of licence. The author is accused of writing obscenely as well as licentiously. The development of the charge produces a great sensation in court; but immediately arise a countless crowd of defenders of the Fol-Amoureux. They are made to plead in his defence the extreme youth at which he wrote this book, and that at a greater age he had written a repentance of his earlier writings; adding his talents as a French writer, and his honesty in attacking the corruptions of all conditions, political or ecclesiastical, which must of course provoke a multitude of enemies. Divine-Eloquence is brought forth to reply to these arguments, speaks at length in defence of lady Chastity, and criticises the *Romance of the Rose* with great severity.

The controversy once begun, did not stop here. An official of the male sex, Master Jean Joannes, provost of Lille, took up the defence of Jean de Meun, and was followed by two other advocates, Gontier and Pierre Col. We seem to know little of these two individuals, Gontier and Pierre Col, except that the first is said to have been secretary of the king, Charles VI., which sounds rather ominous. Gontier Col demands of Christine de Pisan, in language of indignation, "Is it true that you have lately written, by way of invective, against my familiar instructor (*mon maistre enseigneur familier*), Maister Jehan de Meun, a true Catholic, solemn master and doctor in holy theology, very profound philosopher, and excellent, knowing all which is capable of being known to the human understanding, whose glory and renown lives and will live to ages to come, by the grace of God and work of nature made and compiled in the book of the Rose?" Gontier Col writes directly against Christine de Pisan, and closes his attack in a sort of form of authority—"Written in haste, present Master Jehan de Quatremares, and Jehan Porchier, counsellors, and Guillaume de Neauville, secretary of the king, on Tuesday, the 13th day of September, 1407." In answer to all this, Christine de Pisan comes forward again, and, after excusing herself as a woman for reading a book so full of ribaldry, replies to the defence of the provost of Lille, and the king's secretary, and others. The defence of her sex, by Christine de Pisan, is full of earnestness and full of talent; but though her task, according to our modern feelings, was not a very difficult one, yet in that age it appears not to have been convincing. Gontier Col replied, and the controversy lasted through a few years.

The popularity of the *Romance of the Rose*, however, did not diminish in France. In fact, it appears to have been very great during the fifteenth century. The number of manuscripts of this period, preserved in various collections, as well as of the fourteenth century, is very considerable, a great part of them more or less costly manuscripts, finely illuminated, which must have been made for people of rank and fortune. At least one person undertook to remodel the *Romance of the Rose*, and take from it some part of its objectionable character.

A still greater proof of the popularity of this manuscript in the fifteenth century is the fact that it was one of the earliest books printed, and that it was printed over and over again in black letter during the earlier ages of the French press. At least seven or eight different printed editions appeared in France before the beginning of the sixteenth century. During the years 1525 and 1526, the well-known French poet, Clement Marot, was confined in the prisons of the Châtelet and of Chartres, on the charge of leaning towards the religion of the reformers; and while there it appears that he amused himself with reading the *Roman de la Rose*. Interested in the work itself, which presented in strong colours the reforming notions in religion, as well as politics, of the thirteenth century, and finding the language rather antiquated, Marot revised the text, and produced a new edition, which appeared in 1526, and became the model of all the subsequent editions printed during the sixteenth century, after which date the book had lost its original interest, and became obsolete. Clement Marot's text differs very much in its language and in its phraseology from the texts of the manuscripts of the fourteenth and fifteenth centuries, but it is of no use whatever philologically. The social influence of the *Romance of the Rose* had nearly expired when it fell into his hands—an influence which, no doubt, counted for much in the formation of woman's character and sentiments during the fourteenth and fifteenth centuries in fashionable society in France, and which substituted a more coarse immorality for the refined and delicate, but perhaps not much more moral, chivalry of the earlier period.

CHAPTER XI.

WOMANKIND IN THE FEUDAL CASTLE—WOMAN'S POSITION IN THE HOUSE-
HOLD—CHIVALRY—THE RELATIONS OF THE SEXES - LOVE.

LET us now descend to the reality of Womankind. In a former chapter I
have described briefly and in general terms the change brought upon society
by the feudal system, and especially on woman's position in it. We may
contemplate these, in their full extent, in the literature of the thirteenth and
fourteenth centuries; in the class of romances the subjects of which are
taken from contemporary life; in the tales and histories; in the poetry of
every description.

As a wife, woman had at this time become, instead of the slave and
property of her husband, his equal, and in most of the relations of life an
independent agent. She had become capable of holding independent
power of her own, which was
something more than reflect-
ing that of her husband. She
was now an heiress, carrying with her as her dower
castles, and domains, and provinces, with numerous vassals; she could be guardian
of the manor, regent of the
state, and as such sign deeds,
and share in all the obligations imposed by peace or
war. Many of the great
ladies of the Middle Ages ruled
over extensive territories, and
took a very active part in

A DINNER PARTY OF THE FOURTEENTH CENTURY.

political affairs. In the household her position had more of dignity in it,

and she was looked upon with a different kind of respect.   Instead o.
serving the wine to the guests, she sat at the table, and hers was the place
of honour, by the side of her lord.   The picture of a mediæval party at table
in the preceding page is taken from an illumination of the fourteenth century,
in the Imperial Library in Paris.   It represents a sacred subject, and the
figure at the head of the table is no doubt the Saviour.   When her lord was
absent, the lady of the house was at the head of the board.   In our next cut,
where the chief of the party is a king, he has a lady by his side, and one of the
male guests separates her from another lady.   This second cut is taken from
an illuminated manuscript of the *Romance of Meliadus,* also of the fourteenth
century, preserved in the British Museum (MS. Additional, No. 12,228).

A ROYAL DINNER PARTY.

If a visitor of any rank came to the castle during the absence of the lord
the lady received him, provided for his wants, led him to the table herself,
and seated him by her side as in the place of honour.

This was the case even if the stranger came in the night.   In a fabliau
printed in the collection of Barbazan (iv. 370), the lady of a castle, possessed of rather a contradictory temper, receives a visitor into the castle
in despite of the orders of her husband.   This example we may consider as
belonging to the thirteenth century.   In one of the stories in that curious
collection, the *Cent nouvelles Nouvelles* (Nouv. 81), a knight and his company, overtaken by darkness and inclement weather, reach the gate of a
castle.   It was "late," for it was nine or ten o'clock in the evening, and
the people of the castle were already hastening to their beds.   The lord

of the castle was absent, but when they announced the arrival of the visitors to the lady, who was in her chamber undressed for bed, she said, " They are welcome ; quick, kill poultry, and bring forth whatever we have for their supper." And in haste she took her night robe, and thus, dressed as she was, she came courteously to meet the aforesaid lords, with two torches before her and a single woman with her, " a very handsome damoiselle " ; the

RECEIVING A VISITOR.

others were preparing the chambers. She came to meet her guests on the bridge of the castle, and the gentle knight advanced, and, thanking her, kissed her, as did the others also. And so they were received into the castle, and treated to supper before going to bed. It seems, indeed, to have been the special duty, or, at least, the general custom, for the lady of the

20

castle to go to the gate to receive the visitor. In one of the drawings in a fine
illuminated manuscript in the British Museum (MS. Reg. 15 E. VI., fol.
159, r°), a noble knight, who has left his military escort outside and passed the
outer gate, is met by the lady châtelaine, who advances from the inner gate
towards him.   In the book of the *Très chevalereux Comte d'Artois*, when
the Count d'Artois pays a visit to the Countess of Boulogne in her castle, she
similarly comes out, with her fair daughter, to receive him at the gate, and she
takes him by the hand and leads him into the hall, where he finds dancing
and minstrelsy.   The manner in which the countess in this case received
the visitor is shown in a drawing in the illuminated manuscript, a copy of
which is given in the cut on our last page.   It will be seen that the Count
d'Artois and his esquire are entering by the outer gateway, while the ladies
are issuing from the interior of the castle.   Sometimes, of course, it must
have happened that the lady was found in a state of unreadiness, and then
the guest was introduced into the castle, and awaited her in the hall.   Such
is the case in the *History of the Châtelain de Coucy and the Lady of Fayel*,
where, on the unexpected arrival of the former in the absence of the
husband, he is obliged to wait in the hall while she hurries to her chamber
to dress; but this operation is soon performed, for, as the author says, "a
fair lady is soon arrayed"—

Car belle dame est tost parée.

But this delay in receiving the guest appears not to have been considered
courteous, and occurs seldom in the romances or tales.   The knight of La
Tour-Landry urges that "all women should come to receive their friends in
the state in which they happen to be," and he tells a story of a knight who
was accustomed to make distant voyages, and who had two fair nieces, well
married, to both of whom he was much attached.   In one of his voyages he
bought for each of them a very rich robe, and on his return he proceeded
direct to the house of one of his nieces, and announced his arrival.   The
lady shut herself up in her chamber to dress fine, and sent word to her
visitor that she would come soon.   The knight was thus kept so long
waiting, that he lost patience, and so, remounting his horse, hastened to the
house of the other niece, who had at that moment a caprice of making
bread, and was thus occupied with her hands all covered with paste.   So
soon, however, as she heard that her uncle was at the gate, she hurried, just
as she was, to welcome him, led him to his chamber, and so soon as he was
safely lodged, went to her own chamber to dress, that she might appear
before him in a guise better fitted to do him honour.   The uncle was so

charmed with her behaviour, that he gave her the two robes, and withdrew his love from the other.

When a guest departed, it appears to have been the practice for the lord and lady of the castle to conduct him to the gate. A scene of this description is represented in the accompanying copy of one of the beautiful

THE GUEST'S DEPARTURE.

illuminations to the *Roman de la Violette.* Gerard of Nevers, the hero of this romance, has delivered the family of the castle of Bien-Assis from the persecutions of a brutal giant, and is here represented taking his leave of its lord and lady at the gate. It must be explained that their beautiful daughter has fallen violently in love with Gerard, whose heart, however, is otherwise engaged. As he mounted his horse, the young lady, who appears to have been in bed, was suddenly informed of his departure, and throwing over her body a *bliault*, or loose robe, she hastened down into the yard. We have here a good picture of a lady in undress. Her condition may be best described in the words of the original :—

Gerars monte, plus ne demeure,	Gerard mounts, he waits no longer,
Sonr le choval, l'espée çainte.	On his horse, his sword girded on.
La fille au signor vint deschainte,	The lord's daughter came ungirt,
Acourante, quant ot la nouviele.	Running to him, when she heard the news.
Em pur son bliaut fu la biele,	In her mere bliault was the fair one,
Sans gimple, un chapel d'or el chiof;	Without wimple, a chaplet of gold on her head ;
Mais dire vous voel de rechief	But I will tell you again
K'encor estoit ses chiés plus sors	That her head was still fairer
Et plus reluisans que li ors	And more shining than the gold
Qui fu el chapiel, che m'est vis.	Which was in her chaplet, it appears to me.
La freche colors de sen vis	The fresh colours of her face
Fu assés miex enluminée	Was much more brilliant
Que res en Mai, la matinée.	Than a rose in May, in the morning.
* * * *	* * * *
Le cors avoit bien fait et gent,	Her body was well-made and graceful,
Les mains bien faites et les bras.	Her hands well-made and her arms.
Un poi ot soslevé ses dras,	She had lifted her clothes a little,
Se li paroit li piéehouriés	So that her little foot appeared,
Blans et potis, bien fait et ués.	White and small, well-made, and clean.

It may be remarked that the text of this romance is of the thirteenth century, while the illuminations belong to a prose version of it in a manuscript of the fifteenth.

As the lady of the castle sat by her husband at the table, so also when not at their meals they sat side by side on one seat, similar to what we now call a settle, as shown in the accompanying cut, which is taken from an illuminated manuscript of the fourteenth century in the Imperial Library in Paris. When a visitor came, or when she would converse with a gentleman whom she held in esteem, the lady of the

THE KNIGHT AND HIS LADY.

house took him by the hand, and placed him in the seat of honour by her side.

The lady of the castle, too, had the direction and control of the whole family, which was often very numerous. This arose out of the spirit of feudalism itself, under which it had become the practice for the vassals, or feudatories, to send their sons to be educated in the family of their suzerain, while the daughters were similarly placed with the lady of the castle, who had thus in attendance upon her a retinue of young damsels, all claiming the honourable title, for none were admitted to it who were not of gentle blood, of *chambrières*, or chamber-maidens. These formed a very important part of the household.

DAMOISELLES AND DAMOISEAUX.

They were all, as daughters of gentle blood, entitled to be called *damoiselles, i. e.*, little dames, as those of the other sex were to that of *damoisel*, or little lord, and their intercourse among themselves, and with the *damoiseaux*, including the daughters and sons of the lord of the castle, was on a perfect footing of freedom and equality. During the earlier part of the day, these *chambrières* remained by themselves, in their chambers, or in that of their lady, employed in work of different descriptions, but all tending to the production of articles of dress or decoration of the person. After dinner, until the time of supper, they joined in society with the young *bachelors,* as all those were termed who had not yet attained the rank of knighthood, in the chambers, or in the garden, where they indulged in a variety of games and amusements. The preceding cut, from an illumination in the manuscript of the *Livre du très chevalereux Comte d'Artois,* of the fifteenth century, furnishes a good picture of a party of these damoiselles and damoiseaux engaged in conversation in the chamber. It will be observed that all the damsels, with one exception, present the same character of formality and demureness in the posture in which they are seated, and especially in the manner in which they hold their arms and hands. There is a character of conventionality about them which has evidently been taught,

A SOCIAL PARTY IN CONVERSATION.

even to the holding of the hands crossed. This fashion continued long to exist, for in one of the comedies of Larivey (the latter half of the sixteenth century), "Le Laquais," one of the characters, act iii., sc. 4, says, "Poor girl, she would be a very fool to remain for ever with her *hands in a cross* on her apron, till her father marry her." The same conventionality is seen in the second group, which is taken from an illuminated manuscript of perhaps rather earlier date, in the Imperial Library in Paris.

Several short codes of instruction in behaviour for young ladies in the Middle Ages have been preserved, and they are in many respects curious. The earliest apparently of these is in verse, by one Robert de Blois, and belongs to the thirteenth century. It was printed by Barbazan, under the title of *Le Chastoiement des Dames.* Robert exhorts the fair sex not to talk too much; to be courteous and modest before gentlemen; when walking out, not to go on a trot, or a run, but to walk straight forward at a steady pace, and not to advance before their companions. "Running and trotting, your own heart will tell you, are not becoming in a lady."

> En vostre cuer pooz penser
> Que le corre ne le troter
> A dame jà bien ne serra.

The ladies are not to amuse themselves by turning their eyes right or left as they walk along, but to look straight before them, and to salute courteously all they meet. They are not to let men put their hands into their bosoms, or kiss them ; and the poem goes on to treat almost entirely of love matters, which seem to have been the great subject of conversation and thought. The worthy Knight of La Tour-Landry, in the middle of the fourteenth century, instructs his daughters in a somewhat similar spirit; and that curious book, the *Menagier de Paris*, written about the year 1343, is still more particular. "If you are walking out," the author says, " go with your head turned straight forward, your eyelids low and fixed, and your look straight before you down to the ground at four toises (twelve yards), without turning your eyes on man or woman, to the right or to the left, or staring upwards, or moving your eyes about from one place to another, or laughing, or stopping to talk to anyone in the streets." Mr. Furnivall has printed in his *Babees Book*, a similar little code of instructions for damsels of the first half of the fifteenth century, written in English verse, and entitled in the manuscript, "How the good wyfe taughte hir doughtir." These counsels are of a description similar to the others, and they all show the character of demureness and conventionality which was, during the Middle Ages, considered to be most becoming in the fair sex, at least when young. Our third example of females conversing, taken from

LADIES IN CONVERSATION.

a manuscript of Froissart, of the fifteenth century, exhibits somewhat more energy of action.

Among the higher branches of the family, and where the intercourse was more private, the freedom of manners was, as may be supposed, greater, and the whole scene presents more of ease. Our next group belongs to an earlier period, for it is taken from a manuscript of the thirteenth century, at present in the Imperial Library at Paris (No. 1104, Fond St. Germain des Prés). The rank of the lady is here shown by her head-dress; that of her companion by the hawk he holds on his fist, a sure sign of gentility

MEDIÆVAL CONVERSATION.

during the feudal period. The marks of rank appear rarely to have been laid aside, even in the most familiar intercourse, in feudal society. Our next cut is taken from a manuscript in the Imperial Library in Paris (No. 8392), containing a treatise entitled the *Livre des Merveilles du Monde*, stated to have been executed by Nicolas Flamel in 1350. The ladies are all of noble rank, and even in their familiar intercourse wear their crowns and coronets. It is an interesting picture of ladies of rank and their children as they appeared in the middle of the fourteenth century.

Under all these circumstances just mentioned, there arose a peculiar tone of sentiment between the two sexes, one which had not been known in the same form before. The lady of the castle, as the head of the household, represented Womankind in full consciousness of independence and self-confidence, and this consciousness had been communicated to the rest of the sex within the castle-walls. When woman obtains this position, it immediately makes itself felt upon the other sex, and under it the harshness and ferocity which were naturally among the first characteristics of fendalism, were gradually exchanged for elegance of manners and sentiments which were new to society. Out of this new state of things arose two words which will never be forgotten. The first of these is *courtesy*. Every great baron's household was a court, and courtesy meant simply the manners and sentiments which prevailed in the feudal household. One of the modern, but almost mediæval, Latin writers has said, using the Latin form of the word, " *Curialitas est quasi idem quod nobilitas morum* "—" Courtesy is the same thing as nobility of manners." Courtesy was, over everything, that which distinguished the society inside the castle from that without, from the people of the country, and from the *bourgeoisie*, and the Middle Ages universally allowed that it was the influence of the female sex which fostered it. A little poem of the thirteenth century, published by my friend M. Jubinal, in

LADIES AND THEIR CHILDREN.

his volume of *Jongleurs et Trouvères*, expresses this sentiment in strong terms :—

Assez i a reson por qoi	There is reason enough why
L'en doit fame chière tenir;	We ought to hold woman dear ;
Quar nous véons poi avenir	For we see happen very little
Cortoisie, se n'est par fames.	Courtesy, except through women.
Bien sai que por l'amor des dames	Well know I that for the love of the ladies
Devienent li vilains cortois.	The very clowns become courteous.

I know nothing more beautiful than the sentiment of the chapter of the book of the Knight of La Tour-Landry, in which he recommends the duty of courtesy to his daughters.

The other word which we owe to the influence of Womankind on feudal society is *chivalry*. It indicated a spirit which arose from the same source. "Woman," says the poem just quoted, "is of such nature, that she makes the coward bold."

> Fame si est de tel nature,
> Qu'ele fet les cœurs hardis.

Woman's position once established in the form it had now taken, its influence was natural. Dame and damoiselle learnt to value the other sex chiefly for his bravery and for his skill in battle—he soon learnt to treasure the approval of that sex whose smiles he had sought within the castle walls, for the acts of prowess which had distinguished him outside. Mixed up with this was the spirit of gallantry which, as we have seen in a previous chapter, had made its way from the south, from Italy and la belle Provence. The knight learnt to look upon woman as his patron and mistress, and upon himself as her servant, and as bound to offer himself in her defence. It was this feeling of devotion which obtained the name of *chevalerie*, it was the moral duty of the *chevalier*. The duties of the knight towards the lady are thus defined in the *Ordene de Chevalerie* of Hugh de Tabarie, printed in Barbazan—

Dame ne doit ne damoiselo	He ought neither dame nor damoiselle
Por nule rien fourconsillier;	To misadvise on any account;
Mais, s'eles ont de lui mestier,	But, if they have need of him,
Aidier leur doit à son pooir,	He ought to aid them with all his power,
Se il vent los et pris avoir;	If he will have praise and respect;
Car femes doit l'en honourer,	For we ought to honour women,
Et por lor droit grans fez porter.	And for their right undergo great fatigues.

But though all these principles of chivalry and gallantry were universally acknowledged and talked of, the things themselves soon sank into forms and matters of show and ostentation, and they were displayed to most advantage in the romances. Chivalry, in show, belonged to the tournament and the joust, of which the ladies were looked upon as the special patrons, and he was considered the most gallant who most skilfully carried off their favours. It was his lady who sent him into the combat, and she sometimes led him to the field by his bridle, or even by a chain, and he proclaimed himself her servant. The knights were all, as they pretended, the "servants of love," or "of beauty." At the great tournament in Paris in 1389, given

by Charles VI., on the second day the knights who were to combat were conducted to the field by twenty-two damoiselles. It was the office of the ladies—sometimes especially of the damoiselles—to dress the combatant. They sometimes armed the knight for the combat, as in the *Roman de la Violette*, where (l. 227) the knight's daughter gives Gerard his helm—

> La puciele l'ielme li baille.

Generally each lady had her particular favourite, to whom she gave some object for which he was to fight. Sometimes the favour was a scarf, or some article of the lady's own dress, which he hung to his lance or helmet, or attached to some part of his armour. In more than one instance the lady gives as her favour to the knight of her choice her *chemise*. More frequently the token was a sleeve. In the romance of Flamenca, the king carries Flamenca's sleeve on his lance, and thus excites the queen's jealousy. In the *History of the Châtelain de Coucy*, on the announcement of a great tournament which was to be given at the castle of Fayel, the lady of the castle, at his request, promises to make him a large embroidered sleeve, that he may be her champion in the combat, to which he comes in very rich armour. After the service of mass, the ladies, who were the witnesses and judges of the tournament, mount to the stage which was prepared for them—

Tost fu mainte dame montée	Soon was many a lady mounted
Pour véoir et pour esgarder	To see and to consider
Ceulx qui veullent honnour garder,	Those who will keep honour,
Et mettre cuer et corps et ame	And employ heart and body and soul
Pour l'amour d'onnour et de dame.	For the love of honour and of the ladies.

In the hottest of the combat, when the Châtelain de Coucy was bidding fair for the victory, then the heralds shouted out to the lady spectators—

Dames, or povés esgarder.	Ladies, now you may look at them.
Donner les doit-on par soulas	You ought to give them for encouragement
Manches et aguilliers et las,	Sleeves, and needle-cases, and laces,
Les savoureus baissiers promettre.	Promise them the delicious kisses.

We give a coloured plate, from an illumination of the fifteenth century, representing these lady spectators and judges on their stage. In the earlier period, men sat indiscriminately with the ladies on this stage, but in the fifteenth century, when feudalism was at its last gasp, if not earlier, it appears to have been reserved entirely for the ladies.

It was the right of the ladies also to judge and pronounce who of the

combatants in the tournament merited the prize.   At the tournament in
Paris in 1389, according to the monk of St. Denis, who has left us an

DISTRIBUTING THE PRIZES OF THE TOURNAMENT.

account of it, the ladies met after supper on each day, and adjudged the
prize of valour, and their judgment was immediately confirmed by the king.

The prize, which was presented by one of the ladies, was usually in the form of a crown or chaplet, which was called the *chapelet d'honneur*, but it was sometimes in the form of a collar. When the *trcs chevalereux* Comte d'Artois, as his book tells us, proved himself the most valiant combatant in the tournament at Boulogne, the prize, which consisted of a collar of gold, was placed round his neck by the fair hands of the beautiful daughter of the Count of Boulogne, and in performing this duty she addressed to him the words, "*Monseigneur, comme ou mieulx faisant de toute la journée, les dames vous font présent de cest chappeau, en vous priant que le vuilliés prandre cn gré.*"

Scenes like this were not unfrequently pourtrayed upon the ornamental objects belonging to the ladies' toilette, and especially upon the covers of their mirrors, which were usually of ivory. One of these, of the latter part of the thirteenth century, has been engraved by Paul Lacroix and Seré, in their great work *Le Moyen Age et la Renaissance*, from which it is copied in the accompanying cut—it represents the ladies adjudging and distributing the prize of valour to two combatants in the tournament. The prizes are either chaplets or collars, and the proceedings are directed by the queen of the tournament, who stands above with a sceptre in her right hand, and a falcon on her left. To judge by what is taking place in the centre of the picture, we may suppose that at this time ladies were not the only persons admitted on the stage. Perhaps it is another successful competitor, for one of the advantages gained by the victor was the right of kissing at his will the fairest of the ladies present.

The ladies of these periods were generally so fully persuaded that the merit of the other sex consisted chiefly in bravery and warlike exploits, that sometimes a fair maiden became inaccessible to all softer charms, and, resolving to have at least a brave husband, offered herself as the prize of the tournament. Of course she was a damoiselle of rank and wealth, and worth fighting for. This was the case in our own country, according to the history of the Fitz Warines, with the fair Melette of Whittington, who refused to take for her husband anybody but one who should be "handsome, courteous, and accomplished, and the most valiant of his body in all Christendom." Her uncle proclaimed a tournament, and offered Melette, with the manor of Whittington, as the prize. Guarin de Metz so distinguished himself on the first day that he gained the lady's love, and, the next day, she sent him her glove for a favour, and asked him to defend it. Somewhat similarly, in the charming *romance* or ballad of "Bele Idoine," the king, her father, proclaims a tournament, at which Idoine is to be the prize.

But these were comparatively rare cases. The damoiselles of the feudal period were very susceptible to the passion of love, which was, indeed, the ruling spirit of the society within the castle—the moving power of life—as we are told in the opening lines of the *History of the Châtelain de Coucy*—

> Amours, qui est principaument
> Voie de vie honnestement,

The young damoisel in the household of the castle was constantly making

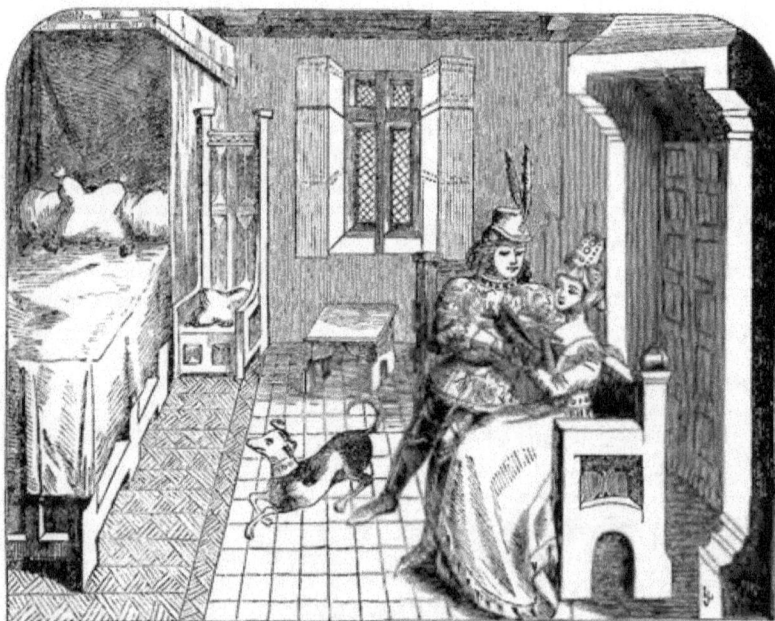

A BED-CHAMBER SCENE.

love to the damoiselle, and labouring to seduce her, and she was but too ready to listen to him. Feudal society was, in comparison to what had gone before it, polished and brilliant, and presented many great qualities, but under the surface it was not pure. This may be accounted for by many circumstances in the texture of mediæval society.

First, nearly the whole society in the castle mixed together on something like a footing of equality, and where the lord of the castle appointed one of the young bachelors to serve one of his daughters, it might, and, according to the romances, sometimes did, end in marriage. During a considerable portion of the day, the damoiselles and the damoiseaux were engaged in playing together at different amusements and games, and we can perceive in the description that these were often suggestive of anything but chaste feelings, while the language in common use among both sexes was far from delicate. All these were combined with an extreme intimacy between the two sexes, who commonly visited each other in their chambers or bedrooms. Thus, in the poem of Gautier d'Aupais, the hero is represented as visiting in her chamber the damoiselle of whom he is enamoured. Numerous similar examples might be quoted. One of these is given in the accompanying cut, from an illumination in a manuscript of the fifteenth century in the Imperial Library in Paris, containing the romance of *Othea*. The lady is receiving a visit from her lover in her chamber. The scene is especially interesting as showing the interior of a chamber of a castle at this period, and the manner in which it was furnished. At times, one of the parties is described as being actually in bed, as is the case in the romance of *Blonde of Oxford*, where Blonde visits Jehan in his chamber where he is in bed, and stays all night with him, in perfect innocence, as we are told in the romance. We must remember that it was the custom in those times for both sexes to go to bed perfectly naked.

Then, as they have been described in an earlier chapter, theories about love, and sentiments of a very free character, springing probably out of the old licence of the lower empire, had established themselves in the south of France—in Provence—and had spread through the whole extent of feudalism. Making love was considered the great business of social life, and rules and forms were laid down for carrying it on properly. The manner in which, in the story of Jehan de Saintré, the dame des Belles Cousines, instructs the youth in love is quite edifying. In the romance of *Floire and Blanceflor*, the king, Floire's father, puts them to schooling together when still very young, and love was one of the first sciences they began to learn.

Et quant à l'escole venoient,	'And when they came to school,
Lor tables d'yvoire prenoient.	They took their tablets of ivory.
Adont lor véissiez escrire	Then you would see them writing
Letres et vers d'amors en cire.	Letters and verses of love on the wax.
Lor greffes sont d'or et d'argent,	Their styles are of gold and silver,
Dont il escrivent soutiument;	With which they write cunningly;

Letres et salus font d'amors,

Du chant des oisiaus et des flors.

D'autre chose n'ont il envie.

Roman de Fl. et Blancef., l. 250.

They make letters and saluts (*a sort of verse*) of love,

Of the song of birds, and of flowers.

They have no desire of aught else.

Thus, it became one of the great accomplishments of a young bachelor, as well as of a knight, to compose love verses upon his lady. When Gautier d'Aupais could make no impression on the hard heart of the object of his affection, he consulted a minstrel, who advised him to compose a song in her praise, setting forth his passion, and that he should cause it to be sung in her presence by some one whose profession it was to sing. Gautier did so, and was successful. This knightly love-poetry formed once a large body of literature, and much of it is preserved. The chansons of the Châtelain de Coucy form a substantial volume. These compositions were distinguished by the title of *Romances.* My friend, M. Paulin Paris, has given a selection of them in his charming little volume, *Le Romancero François*, which includes romances by kings and dukes and great barons. Such poets were still more numerous in Provençal, and among them we have to reckon our own lion-hearted king, Richard I.

We may easily understand how all these causes would join in giving a great licence of tone and character to female society during the feudal period. In the history of the Fulke Fitz Warines, the intrigue of Sir Arnauld with the fair damoiselle, Marion of the Heath, in Ludlow Castle, is not told as an occurrence which was at all unusual.

CHAPTER XII.

WOMANKIND IN THE FEUDAL CASTLE—MARRIED LIFE—WOMAN'S WORK—
WOMAN AS THE PHYSICIAN.

THE same freedom which has been described in the last chapter as prevailing in the relations between the sexes, continued after marriage. The wedded lady seems to have claimed the right of having a lover as well as a husband, and sometimes more than one. In the story of Aucassin and Nicolette, the former speaks with a sort of admiration of " the fair courteous dames, who have two lovers or three along with their husbands "—*les beles dames cortoises, que eles ont ii. amis ou iii. avoc leur barons.* The good knight of La Tour-Landry, in a discussion on this subject with his own lady, advances curious reasons why married women might love *par amours* other men beside their own husbands. "Why," asks the knight, "should not ladies and damoiselles love *par amours?* For it seems to me that in true love there is nothing but good, and just as the lover is more worthy for it, and shows himself more gay, and handsomer and better arrayed, and is more encouraged to follow arms and honours, and taketh, therefore, better manner in himself and better bearing in all conditions of life, in order to please his lady and his love, just so does she who is loved of him, to please him, since she loves him. And so I tell you that it is great alms when a dame or a damoiselle is the means of making a good knight or a good esquire." * These lines of the knight of La Tour-Landry breathe the whole spirit of feudal chivalry. Bravery and skill in battle on the part of the object were always a sufficient excuse for the lady's love, and he was proud of displaying the favours which not only gratified his passion, but which were his incentives to great actions, for, as the knight observes a little further on, " it must be a great act of goodness on the part of the ladies to make out of a

* *Le Livre du Chevalier de La Tour-Landry,* edited by M. Anatole de Montaiglon p. 247.

22

man of nothing a man of valour and worth." The lady des Belles Cousines took the young Jean de Saintré into her favour, instructed him in the amorous science, sent him out to tournaments and battles, where he earned glory in her name, and then, when she thought he had done enough, she made him her lover. It is the perfect spirit of the Provençal doctrine of love.

In an early fabliau composed by a trouvère named Pierre Danfol, printed in the collection of M. Méon, a knight of Normandy pays his court to a lady, who refuses him her love until he proves himself valorous enough to deserve it.

Si li dist, en riaut, sanz ire,	And she said to him, laughing, without anger,
Que de s'amor n'ert-il jà sire,	That of her love he will never be lord
De si que sache, sans dotance,	Until she know, without doubt,
Commant il porte escu et lance,	How he carries shield and lance,
Et s'il en set venir à chief.	And if he know how to conquer with them.
Méon, Fabliaux, tome i., p. 175.	

The knight offers, and receives her permission, to challenge her husband to a tournament, which is held in her presence, and in which the husband is overthrown. The lady is sorry for her husband's mishap, but she greatly rejoices at the success of her knight, and gives him her love without further hesitation. According to another fabliau in the same collection, there was a knight who was a great coward, and who was, therefore, despised by his wife. Three other knights aspired to her love, and she determined at last to take one of them. On the eve of a tournament the lady sent to the three knights her chemise, with a message to the effect that she would give her love to him who would enter the combat with no other defensive armour, except his helmet, his chausses-de-fer, his shield, and his sword. The two elder knights declined the enterprise, but the youngest accepted the chemise, kissed it with transport, and, rushing eagerly into the combat, came out of it victorious but covered with wounds, and sent the chemise, bathed in his blood, as an offering to his lady. She threw it over her dress, and boasted of it openly in the presence of her husband. A similar case had been laid before the courts of love in Provence for their judgment on the merit of the lady's act.

Sometimes the lady's love was the reward of perseverance, and of the display of the lover's devotion to her. The Châtelain de Coucy, according to the history, loved the fair lady of the castle of Fayel, and paid a visit to the castle in her husband's absence. The lady rejected his suit, as being contrary to her duty, and sent him away. Then he went about to jousts and tournaments, and gained so much fame, that his praise was heard even in the castle of Fayel, and the lady listened to it with pleasure, as she knew that all these brilliant feats had been performed for her sake. And he wrote songs upon his lady, which were sung before her by a jongleur, or minstrel, and, when she knew the meaning of them, her heart was still more softened. Nevertheless, in another visit to the castle of Fayel, the châtelain's suit was again rejected, though somewhat less obdurately. But he persevered, frequented the tournaments more than ever, and made songs upon his lady, which he sang himself. Gradually she became more yielding, and dreaded less the blame she might incur, until at last she threw aside all her scruples, admitted him secretly by night into the castle garden, and gave herself up to love :—

Dist la dame: " Certes bien croy,	Said the lady : " Truly I believe well
Que loiaus serés envers moy;	That you will be loyal towards me ;
En moy arés loial amie,	In me you will have a loyal lover,
Car pooir n'ay que le desdie,	For I have not power to deny it,
Car ce qu'amours vient à plaisir,	For that which becomes love's pleasure,
Convient-il chascun obéir."	Every one must obey it."

Hist. du Châtelain de Coucy, l. 3561.

A bad or tyrannical husband was another excuse readily allowed. One of the romances in the *Romancero François*, that of Belle Emelos, by Audefroy-le-Bâtard, tells us how the fair Emelos, married to a duke, who beat and ill-treated her, sat disconsolate in the castle-meadow, thinking and talking of her lover, Guy. Her husband overhears her, and goes and beats her, in great anger ; but at the same moment Guy comes, sees what has taken place, draws his sword and slays the duke, and carries the lady away on his palfrey. In another in the same collection, Belle Isabeaus, who loves Gerard, is forced by her parents to marry one whom she does not love. Gerard goes to visit her, finds her alone in a garden, and, in the midst of their transports, the husband becomes unexpectedly a witness, and in his grief drops dead on the spot. They bury the husband, and Gerard takes his place. The excellent editor of this poem remarks, *un peu malicieusement*, that there have been few husbands who acted on such an occasion so conveniently.

Jealousy was another quality unbecoming in a husband of gentle blood. Jealousy belonged to the bourgeois, and not to the knight. This passion forms the groundwork of the *Roman de Flamenca*. The fair Flamenca, daughter of Gui de Nemours, is married to Archambaut, lord of Bourbon, and the nuptials are celebrated with a splendid festival, accompanied by a graud tournament, in the course of which Archambaut is made jealous of his young wife. This jealousy becomes a ruling passion with him, and he shuts his wife up in a tower of his castle, which he never allows her to quit, unless on Sundays and the church festivals, when she went to church under his own escort, or when he took her to the baths of Bourbon, with two of her damoiselles, locked them up in their bath, and carried the key with him till he let them out. Flamenca long pined under this confinement, and under the ill-treatment to which she was subjected ; until at length a young knight of Burgundy, named William, heard of her story, and he resolved to offer her his love, and to deliver her. He eventually caused to be made secretly a subterranean passage leading into the bath, which now becomes the safe scene of their interviews, while Archambaut believes that his wife is alone, accompanied only by her two damoiselles. The lady soon yields herself to William's embraces, and finally he carries her away. Previous to the interview in the bath, when William's love is accepted, he obtains Flamenca's permission to bring with him two of his esquires, and, while the principals are engaged in the chief room of the baths, the maidens, at the bidding of their mistress, yield to the esquires in rooms adjoining. The damoiselles are always found aiding and advising their ladies in these intrigues. The chambrière of the lady of Fayel performs this office towards her mistress, and even risks her own reputation to cover her lady's amour with the Châtelain de Coucy.

All these facts, and many of a character which I could less easily quote, show us that, under the external pride and pomp of the mediæval castle, the degree of morality which prevailed in its society was not very high. There was, indeed, no real check upon it, for even religion, as it was then cultivated, and especially the system of confession and absolution, was calculated rather to screen immorality than to prevent it. The following tale, found in manuscripts of the fourteenth century, is printed in my *Selection of Latin Stories :*—" A certain esquire had committed adultery with the wife of his lord, and began on this account to be an object of scandal; and when the knight, his lord, heard of it, he took with him the said esquire to a man possessed with an evil spirit (*dæmoniacus*), who was in the habit of accusing many people in public of the sins which they had committed secretly. The squire, knowing, therefore, that he was taken to the dæmoniac for this cause, and conscious of his guilt, obtained licence from his lord, for a case of urgent necessity, to go to a neighbouring town, and there he made a full confession to the priest of this as well as of his other sins, and having received from the priest penance and very severe discipline (flogging), returned to his lord. And when they came to the aforesaid dæmoniac, the knight interrogated him as to the character and deeds of his esquire. To whom the dæmoniac replied, 'Yesterday morning, when he started with you, I knew him and his deeds well; but now they are known only to him who has made his back bloody, nor am I able to say or know more of him.' " This anecdote was told by the priests themselves, as a good illustration of the efficacy of confession.*

This laxity of manners also explains why, during the feudal period, illegitimacy of birth was considered so little dishonourable, that the word which designated it was commonly adopted as a surname. The first of our own Norman kings was William the Bastard; and one of the most distinguished of the knightly poets of the Romancero, at the beginning of the thirteenth century, who appears to have lived in Artois, was Audefroy le Bâtard.† In one of the " romances " of the latter century, the fair Beatris, a daughter of high family, is already pregnant by her lover, the knight Ugon, when she is sought in marriage by the duke Henri. Her father will force her to marry the duke, but she scuds to her lover, who meets her at night in the garden of her father's castle, carries her off to his own territory, and there marries her.

As it appears from this story, the father still claimed the absolute right of disposing of his daughters. In the *Roman du roi Flore et de la belle Jeanne*, of the commencement of the thirteenth century, we are told of a knight who had a beautiful daughter, named Jeanne, and a faithful and favourite esquire named Robin, to whom he proposed to give his daughter in marriage, as a mark of his esteem, though in regard to position the match was very unequal. The knight's lady, when she was told of his intention, protested against it, but without effect, and she appealed to her relatives, who refused to interfere, telling her that her husband was a knight, brave and powerful, and that he had the right of disposing of his daughter at his will (*il puet faire de sa fille sa volenté*). The knight sent for his chaplain, caused him to perform the ceremony of betrothal, and fixed the day of marriage.‡ In the whole of these proceedings the damsel appears not to have been consulted. In the romance of *Belle Idoine*, who is a king's daughter, but who loves

---

* *A Selection of Latin Stories, from Manuscripts of the Thirteenth and Fourteenth Centuries* (published by the Percy Society), p. 33.

† Among the members of the knightly family who lived together in his household, Adam du Petit Pont, towards the middle of the twelfth century, enumerates illegitimate children of the husband and illegitimate children of the wife. See Scheler, *Lexicographie Latin du xiiᵉ et du xiiiᵉ Siècle*, p. 123.

‡ This ceremony is represented in the cut on the next page, taken from a French illuminated manuscript of this period.

a gallant knight, the Count Garsiles, the damoisolle is betrayed by her *maistre*, or duegna, to the king her father. The latter, angry that his daughter should have formed relations of this kind without consulting his will, not only stripped and beat her severely, but shut her up in a tower, where she remained three years. I could give many examples of the

BETROTHAL OF YOUNG NOBLES.

exercise of this sort of paternal authority, but the father became gradually less arbitrary. In the pretty little novel of the Countess of Ponthieu, of the thirteenth century, when the count agrees to give his daughter in marriage to Thebaut, lord of Dommare, he said, " I will give her to you, *if she will it;*" and so, when Flamenca is given by her father to Archambaut, her consent is made a condition of the gift. However, to judge by the contemporary records of the history of manners which I am using, it had become by no means an uncommon thing for the daughter to make her own choice, and contract a runaway match. The opposition of the father usually arose from pride, or from selfishness; he was unwilling that his daughters

A ROYAL WEDDING.

should marry below his own rank and position, and he was desirous of disposing them in a manner which would bring, either by family alliance (which was of great importance in feudal times), or by the acquisition of wealth, advantage to himself. Love between those who were not equals in rank and wealth was very natural where, as already stated, the sons and daughters of the vassals were collected together in the household on a footing of social equality. Many examples might be quoted from mediæval literature and romance.

The act of betrothal, which in earlier times was one of so great consequence to the fathers of the two individuals most interested in it, and which was frequently performed in their childhood, had now lost much of its importance. It was still performed ceremoniously by a priest, in the presence of the parents and of witnesses, as shown in the picture we have given above. In the case of Jeanne and Robin, told before, the betrothal took place only six days before the marriage; but the usual time seems to have been a month. This was the case with the *très chevalereux* Comte d'Artois. The cut on the preceding page, copied from a fine illuminated manuscript of the latter half of the fifteenth century, in the British Museum (MS. Reg. 14 E. IV., fol. 284, r°), represents a royal marriage ceremony, no doubt much in the manner in which it was performed throughout the feudal period. Many of the relations of marriage appear to have been still under the influence of the clergy, which, as they were easily ruled by interested motives, had long been a subject of complaint. In England, already in the reign of Edward II., a popular poem on the corruptions of the time puts forward as a subject of complaint the facility with which, through the intervention of the priesthood, a man who had the means could get rid of his own wife, and take another man's in her place.*

> If a man have a wyf,
> And he love her nowt,
> Bryng hyr to the constery (*consistory court*),
> Ther trewth schuld be wrowt.
> Bring twei fals wytnes with hym,
> And hymself the thrydde,
> And he schal bo deperted (*divorced*),
> As fair as he wold bydde,
> 　　From his wyf;
> He schal be mayntend fulle wel
> 　　To lede a sory (*disreputable*) lyf.
>
> When he is deperted
> From his trew spowse,
> Take his neyzhebores wyf
> And bryng her to house (*bring her home*),
> Yif he have solver
> Among the clerkes to seude,

* *A Poem on the Times of Edward II.*, published by the Percy Society, p. 17.

He may have hir to hys wyf
To hys lifes ende,
　　　With ouskylle (*with wrong*);
Thei that so fair with falsenes dele (*deal*),
Goddes corse on her bille (*on their mouth*)!

We must not suppose that the ladies of the household were idle. They it was who, as in earlier ages, produced the materials necessary for a great part of the clothing of the family. Adam du Petit Pont, a scholastic writer of the twelfth century, describing a knightly mansion in his native England, says that, as they went round the house, they saw a chamber looking upon the garden, which was the *gynæceum*, or room of the women, and, approaching, they beheld, collected inside, linen warp, woof, and other objects of a similar description, as well as various implements and machines used in working linen and woollen, and also the different stuffs thus produced. In this room the lady of the castle and her damsels passed much of their time, probably the whole of the morning previous to the dinner. A short poem in praise of the sex, entitled *Le Bien des Fames*, printed by M. Jubinal, tells us that—

Mult doit fame estre chier tenue;	Much ought woman to be held dear;
Par li est toute gent vestue.	By her is everybody clothed.
Bien sai que fame file et oeuvre	Well know I that woman spins and manufactures
Les dras dont l'en se vest et cuevre,	The cloths with which we dress and cover ourselves,
Et toissus d'or, et drap de soie;	And gold tissues, and cloth of silk;
Et por ce di-je, où que je soie,	And therefore say I, wherever I may be,
A toz cels qui orront cest conte,	To all those who shall hear this story,
Que de fame ne dient honte.	That they say no ill of womankind.

In the romances, and in the illuminations of manuscripts, the ladies of the castle are sometimes introduced at their work. In the latter the process of spinning thread is, perhaps, the one most frequently represented. The following cut, taken from a manuscript of the Bible of the fifteenth century, in the Imperial Library in Paris, represents a lady thus employed. The distaff, or, as it is called in French, *quenouille*, was still so completely the woman's implement, that during the feudal period property which went in the female line was said to descend to the *quenouille*, or distaff, and an heiress was called in France an heir *de quenouille*. The crown of France, strictly subjected to the Salic law, was said legally never to go to the distaff (for, in the primitive ages, queens were employed in spinning, like the rest of their sex). For the same reason, as spinning was one of the first works in which

23

the damoiselle was instructed, and in which they were all proficient, the word *spinster* has become the legal designation of a woman who has not been married, not because spinning was not continued after marriage, but because it was looked upon as the young un-married woman's chief occupation. In fact, according to old tradition and legend, it had been almost created with her. The old popular proverb told of the time "when Adam dolve and Eve span;" and in that charming illuminated manuscript known as Queen Mary's Psalter (MS. Reg. 2 B. VII., fol. 4, v°., of the begin-ning of the fourteenth century), the first pair are represented thus employed, Eve seated with her distaff, with the marginal explanation, "here Adam digs ground in the world, Eve spins to make dresses":—

A LADY AT THE DISTAFF.

Icy fuyit Adam en secle tere,
Eve file pur robes fere.

Even in the oldest of Greek legends and traditions woman is known as the spinster. The old French poet, François Villon, speaking of Sardanapalus, says that he—

En voult devenir moulier (*woman*),
Et filer entre pucellettes.

The accompanying cut, taken from an illuminated manuscript of the fourteenth century, in the British Museum (MS. Reg. 10 E. iv.), represents a lady spinning on the wheel.

Our next cut repre-sents one of the ladies of the household carding or combing her wool. This also was an important part of the ladies' work, and a pair of cards was

A LADY SPINNING.

as necessary an article of the furniture of a house as a distaff or a spinning-wheel. In the English wills and inventories of the fifteenth century, we find frequent mention of a "pair of cards." Every household of any importance had also its loom or looms, and weaving appears to have been looked upon as a superior grade of ladies' work, and in illuminations it is generally ex- ercised by the lady of the house. Our cut below is taken from an illumination of the French trans- lation of Boccace, "des Nobles Femmes," in which it illus- trates the story of the wife of King Tarquin. As was the custom of the Middle Ages, and especially of the earlier period, the queen herself and her damoi- selles employed themselves in

A LADY CARDING WOOL.

the same kind of domestic occupations, and she here presides at the loom, while one of her companions is occupied with her cards or combs, and her carding-stock, and the other with her distaff.

Among the works of Christine de Pisan is a book entitled *The Epistle of the Goddess Othea* (*l'Epistre Othea la Deesse*), which con- sists of a series of wise sayings for children, illus- trated from fable and my- thology, and is pretended to have been compiled for the instruction of Hector of Troy, when he was fifteen years of age. Each saying is given in verse, and is called the *texte*, while the illustration follows in prose. The fol- lowing is one of these *textes*, and tells us how the maiden,

A QUEEN AND HER DAMOISELLES.

Yraigne (*Arachne*), was turned into a spider for her boasting :—

Ne te vantes, car mal en prist A Yraygnes, que tant mesprist, Que contre Pallas se vanta, Dont la deesse l'enchanta.	Be not a boaster, for ill came of it To Yraigue, who erred so much, That she boasted herself against Pallas, For which the goddess put an enchantment upon her.

The *glose*, or comment, which follows tells us that " Yraignes, according to the fable, was a damoiselle very skilful in the arts of weaving and spinning (*de tissir et de fillerie*), but too proud of her accomplishments; and, in fact, she boasted herself against Pallas, for which the goddess was angry against

THE STORY OF THE DAMOISELLE YRAIONE.

her, and transformed her into a spider for her boast, and said, ' Since you boast so much of your spinning and weaving, you shall for evermore spin and weave (*filleras et tistras*) work of no value.' And thus came into existence the spider, which still goes on spinning and weaving, but produces nothing of any worth." There is in the British Museum (MS. Harl., No. 4431) a beautiful manuscript of this book, in which the text just translated (fol. 126, rᵒ) is illustrated by a picture which is copied in our cut, and represents Yraigue at work, both in her original form and in that which she was made afterwards to assume. The lady with the crown is, of course, the goddess. The manuscript is of the earlier part of the fifteenth century.

In the literature of the Middle Ages, the ladies are not unfrequently spoken of as engaged in weaving woollen or linen. Thus, in a fabliau of the trouvère Rutebeuf, a woman pleads as an excuse for remaining up late at night, that she was obliged to finish a piece of linen cloth she was weaving—

Sire, fet-elle, il me faut traimer	Sir, I am obliged to work
A une toile que je fais.	At a linen cloth which I am making.

In my *Collection of Latin Stories* (p. 9), there is a tale of a woman whose husband was on the point of death, and who had already lost the use of his tongue and other members, and she told her maid to go in haste and buy three yards of coarse cloth of borel to make him a shroud. The girl replied, "Madame, you have plenty of linen cloth [of course, of her own making], give him four yards or more for his shroud." To which the high dame replied indignantly, "Three yards of borel are enough for him." And the dispute between mistress and maiden rose so high, that the dying man was roused to make use of his tongue also. Our next engraving represents a domestic loom of a later period: it is taken from one of the

A LADY AT HER LOOM.

early illustrations to Erasmus's well-known book, *The Praise of Folly.*

When the ladies had thus woven their cloths, they either laid them by, or immediately made them into the articles of clothing which were wanted. In the romance of *The death of Garin le Loherain*, the Count Fromont, entering the chamber of the fair Beatrice, finds her occupied in sewing a very rich *chainsil*, or chemise—

Vint en la chambre à la bele Beatriz;
Ele cosoit un molt riche chainsil.

Among the subjects of the side compartments of a print by Israel van Mechelin, we see a lady, apparently the mistress of the family, engaged in cutting up a piece of cloth to make it into garments, while two of her damsels are at work at their distaffs. It is given here in the cut in the margin.

LADIES AT THEIR WORK.

In the romance of *La Violette* a burgher's daughter is described as seated in her father's chambers, making a stole and amice in silk and gold, and as working with great care "many a little cross and many a star." And in the fabliau of *Guillaume au Faucon* a young bachelor, who enters suddenly the chamber of the ladies, finds them occupied in embroidering on a piece of silk the ensigns of the lords of the castle. It appears, indeed, to have been a point of pride among the ladies of the castle to be skilful in the art of embroidery. The cut in the margin, taken from a beautiful illuminated manuscript of the fourteenth century in the British Museum (MS. Reg. 2 B. vii.), represents a lady thus employed. Sometimes the daughters of a high family learnt still richer and more delicate work. In the fabliau of Richaut, printed in the collection of Méon, we are told of a knight's daughter who was entrusted to a burgher to learn *orfrois*, or the art of embroidering in gold and silver.

EMBROIDERY.

C'est la fille à un chevalier	She is the daughter of a knight
Prou et cortois,	Noble and courteous,
Qui l'a mise chiés un borjois,	Who has placed her with a burgher,
Qui l'aprunt à ovrer orfrois	Who teaches her to work *orfrois*
Avec sa fille.	Along with his daughter.

The art of embroidery was indeed often carried to a great degree of perfection by the mediæval ladies, who sometimes executed in this work figures and even elaborate pictorial scenes. We have an example of female skill in this kind of art in the well-known Bayeux tapestry. Robes were often ornamented with such pictorial scenes. In one of Marie's lais, the "Lai de

Laustic," the lady, shut up through the jealousy of her husband, communicates with her lover by means of pictorial embroidery of this description :—

" Le laustic li tramoterai,	" The nightingale I will send to him,
L'aventure li manderai."	And I will send him an account of the
	adventure."
En une piéce de samit	In a piece of samit
A or brusdé e tut escrit	Embroidered in gold and all pictured
Ad l'oiselet envolupé ;	She has wrapped up the little bird.
Un sien vallet ad apelé,	She has called a valet of hers,
Sun message li ad chargi,	Has entrusted her message to him,
A sun ami l'ad enveié.	Has sent him to her lover.

Poesies de Marie, ed. Roquefort, tom. i. p. 324.

In the romances, damsels are introduced occupied in such work, and also in embroidering portraits of their friends or lovers, usually on samit, a rich stuff of silk. The ladies in the early period similarly wove of silk girdles, ornaments for the head, ribands, and other articles, which were carried at tournaments by the knights on their armour or casque as favours. This was called a *cointise*, or *mignardise*. The heroines in the romances excelled at such works. One of them, in a passage of the *Roman de l'Escoufle*, quoted by Francisque Michel in his important work, *Recherches sur le Commerce des Etoffes de Soie*, boasts :—

Bien sachiés que jou referoio	Know well that I could make
Joiaus de fil d'or et de soie,	Trinkets of gold-thread and of silk,
K'il n'est fame ki tant en sache	That there is not a woman who knows so much
D'orfrois, de cainture, d'atache,	Of orfray, of girdles, of bands,
De ce faire ni-je tot le pris.	I stand highest at this work.

The dame or damoiselle making such things for her lover often wove in with the silk and gold thread some of the hair from her own head. This mark of attachment, as may be supposed, was highly valued. In the history of the Châtelain de Coucy, when the lady of Fayel knew that the châtelain was going to leave, " she worked for him a net of silk very fine and well made, and there was some of her hair worked among the silk ; the work of which seemed very handsome and rich, and with it he bound a very rich *bourrelet* over his helmet."[*]

The mediæval ladies were possessed of another accomplishment, and one

---

[*] La dame de Faiol fist un laqs de soye moult bel et bien fait, et y avoit de ses cheveux ouvrez parmy la soie; dont l'œuvre sembloit moult belle et riche, dont il lioit un bourrelet moult riche par-dessus son heaume.

of great importance in those days—they were physicians, and, to a certain
degree, surgeons. The question of allowing women to practise as doctors
has been a subject of great discussion of late, but in and before the feudal
period it was regarded as one of the natural duties of the sex, for men
skilled in these professions were not usually at hand. In the pretty little

THE LADY AS PHYSICIAN.

novel of *Aucassin and Nicolette* of the thirteenth century, the former
having fallen from his horse on his shoulder, the damsel Nicolette subjected
the injured part to a skilful manipulation, and found that the shoulder was

dislocated. "She handled it so with her white hands and laboured so much, that, by God's will, who loves lovers, it came into its place; and then she took flowers and fresh grass and green leaves, and bound them upon it with the flap of her chemise, and he was quite healed." In another little novel or romance, that of *Amis and Amilon*, when the latter is struck with leprosy, the wife of his friend Amis takes him into her chamber, strips him of all his clothing, bathes him herself, and then puts him to bed. So, in the *Roman de la Violette*, the damoiselle of the castle takes Gerard, who is carried in desperately wounded, into a chamber, and there divests him of his armour, undresses him, and puts him to bed. The damoiselles then examine all his wounds, apply to them ointments of great efficacy, and he soon recovers. In the romance of *Elie de Saint Giles*, the fair Rosemonde causes Elie, wounded, to be carried into her chamber, takes with her fair white hands precious herbs from her coffer, applies them to his wounds, prepares a bath for him, and places him in it. Many similar examples might be quoted. The accompanying sketch of the interior of a chamber is taken from the illuminated manuscript of the *Historia Scholastica*, of the date of 1470, in the British Museum (MS. Reg. 15 D. I.), but it is here copied from Shaw's *Dresses and Decorations*. It illustrates the history of Tobit, who is represented lying blind and sick on his couch, while his wife, Anna, is preparing a medicine for him, in doing which it will be remarked that she is following the directions of a book. Collections of medical receipts are found in abundance in all periods of the Middle Ages; and it must be borne in mind that, in those ages, women, and not men, were usually able to read and write.

CHAPTER XIII.

WOMANKIND IN THE FEUDAL CASTLE—WOMAN'S AMUSEMENTS—THE GARDENS OF THE CASTLE—PET ANIMALS.

It was in the earlier part of the day that most work appears to have been done by the ladies of the feudal household. Our mediæval forefathers began their day with sunrise, and considered that it ended about eight or nine o'clock in the evening, when they usually retired to bed. They rose very early, and, after performing their religious duties, they, to use their French phrase, *déjeunaient*, which our English translated literally by *they broke their fast*, but *breakfast* appears not to have been looked upon in the light of a meal. The two meals of the day were *dinner*, about the middle of our forenoon, and *supper*, which was taken at about four or five o'clock in the afternoon. In the later part of the feudal period, when people of fashion began to prolong the day into the night, they had a second and later supper, probably about the older hour of bed-time, which they called the *arrière souper*, and which was known in England as the *rere-supper*.

The part of the day before dinner appears to have been employed by the women of the castle chiefly in work. At the dinner-table, in the great hall, the whole household assembled. The meal was closed by the washing of hands, and then every one was at liberty to remain in the hall, or to seek amusements through the chambers or in the other parts of the castle. The knights and ladies of more matronly bearing appear to have remained for some time in the hall, or to have sometimes adjourned into a less public apartment, where wine and ale were served round to the former, while minstrels chanted to them, accompanied by the harp, legends from their own family history, or scenes from the romances, or other subjects of interest, or told and even acted tales, with a variety of performances which, like the tales, were commonly of a very licentious description, and speak little for the delicacy of feudal society. One of the amusements of these old heroes, which seems to have prevailed chiefly in the earlier ages of feudalism, was especially characteristic, and belonged to those great northern races from whom we claim our own descent. When the primeval warriors sat round their hall drinking their ale or mead, one of their great amusements was uttering extravagant boasts of the feats which each had done, or would do, and passing satirical jokes upon others. This proceeding was called *gabbing*, and the boasts and jests were called *gabs*. The word is preserved in our Anglo-Saxon under the forms—*gabban*, to joke or jeer; *gabbung*, joking; *gabbere*, a joker;—and it took its place in the French language of feudalism as *gaber*, to joke or banter; and *gab*, *gabois*, or *gaberie*, a joke or pleasantry. It was considered to be a great accomplishment in a gentleman to excel at a *gab*. In the Romances of the Round Table, Sir Keu was celebrated as the most accomplished gabber in King Arthur's court, and was the terror of all who could not bear a sarcastic joke with equanimity. There is preserved a curious little poem in Anglo-Norman, of the twelfth century, which relates how Charlemagne and his douze pairs went on a pilgrimage to Jerusalem, taking in their way Constantinople, where they were courteously received by the Emperor, or, as he is here called, King, Hugo. At night they were placed in a good chamber with beds enough for them all, and, plentifully supplied with wine, they lay down, drank their wine, and began to gab, Charlemagne claiming the right to say his gab first—

E dist Carlemaines, " Ben dei avant gabber."

The emperor's boast was, that if the strongest of Hugo's knights, doubly cased in armour, were placed on his steed before him, he would strike him on the helmet with his good sword with such force, that the blade would pass through the whole length of his body, armour and all, and through the horse, and afterwards into the ground, up to the handle. The *gabs* of the other paladins were still more extraordinary; Oliver made boasts in regard to the emperor's daughter which I will not here repeat. But King Hugo had been suspicious of his guests, and had placed a spy in their chamber, who repeated to him all they had said, and the results of this form the subject of the poem. It may be remarked, that in the latter ages of the word *gab*, the ladies, who had not been admitted into the gabbing of the primitive period, were as skilful in its use as the other sex, and perhaps more so. Many of the domestic games of the feudal period were formed chiefly for the purpose of this spirit of gabbing, though the gabbing took rather a different form. A poet of the thirteenth century tells us a story of one of these games, which was called *Le roi qui ne ment pas*, the king who does not lie, in which, as it might happen, a lady or a gentleman was placed on the playful throne, and each of the others had the right of putting a question and receiving a truthful reply. The questions and answers were generally satirical—veritable gabs—and, in the case to which I allude, are now not capable of being repeated. This was the character of most of the popular games of the feudal period. This same spirit of gabbing continued beyond the Middle Ages. In the fourteenth century we find it in games of chance, in which sarcastic characters were drawn upon rolls of vellum or paper, with marks attached to each, and you drew by chance, and took what you got, and were no doubt laughed at for it. The roll was called a *Rageman Roll*,—Rageman perhaps meaning the devil, who was supposed to direct the chances of the game, which were of a rather disreputable character. The spirit of this game continued to the age of Elizabeth and James I., when it appeared under the shape of roundels, discs of wood for serving fruit or confectioneries round to the festive party, which you turned up after having eaten the fruit, or sweetmeats, and found on the under surface a satirical motto, which was supposed to apply to yourself. It was especially a lady's game. I have printed two of the Rageman's Rolls, one in French, the other in English, in my *Anecdota Literaria*.

After the washing of the hands after dinner, a drink was usually served round, and then, as stated before, the younger portion of the family of the castle rose from the table, and proceeded in groups to amuse themselves in different ways. Some went in couples, apart, making love. Many formed parties, who conversed, told stories, and sang songs. Minstrels, and jongleurs, and mountebanks found a welcome in the castle, and always received their reward. Others spread through the chambers, and in the gardens, and out into the meadows, and joined in dances, and in games of various descriptions. When Jean of Dammartin was finally retained in the household of the Earl of Oxford, and in the service of the fair Blonde, the poet who composed the history tells us how—

Après manger lavent leurs mains,	After dinner they wash their hands,
Puis s'en vont juer, qui aius ains,	Then go to play, in emulation of one another,
Ou en forès ou eu rivères,	Either in the woods or on the banks of rivers,
Ou en deduis d'autres manières.	Or in pastimes of other kinds.
Jehans au quel que il veut va;	Jean goes to whichever he pleases:
Et quant il revint souvent va	And when he returns, he often goes
Jouer as chambres la contesse,	To play in the chambers of the countess,
O les dames, qui en destrèce	With the ladies, who in confinement
Le tienent d'uprendre François.	Hold him to learn French.

De jus de cambres seut assés,	Of chamber games he knew plenty,
D'eschés, de tables, et do dés,	Of chess, of tables, and of dice,
Dont il sa damoisele esbat;	With which he amuses his damoisello;
Souvent li dist eschek et mat,	He often says to her check and mate,
De maint jeu à juer l'aprist.	He instructs her in many a game.

Roman de Blonde, l. 387.

In the *Roman de la Violette*, the young gentlemen and ladies are described as, after dinner, spreading similarly through the castle, attended by minstrels with music. The ladies of the feudal ages were passionately fond of dancing. They danced in the chambers, and in the gardens, and they even wandered into the fields to dance. The favourite dance was the *carole*, in which those who joined in it danced in a ring and accompanied

A DANCE AT COURT.

their movement with singing, and this dance was so universally used, that the common word for, to dance, was *caroler*—to carol. In the Romances of the Round Table, one of the heroines, the lady of the Terre-Lointaine, lost in

admiration at the fair dancing in the meadow of the Forêt Perilleuse, says
to the enchanter, Guinebaut, "Think you not, fair sir, that one would be
very happy to follow these fair caroles all the days of one's life?" and, to
please the lady, Guinebaut placed the carole under a charm, which pro-
longed it to a very indefinite period. The foregoing cut is taken from
one of the illustrations in the illuminated manuscript of the *Roman de la
Violette*, and represents a carol at one of the grand feasts of the royal court
of Louis-le-Gros. Every reader of the *Roman de la Rose* will remember
the description of the gay carole led by Liesce (*Joy*) in the garden of
Deduit.

Besides the carole, the Middle Ages had a variety of other dances, the
names of many of which might be collected, but it would be difficult to
describe them. A long list will be found in Rabelais. The well-known

MONKS AND NUNS AT THE DANCE.

manuscript in the British Museum known as Queen Mary's Psalter, which
furnishes us with so many illustrations of the manners of the early part of
the fourteenth century, gives us several pictures of a dance of a very
peculiar character. The dancers are four in number, two of each sex; but
perhaps this number may be ascribed merely to the caprice of the artist,
dictated by the space in which he had to confine the figures. They hold
each other not simply by the hand, but by a ribbon, or band. In the
different pictures in the manuscript, the characters who perform the dance
are curiously varied. Thus, in one (fol. 174) they are youths and maidens;

in another (fol. 179), demure-looking citizens and their wives; in a third (fol. 180), we see the dance performed by monkeys; and in a fourth (fol. 229), by female saints, the musicians in this latter being repre-sented by angels. In the one which is copied in the opposite cut (fol. 170), the dancers are monks and nuns, the first monk, with the cowl on his head, having some-what the air of a superior, perhaps an abbot.

The ladies of the feudal ages were partial, also, to games of skill, especially to tables and chess, the former of which was played with dice, and appears to have resembled our backgammon. The game of tables appears to have been of great antiquity among our race, but before the ages of feudalism it seems to have been confined chiefly to the male sex; in the feudal castle the ladies embraced it eagerly, and in the illumi-nated manuscripts, when we find a party engaged in this game, it is almost invariably a lady and a gentleman. The cut given above, taken also from Queen Mary's Psalter (British Museum MS. Reg. 2 B. VII.), represents another game of this kind, called the game of *dames*, which is still known in France by the same name; though, in England, this name was changed before the sixteenth century into that of *draughts*, which is said to have been given to it because, in playing, the pieces are *drawn* from one square to another. The game of dames, as being much less exciting than tables, was

A PARTY AT DAMES.

A PRINCELY PARTY AT CHESS.

therefore far less popular, and is not so frequently mentioned in the old writers.

The prince of games was always that of chess. Among the first things included in a liberal education for either sex was skill in playing at tables

A PARTY AT CHESS.

and chess, and a party at chess is not unfrequently represented in the illuminations of manuscripts. It usually consists of a gentleman and a lady playing together. Walter Mapes, in his book, *De Nugis Curialium*, tells a story of a Breton prince, who was accustomed to play at chess with his lady; and, in the Romances of the Round Table, the enchanter, Guinebaut, gives to a fair lady a chess-board and men, made half of gold and half of ivory, which possessed the quality, that, when a gentleman and lady played at it, the lady always gained the victory. Our first cut represents Otho, marquis of Brandeburg, engaged at chess with a lady. It is taken from a manuscript of the fourteenth century in the Imperial Library in Paris (No. 7266). The next cut, taken from a finely-illuminated manuscript of the romance of the *Quatre Fils d'Aymon*, in the Bibliothèque de l'Arsenal, at Paris, executed in the fifteenth century, repre-sents a nobleman and one of the great ladies of his household playing at chess together, apparently in a sort of alcove adjoining the garden, which latter forms the background of the picture. The heroes and heroines of the mediæval romances are frequently introduced playing at chess.

Other amusements of the squires and damoiselles of the castle consisted of what we should now call romping games, allied with our hunt-the-slipper, hide-and-seek, etc., and these appear to have been rather numerous. They were generally of such a character as to admit of both sexes displaying their skill in the accomplishment of gabbing, already alluded to, and we have no want of evidence that this was often carried far beyond what would be allowed by modern delicacy. One of them, entitled *Le roy qui ne ment pas*, has already been described. The names of others of these games are sometimes mentioned, but, with a few exceptions, we are not well acquainted with their character. In a story in the Ménagier de Paris, compiled in 1393, the ladies, visited unexpectedly after supper, were found, some playing at *bric*, others at *qui féry?* (who struck?) others at *pince-merille*. The first of these games, which was played with a small stick, or wand, is mentioned by Rutebeuf in the thirteenth century. "*Qui féry?*" appears to have been the game which was called in English hot-cockles. The exact character of the game of *pince-merille* appears not to be known; but *tiers* is understood to have been a sort of blind-man's-buff. We might add other names to these, and, in fact, the games of this description appear to have been very numerous. The reader of Rabelais will remember the immense list of those which were taught to the youthful Gargantua. The games played by the ladies of the castle sometimes descended to a still more popular character, and became identical with the children's games of modern times. The accompanying cut, taken from a manuscript of the fourteenth century in the British Museum (MS. Harl., No. 6563), represents two females playing at ball.

DAMOISELLES PLAYING
AT BALL.

The ladies and damoiselles of the castle are everywhere described as exceedingly fond of wandering in their gardens, and through them into the meadows, and listening with great pleasure to the song of the birds. They had a fashion, which prevailed very generally at the season of the year, of dressing their heads with garlands and chaplets of flowers. When Jean of Dammartin sought Blonde of Oxford one day, and looked from the chamber, he saw her in a meadow, where she was making a chaplet—

> Adonc de la chambre s'avance,
> De là la vit en j. prael
> U ele faisoit un capiel.
> *Blonde of Oxford*, l. 850.

25

In a poem in praise of the fair sex, published by M. Jubinal, from a manuscript of the thirteenth century, we are told that woman makes chaplets of flowers for those who love—

> Si fet fere chapiaus de flors
> A cels qui aiment par amors.
> *Jubinal, Jongleurs et Trouvères,* p. 85.

In another piece, published by the same editor, the lady is crowned with a chaplet of flowers of very great beauty—

> Uns chapiaux de flours acorone
> La dame de moult grant biauté.
> *Lettre à M. de Salvandy,* p. 160.

These chaplets of flowers were not worn only by the gentler sex, for we are told in the romance of Lancelot, that "there was no day in which Lancelot, whether winter or summer, had not in the morning a chaplet of

DAMOISELLES MAKING GARLANDS.

fresh roses on his head, except only on Fridays, and on the vigils of the high feasts, and as long as Lent lasted." In the *Roman de la Rose,* Deduit, or Pleasure, the lord of the garden, has a garland of roses on his head, which his lady-love, Liesce, Joy, had made for him :—

> Par druerie et par solas
> Li ot s'amie fet chapel
> De roses, qui moult li sist bel ;

and so has Love. It appears to have been customary at this time for the damsel to make a chaplet of roses to place on the head of her lover.

The accompanying cut is also taken from the manuscript known as Queen Mary's Psalter (MS. Reg. 2 B. VII.), of the beginning of the fourteenth century, and represents a party of damoiselles, apparently in the open meadows, gathering flowers, and making their garlands.

It will be remembered how Emelie, in Chaucer's Knight's Tale, rises at daybreak to descend into the garden, and make herself a garland—

> Iclothed was sche fressh for to devyse.
> Hire yolwe (*yellow*) heer was browdid (*platted*) in a tresse
> Byhynde hire bak, a yerde long, I gesse.
> And in the gardyn, at the sonne upriste (*at sunrise*),
> Sche walketh up and doun wheeras hire liste;
> Sche gadereth floures, partye whyte and reede,
> To make a certeyn gerlaud for hire heede,
> And as an aungel hevenly sche song.

In the Lay of Aristotle, the mistress of king Alexander is described as descending early in the morning to walk in the garden, and make herself a

THE LADY AND HER DAMOISELLES IN THE GARDEN.

chaplet of flowers. Quotations illustrative of this custom might be multiplied almost without end. Our next cut is of rather a later date: it is taken from the manuscript service book of the fifteenth century, known as the "Heures" of Anne of Brittany, now in the Bibliothèque Imperiale in Paris.

The lady of the castle is here making the garland, while her damoiselles are gathering the flowers.

We can understand the love of the ladies of the castle, and of the other sex also, for the pleasures of the gardens and of the fields, after being confined in the close and dull rooms of the feudal building. This feeling appears, indeed, to have been shared by both sexes, and hence we find not unfrequently the lords of the castle resorting to the garden to play at tables or at chess, or even to hold meetings of a more serious character. All, at times, sought their happiness in its charms. The knight of La Tour-Landry opens his subject by telling us how, in the year 1371, at the approach of the month of May, sad and full of thought, he went into his garden, and seated himself in the shade, and how he listened to the singing of the birds until his heart became lightened, and his joy returned.

The garden was perfectly private, and with this object it was inclosed by walls. In Chaucer's Tale, the knight January

> —Had a gardyn walled al with stoon,
> So fair a gardyn wot (*know*) I no wher noon.

And Chaucer dwells warmly on—

> The beauté of the gardyn, and the welle (*fountain*)
> That stood under a laurer alway green.

In the romance of *Les Enfances Guillaume*, the messenger of Guillaume finds the young princess Orable at Orange, then in the power of the Saracens, seated in a garden planted with yews, laurels, and pine trees. In the midst of it flowed a clear fountain, bordered with herbs which possessed such sovereign virtues that no disease or wound was proof against them. The knowledge of the healing virtues of herbs was one of woman's qualities.

A fountain was considered a necessary part of the knightly garden. In the description of the garden in the *Lais de l'Oiselet*, we are told—

Et enmi ot une fontaine,	And in the middle there was a fountain,
Dont l'iaue estoit et clere et saine ;	The water of which was both transparent and salubrious;
Et surdoit de si grant randon,	And issued with so great force,
Com s'ele boulist do randon ;	As though it boiled violently ;
S'iert ele plus froide que marbres.	And it was colder than marble.

This fountain was shaded by beautiful trees, so thickly leaved that the sun's rays could not penetrate to it. In the garden where the two maidens went to amuse themselves in the fabliau of *Hueline and Aiglantine*, the fountain was under a pine. The garden is generally described as being extensive. It appears to have been situated usually outside the walls of the castle, or castellated mansion, but we have few early descriptions to enable us to fix its exact position, especially in the large castles, (though it was evidently easy of access from the chambers of the ladies, and it usually communicated with the fields. From the *History of Fulk fitz Warine* (p. 42), we learn that in the great feudal fortress of Ludlow, in the twelfth century, the gardens lay in the fields under the rock on which the castle was built, and they probably extended to the bank of the river Teme. Their position will be well understood by any one who has visited Ludlow. We learn from other sources that people always chose for the site of the garden, when they could, the bank of a river, and a castle was, indeed, usually built where a river flowed near at hand. In the *Lai de Gugemer*, by Marie de France, the garden lies at the foot of the donjon or main tower, is inclosed by a wall, and is bounded by the sea.

En uu vergier souz le dongun,	Iu a garden under the doujon,
Un clos aveit tut envirun ;	It had an enclosure all round ;
De vert marbre fu li muralz,	The wall was of green marble,
Mult par esteit espès o halz ;	It was very thick and high ;
N'i out fors une sule entrée,	There was only one sole entrance,
Cele fu noit e jur gardée.	This was guarded night and day.
De l'altre part fu clos de mer.	On the other side it was enclosed by sea.

Poesies de Marie, tom. i., p. 64.

Probably some of those little postern-gates which still remain in the walls of our ruined castles, served the ladies of the household for private access to the gardens. There are more than one in the line of walls in Ludlow castle facing the gardens, as just described. It is certain that the apartments of the ladies had easy and private communication with the garden. In the story of the Chastelaine de Vergi, the lady of the castle appointed the knight, her lover, to conceal himself in a corner in the garden until he saw a little dog pass through, and then she would admit him into her chamber. In one of the episodes of the Romances of the Round Table, the second Genevieve, after she is undressed, is conducted by her maid into the garden before being put to bed. This incident belongs either to the twelfth or to the thirteenth century.

A very famous description of a garden in the mediæval literature was that in the *Roman de la Rose*, the hero of which, L'Amant, the Lover, in his wandering, comes upon an extensive garden, surrounded by a lofty wall. It is, as stated in a former chapter of the present book, the garden of Deduit,

Pleasure. L'Amant follows the wall round, and at length comes to a small entrance-gate, at which he knocks, and, after much importunity, obtains admission from dame Oyscuse, lady Idleness, a fair and noble maiden, who held the key of the gate. Eagerly the lover entered the garden, and thought he had found his way into Paradise, so beautiful was the scene, and so lovely and varied the song of the birds which abounded in it. Proceeding in search of Deduit, the lord of it, he found him with a fair party of companions indulging in all the amusements which a beautiful garden usually afforded. They were engaged in dancing a carol, which a very fair lady named Liesce, Joy, led with her song. Here the fair dame Courtoisie invited him to join in the dance. Then L'Amant went to examine the garden, and tells how it was filled with trees and flowers, and how he came to a beautiful fountain, under a magnificent pine, and enclosed in marble. It was the Fountain of Love. In the noble illuminated manuscript of the *Roman de la Rose* in the British Museum (MS. Harl. No. 4425), the illuminator has given a pictorial representation of this scene in the garden, which we have copied as far as could be done in our coloured plate. It would be impossible to reproduce the minute delicacy of the original, nor have we attempted to give *all* the leaves, flowers, and birds which are introduced into it. A party are seen singing and playing on the vicille, or fiddle. The lower part of the picture, which represented the garden wall and gate, and L'Amant obtaining admission, has been here omitted.

Chaucer, who appears to have had a great sympathy for the pleasures of the garden, dwells upon them often in his poems. In the *Frankeleynes Tale*, the friends of the lady Dorigen, seeking to rouse her from her melancholy, take her " by riveres and by welles " (*fountains*), and to other pleasant localities, where they dance, and play at chess and tables—

> So on a day, right in the morwe tide,
> Unto a gardeyn that was ther beside,
> In which that they had made her ordinance
> Of vitaile, and of other purveaunce,
> They gon and plaie heer all the longe day.
> And this was on the sixte morwe of May,
> Which May had painted with his softe schoures
> This gardeyn ful of leves and of floures;
> And craft of mannes hand so curiously
> Arrayed had this gardeyn of suche pris,
> As if it were the verray paradis.

The games and amusements of the garden are frequently alluded to in the mediæval writers. The curious story of the Emperor Constant, published in the *Nouvelles Françoises en Prose du XIIIe. Siècle*, records how "the emperor's fair daughter, after she had dined, went into the garden, with four of her maidens, and began to chace one another, as maidens play together sometimes."

The garden was also a common scene of love intrigues, and often plays

MAULGIS WITH THE FAIR ORIANDE IN THE GARDEN.

that part in the mediæval romances and histories. It was in the garden that the fair dame of Fayel met the Châtelain de Coucy, and granted him her love. In the romance of *Maulgis et la Belle Oriande*, the hero and heroine are introduced making love in the garden. "They met in a garden to make merry and amuse themselves after they had dined, and it was the time for taking a little repose. It was in the month of May, the season when the birds sing, and when all true lovers are thinking of their love." The scene is represented in the accompanying cut, taken from an illuminated manuscript of the romance, of the fifteenth century, preserved in the Bibliothèque de l'Arsenal in Paris. The two lovers are sitting on a grassy bank, supported by a low wall. The garden itself is square, enclosed by walls and towers, with two entrances—one from the castle; the other, through a gate between two towers, from the fields. A pear-tree, in the garden of her father, was the place of meeting of Blonde of Oxford with her lover Jean of Dammartin, and it was thence that he finally carried her away. Similarly, among the songs of the *Romancero François*, the fair Béatris appoints her lover, Count Hugo, to meet her in the garden of her father's castle, and it is from thence she elopes with him. And I might produce many other similar examples.

Our next cut is taken from a manuscript of the fifteenth century in the British Museum (MS., Reg. 15, D. III., fol. 298). It also represents a lady and a gentleman, dressed in the full of the fashion, meeting in a garden.

But one of the most favourite pleasures of the garden appears to have been listening to the singing of the birds. The people of the Middle Ages appear to have had a great taste for singing birds. One of the early lays relates how King Arthur, with his queen, Geneviève, and a party of his courtiers, one day rode out of Cardoil to take their disport in the forest; and, when he entered it,—

Lou chant des oisiax escouta,	He listened to the song of the birds,
Qui moult chantoient doucement.	Which sang very sweetly.
Tant i entendi longuement,	He listened to it so long,
Por ce qu'il en oi plenté,	Because he heard abundance of them,
Que il entra en un pensé	That he fell into a musing
D'une aventure qu'il savoit,	On an adventure which he knew,
Qui avenue li estoit.	Which had happened to him.

Méon, Nouveau Recueil, i. 128.

The writer of the *Roman de la Rose* has given a long enumeration of the variety of birds which filled the garden of Deduit with their songs, and appears to have been chiefly anxious to prevent any one supposing that any bird of which the name was known was absent. There might be seen, he assures us, and heard, nightingales, jays, starlings, wrens, turtle-doves, goldfinches, swallows, larks, titmouses, "calendres," blackbirds, "mauvis," and he even places parrots among them. We can hardly suppose that parrots were seen flying wild and *singing* in a mediæval garden. But a writer of a much more serious character than Guillaume de Lorris has gone still farther in the introduction of strange birds into the mediæval grove. John de Garlande, a scholar of the thirteenth century, says that the fowler (*auceps*) went into his grove to catch, among other birds, a phœnix!

The ladies of the castle, and of the aristocratic class generally, were much attached to pet animals, and especially to birds. In the engravings we have already given, we have seen frequent examples of the small pet

A GARDEN SCENE.

dog, or, as it was usually called by the diminutive of affection, *chiennez*, which seems to have been the ordinary companion of dame or damoiselle. The cat appears never to have been taken as a pet, except among old women who were reputed as witches. A present of a tame bird seems always to

26

have been considered acceptable to a lady. In the *Roman de la Violette*, while Euriaus is lamenting over her griefs, a lad brings her a tame lark :—

Atant un varlés li aporto	At that moment a valet brings her
Une aloie qu'il avoit prise,	A lark which he had caught,
Et l'avoit à chanter aprise.	And had taught to sing.
Euriaut a donné l'aloe,	To Euriaus he has given the lark,
Et de chanter forment li loe.	And highly praises its singing.
La damoisiele prist l'oisiel,	The damoiselle took the bird,
Qu'ele ot rechut del damoisiel	Which she had received from the damoisel,
En son devant le prist à paistre.	And placed it in her lap to feed.

Roman de la V., l. 3898.

This bird was sufficiently tame not to be confined in a cage, for subsequently it flew away, carrying with it a jewel which became, in the course

of the story, the cause of further grief. We see, however, in illuminated manuscripts, that birds in cages were far from uncommon, and in a picture given in a former chapter we have had, in a lady's chamber, a cage with a couple of birds in it. The accompanying cut, taken from a manuscript of the fourteenth century in the library at Paris, gives another example. Hawks and falcons were sometimes made pets, but the favourite bird for the cage was the pie, or magpie, the cunning of which and its skill at learning to talk have made it the hero of many mediæval stories. One of these is told by the knight of La Tour-Landry. There

BIRDS IN A CAGE.

was a fair lady who had a pie in a cage which talked of everything it saw, and the lord of the household happened to have a fine eel, which he kept in his pond with great care for a feast which he intended to give to some of his friends. During his absence, the lady was seized with a longing for the eel, and it was agreed between her and her "ménagière" (housekeeper) that they should eat the eel, and tell their lord that the otter had stolen it; so when the lord returned, and inquired for his eel, he would have been deceived, but the pie never ceased crying out, " My lord, my lady has eaten the eel !" In their anger, the lady and her accomplice plucked all the feathers from the pie's head. And the poor pie was greatly mortified, and from that time, whenever a bald man approached, he shouted out in compassion, " Ah ! you have been telling about the eel !" A jay was also a common cage-bird on account of the same capacity of learning to talk. A curious English political poem of the reign of Edward II., printed by the Percy Society, rather cleverly compares an ignorant priest to a jay in a cage—

Certes also hyt fareth
By a prest that is lewed (*ignorant*)
As by a jay in a cage,
That hymself hath beshrewed (*cursed*);
Gode Englysh he speketh,
But he not (*knows not*) never what.
No more wot (*knows*) a lewd prest
His gospel wat he rat (*which he reads*)
By day.
Than is a lewed prest
No better than a jay.

The parrot, for a similar reason, was a great favourite, but it was a bird not easily obtained, and therefore of rarer occurrence.

In a former cut we have seen a tame squirrel in a cage, and singularly, though of so old a date as the fifteenth century, the cage is of the same revolving construction which has continued to the present day. The cut which we give here, taken from one of the compartments of the Tapestry of Nancy, executed also in the fifteenth century, represents a lady holding a tame squirrel attached by a cord. Tame squirrels are introduced more than once in old mediæval stories.

THE TAME SQUIRREL.

CHAPTER XIV.

WOMANKIND IN THE FEUDAL CASTLE—THE FEUDAL LADY OUT OF THE
CASTLE—WALKING, RIDING, AND DRIVING.

SOCIAL life within the feudal castle was, as we have already seen, sufficiently
free and easy ; but when dames or damoiselles left the precincts of the castle,
they were more studious of personal behaviour, less natural, and more osten-
tatiously proud.   A wide gulf lay between those of gentle blood and the
bourgeoisie and, still more, the peasantry.   The lady could only even be
personally waited upon by those who were of gentle birth, like herself.

The more formal rules of behaviour among the higher class of the
gentility were, of course, taught orally, and we have, therefore, no direct
account of them, but the feudal or semi-feudal age has left us some popular
written codes of the teaching of good manners, which, though intended for
the edification of the *bourgeoisie*, were, no doubt, imitations of the manners
of the castle.   These are found in France and in England.   The author of
the *Menagier de Paris*, compiled in 1393, gives his young wife, to whom it
is addressed, especial advice as to the manners of a lady in walking in
public.   "As you go," he says, "look straight before you, with your eyelids
low and fixed to the ground at a distance of five toises (thirty feet), and not
looking at or turning your eyes to man or woman who may be to your
right or left, nor looking upwards, nor changing your look from one place
to another, nor laughing, nor halting to speak to anybody in the street."
Other similar directions breathe the same spirit.   An English metrical code
of instructions, compiled probably some thirty or forty years later, is printed
in Mr. Furnivall's *Babees Book* under the title of *How the good Wiif taughte
her Doughtir*.   Among other things, which show rather a deficiency in
refinement, the young maiden is taught to be "of seemly semblant, wise,
and of good manner ; " and she is told how she is to walk in public :—

And whan thou goist in the way, go thou not to (*too*) faste ;
Braundische not with thin heed ; thi schuldris thou ne caste ;
Have thou not to manye wordis ; to swere be thou not leefe (*ready*) ;
For alle such maneres comen to an yvel preef (*result*).

In the illuminations of mediæval manuscripts, we now and then see the feudal gentry and ladies in their more ceremonious behaviour, as they exhibited themselves to the outer world. My old friend, M. du Sommerard,

OUTSIDE THE CASTLE.

of the Hôtel de Cluny, published in his Album, from a manuscript now in the Bibliothèque de l'Arsenal at Paris, which was written and illuminated in the fifteenth century for a prince of the house of Burgundy, a picture representing the lords and ladies of a noble or princely household walking out from the castle into the town, and it is known that at this period the court of Burgundy was allowed to be the perfect model of courtly etiquette. This picture is copied in the cut on the preceding page. There is one part of this illumination especially to be remarked, and to be recommended to the attention of modern artists, who are given to represent our forefathers in these old times as walking arm-in-arm, which is a comparatively modern custom. As here represented, when two persons of different sexes, or even if they were of the same sex, walked together, they held each other by the hand. To judge from the literature of the time, it was the height of refinement in the twelfth and thirteenth centuries, to hold each other by the finger only. Even the sainted ladies in Paradise are described as walking in couples, and holding each other by the finger,—

> L'uno tiut l'autre par le dois.
> *La Court de Paradis, in Barbazan,* iii. 139.

And so in the *Roman de la Violette*, at the great festival given by the king, after having taken part in various enjoyments, the guests distribute themselves through the hall in couples (a lady and a gentleman) who take each other by the finger—

Quant il orent assés deduit,	When they had enjoyed themselves enough,
Par la sale s'acoinsent tuit;	They all went in couples through the hall,
Li uns prent l'autre par le doi,	One takes the other by the finger,
Si s'arangierent doi et doi.	And so they arranged themselves two and two.

Roman de la Violette, p. 10.

And in the still earlier period, the hero Ogier le Danois walks with the Princess Gloriande, holding her in the same manner—

Donques enmainne le bon Danois Ogier,	Then leads away the good Dane Ogier,
E Gloriande, qui par le doit le tient.	And Gloriande, who holds him by the finger.

Roman d'Ogier, p. 110.

At the same time, however, and especially in the later feudal period, the ladies and gentlemen, or two or more ladies together, took each other by the hand, and this is the fashion represented in the picture just described, and in other contemporary illuminations. It is often alluded to in the mediæval writers. The reader of Chaucer will remember the scene in *The Flower and the Leaf*, in which the knights are seen strolling into the beautiful fields, to join the ladies who were there following their recreations ;—

> And every lady tooke, fulle womanly,
> By the hond a knight, and forth they yede *(went)*.

And, a few lines farther on,—

> And at the last I cast mine eye aside,
> And was ware of a lusty company,
> That came rominge out of the fielde wide,
> Honde in honde a knight and a lady.

In the Romances of the Round Table, at the festival given by King Leodegan, when visited by King Arthur, the latter mounted hand in hand with the fair princess Genievre, afterwards to be his queen, from the gate up into the palace. So with Gauvain and the maiden in the dit, or lai, of the *Chevalier à l'Espée*, printed in the first volume of Méon's collection of fabliaux—

> Encontre lui sailli Gauvain
> Et la pucele main à main.

It also reminds us in some measure of the picture given above. When ladies walked together, they also usually held hands in this same manner. In the accompanying cut, taken from one of the illuminations of Queen Mary's Psalter, of the beginning of the fourteenth century, a party of damoiselles are seen walking in the fields thus holding each other by the

DAMOISELLES OF THE CASTLE WALKING IN THE FIELDS.

band. It was less common with the men, and seems always to have been regarded as a mark of more than ordinary friendship. In the romance of *Ogier le Danois*, when the Emperor and Ogier become reconciled, the sincerity of their friendship is shown by their walking together hand in hand. Or they walked thus when employed on some ceremonious occasions, as when, in the Romances of the Round Table, the twelve princes of Rome go on a message to King Arthur from the Emperor Lucius, they approach him drawn up two and two, each couple holding by the hand.

Seats were not abundant in the feudal ages, but the ladies appear to have been remarkably skilful at sitting down or squatting on the ground. This was the constant practice when the knights and ladies were taking their recreations in the fields, or in their garden. In the Romances of the Round Table, in the scene between Merlin and Viviane, when the knights and ladies, esquires and maidens, have ceased dancing, the ladies and maidens sit down upon the grass to look on at the exploits of their companions of the other sex at the quintain, and at other such games; and in a somewhat similar scene, which is laid in the Forêt Périlleuse, where King Bohor and his brother, the enchanter Guinebaut, and their companions, find a knight of great distinction, and his lady of no less beauty, seated on thrones, and witnessing likewise a fair party of dancers, the lady rises to salute the king and his friends, and invites them to sit on the grass. A song by one of the trouvères of the thirteenth century, Guillaume de Vinier, begins by telling us that the songster " found two ladies seated in a verdant meadow."

> Dalés un pré verdoiant
> Trovai deus dames seant.

Just in the same manner, in a poem entitled *De la Fols et de la Sage*, of the thirteenth or fourteenth century, the writer pretends to see " two ladies near him seated on the grass," and he proceeds to repeat their conversation—

> Encor m'est-il avis que je doie veoir
> Deus dames delez moi deeus l'erbe seoir.
>
> *Jubinal, Nouveau Recueil*, ii. p. 74.

Not only a seat on the grass, but a meal on the grass, was often a necessity in feudal travelling, when places of entertainment were not found everywhere, and the knightly travellers were obliged to carry their provisions with them on mules or horses of burden. A picture by an Italian artist of the fourteenth century, in a manuscript preserved in the Imperial Library in Paris, represents the miracle of the multiplication of bread described in the Gospel. The accompanying cut gives the portion of it in which the females are seated on the ground receiving their bread, and furnishes a good illustration of the mediæval manner of squatting on the grass. But with the feudal travellers it was performed with somewhat more ceremony, and, in fact, it became sometimes a veritable pic-nic, at least in form. In the romance of *Garin de Montglane*, Garin and his love, the fair Mabile, on their way to the court of the count of Limoges, are obliged not only to feed, but to sleep, on the grass. The preparations for the first are thus described in the romance:—The valet drew from the coffer, or

A MEDIÆVAL PICNIC.

chest, a table-cloth (*nape*), and spread it on the grass. Then he took out bread, and wine, and fish, and pigeon-pies (*pastés de colombiax*), of which latter "there was plenty." He next sought water, to wash. When the repast was finished, as night began to approach, the valet proceeded to make the beds, "as he had been well taught," of fine hay newly made ; he made a thick layer of it, and spread over it white sheets, and a fair coverlet of scarlet and gris.* To gratify any of my fair readers who may be curious

* *Escarlate* was a cloth of that colour, and *gris* was another.

to know the exact manner of this process of bed-making in the fields, in the earlier part of the thirteenth century—for to that period the romance belongs—here are the very words of the original—

> Li vallez fist los lis, qui bien en fu apris,
> De beau fain qui estoit novellement cueillis;
> Graut couche li fait, si li a blans dras mis,
> Et son bel covertoir d'escarlate et de gris.

In illustration of this story, I give here a representation of a mediæval

A MEAL ON THE GRASS.

pic-nic, taken from an illuminated manuscript of the romance of Tristan, of the fifteenth century, preserved in the French Imperial Library (No. 6774).

It was not only in the fields, and in the open air, that the ladies sat upon the ground. The readers of good old François Villon, who wrote in the middle of the fifteenth century, will remember the lines of the *Grand Testament*, in which, speaking of the ladies of Paris, he says,—

Regarde-m'en deux, trois, assises
Sur le bas du ply de leurs robes,
En ces monstiers, en ces eglises.

In the Middle Ages, pews were less in use than in modern times, except as

LADIES IN CHURCH.

belonging to favoured individuals, or to those who were able to buy them, but open seats were still less known, and the ladies, and some of the men also, when listening to the sermon of the preacher, squatted on the ground as they did in the fields. This manner of sitting, or squatting, in church, is well represented in our cut, taken from a manuscript in the British Museum (MS. Harl. No. 2897, fol. 157, v°), which is ascribed to the reign of Henry IV., that is, the earlier part of the fifteenth century. It was, literally, open churches and free sittings. The same volume contains several other similar groups; and another manuscript in our great national collection (MS. Reg. 20 C. VII., fol. 77, r°), which appears to belong to the latter years of the century previous, gives us a similar group of persons sitting on the ground to listen to the preacher.

Before the feudal period, women in general were probably not much accustomed to riding, or, when they rode, they were rather carried by the

THE JOURNEY TO MONTARGIS.

horse, as a beast of burden, than as an animal over which they had command. We have already given examples of ladies riding, both sideways and astride, taken from Anglo-Saxon manuscripts, but it is probable that in Western Europe this was not a very common practice before the feudal period, when Womankind rose to a higher and more independent position in society. And even then it was probably not till a rather late period that the practice became general. It is introduced not unfrequently in the great romances compiled in the latter part of the twelfth and in the thirteenth centuries, but the conducting of the lady on horseback appears in them almost as a ceremony. The ladies appear riding in some of the illuminations to these romances, which, however, are chiefly of the fifteenth century. This is the date of the manuscript of the *Roman de la Violette*, or of Girard de Nevers, which has furnished the accompanying cut, representing Girard and his party on their way to the tournament of Montargis. It is a very good picture of a party of knights and ladies of this date riding on a journey. In one of the poems printed by Jubinal in his *Nouveau Recueil*, the Dit des Anelés, the story turns on the pilgrimage to St. James in Galicia by a knight and his lady. The knight takes his wife with him reluctantly, on account of the hardships and dangers of such a journey; they were well mounted, and were accompanied by an esquire, and by a valet who led the sumpter horse.

> Moult bien furent montez, s'orent i. escuier,
> Et i. loial vallet qui menoit le sommier.

A lady riding prided herself on her dress, and on the richness of her trappings. In the Romances of the Round Table, the damoiselle whom Gauvain encountered in the forest was mounted on a rich palfrey of Niort (a place which appears to have been celebrated for its breed of horses), and she had an ivory saddle, with stirrups of gold, and housing of scarlet. The bridle was of gold, with gold fringe. She wore a bliault or surcoat of white satin, and a wimple of linen and silk, and her head was inclosed in a fine tissue, which formed a protection against the sun. In the romance of Gaufrey (one of the Romans de Geste), the Princess Flordespine is mounted on a valuable mule, the saddle of which was of ivory, inset with gold; on the bridle was set a gem of such power, that it gave light in the darkness of night, and whoever bore it was safe from all disease. The housing was of marvellous workmanship; and attached to it were thirty small bells, which, when the mule went on a gentle amble, produced a wonderful melody. At a later period than this, Chaucer says of his wife of Bath—

> Uppon an amblere esely sche sat,
> Wymplid ful wel, and on hire heed au hat
> As brood as is a bocler or a targe;
> A foot-mantel aboute hire hupes large,
> And on hire feet a paire of spores scharpe.

Among the pictures in an illuminated manuscript in the British Museum (MS. Reg. 20 C. VII., fol. 185, v`), of the latter end of the fourteenth

century, there is one representing the ceremonious entry of the Duchess of
Burgundy into Paris in 1369. The duchess, in her rich costume, is seated
upon her palfrey. Her lady of honour, who rides behind her, is similarly
mounted. I give, in the accompanying cut, a similar subject taken from an
illuminated manuscript of Froissart in the Imperial Library in Paris. It is

QUEEN ISABELLE AND HER LADIES.

of the fifteenth century, and represents the entry into Paris of Isabelle of
Bavaria, the queen of Charles VI. These pictures might almost be taken
as representing scenes of older romance. In the great romance cycle of
Garin le Loherain, we are told how the noble Princess of Maurienne, the
fair Blanchefleur, afterwards the queen of Pepin, made her entry into Paris.
"She had her head bare, and a robe of red samit, or satin, covered gracefully her limbs. The palfrey which carried her had the whiteness of the
fleur-de-lis; its housing was of the utmost richness; and the bridle alone
was worth the weight of a thousand pounds sterling." I will not follow the
poet in his description of the personal beauty of the lady, or of the richness
of her dress.

The ladies of the feudal period, as appears by the pictures in the manuscripts, rode in two manners, either sideways or astride. Usually—probably

riding steady animals—they rode sideways; but when dames of what we may perhaps term a "faster" character mounted spirited horses, and especially when they joined in hunting, they rode astride. It is curious that, in the illuminated manuscript of Chaucer's *Canterbury Tales* in the possession of the Duke of Sutherland, the wife of Bath, who claims the possession of a masculine character, is represented riding astride, while the prioress and the nun ride sideways. In my next chapter I shall give some pictures of mediæval ladies riding in this manner. But there is one circumstance especially deserving of remark. In all the illuminations of manuscripts with which I am acquainted, whether Anglo-Saxon, Anglo-Norman, French, or English, older than the beginning of the sixteenth century, the lady, when riding sideways, always sits with her legs on the right side of the horse, with her left hand towards its head. Here is a little picture of the Virgin Mary conducted by Joseph into Egypt, in which she sits in this manner. It is taken from a manuscript of the thirteenth century, in a private collection in Paris. We have seen the Anglo-Saxon ladies so seated. We have just seen the ladies on their way to the tournament of Montargis, and Queen Isabelle and her attendants, riding in the same manner. I know only of one example to the contrary. A manuscript in the British Museum (MS. Harl., No. 2278), of the latter half of the fifteenth century, contains a copy of the poet Lydgate's *Life of St. Edmund*, rather copiously illuminated.

THE JOURNEY INTO EGYPT.

In one of these illuminations (fol. 92, r'), illustrating one of the posthumous miracles of the saint, we see a lady riding on a horse, on the same side as ladies ride at present. But the story of the miracle is, that three ladies, one of whom was deaf, the other dumb, and the third deprived of the use of her hands and feet, went together to the shrine of the saint to be cured; and, as the only way of conducting thither the last of these, they put her upon a horse. She is not, properly speaking, riding, but is placed upon a strong beast, in a knight's saddle, in an awkward position, and has evidently no command over the horse. There can, I think, be no doubt that, down to the end of the fifteenth century, or, I may say, to the reign of Henry VIII., ladies riding sideways always sat with their legs on the right side of the horse, and with their left hand to its head. I have not yet been able to ascertain the exact time at which the change took place, or how it arose, but I suppose the cause to have been that, about this time, the ladies abandoned the slow and easy-going animals they had formerly employed, to ride more spirited horses. It seems evident that, to possess a full command over the horse, the rider must have her right hand to his head. My conjecture as to the

QUEEN MARY AND QUEEN ELIZABETH.

date of the change seems to be justified by a fact. The two daughters of Henry VIII., Mary and Elizabeth, became both queens of England, and had, therefore, their great seals, on one side of each of which the queen is represented on horseback. Both are seated on the left side of the horse as at present, as will be seen in the accompanying cut, in which the queens are represented as they appear on their great seals.

During the ages of which we have been speaking, the ladies rode either the mule or the palfrey. Previous to the feudal period the mule appears to have been little known in Western Europe, for the only name the Anglo-Saxons had for it was *mul*, which, of course, is merely the Latin *mulus*, and we only find it used in translating the Latin word in ecclesiastical writings. The animal, itself, was apparently of an inferior breed, and used only for menial purposes. The more honourable use of the mule was, probably, derived from the Saracens of Spain. I am informed by a friend, Dr. Hyde Clarke, who has lived long in the East, that the mule of the East is a much finer animal than the mule of our northern climates, and that it is especially calculated for a lady's riding. "A fine mule," he tells me, "is showy, will go at a good rate, with a steady pace, and an easy seat, and work his way over mountain-paths, and rocky defiles, and among muddy and stony ways." In the Carlovingian romances, which represent especially the tradition of the Saracenic period, ladies of the highest rank are introduced riding upon the mule (*mulet*). Thus, in the romance of *Huon de Bordeaux*, the Duke Huon, after marrying a Saracen princess, when starting on his way home, mounts his fair Duchess on a mule,—

> Il fait la dame sor i. mulet monter;—

and in the romance of *Gaufrey*, as just quoted, the Princess Flordespine is mounted on a mule. So, in *Parise la Duchesse*, the duchess is mounted on an "ambling mule,"

> Sor i. mulet anblant font la dame monter,

and again, further on,—

> Sor i. mulet anblant ont la dame monté.

Twice in the romance of *Garin le Loherain*, a lady of high rank is introduced mounted on an "Arabian mule." I might bring forward other examples of this use of the mule from the romances, and from the mediæval poetry of rather a later date. In the little poem of *Hueline and Aiglantine*, printed in Méon's collection, we are told that:—

Dame Eglantine et une mule,	The lady Eglantine had a mule,
Miendre de li ne fu ainz nule,	Better than it there was never none,
Tote blanche con un cristax ;	All white as a crystal ;
Qui sor li siet ne sant nul max.	Whoever sits upon it feels no evil.
Soef la porte l'ambléure,	It carries her gently at an amble,
Qu'il ne set nule autre aléure,	For it knows no other pace,
Mais tant par vet sinplemant	But goes so very easily
Que rosée ne sant noiant.	That she does not even feel the dew.
Frain a où chief de grant paraje,	It has a rein at the head of great quality,
Qui moult fu fait de grant barnaje;	Which was made with very great richness;
Le chevece fu tote d'or,	The bridle was all of gold,
En Eegipte la firent Mor ;	The Moors made it in Egypt ;
Les regnes sont á or batues,	The reins are of beaten gold,

28

De fil de soie bien tissue.	With silk-thread well woven.
Sele ot belo, et bien ovrée,	Sho had a fair saddle, and well worked,
De tote part bien atornée,	Well adorned in every part,
Et moult i ot assises pierres,	And very many gems were set there,
Esmeraudes qui furent chieres.	Emeralds, which were of great worth.
De paile fu la coverture,	The housing was of silk,
Qui cele a, d'autre n'a cure ;	She who has it, cares for no other ;
Car tant par est de grant bealté,	For it is of so very great beauty,
Que jà sa per ne troverez.	That you will never find its equal.
Li euel sont de blanc argeut,	The rings are of white silver,
Sororé sont et avenant.	They are doubly gilt and handsome.
Li estrier sont d'or noielé,	The stirrups are of gold nielloed,
Bien forbi et bien atorné.	Well polished and well arranged.
Uns esperons ot la pucele	The maiden had a spur,
Dont ne vos os dire novele,	Of which I dare not give you a description,
Car plus sont chier si esperon	For her spurs are of more worth
Que li roiaumes Salemon.	Than Salomon's kingdom.

Méon, Nouveau Recueil, tom. i., p. 359.

It will be seen that, when ladies rode abroad, they prided themselves on the beauty of their trappings.

As the age of feudalism advanced, the mule appears gradually to have gone out of use for riding, and the ladies took to the palfrey. The palfrey always held a high place in the stable, and the great ladies often rode it; but the mule seems to have been considered as having a steadier and more certain pace. In that branch of the great romance cycle of the family of Lorraine, which tells of the death of Begon of Belin, the fair duchess Beatris, grieved at seeing her husband Begon in sorrowful mood, says, to console him, "Why are you thoughtful, sire Begon ; you, so high, so noble, so bold a knight ? Are you not a rich man in the world ? Gold and silver fill your coffers ; vair and *gris* (the richest cloths) your wardrobes ; on your perches, you have hawks and falcons ; in your stables, abundance of steeds, palfreys, mules, and horses of value." Begon's reply reveals one of the finer features of the spirit of feudalism. "Lady, you say true ; but you have mistaken in one thing. Wealth does not consist in rich cloths, in money treasured up, in horses of value, or great palfreys. It consists in friends, in kindred ; the heart of a single man is worth the gold of a whole country." We see here the palfrey and the mule reckoned among the most valuable animals of the baronial stud, and the former placed first. In this same cycle of romance, as already stated, we have the Princess Blancheﬂeur entering Paris mounted on a palfrey. In the later poetry, ladies are continually introduced riding upon palfreys, and the mule was soon abandoned. Women rode more generally, and more spiritedly ; and while, on one hand, the practice of riding astride was no longer considered becoming, on the other, as I suppose, as the fair riders felt the want of greater command over the horse, the seat was changed from the right side of the horse to the left. As I have just remarked, so far as I have yet been able to trace it, the change appears to have taken place about the beginning of the sixteenth century.

In primeval times, women were, probably, carried in carts or waggons, when the family moved from one place to another, if the latter were rich or

THE LADY VENUS IN HER CHAR.

powerful enough to command such means of locomotion, and these were no doubt, very clumsy and inconvenient. In later times, when ladies rode, this mode of carriage still continued in use; but, apparently, only on special occasions. The carriage, itself, was called, in Latin, *carra;* and in French, and later English, a *car*, or *char*, for the modern languages had a tendency to soften the pronunciation of the *c*. Ducange quotes an early Latin treatise on the miracles of St. Liudegar, the writer of which, speaking of a lady and her daughter, says, "The mother and daughter, placed together in a char (*in una carra mater simul et filia positæ*), were brought to our church." In the feudal period, these chars became objects of pride and ostentation, and were used on great ceremonial occasions. A curious poem, entitled, *Le Tournoiement aus Dames*, which M. Paulin Paris thinks may be ascribed to so early a period as the year 1185, tells us how knighthood, having so far fallen into neglect that tournaments had ceased, the ladies consulted together, and decided on holding a tournament of their own. Among those who attended this tournament are introduced the names of nearly all the great ladies of France. .Among others was the Countess of Britany, who summoned all her ladies to come in chars, for the purpose, as she said, of making greater pomp—

La contesse... si a mandée	The countess has summoned
Toutes ses dames sanz eschars	All her ladies, without sparing,
Qu'elles vienent dedenz les chars,	That they come in chars,
Qu'ainsi, ce dist, le voudra fere,	For thus, she said, she would do,
Por plus le beuban contrefere.	To better represent the pomp.

In the thirteenth century, these chars were evidently looked upon as marks of pride, and as belonging only to people of rank and gentility; for Philip le Bel, King of France, by an ordonnance given in 1294, forbade the use of chars to the wives of citizens. We have seen in a former chapter, in the *Roman de la Rose*, how the lady Venus ordered her six doves to be harnessed to her char. Venus's char is represented in the preceding cut, taken from the beautiful illuminated manuscript of that book in the

A LADY'S CHAR OF THE FOURTEENTH CENTURY.

British Museum. On the reconciliation of Richard II. with the citizens of London, when the king and his queen entered the city in pompous procession, she had, in her train, two chars filled with her court ladies. One of them was overturned, and Richard of Maidstone tells us, exultingly, how, in their fall, the ladies exposed their persons unbecomingly to the gaze and jeers of the multitude, as he looked at it as a judgment of heaven upon the extravagance of the times, of which he considered the use of chars as one of the signs.

Our next cut is taken from a manuscript of the fourteenth century, known as the *Luttrell Psalter*, some of the illuminations of which have been engraved by the Society of Antiquaries. It will be seen that it is a long cumbrous vehicle, dragged along by a long team of horses, with two drivers or postillions. From their heads seen through the windows, the carriage appears to be filled with ladies of rank.

A LADY IN HER CAR.

In the fifteenth century, the use of the char appears to have become common, and we meet, more frequently, with pictorial representations of it in the illuminated manuscripts. The one given in our cut above is taken from a manuscript in the British Museum (MS. Reg. 14, E. V. fol. 408) of the fifteenth century. It is the usual form of the char, as we see it in manuscripts, and as it probably remained unaltered from a very

early period. It is an open carriage, or van, with a body like that of a
waggon, and an arched roof supported upon wooden posts. Inside were
seats and cushions for the ladies, and other conveniences and luxuries. The
whole carriage was sometimes adorned with rich ornaments, and covered
with curtains. The seat for the driver was outside, in front, or often he
sat, like a postillion, on one of the horses. Our next cut furnishes a good

TULLIA DRIVING OVER HER FATHER'S BODY.

example of the ladies' char. It is taken from a finely illuminated manuscript of the French translation of *Valerius Maximus*, of the latter part of
the fifteenth century, preserved in the Imperial Library in Paris (No.
6984), and represents the story of Tullia, the queen of Tarquin the Proud,
ordering her charioteer to drive over the body of her slaughtered father,
Servius Tullus.

CHAPTER XV

It is a curious fact, that the writer of the *Ménagier de Paris*, so often quoted in these chapters, which consists of a code of instructions for his wife in the regulation and management of herself and her household, places hawking as one of the accomplishments of the lady, and under her especial direction, and gives her a rather long treatise on the subject; and that the earliest treatise on hunting and hawking, written in the English language, was the work of a fair lady of knightly family, who was, moreover, the superior of a monastic house. This was dame Juliana Berners, prioress of the nunnery of Sopewell, near St Alban's, and supposed to have been the daughter of King Richard the Second's favourite, Sir James Berners, and to have lived during the first half of the fifteenth century. However, we have other reasons for knowing that, both in France and in England, the feudal ladies, were passionately fond of the chace. A great and learned ecclesiastic of the twelfth century, John of Salisbury, who condemns the practice of hunting as one of the most oppressive manifestations of feudal tyranny, bears witness to the eagerness with which the ladies of his time followed the sport of hawking; and, to come to a later period, it was at a grand hunting party, given by King Louis XII. to the Archduke Maximilian, that the wife of the latter, Marie of Burgundy, was thrown from her horse, and killed. Catherine de Medicis was a great huntress of the stag, and a little poem in French, belonging to the early ages of printing, entitled, *The Women's Wishes (Les Souhaitz des Femmes)*, makes the knight's lady wish for the green woods, with her hounds in leash, to hunt the stag, and that her husband might be bold in courage.

> Et moy, qui suis chevaleresse,
> Je souhaitte au vert boscage
> Au cerf chasser limiers en lesse,
> A mon mary hardy courage.

The coarse caricaturist of feudal society in its last stage of decadence, François Rabelais, describing the freedom of manners of the people of his model convent of Theleme, says, "If any one of them said, ' Let us go to the sports in the fields,' they all went. If it were to hawk or to hunt, the ladies mounted on fair hackneys, with their richly-caparisoned palfrey, carried each on her fist, genteely gloved, either a hawk, or a laneret, or a merlin." *

Hunting was, indeed, one of the great safty-valves of feudalism, and one which had been received from a period far more remote. It was the active occupation of the old primeval chieftain when not engaged in war, and it similarly relieved the male inhabitants of the castle from that tedious inactivity which they felt as the greatest of curses. In other words, it kept them from worst mischief. One of the cynegetical writers of the Middle Ages, Gaston Phœbus, speaks rather boastingly of hunting in a moral point of view. By hunting, he says, you avoid " the sin of idleness "—(*le péché d'oyseuse*)—" and," he says, " since he who flies the seven mortal sins, according to our faith, is to be saved, therefore every good hunter will be saved "—(*Car qui fuyt les sept péchiez mortels, selon nostre foy, il devroit estre sauvé; donc bon veneur sera sauvé*). I do not make myself responsible for the truth of the reasoning, although it is put very logically.

But, like everything else under the feudal system, hunting was now placed under exact rules and forms, which had not been defined before, and these were soon committed to writing, for the instruction and use of the feudal household; for skill in hunting and falconry had become one of the great accomplishments of a gentleman, and among the finest features of a noble character stood prominent the love of hounds and hawks. At first, these treatises were short, and composed in verse, for the purpose, no doubt, of committing them to memory. The oldest known treatise of this description, which is in French verse, and belongs to the close of the thirteenth century, is entitled the " *Dict de la chace dou cerf*" (the ditty of stag-hunting). In the century following, these treatises became more elaborate, and some of them became very celebrated and popular. Among the first comes the work of an anonymous writer, the *Book of King Modus* (*Livre du roy Modus*), compiled in 1328. Gaces de la Vigne wrote a French treatise on hunting in 1359; Gaston Phœbus, already mentioned, in 1387; and Hardouin, lord of Fontaine-Guérin, in 1394. All these were very

* Si disoit, allons à l'esbat ès champs, tous y alloient. Si c'estoit pour voller ou chasser, les dames montées sus belles hacquenées avecques leurs palefroy gourrier, sus le poing mignonnement enguantelé portoient chascune ou un esparvier, ou un laneret, ou un esmerillou.—*Rabelais, Gargantua*, liv. i., c. 57.

aristocratic authors. These French books were accepted as authorities on the subject in England, but some of our Englishmen became, in course of time, ambitions of furnishing us with treatises of our own, though these, also, were at first written in French. The earliest bears the name of Twety, who is said to have been chief huntsman to King Edward II., though his book appears to have been compiled from the works just quoted. It was written originally in French, but there is an English translation of it, preserved in manuscripts of the fifteenth century. Then comes a treatise on hunting, called the *Master of the Game*, which is dedicated to the Prince of Wales, afterwards Henry V., and is said to have been compiled by that Edward, Duke of York, who was slain at Azincourt. Lastly comes the treatise of dame Juliana Berners, already spoken of, which was the first book on the subject *printed* in the English language.

With the feudal sentiments attached to it, hunting received several technical and more or less ceremonious names. The most comprehensive was that of *chace*, or *chasse*, in mediæval Latin, *chacea*, or *cacea*, signifying an extent of territory abandoned to wild beasts; but the derivation of the word appears to be unknown. There was, however, an older and a more dignified word, formed from the purer Latin *renatura* (hunting), which had, probably, been the name in use in Gaul ever since the Roman times, and which, in French, was moulded into *venerie*. This became what we may, perhaps, call the higher title of the science, and was the more fashionable one for books on the subject: that of Twety was entitled, *Le Art de Venerie*. *La chasse* was the more comprehensive name in use in Norman England, as in France, and embraced animals which were not objects of the chase acknowledged under the title of *renatura*. We Englishmen have preserved, through all changes, our own Anglo-Saxon word, *huntung* (hunting).

Venerie, therefore, which was considered in feudal times as the noblest division of the art, included only the animals which were acknowledged in the earlier mediæval *renatura*, and which were those hunted in primitive times. There were only four beasts of venerie; the hare, the hart, the wolf, and the boar, which are thus enumerated in verse in the English translation of Twety.

> To venery y caste me fyrst to go,
> Of wheche iiij. bestis be, that is to say
> The hare, the herte, the wulf he, the wylde boor also;
> Of venery for sothe ther be no moe.

There were five other beasts " of chace;" the buck, the doe, the fox, the martin, and the roc; and some others, of less account, which might be included within the province of the hunter.

These animals, of course, were hunted with hounds, of which there were several kinds employed in the Middle Ages. Among them, one of the best known, was the *rache*, or scenting-hound, which appears to have been a strong dog, and which was used especially in hunting the stag. It was, no doubt, our modern hound. The greyhound was, as now, the dog used for hunting the hare, and it was the favourite of the ladies. In an early English manuscript of poetry in the Cambridge University Library (Ff. v. 48, fol. 119), we are told of a lady riding forth on her palfrey attended by both these kinds of dogs, greyhounds and raches :—

> She was as feyre and as gode,
> And as riche on hir palfray;
> Hir greyhoundis fillid with the dere (*deer's*) blode,
> Hir rachis coupuld, be my fay (*by my faith*).

Here the greyhounds were, evidently, employed in the chace of the deer, as well as the raches. Another dog, the spaniel, was used in hawking, and, of course, was a ladies' dog. One of the early English treatises on the

HUNTING THE STAG.

chace, tells us that, " hys crafte is for the perdrich (*partridge*) and the quail; and, when taught to couche (*set*), he is very serviceable to the fowlers who take those birds with nets." The spaniel was also used for hunting the hare. The author of the *Ménagier de Paris* gives his wife especial instructions for selecting and teaching their spaniels according as they were intended for coursing the hare, or for hawking.

It is probable that the lady of the castle, however spirited and cou-

rageous she may have been, did not go personally to hunt the wild boar or
the wolf. But we have already seen that the feudal ladies did hunt the
stag, and we can produce pictorial evidence of the manner in which they
entered into the sport. The illuminator of a manuscript in the British
Museum (MS. Reg. 2 B. VII.), so often spoken of by the name of Queen
Mary's Psalter, took a fancy to adorn the foot-margins of his pages of
vellum with subjects chosen from the field-sports of the day, as well as with
others of a kindred character. The manuscript and its illuminations
belong to the beginning of the fourteenth century, perhaps, to the reign of
Edward II. One of these, which is copied in our cut, represents a lady and
her damoiselle engaged in the chase of the stag. The lady is mounted astride
on her palfrey, and is blowing the mote with her horn like a true hunts-
woman. Her rache, probably, is attacking the animal courageously; but
the skill of the damoiselle, with her unerring arrow, has most effectually
decided his fate. The use of the horn was sufficiently elaborate, and required
skill and experience on the part of the blower, whether gentleman or lady.
It formed a sort of instrument of communication, not only among the
hunters themselves, but between them and their dogs, and the language in
which it was used, like almost everything feudal, was French. Twety is
very particular in his instructions on this point. When the hunter has got
sight of the hart, he is taught to " blowe after one mote, ij. motes, and if myn
howndes come not hastily (*immediately*) to me as y wolde, I shalle blowe iiij.
motes, and for to haste hem to me, and for to warne the gentelys that the
hert is sene, than shalle I rechace on myn howndis iij. tymes, and whan he
is ferre fro me, than shalle y chase him in this manner, *Trout, trout, tro ro
rot, trout, trout, tro ro rot, trou ro rot, trou ro rot;* "   . because " that
the hert is sene, and y wot (*know*) nevere whedir that myn houndys be
become fro myn meyné (*company*)." Other combinations of motes are
ordered for different incidents of the chace. And so with the hare, " if ye
hounte at the hare, ye shalle sey, atte uncouplyng, *Hors de couple, avaunt;*
and after iij. tymes, *Sohow, sohow, sohow!* and ye shalle seye, *Sa, sa, cy,
avaunt, sohow.* And if ye se that your houndes have good wyl to renne, and
be feer (*far*) from you, ye shalle sey thus, *How amy, how amy, swef, mon amy,
swefe.* And if ony fynde of hym where he hath ben, as Rycher or Bemond,
ye shalle seye, *Oiez à Bemond le vaillaunt, que quide trovere le coward, ou le
court cow!*" *i.e.,* " Hark to Bemond the valiant, who believes he has found
the coward with the short tail." Richer and Bemond, it must be understood, were names of dogs, and coward was a popular name for the hare.

The ladies of the castle, undoubtedly, took an active part in the hunting

of the hare; but their exploits in coursing are not frequently alluded to,
and I have not seen any mediæval drawing representing it. Another animal,
however, which might almost be classed with it, seems to have been an
object of great amusement to the ladies of the castle; at least this may be
presumed from its not unfrequent appearance among the sports in the

THE CHACE OF THE RABBIT.

margins of Queen Mary's Psalter. This was the rabbit which was
called in French, a *connil*, and in English, a *coney*, from the Latin word,
cuniculus. In one of the illuminations alluded to, which is given in the
cut above, two ladies are seen in the warren hunting the rabbit. The
first, and, perhaps, we may say the principal lady, is armed with a bow,

RABBIT-HUNTING EXTRAORDINARY.

and what was called a bolt (in French, a *boujon*), an arrow with a large
head, for striking birds and small animals, which seems to have been the
peculiar weapon of the fair sex. The *Ménagier de Paris* recommends this
weapon to the ladies for shooting at blackbirds, thrushes, jays, and wood-
cocks, when they sought shelter from the hawk in a bush. The other lady

is armed with a simpler weapon, apparently a mere club, with which she
seeks to knock the rabbits on the head. The latter appear to be under no
great fear of their assailants. The feudal ladies seem to have been well-
practised in the use of the bow. Another cut, which we here give from the
same manuscript, was evidently drawn with a satirical aim. The lady has
taken her little pet dog to the chace, and has started the game without
difficulty; but she finds it much less easy to encourage her animal to the
attack, while the rabbits, which look more formidable by their magnitude,
appear to be rather amused than otherwise with his comical figure and
costume.

There was another way of taking rabbits, which appears to have been a
favourite among the ladies, that of drawing them out of their burrows with
ferrets. The use of the ferret for this purpose is certainly of great antiquity,

FERRETING THE RABBIT.

for Pliny (Hist. N., lib. viii., c. 81) speaks of it as common among the
Romans in Italy; and we can have no doubt of its being general in the
Middle Ages. Ducange quotes a record of Dauphiné which furnishes us
with the sum at which, at one time at least, these animals were valued, for it
states that for four ferrets for catching rabbits was paid the sum of twenty
deniers (*pro iv. furetis ad capiendum cuniculos xx. den. gr.*). An act of the
thirteenth year of the reign of Richard II. prohibits any priest or other
clerk, not possessed of a benefice to the yearly amount of ten pounds, among
other things, from employing ferrets to take rabbits, under a penalty of one
year's imprisonment; and it appears from Branthôme's account of the
transactions of François I. with the Pope, that the Italian clergy at that
time were fond of hunting rabbits with ferrets. Our next cut, taken from

Queen Mary's Psalter, will leave no doubt of the use which the English ladies made of the ferret in the time of Edward II.

The ladies were, no doubt, fond of their dogs; but they were no less attached to their hawks or falcons. In the book of *Le Roy Modus*, two ladies are introduced disputing, in verse, on the superiority of the pastime of dogs or of birds, and they decide in favour of the latter. A great English theologian of the twelfth century, John of Salisbury, as already cited, has left us a very ungallant reflection on the love of the ladies for hawking. He alleges, as a proof of the frivolous character of this pastime, that the "less worthy" sex was the most skilful of the two in bird-hawking, which, he says, we might make an accusation against nature herself, that "the less worthy are always the more prone to rapine." What he adds further gives us rather a curious glimpse of social life at that period. "Although many exercise hunting that, under pretext of it, they may be more sparing in their expenditure, be more rarely at home, more frequently guests at the table of others, and avoid a multitude of visitors; while they wander about the woods, wilds, and lakes, clad in meaner clothes, and satisfied with more frugal fare; while they console with the show of pleasure, or rather of vanity, their companions and followers, whom the hunger of fasting emaciates, and the torments of nakedness afflict, and whom excessive labour exhausts."[*] Thus the feudal chieftain sought, in the chace, a means of escaping for a time the profusion and display of the castle.

That falconry was considered in the Middle Ages as especially the province of the ladies of the household is evident, from the circumstance, that the author of the *Ménagier de Paris* makes it an important part of his domestic instructions to his wife. Hawking was a sport of great antiquity in Western Europe, and appears to have come to us from our Northern and Teutonic ancestors. It was in high repute among the Anglo-Saxons, and the name of the bird not uncommonly entered into the composition of proper names. It was eagerly adopted into feudal society, and became, as

---

[*] "Quod vel ex eo mecum conjicies quod deterior sexus in avium venatione potior est. In quo poteras naturam arguere, nisi nosses quia deteriora semper proniora sunt ad rapinam. Inanis etenim est et admodum laboriosa, et quae damna sumptuum nunquam successuum utilitate compensat. Licet plurimi venationem exerceant ut sub eo praetextu sumptus faciant parciores, domi rarius, saepius in mensa aliena, multitudinem vitant, dum silvas, saltus, lacusque circumeunt, pannis induti vilioribus, frugalioribus contenti cibis; dum consortes et famulos quos macerat jejuniorum inedia et tormenta nuditatis affligunt, quosque labor immoderatus exhaurit, voluptatis aut potius vanitatis imagine consolentur.—*Johan. Saresb. Policraticus,* lib. i., c. 4.

already stated, a favourite occupation of the ladies. The hawk became more especially the personal companion of its master or mistress, as much of its utility depended upon its familiarity, and hence, he or she had to attend personally to its breeding or feeding. The author of the *Ménagier de Paris* is especially minute in his directions to his lady on the treatment of the hawks in their domesticity. It was of the utmost importance that the hawk should remain constant to the fist till directed to fly at its prey, and be always ready to return when called. The lady of the *Ménagier de Paris* is told that, while her hawk is still in its infancy, she must " continue to hold it often on the fist, and among people, as much and as long as you can." And farther on in these instructions, the husband goes on, " But at this point in the breeding of the hawk, it is well, more than before, to hold it on the fist, and carry it into the courts of law, and among people in the churches and other assemblies, and in the streets, and hold it, day and night, as continually as one can." Another early French writer on hunting and hawking, Gaces de la Vigne, recommends people to carry the falcon on the fist wherever people were assembled, in church, or elsewhere :—

> Là où les gens sont amassés,
> Soit en l'église ou autre part.

As hunting and hawking were not permitted, except among the aristocratic class, it became a distinctive mark of a gentleman or lady to carry a hawk on the fist, whether riding or walking, and they are thus constantly represented in the pictures and illuminations. So far was it from being considered at all blamable to enter the churches in this way, that the ecclesiastics and monks of rank and position adopted the fashion themselves, and appeared in their places in the sacred edifice with the hawk on the fist. It is true that this practice was condemned by the stricter part of the clergy, but it was persisted in, in spite even of the canons of the church. Several figures of women as well as men with the hawk on the fist will be seen in

THE LADY AND HER HAWKS.

the illustrations to our previous chapters. The accompanying cut, taken from the illuminations of a manuscript in the British Museum (MS. Reg. 10,

E. IV.) of the fourteenth century, represents a lady tending her hawks on the perch; she wears the large thick gloves, which protected the hand when the bird was seated on it.

In reading these early books on falconry—the *Ménagier de Paris*, for example—we cannot but be astonished at the elaborate manner in which the birds were bred, and the rich and delicate meats with which they were fed. Every part of the treatment of the hawk was conducted with the utmost ceremony, and, when in use, it carried small bells on its legs, which were made of silver, as finely toned as possible, and two straps of leather, called

THE HAWK STRIKING THE HERON.

jesses, attached to them, by which it was held down to the hand. It wore also a little cap, or hood, by which it was hood-winked when not flying at the game, and which was taken off when the game was started. Different species of the hawk were allotted to persons of the different grades and ranks of society. Thus, we are told that the eagle and the vulture belonged to the emperor, from which we must, no doubt, understand that the emperor was not expected to go often a hawking; or, perhaps, he descended a step from his rank, and used the gerfalcon, which was allotted to the king. A merlin was the ladies' hawk, and the hobby that for a young man.

The accompanying cut, also taken from Queen Mary's Psalter, represents a party of ladies hawking on foot. One of them holds the bird hooded on her fist, to which it is attached by the jesses, which were knotted between the fingers. The other has let her hawk go, and it has struck a heron. They are accompanied by a leash of dogs, which we may suppose to have been intended for spaniels.

The dogs were very commonly dispensed with when hawking on the river, which was the favourite scene of this diversion, especially with the ladies, and the favourite game with them was the heron. This was so much the case, that the common phrase for going a hawking was, "going to the river" (*aller en rivière*). A political poem, entitled, *The Vows of the Heron*, printed in my *Political Poems and Songs*, describes the season for this sport as being "in the month of September, when summer is in the decline, when the gay small birds have lost their note, and the vines dry up, and the grapes are ripe, and the trees shed their leaves, and the roads become covered with them" :—

> Ens el mois de Setembre, qu'estés va à declin,
> Que cil oisillon gay ont perdu lou latin,
> Et si sakent les vignes, et meurent li rosin,
> Et despoillent li arbre, et coeuvrent li chemin.

Then Robert of Artois, who was an exile at King Edward's court in London (it was the year 1338), was seized with the desire of going to the chace, because he called to mind the very noble country of France the lauded, from which he was banished. That day he went hawking (*à la voler*—the common phrase for hawking was "flying," *i.e.*, flying the hawk), over fields and over heaths, he carries a little falcon which he had bred, they call it a muskadin falcon in that country ; he went hawking along the river until he has caught a heron.

> Che jour ala voler par camps et par larris,
> Un petit faucon porte, qui de lui fu nourris,
> Un faucon muskadin l'apellent on pais ;
> Tant vola par rivière qu'il a un heron prins.

The ladies did not always hawk on foot ; and a picture in the manuscript, known as Queen Mary's Psalter, which we copy on the next page, gives an interesting group of a party on horseback, consisting of two ladies following the sport, attended by a gentleman. Their game is here water-fowls, and it was still *en rivière*. As it will be seen, instead of dogs to rouse the game, they have here a man, or a lad, who is employed to frighten them. It may be remarked, that, in the early Anglo-Saxon manuscripts, wherever a hawking scene is introduced, it is always laid on the bank of a river.

It will be seen in this cut, as well as in a former cut in the present chapter, that, as I have said before, the ladies, when they rode on hunting, sat upon the horse astride. In another manuscript in the British Museum

(MS. Reg., 20 D. I.), written in the fourteenth century, apparently towards the south of France, the ladies appear all riding astride in men's saddles.

There were other methods of rousing the water-fowl, one of which was by the beating of a tabor. An English chronicler of the twelfth century, Radulphus de Diceto, tells an anecdote of a youth belonging to the household of the Bishop of London, who went hawking along the river for teal, and rose one "by the sound of that instrument, which is called by those who hawk on the banks of the rivers a *tabor*" (*juxta sonitum illius instrumenti*

LADIES HAWKING.

quod a ripatoribus vocatur tabur). This use of the tabor was so common, and lasted during so long a period, that we see a picture of men hawking with the tabor among the misereres, or carved seats, in the cathedral of Gloucester, which are of the fifteenth century; and ladies hawking with the tabor are introduced among the illuminations of a manuscript in the fourteenth century, in the British Museum (MS. Reg. 10 E. IV.), of which we give the part representing the damoiselle raising the game in the opposite cut.

The hawking season began with the month of August, and during the

early part of that month appears to have been confined to partridges—at
least, so says the *Ménagier de Paris*—and the time of the day recommended
for the sport was from very early in the morning to tierce, or nine o'clock.
The feudal ladies were early risers. In the month of July, we are told, the
heat was too great. The partridge was an especially favourite bird with the
ladies to hawk. In the middle of August the quail came in, and the two
following months appear to have been the busiest of the year. After the
end of September, when partridges and quails began to fail, the hawking
became more general and indiscriminate, and the ladies were allowed to

BEATING THE RIVER.

"fly" at almost anything in the shape of a bird, including fieldfares,
thrushes, and even magpies and jays.

The early printed volume, already spoken of as bearing the name of
Juliana Berners, is not limited to hunting and hawking, but it contains also
a treatise on fishing, at least on fishing with the angle. There seems, however, to be some doubt whether this treatise be the work of dame Juliana or
not, and perhaps it will be safest not to insist upon the authorship. Here it
is pleaded in favour of this recreation that, instead of fatiguing those who
partake in it, like hunting and hawking, and leading to disappointments, it is
a pastime soothing to the spirit, which leads to the tranquil enjoyment of the
beauties of nature, and which is the most profitable to mind and body of all
games. If the angler at last be unsuccessful, and return home without any
fish, he is not without good consolation; for " atte the leest he hath his
holsom walke and mery at his ease, a swete ayre of the swete savoure of the
meede (*meadow*) floures, that makyth hym hungry; he hereth the melodyous

armony of fowles; he seeth the yonge swannes, heerons, duckes, cotes (*water-hens*), and many other foules wyth theyr brodes (*broods*), whyche to me seemyth better than alle the noyse of houndes, the blastes of hornys, and the scrye (*screaming*) of foulis, that hunters, fawkeners, and foulers can

LADIES FISHING WITH THE ANGLE.

make. And yf the angler take fysshe, surely thenne is there noo man merier than he is in his spyryte." A manuscript copy of this treatise, the language of which I will modernise, adds here another advantage of the practice of angling :— " Also, whoso will use the game and disport of angling, he must take heed to this sentence of the old proverb, which is in these verses :—

> Surge, miser, mane, sed noli surgere vane :
> Sanctificat, sanat, ditat quoque surgere mane.

That is to say, he must rise early, which thing is right profitable to men in this wise: one is for health of the soul, for it shall cause a man to be holy if ever he shall be well set to good; the second is, it shall cause bodily health, and shall cause him to live long; the third, it shall cause him to be rich worldly and ghostly [*i.e.*, in this world and spiritually], in goods and goodness." I give the concluding bit of advice, again in the orthography of the original, on account of its quaintness: it was not, probably, always followed by the hunter and hawker from the feudal castle. "Also, that ye broke noo mannys heggys (*hedges*) in goynge abowte your dysportes, ne (*nor*) opyn noo mannys gates but that ye shytte (*shut*) theym ageyn. Also, ye shall not use this forsayd crafty dysporte for no covetysenes to thencresynge (*the increasing*) and spayringe of your money only, but pryncypally for your solace and to cause the helthe of your body, and specyally of your soule." The writer explains his (or her, if it be dame Juliana,) meaning further by insisting that, as you avoid taking any companions with you when you go to the river to angle, you are less liable to interruption, and therefore may say your prayers at your ease. Such seems to have been the tone of popular sentiment in England towards the middle of the fifteenth century.

The accompanying cut represents ladies fishing. It is taken from a French illuminated manuscript of the fifteenth century in the Imperial Library, the subject of which is a very tiresome poem, or romance, entitled, *Le Roman de très-douce Mercy au Cœur d'Amour épris*, which I could not recommend any of my fair friends to attempt to read. It will be sufficient to say that the cut is taken from one of the illuminations to this volume.

CHAPTER XVI.

THE notion of the particular elements which together constitute female beauty has varied at different times and among different peoples, and the knowledge of this variation is by no means an unimportant article in social history. Certainly, beauty was a word much in use among the society of the feudal castle, the quality itself was much thought of and much talked of, and the literature of those ages, their romance and their poetry, abound in descriptions which enable us to form some idea of mediæval taste in this respect. Thus certain colours were preferred in the complexions, and certain forms were admired in the limbs. The favourite colour for a lady's hair, for example, was blonde, or what we should call fair, neither dark nor golden, but very light brown, nearly such as we should call auburn. It constantly occurs in the romances. Thus, in *Girart de Viane*, speaking of the fair Aude, the poet tells us,—

Un chapelet ot en son chief posé,	She had a chaplet placed on her head,
A riches pierres ke getent grant clarté;	Of rich gems which shed great brightness;
Blonc ot le poil menu recorcelé,	She had blonde hair formed into a small circle,
Les oelz ot vairs comme faucon mué,	Her eyes she had vair like a falcon in mew,
Et la viairo frais ot encoloré.	And her face fresh and coloured (red).

Vair, which is interpreted as blue or azure, was the favourite colour of the eyes. A lady in the fablian of *Gonbert et les deux Clercs*, has " eyes *vair* as crystal."

> Les iex ot vairs como cristal :

and another, in a fablian quoted by Roquefort,—

Ot vairs iex rians et fendus,
Les bras bien fes et estendus,
Blanches mains, longues et ouvertes;
Aux templieres que vi apertes
Apparut qu'ele or teste blonde.

Had *vair* eyes, laughing and large,
Her arms well made and long,
White hands, long and open;
By her temples which I saw uncovered
It appeared that she had a blonde head.

In England at this time, a favourite colour of the eye appears to have been grey, though possibly the English *grey* may have been nearly the same as the French *vair*. In one of the pieces printed in my *Specimens of Lyric Poetry of the Thirteenth Century*, the lover describing his mistress, says:—

Hyre oyghen aren grete ant gray ynoh,
That lussum when heo on me loh
Ybend wax eyther breghe.

Her eyes are great and grey enough,
That lovely when she on me laughs
Either brow becomes bent.

Specimens of Lyric Poetry, p. 34.

The brows of this English beauty, the poet tells us further, were "white between and not too near." Her nose was set well, and her locks "were lovely and long." Her chin was dimpled, and her cheeks white and red as the rose when it begins to bloom. Her lips were red, and her teeth "white as bone of whale." The ivory used by the northern nations, and by our forefathers in early times was made from the teeth of the walrus, and therefore the usual name for ivory in English, especially in poetry, was "whalebone." These teeth were "evenly set and arrayed." She had a swan's neck. Her hand was lily-white; and her arms were an ell long.

Such descriptions as these might be multiplied to almost any extent, but one or two more will contribute to make us better acquainted with the character of woman's beauty as it was understood in feudal times. In the *Lais* of Marie de France, we are told of the lady of the seneschal of the king of Nantes,—

La dame est bele durement,
E de mut bon affeitement;
Gent cors out e bele faiture,
En li former must nature.
Lee oilz out veirs, e bel le vis,

Bele buche, neis bon nsis;
E' l'réaume ne out sa pore.

The lady is excessively beautiful,
And of very good manners;
She had an elegant body and good make,
To form her nature exerted herself.
She had *vair* eyes, and a handsome countenance,

A beautiful mouth, a nose well seated;
The kingdom had not her equal.

Marie, Lai d'Equitan, Poesies, ed. Roquefort, i. 116.

In the romance of *Blonde of Oxford*, the lady's locks differ a little from those just described, for they were like shining gold, and so long that they reached twice round her head,—

Il samble quo tout si chevoil
Soient de fin or reluisant,
Et si loue sont, qu'en déduisant
Li vout it. tours ontor la testé.

It appears as though all her hair
Were shining with fine gold,
And they are so long, that in her play
They go twice round her head.

The ears which supported it were fair and white, and delicate. Her forehead was white and smooth, and without a wrinkle. The eyebrows were brownish (*brunet*), narrow, and delicate, and the nose was well formed; but the eyes were beyond all admiration.

Il sont vair et cler et luisant,
Et plain d'un regart atraiant,
Si soutil et si engigueus,
Qu'il n'est nus, taut fust malineus,
Santé ne li fust revenue
S'il apercevoit sa véue.

They are *vair* and trausparent and bright,
And filled with an alluring look,
So keen and so seducing,
That there is no one, however ill be might be,
But he would recover his health
If he obtained a look from her.

Her face was redder than a rose, and was beautifully set off with white. Her two lips were reasonably plump, not thin, and redder than cochineal,—

Ses deux levretes ne sunt pas
Tenuenes, mais par raison grossetes,
Et plus quo graine vermilletes.

The poet carries this description through several pages. The charms of the beloved of Gautier d'Aupais are told in fewer words. She had a round face, which was, like the others, red; her eyes *vair* and laughing; her nose long and well formed; her mouth red, and her chin dimpled; her neck fuller and whiter than a flower in the meadow.

Ele ot plain le visage, si fu encolorez;
Les iex vairs et riant, lonc et traitis le nez;
La bouche vermeillete, le mentou forcelé;
Le col ot plain et blanc plus que n'est flor de pré.
Gautier d'Aupais, ed. Fr. Michel, p. 6.

All these descriptions belong to the thirteenth century, the classic age of feudal literature. A poet of the same period, Guillaume de Lorris, the author of the first part of the *Roman de la Rose*, has described with sufficient brevity the charms of dame Beauty herself (edit. of M. Francisque Michel, tom. i., p. 32).

El ne fu oscure, ne brune,
Aine fu clere comme la lune,
Envers qui les autres estoiles
Resemblent petites chaudoiles.

She was neither dusky nor brown,
But was bright as the moon,
In comparison to which the other stars
Resemble small candles.

Tondre ot la char comme rousée,	She had flesh tender like the dew (?),
Simple fu com une espousée,	She was simple as a bride,
Et blanche comme flor-de-lis;	And white as the fleur-de-lis;
Si ot le vis cler et alis,	And she had her face bright and smooth,
Et fu greslete et alignie,	And was slender and elegantly formed,
Ne fu fardée ne guignie,	Nor was she painted or disguised,
Car el n'avoit mie mestier	For she had no need
De soi tifer ne d'afetier.	To dress herself out or set herself off.
Les cheveus ot blons, et si lons	She had blond hair, and so long
Qu'il li batoient as talons;	That they swept at her heels,
Nés ot bien fait, et yex et bouche.	She had a nose well formed, and eyes and mouth.

Among this old literature we meet with short pieces in verse enumerating, usually in trios, the beauties of women, but they are often rather coarse. One of these which has been preserved belongs to the fourteenth century, and is remarkable for its length. It has been printed by Méon in the second volume of his supplement to the Fabliaux of Barbazan. The writer, who tells us that he composed it in the year 1332, has made a list of seventy-two " beauties" which are found in ladies,* and has arranged them in double trios of beauties of contrary character. Thus, the first division consists of three which are beauties in being long, and three in being short. The former are a long nose, long arms, and a long waist; and among the latter are short breasts. It must be acknowledged that even this writer is sometimes, to say the least, a little indiscreet in his enumeration, too much given to reckon up the qualities of his ladies as he would those of a horse, and he is sometimes a little obscure. Among the beauties by being slender are the body and the fingers; by being soft, the hands; by being vaulted (votis), the neck and feet; by being, on the contrary, hollowed (fosseleus, i.e., dimpled), the chin—a dimpled chin was always considered a beauty; by being high, the forehead; by being small, the ears, the mouth, and the feet. The latter are recommended to be "round like a walnut."

Petiz piez rons comme une nois.

When, in the passage quoted above from the Roman de la Rose, Guillaume de Lorris says of Beauty that she was neither painted nor disguised by artificial embellishments, he no doubt intended to give utterance

---

* Ci sont les Divisions des Soixante et Douze Biautès qui sont en Dames.—Méon, Nouveau Recueil, i. 407. These " Seventy-two heauties " appear to have been in a manner proverbial in the Middle Ages, and so late as the age of printing we find them still in record. A tract, printed apparently in the fifteenth century, and reprinted by M. de Montaiglon in his Anciennes Poésies Francaises, vii., 287, entitled La louenge et beauté des Dames, concludes with this popular list.

to a satire on a practice which prevailed extensively in his time. We have already seen that the practice of seeking to procure beauty, or at least to improve it, by painting the face, dyeing the hair, and other similar means, had existed from a very early period, and we shall find, as we go on, that these practises were used almost to an excess during the feudal period. We trace in the age of which we are speaking, another practice with which we are well acquainted in modern times. The ladies of this early period sought to give artificial odours to their persons, as well as artificial beauty. The art of perfuming is said to have been practised throughout the East from a very remote date, and it seems to have been brought thence into Western Europe. But the perfumes used among the feudal ladies, were not very refined in their character, for, as far as we know, they consisted only of saffron. At least, this was the favourite perfume. It is said of a lady in the romance of the *Sept Sages* :—

Deus aniaus ot en sa main destre,	She had two rings on her right hand,
Et trois en ot en la senestre;	And three she had on her left;
Et si ot guimple ensafrenée,	And she had a wimple perfumed with saffron,
De soie qui fu desguisée.	Which was worked of silk.

Li Roumans des Sept Sages, ed. Keller, p. 174.

The wimple, or covering for the neck, appears to have been the part of the dress in which the perfume was usually lodged. In a curious little poem of this period, which has been printed by M. Robert, in a small collection of Fabliaux, under the title *Du Mercier*, this personage, who in the Middle Ages was a dealer in a very miscellaneous assortment of articles, has " wimples perfumed with saffron."

J'ai les guimples ensaffrenées.

The notion of perfuming with saffron would now be considered very primitive, yet this plant was formerly a great favourite both for its flavour and for its smell, and this is still the case in some parts of the country. I am told that in Cornwall people still use it plentifully, both to flavour their cakes, and to lay in their drawers with linen as we do lavender.

With feudalism came in that system of ever-varying fashions in dress and costume, which has been continued to our own times. In the olden time, the forms of dress had not been subjected to capricious changes, but they were distinguished, according to the rank and position of the wearers, chiefly by the quality of the materials and the richness of their jewelry. But with feudalism came new classes of feelings and sentiments. All that part of society which came under the description of knightly, was in principle equal, although the pride of individual distinction had never perhaps existed to a greater extent. The knight, when on service, which was the case during the greater part of his time, bore his badge of personality on his shield, or on his helmet. Now that feudalism had brought Womankind into a much more prominent and important position in society, she required also some outward mark of her personal rank and importance, and sought it in the richness or form of her dress. It is the usual case, in uncivilized or only partially civilized society, that the man lays the work upon the woman, and assumes the right of displaying pride and vanity to himself. This feeling we have seen to exist to a great degree in society in Western Europe previous to the feudal period; and it must be acknowledged that, in the earlier developments of the love of extravagance in dress, the feudal ladies only followed the example set them by the other sex. The satirical writers and the religious preachers of the eleventh and twelfth centuries were far louder in their outcries against the extravagant finery of the knights and esquires than against that of the ladies and damoiselles, and, to judge from some of their descriptions, not without reason. The different form of society, too, gave to both sexes far more frequent and more exciting occasions for exhibiting this description of pride. The dull indoor amusements, the heavy eating of the dinner-table, the drinking which followed, the games in which the men almost exclusively partook, had given place to the more brilliant gaiety of the castle, to the carole, and above all to the tournament.

It appears that this love of new fashions and extravagance in dress, had risen to a great height at the close of the twelfth century, and the protest against it, in contemporary writers, goes on increasing during the three centuries which followed. Many writers bear witness to the gaiety of the ladies of the thirteenth century. Gautier de Coinsi, a religious poet who lived in the earlier half of that century, describing a maiden who was modest and prudent, and telling how she avoided the society of the gayer portion of her sex, says of the latter, —

Les autres puceles voit rire,	She saw the other maidens laugh,
Alor as baules, as queroles,	Go to dances, to caroles,
Et contenances fere foles.	And behave themselves like mad women.
* * * *	* * * *
Qu'as autres point ne s'aparoille,	That she associate not with the others,
Qui deus et deus s'entracompaignent,	Who go about together two and two,
Qui s'abelissent, qui se paignent,	Who deck themselves out, who comb themselves,
Qui se fardellent et qui s'oignent,	Who paint themselves, and who anoint themselves (*with oil*),
Qui s'ascement, et qui se joignent,	Who adorn themselves, and who make themselves young,

Envolepent et enpipodent,   Who ———— and squall (?),
Qui s'emmuselent, chiflent, godent   Who muzzle themselves, warble, fondle
As chevaliers avul cels sales.   With the knights down in those halls.
                    Méon, Nouveau Recueil, tom. ii. p. 39.

Jean de Meung, too, the second writer of the *Roman de la Rose*, who
flourished in the reign of Philippe le Bel, the latter part of the thirteenth
century, gives a rather striking description of the manner in which the
ladies decked themselves out, when they "went to the caroles, or to the
other gay assemblies."

                    —Quant vous alés as karoles,
                    Ou à vos assemblées foles.
                              Roman de la Rose, l. 10009.

Not long after the middle of the fourteenth century, the knight of La
Tour-Landry, in his "Book," tells his daughters, for their instruction on
this subject, a curious anecdote, as a warning against being too ready to
adopt new-fangled fashions, and especially those of other countries. A noble
baroness of the duchy of Guienne one day addressed the lord of Beaumanoir,
and said, "I come from Britany, and I have seen my cousin, your wife, who
is not so arrayed, nor her dress made of such materials, as the ladies of
Guienne, and of many other places; for the borders of her robes and head-
dresses are not so large or of the fashion which is now in vogue." * The
knight replied, "My lady, since she is not arrayed in your fashion and like
you, and her borders seem to you small, and you blame me for it, know
that you shall blame me for it no longer; for I will make her more elegant
(*cointe*) and as well arrayed in noble ornaments of the new fashion, as you
or any of the others, for you and they have only the half of your bodies
(*corsés*), and your hoods (*chapperons*), lined with vair and with ermine, and
I will do still better, for I will have her dresses and hoods lined on the
other side, the hair outward, and so she shall be better furred and lined than
you or the others."† The knight then goes on to complain that these new

---

* The English translator of the knight's book, somewhat less than a century afterwards,
found a difficulty in representing here the words of the original relating to costume; his translation is, "For her hodes, taylles, and sleves be not furred ynowgh after the shape that rennithe
now."—*The Booke of the Knight of La Tour-Landry*, p. 30 (in my edition).

† The English version, quoted in the last note, gives this as follows:—"Sethe she nys not
arrayed on youre gise, and that ye thenke her array and her furre to litelle, and that ye blame
me for it, forsothe ye shall have no more cause to blame me, for y wolle make arraye her as
nobly as ani of you alle, and as queintly; for ye have but halfe youre hodes and cotes furred
with ermyn or menever, and y wol do beter to hor, for y wolle furre her gowne, coleres, sleves,
and cotes, the here outwarde; thus she shalle be beter purfiled and furred thanne other ladies
and gentille women." It is evident that a change had taken place in the details of the costume
between the period at which this book was written, and that at which it was translated into
English.

guises had been borrowed from the English, and that they had been first adopted by the disreputable women who followed the camp—that these were the first who figured in the great purfiles and corsages, slit at the sides and "lès flontans" (*car ce furent celles qui premièrement admenerent cest estat au Bretaigne des grans pourfilz et des corsès fendus és costez et lès floutans*). The reader of Chaucer knows how, a little later on in the century, the "persone" in the *Canterbury Tales*, inveighs against the wild extravagance of contemporary fashions in dress.

The great variety of stuffs and materials for dress which are mentioned as existing in the twelfth century, is a proof not only of the extensive usage which was made of them, but of the consequent activity in the different branches of their manufacture; and there is also abundant evidence, that during this period a great variety of fashions sprung into existence, not in the articles of dress, for they seem to have remained permanently the same, but in their forms and make. Towards the close of the century the complaint against this extravagance in both sexes became greater, and it went on increasing during the century following. We must not, however, suppose, with most of our popular writers on the history of costume, that there was quite a uniformity in this change of the fashions of dress, or that at any particular date the costume was everywhere the same. On the contrary, there was no *law* of fashion, but each high dame seems, to a certain degree, to have chosen her fashion for herself, although at any particular period a certain general character prevailed. This is easily understood. The whole extent of feudalism formed, in some respects, one great domain, in which each feudal castle was a sort of little state, complete in itself. The communication between the different castles was not frequent, or rapid, especially among the females of the household, and less so if far apart, and it was only at times that the lady of the castle presented herself at the "royal court." The articles of dress of the feudal ladies, in each great castle, were usually made within the household, according to a general form, but the higher ladies sought to show their rank always by the superiority of the material, and sometimes also by some variation of form, which would of course soon be imitated by others. When the lady of the castle went to the king's court, she saw there similar variations, or peculiarities, in dress, perhaps on a much more striking scale, and she eagerly carried them home with her to introduce them into her own lesser court. But every lady did not necessarily adopt this same fashion, which probably consisted chiefly in the higher value of the materials, and was only, therefore, within reach of a few. The increasing extravagance of the ladies' costume, of which the clergy especially complained, consisted of the spreading eagerness of women of lower rank and position, to spend far beyond their means in rivalling the costly dresses of the great ladies of the court. At all periods we find a great variety of ladies' costume existing contemporaneously, as every one knows who has carefully compared the illuminated manuscripts; but, from one time to another, some special novelty in the style of dress was more extravagant or became more the rage than usual, and thus marked a sort of period in the history of fashion.

The description which Guillaume de Lorris gives, in the *Roman de la Rose*, of the dress of the lady Riches, may be taken as a good picture of the costume of the lady of the highest and proudest class in mediæval society. Its beauty consisted chiefly in the costliness of the materials, and in the rarity of the gems which adorned it. Her robe was of purple, which at this period was the name of an extremely rich material, we may suppose of this colour :—

Richesse ot une porpre robe,	Riches had a robe of purple,
Ice ne tenés mie à lobe;	Do not take this for a joke ;
Que je vous di bien et aficho	For I tell you distinctly and affirm
Qu'il n'ot si belo ne si riche	That there was no one so beautiful or so rich
Ou monde, ne si cuvoisie.	In the world, or so gay.
La porpre fu toute orfroisie,	The purple was all covered with orfrays,
Si ot portraites à orfrois	And it had pictured in orfrays
Estoires de dus et de rois.	Histories of dukes and kings.

Roman de la Rose, ed. Michel, tom. i. p. 35.

It was the custom, in some of the richer dresses, to adorn them with this pictorial embroidery. The lady Riches had round her neck a collar of gold, set with precious stones, which were very brilliant. The girdle, which encircled her robe, was wonderfully costly. The stones which adorned it were all possessed of strange virtues, for gems were in those days believed to be endowed with magical qualities, and their individual value was regulated by the quality each was supposed to possess. The stone which was set on the buckle of her girdle had the quality, that whoever wore it on the person was protected against the effects of poison or venom : it was worth all the gold of Rome. The stone on the tongue of the buckle protected against the toothache, and strengthened the sight. The nails of the girdle were of pure gold. Madame Riches had on her blonde tresses a circle, set with stones of immense value, with a wonderful carbuncle in front.

Mais devant ot, par grant mestrise,	But there was in front, with great skill,
Une escharboucle ou cercle assise,	A carbuncle set in the circle,

Et la pierro si clore estoit,	And the stone was so bright,
Que maintenant qu'il anuitoit,	That, when it was night,
L'en s'en véist bien au besoing	One could see well by it at need
Conduire d'une liue loing.	To go a league distance.

Our information on the different articles of dress worn by the ladies in the twelfth and thirteenth centuries is sufficiently exact. The first was the *chemise* (*camisia*), which was called in English, as far back as the fourteenth century, a shift, and was worn next the skin. The collar of the chemise was allowed to pass the rest of the dress, and was sometimes turned down. It appears to have been usually plaited; and dandies of either sex seem to have prided themselves upon the neatness with which it was arranged. Over the chemise was worn the *cote*, a long tunic with sleeves fitting close, which were the only part of it visible, as the rest was covered by the *surcote*, or super-tunic, worn over it, as its name indicates. The surcote was, perhaps, the most important article of the dress. It was sometimes without sleeves, sometimes with half sleeves which descended a little below the elbow, and sometimes with false sleeves, which fell over the back. Under Philippe le Hardi, in the latter half of the thirteenth century, the cote and the surcote were made of very rich materials, and of brilliant colours, and it was customary to embroider them in silver and gold with the arms of the wearer, if she were a person of distinction. A cote of cloth of gold well shaped—

Cote de drap d'or bien taillò—

was part of the dress of Blonde of Oxford, in the romance, which carries us back to the thirteenth century. Over these was thrown the mantle, which seems to have been known at times by the name of the material of which it was made, especially when that material was more than usually precious or rare. Thus in the thirteenth century it was sometimes called a *siglaton*, this being the name of a very precious stuff brought from the east; and in the twelfth century it was called a *cape*, a word said to be derived from the Latin *capella*, a goat, because it was made of the hair of that animal. The *bliault* was another outer garment, perhaps more complete than the mantle. We have seen in a former chapter,[*] a young lady leaving her bed, and descending, dressed only in a bliault, to bid farewell to her lover, and we have there given a picture of the lady in this costume. It must be understood that at this time it was the custom, with both sexes, to lie in bed at night perfectly naked. The text of the *Roman de la Violette*, in which this

---

[*] See before, p. 155 of the present volume.

incident occurs, is of the thirteenth century, but unfortunately the illuminated manuscript of the romance, from which our picture is taken, is only of the fifteenth, though probably the character of the bliault had undergone little change. We see in a little nouvelette of the same thirteenth century, that of *Aucassin et Nicolette*, the fair damsel Nicolette rising from her bed, and making her escape from her chamber in the same simple disguise—*ele se leva, si vesti un bliault de drap de soie que ele avoit molt bon.*

The dressing of the head was perhaps the most important part of the fashionable costume of this period, and performed a great part in its changes. One of the great fashions of the latter half of the twelfth century was the *chapel de paon*, a crown or hat ornamented with embroidery, and surmounted by a peacock's feather. Embroidery of gold and pearls, which was now much employed on the robes of silk and velvet, was also used largely in the coiffure of ladies of rank and beauty. The *tressor*, or *treceour*, was an ornamental fillet or wreath, answering to the *benda* of Provence and Italy, employed to bind the hair; and among other principal articles of the head dress of ladies of rank were the *couvrechefs*, usually made of silk tissue, the wimple (*guimple*) also of silk, and the circlet of gold and silver. The ladies had also a veil, which descended from the summit of the head to the shoulder, and left but a small portion of the hair uncovered.

Gloves were in common use at this time, and were made of different materials—sometimes of sheep's leather, at others of kid, and at others of "vair" and of "gris," and of such rich materials. They were generally formed to cover the wrist. In the Middle Ages it was the height of ill-manners to keep the gloves on the hand during visits, or in soirées, or in balls, or in the presence of great people, and when two persons met in the public road, they drew off their gloves before touching hands. To omit this would be looked upon as nothing less than a personal insult. Shoes also, though usually made of leather, were sometimes made of other materials, though they do not appear to have differed much in form. The old writers speak especially of two descriptions of shoes in use among the mediæval ladies, which they call *escarpins* and *estivaus*. The former were apparently low shoes for undress and common use. In the romance of *Garin le Loherain*, a lady is made to leave her chamber in grief and negligently dressed :—

Tete doleute hors de sa chambre issi,	All full of grief she issued from her chamber,
Desafublie, chaucié en escharpins.	In undress, shoed with escarpins.
Sor ses cspoles li gisoient li crius.	Her hair lay scattered over her shoulders.

The *estival* (in Latin *æstivalis*) was a sort of buskin, often ornamented with ermine or fur, and worn by ladies when affecting elegance of dress.

One of the most important parts of the lady's dress was her girdle, which was buckled round her waist, and was often made of very rich materials. The beauty of the girdle was considered especially as a mark of dignity, and

QUEENS BERENGARIA AND ISABEL.

as belonging to married ladies. To it was suspended the *aumonière*, or purse, and the keys, the especial signs of the matron's authority. Until the fourteenth century, illuminated manuscripts, except of the church books, are not very numerous, and we get few pictorial illustrations of the details of female costume. For the earlier part of the thirteenth century we may rejoice in the preservation of the sculptures of two queens of England—Berengaria, the queen of Richard Cœur-de-Lion, and Isabel of Angoulême, the third and last wife of King John, and mother of Henry III. Both, which are represented in the cut on the preceding page, are sculptures of the reign of the last of these monarchs. The latter is at Fontevraud in Anjou ; and the former was preserved in the abbey of l'Espau, near Mans. They are good examples of the ordinary dress of the lady of rank of this period. The garment enclosing the body is the surcote, or outer tunic, but the camise or chemise, is open above round the neck. The mantle hangs loose, and in the case of Queen Isabel both surcote and mantle have embroidered borders. The fermails, or brooches, at the neck, are both of gold, and that of Berengaria is especially large and rich. Queen Berengaria has also her *aumonière* attached to her girdle.

This latter article of dress, the girdle, still held its importance, and it was looked upon as a great act of presumption in women of the lower or less reputable classes of society to wear it. It is related of Queen Blanche, the mother of St. Louis, that, one day at church, having received from the priest the kiss of peace, she passed it on, as was the custom, to a woman by her side, richly clad, and whose respectability seemed to be assured by the beauty of her girdle. She was informed afterwards that this woman was a prostitute, and, greatly disgusted at having come in contact with such a person, she made an order—it was during her regency—forbidding in future females of that class from wearing the girdle used by honest women. For a similar reason, more than half a century before, Louis VII. had forbidden women of this description from appearing in the *cape*. The order of Queen Blanche was renewed by subsequent monarchs down to a comparatively late period, and it, or perhaps rather the sentiment it reveals, is understood to have given rise to the old French proverb, *Bonne renommée vaut mieux que ceinture dorée*, good repute is worth more than a gilded girdle.

This eagerness of the women of the lower class to imitate the dress and extravagance of those of higher rank was that which most provoked the indignation of the moralists, and especially of the clergy, and it appears to have gone on increasing during the whole of the thirteenth century. At length, in the reign of Philippe le Bel, the expostulations of the church became so pressing, that that monarch passed, in 1292, a law regulating the number of the dresses and the value of the materials of which they were to be made for each different class of society. It was the first of the sumptuary laws, and was followed at different times by many others. The provisions of this law are curious enough : neither man nor woman of the bourgeoisie was to wear *vair*, or *gris*, or ermines, nor were they allowed to wear gold, or precious stones, or crowns of gold or silver. The ladies of dukes, of earls, or of barons of six thousand livres of land or more, might have four new robes a year, and no more. The same regulation applied to the other sex. Knights, and of course their ladies, were allowed two robes a year, either by gift, or purchase, or otherwise. No damoiselle, unless she were a châtelaine, or a lady of two thousand livres of land, was to have more than one robe a year. Limits were also placed on the value of the materials. The wives of barons were not to have a robe of material worth more according to the value in Paris than twenty-five sols tournois a yard; the wives of bannerets and châtelains were limited to eighteen sols a yard ; and the wives of bourgeois of the worth of two thousand livres tournois or more, were limited to sixteen sols the yard ; and the poorer class to twelve sols. As may be supposed, a law like this was very ineffective, and extravagance in dress went on increasing instead of decreasing.

It was in the head attire that extravagance in form began to show itself. During the twelfth and thirteenth centuries the arrangement of the head-dress appears to have depended very much on the caprice of the individual, at least as to the combinations of the objects of which it consisted, the principal of which have been already described. One of them was the *capele*, or *chapelet*, a circlet which surrounded the head and held in the hair. Blonde of Oxford, at her marriage, was clothed in a capelet of cloth of gold, with a mantle from the neck, the tassels of which were worth fourteen marks.

Uns capeles ses chevex tient,	A chaplet holds her hair,
Qui ert de fin or reluisant.	Which was of fine glittering gold.
Un fremal eut el pis devant,	She had a fermail (brooch) on her breast before,
De chians qu'el aporté avoit;	One of those which she had brought with her;
Li rois nul plus rice n'avoit.	The king did not possess a richer.
Ele eut aumoniere et cainture,	She had aumonière and girdle,
En tant comme li siècles dure	As long as the world lasts
Ne fust sa pareille trouvée.	Its equal may not be found.

Romance of Blonde of Oxford, p. 162.

Towards the end of the thirteenth century, it became the fashion to arrange the hair on the head in a more prominent and bulky form, projecting above the ears on each side, and upon the two bosses thus formed the veil or couvrechef was suspended. To produce this effect, more hair was frequently needed than the head itself produced, and to supply this want false hair was employed. This false hair was called the *atours*, which were sometimes made in the most singular shapes. Early in the fourteenth century these *atours* had assumed the form of two horns, and became an object of great indignation to the religious part of the community. Jean de Meung, the continuator of the *Roman de la Rose*, which was completed in the earlier part of that century, sneers at these horned head-dresses, when he says of the other sex,—

Sus ses oreilles port tex cornes	Over her ears she carries such horns
Que cers, ne bues, ne unicornes,	That stag, or ox, or unicorn,
S'il se devoient affronter,	If they had to face her,
Ne puit ses cornes surmonter.	Could not overcome her horns.

And the same writer speaks of the woman's "horns" at a later period, in his "Testament." An anonymous satirist of the earlier years of the fourteenth century has left us a song against these "cornettes," as he calls them, in which he tells us how the Archbishop of Paris raised his voice against the folly of the woman—

Qui forre son chief at se farde	Who puts false hair on her head and paints herself
Por plere au monde.	To please the world.

The women who adopted such fashions are compared by the satirist to dumb beasts, and he tells us how the prelate had promised a reward to all who would treat them with open derision.

Et commande par aatie	And he commands, in scorn of them,
Que chascum "hurte, belin," die.	That every one cry out, "Push, ram."
Trop i tardon	We are too slow to cry
"Hurte, belin," por le pardon.	"Push, ram," for the pardon.
Se des fames ne nous gardon,	If we are not on our guard against the women,
Ocis seromines.	We shall be slain.
Cornes ont por tuer les hommes.	They have horns to kill the men.
D'autrui chevens portent granz sommes	They carry great masses of other people's hair
Desus lor teste.	Upon their head.

After a little more satire on the vanity of the ladies' costume, the writer continues,—

L'evesque l'a aperceu;	The bishop has perceived it;
Si ne s'en puet estre ten,	And he cannot remain silent,
Ainz en sermone,	But he preaches about it,
Et a toz cels x. jors pardone,	And he gives ten days pardon to all those
Que crierout à tel personne,	Who will cry out at such a person,
"Hurte, belin."	"Push, ram!"

The horns, he says, were made of hemp or flax,—

Foi quo je doi saint Mathelin,	By the faith I owe St. Mathurin,
De chanvre ouvré ou de lin	With worked hemp or flax
Se font cornues.	They make themselves horned.

As I have already stated, the practice of painting the face is one of great antiquity, and was indulged in by the ladies of the Middle Ages largely, both before and after the establishment of feudalism. A short poem of the thirteenth century, which introduces the mercier, or dealer in small wares, enumerating the articles he has for sale, gives the following curious list of the objects employed by the lady at her toilette at that period (it is not always easy to explain them in modern language),—

Si ai tot l'apareillement	I have also all the utensils
Dont feme fait formoment,	Which a woman uses at her toilette,
Rasoers, forces, guignoeres,	Razors, forceps, looking-glasses.
Escuretes et furgoeres,	Tooth-brushes and tooth-picks,
Et bendeax et crespiscors,	And bandeaus, and crisping-irons,
Traineax, pignes, mireors,	Traineaux, combs, mirrors,
Eve rose dont se forbissout ;	And rose-water with which they furbish themselves ;
J'ai quoton dont els se rougissont ;	I have cotton with which they rouge themselves ;
J'ai blanchet dont els se font blanches.	I have whitening with which they make themselves white.

Neither bishop's sermon nor poet's satire appears to have had much effect in moderating the love of the ladies for horns, which seems to have continued during the whole of this century, and into the next. The knight of La Tour-Landry, writing in 1371 or 1372, tells us similarly of a holy bishop in his time who preached against the horned head-dresses of the ladies, when there was present a great crowd of ladies and damoiselles in what was then the new fashion, *et estoient bien branchues et avoient grans cornes.* He told them that Noah's flood was brought on by similar vanities, and that he had no doubt that the demon made his ordinary seat between the woman's horns. In spite, however, of all this outcry and satire, the horns survived, or at least many of the ladies of fashion continued to wear them, and at the beginning of the fifteenth century they seem to have been carried to a greater extravagance than ever. The chronicler Juvenal des Ursins says that, in 1417, "the ladies and damoiselles of the queen's household displayed great and excessive pride, and wore horns wonderfully high and broad, and had on each side, instead of pads, two great ears, so large that when they had to pass through the door of the chamber, they were obliged to turn sideways and stoop, or they could not pass. The anger of the more zealous portion of the clergy was again roused, and fierce were the onslaughts upon the horns.

That, however, there were, during all this period, other and simpler head-dresses in vogue, besides the horns, is evident from the illuminations of contemporary manuscripts. The accompanying cut is taken from an illumination in a manuscript of the *Chronicles of St. Denis*, in the British Museum (MS. Reg. 20, C. VII., fol. 10, v°.), which represents the marriage of King Philippe le Hardi of France with Marie de Brabant, from which I have given here the figures of the queen and her two ladies of honour. The manuscript belongs to the close of the fourteenth or to the beginning of the fifteenth century, and no doubt represents some of the ordinary head-dresses of that period. The next cut is of a rather later date, taken from a manuscript of the romance of King Pontus, and similarly represents the Princess Sidoine and her damoiselles. A ship has brought her, as presents from King Pontus, some of the principal articles of a fashionable lady's attire, including "crowns, or circlets of gold, and chaplets, girdles, *aumonières* of pearls, of gold, and of purple, of *pennes*, of vair and of gris, and of ermines, that it was a great wonder to see." The princess wears what was perhaps one form of the horned head dress.

THE QUEEN AND HER LADIES.

During the whole of the fourteenth century we meet with frequent complaints of the increasing extravagance in dress. The fashions became more varied and capricious, and the fineness of the material increased and came nearer to perfection. A great number of new stuffs are mentioned during this century, but I will not undertake here to describe or enumerate them. The *bliault*, which still continued in use with both sexes, appears now to have been furred. The general dress continued to be much the

same, but one new article of dress was added in the course of the century
under the name of a *garnache*, in the form of a long mantle, with a slit at
the side. This, too, like nearly all the other articles of dress, was worn under
the same name by both sexes. In 1351, the king of France had garnaches
of red velvet, and others of white velvet with sleeves doubled with ermine.
Another new dress, introduced towards the latter part of the century, was
called a *rondeau*, and is better known by the name of a *cote-hardie*. It was
a habit fitting close, reaching only down to the haunches, and buttoned

KING PONTUS SENDS PRESENTS TO THE FAIR SIDOINE.

usually down the breast. Some of the ladies wore over this a very wide
mantle which descended to the ground, and trailed to some distance behind.
Ladies of noble birth now adopted the fashion of having the family arms
depicted on the cloth of their tunics, the usual custom being to carry the
arms of the families *miparti*, the husband's on the one side and the wife's on
the other. Our next cut represents a noble lady of the close of the fourteenth century, taken from a miniature in a manuscript in the Bibliothèque
Imperiale in Paris (Suppl. Lat., No. 1222). It is believed to represent

Marguerite de Clisson, who was married on the 20th of January, 1387, to
Jean de Châtillon, a nobleman who acted a prominent part in the history of
Britany at that period; and the volume, which is a book of prayers, with
its miniature is supposed to have been made at the date just mentioned, on
occasion of the marriage. Marguerite de Clisson wears the rondeau or
cote-hardie.

MARGUERITE DE CLISSON.

Under Charles VI., towards the end of the century, we begin to hear
new and louder cries against the strange fashions affected by the ladies, who
are now accused of transgressing decency in various ways, and especially by
leaving bare their shoulders and breasts, and even their legs and more of
their sides than was to be approved. At the same time there was a general

increase in coquetry, and the custom of carrying perfumes in the dress and the use of paint had become very general. Against the latter, the clergy were especially indignant. Gloves, girdles, and a profusion of jewelry, began also to be greatly affected by all classes. Among people of fashion, the houppelande, which was the most outwardly apparent part of the dress, was covered profusely with ornaments and jewelry, and also with devices and mottoes.

The opening of the fifteenth century found France and Western Europe generally in a melancholy condition, the consequence of long-continued misrule, and war, and misfortunes, which had impoverished the people and ruined their industry. Luxury had found a refuge at the court of Burgundy, and it was from Flanders especially that the pride of Western Europe expected its revival. For a while there was little movement in fashion, but when it began to recover, it became more showy and dashing than ever. A great development of commerce displayed itself early in the new century, and was naturally attended with a similar increase of riches, which was more equally spread than formerly; and thus the richer stuffs and materials came into wider and more general use. Even the gallantry of the men took a gayer turn, and the male costume was almost more extravagant and varied in forms than that of the other sex. The "elegants" of the day covered themselves with embroidery and fine needle-work, and they wore scarfs and chaplets, under the name of ladies' favours. The general character of the costume of the latter differed very much, and their dresses were sometimes immoderately long, and at others equally short.

The dress of the ladies had itself undergone some change. The old surcote, which had still been the fashion of the age of Charles V., continued to be the ceremonial dress of ladies of quality, but they only appeared in it on very solemn occasions, and were represented in it in the effigies on their tombs. The robe and houppelande were the more usual articles of female apparel in the age of Charles VI. The latter, instead of being closed behind as with the men, was now closed before. The girdle, too, was taken from the surcote, and placed over the houppelande, and it was raised higher up to the breast, so as to give the ladies very short waists. The tails of the dress were made extravagantly long, and trailed through dust and dirt, to the great disgust, especially, of the clergy, who attacked the enormous tails of the ladies continually, and one of them has left us in his Latin the following story. It is very edifying according to the ideas of that time. "I have heard," he says, "of a certain woman who dragged white garments

behind her on the ground, and, leaving her tracks behind her, raised the
dust up to the altar and up to the image of the crucifix." (It is evident
that the church must have been ill swept.) "But when she went out of
the church, and lifted her tail up on account of the mud, a certain holy man
saw a devil laughing, and adjured him to tell why he laughed. And he
said, 'Because my fellow was just now sitting on the tail of that woman,
and used it as his chariot; but when the woman raised up her tail, my fellow
was thrown off the tail, and fell into the mud; and that is the reason why
I laughed.'"* Devils were common about the world in those days of
Catholicism.

According to Monstrelet, about the year 1467, the ladies and damoiselles
abandoned these long tails, but instead of them they wore borders and
trimmings of great extravagance, with much broader girdles. Under
Charles VIII., who ascended the throne of France in 1483, the ladies began
to seek more to show the natural form of their body, and wore close-fitting
corsages, with shortened *jupes*, so as to show the lower part of their legs
and feet, but the extravagance in jewelry increased rather than otherwise,
and, above all, the use of paint for the face became more general than
ever.

The horned head-dress of the previous century continued for some time
into the fifteenth, and the exact period of its disappearance is hardly known.
There is a "dite" of honest, rather than poetic, John Lydgate, composed
sometime in the earlier half of the fifteenth century, in which he attacks
the horned head-dresses of ladies, and advises them to cast them away.†
The satire of this poem is very mild, which, perhaps, might be expected
from the circumstance that it is addressed to a royal princess, who is
exhorted,—

> Under support of your pacyence,
> Yeveth (*give*) example hornes to cast away.

The lady's pair of horns certainly passed away about this time. But in
their place there arose upon the heads of the ladies a horned head-dress of
a new fashion and still greater extravagance. We learn from the old
French chroniclers that about the year 1428 there came into fashion a cap
in the form of a single horn, raised on a form of latten or pasteboard, and
trimmed with very fine linen. They called this curious head-covering a
hennin. It became suddenly the great fashion of the day, and it has been

---

* The original, in Latin, is printed in my *Latin Stories* (Percy Society), p. 18.
† It will be found in Mr. Halliwell's edition of Lydgate's *Minor Poems*.

scen in several of the illustrations to our former chapters. The hennin rose from the head, leaning a little backward, to a height of sometimes nearly two feet, diminishing towards a point, and ending a little variously, but always furnished with a quantity of fine linen and gauze, which fell backward like a veil, and then turned back in horns upon the ears, forming a sort of dome over the top, and advancing like a large sheet of paper spread over the face. The ladies of the day are represented as absolutely running mad after these *hennins*, and of course the preachers set their face against them with the utmost zeal. They went so far that they promised at least a spiritual reward to all boys and girls who would shout after them in the open streets, and cry, "Au hennin! au hennin!" And this appears to have been executed so effectively, that the objectionable costume was at length driven out of fashion. The ladies then went to another extreme, and wore little flat hats, covered outside with skin or leather spotted black and blue. Our coloured plate represents the lady's head-dress of the latter part of the fifteenth century; it is taken from one of the illuminations in the well-known manuscript of the *Roman de la Rose* in the British Museum. The lady is dame Nature dispatching Genius, her messenger, to the Court of Love.

Besides these extravagances, the head-dresses of the ladies underwent many changes in the fifteenth century. It was customary not only to wear the hair long, but to carry a great bulk of it upon the head, and the use of false hair became much more extensive than ever, and even wool and other materials were employed in the manufacture of it. The reader of the French poetry of the fifteenth century will remember the lines of Coquillart:—

> De la queue d'un cheval peinte,
> Quand leurs cheveux sont trops petits,
> Ils ont une perruke feneit.

CHAPTER XVII.

WOMANKIND OUTSIDE THE FEUDAL CASTLE—THE TOWN AND THE COUNTRY—PASTORAL LIFE.

BEYOND the walls of the castle, and having no relationship of their own with feudalism, lay two other great classes of the population. First, there were the inhabitants of the towns, the *bourgeoisie*, or, as the French historical writers have called them, the *tiers état*, who embodied, perhaps, to a greater degree than any of the others, the spirit of social and political freedom and progress. These represented the ancient Roman population, recruited as it had been from a variety of sources. The other was to a great extent a servile class, attached to the ground, or personally to the lord, for it represented the original population of the land, reduced to servility through conquest, and largely intermixed in the course of time with slaves reduced to that condition by different means. This mixture formed the population of the country, as it still forms the substance of our rural population. It was not, however, in the Middle Ages, altogether servile, as it included the yeoman and the villain. Among the mass, in both these classes, there was far less of social refinement than among the feudal, or *gentle*, class.

There was a wide social division between this latter class, that of the feudal aristocracy, and the others, upon which it looked down with a proud feeling of scorn, as upon something possessed of a totally different and lower nature. Hence the jealousy with which all marks of outward distinction between the classes were insisted upon, and hence all those sumptuary laws, which fixed the limits within which the burghers and the yeomanry might approach to the finery of the gentry. But the very existence of such a feeling and of these laws showed a tendency, on the one part, to fall from its artificial level, and an ambition on the other to rise up to it. There was an aristocracy springing up among the *bourgeoisie* itself which, though hardly acknowledged by the feudal class, was laid upon very substantial foundations. The constitutions of the towns were republican in their character, and possessed more or less of all the characteristics of republics. Burgher life was a life of turbulence, which was nourished without a check. Trade and commerce, which, of course, led constantly to the accumulation of wealth, while they took the rising burgher from one distant land to another, gave him practical knowledge of men and things which few others possessed, and formed him to habits of business which were invaluable in the administration of public affairs. Schools, which now very generally existed in the towns, were formed for the benefit of the burgher class, and it was from them, too, and from the unaristocratic class, that the schools of the abbeys and of the universities were chiefly supplied with students, for the children of the châtelain seldom went beyond the castle-walls to school. Thus, this unaristocratic portion of society became the depository of school-learning, and made its way into the law, and into the church, and even into the court. Burghers became lawyers, and priests, and statesmen. We have all these combined in the person of Thomas Becket, the great Archbishop of Canterbury. At this time the kings were beginning to see the rising importance of the burgher class, and to encourage them and take them into their favour. This was the case with St. Louis of France and Philippe le Bel, although the latter did issue sumptuary laws. Etienne Barbette, who held the high municipal office of Prevot des Marchands under the latter, was high in the favour of both those monarchs, and St. Louis breathed his last in the arms of his daughter Aelis, who had accompanied his last crusade. She married, in her own class, Jean Sarrazin, one of the richest drapers in Paris, and dying in 1293, was buried in the cloister of the abbey of St. Victor, where her effigy was placed on a tomb raised to her memory. It was in the south that the burgher aristocracy, who took the title of *bourgeois honorables*, or burgesses of the honourable class, appear first, as a body, to have begun to rival and mix with the feudal society, which we can easily understand through the stronger influence there of the Roman sentiment. In the north especially, with the thirteenth century, the power of the bourgeoisie rose rapidly, for there the independence and influence of the towns had been always greater, and commerce and manufactures had flourished. Christine de Pisan, in the latter part of the fourteenth century, complains bitterly of the display of wealth made by the women of Paris. A chronicler of the same period, Meyer, tells us how, when Philippe le Bel visited the towns of Bruges and Ghent, with his Queen Jeanne of Navarre, the extravagance displayed by the wives of the citizens was so great, that Philippe said, he had supposed there had been only one queen there, but he saw more than six hundred. It was only, however, in the course of the fifteenth century, that the higher bourgeoisie and the noblesse began to intermix on an equality. This was encouraged by Louis XI., who gave honours and appointments to men of the burgher class, and encouraged their wives to go to court.

A new word was springing up in the midst of the bourgeoisie, though we cannot say exactly when it came into use. It would have been a greater crime for a burgher to assume the title of *dominus*, or *sir*, or his wife that of *domina*, *dame*, or *lady*, even than to appear in one of those articles of knightly dress which, as far as they were concerned, were proscribed by the sumptuary laws; but there was another title which, according to his old customs, belonged to him. After the burgher had gone through that course of education, and had reached that age which gave him the right of being admitted to the freedom of the town, and therefore of employing men, and thus became entitled to share in the management of the town's affairs, he became a master, and was therefore literally entitled to the title of *magister* (in Latin), corrupted into *maistre* in the vernacular tongue. He thus became a member of the aristocratic class among the townsmen, and, though it was at first little considered by that greatest aristocracy without, within the jurisdiction of the town there was a considerable distinction between this superior class and the class below. This distinction was, of course, prided in by the women, and it was not sufficient to show it by greater display in their dress and living, but they too wanted a title. They assumed, therefore, the feminine form *magistra*, modified in their own language into *maistresse*, and this became the acknowledged word used in addressing or speaking of the wives of the superior class of the bourgeoisie. Thus originated the titles, in French, of *maistre* and *maistresse* (in modern orthography, *maître* and *maîtresse*), and, in English, *master* (corrupted in comparatively recent times into *mister*) and *mistress*. By this title of *maistresse*, or mistress, the women of the town aristocracy were distinguished from the dames, or ladies, of the castle.

It is not to be concealed that during all this time there had been a sinking among the aristocracy, at the same time with the rising among the bourgeoisie. The châtelains had more ways of spending their wealth on a large scale, and their pride, and love of action and display, led them into constant extravagance, while they had fewer means of repairing their losses. After a certain period of feudal history, we begin to hear rather frequently of poor châtelains and of poor knights, and we find them seeking to enrich themselves by alliances with the unaristocratic classes, although they continued to regard them with all their old social prejudices. The story, which is embodied in the fabliau of the *Houce Partie*, turns on an incident of this kind. There was a worthy burgher of Abbeville who, with his wife and only son, removed to Paris, where he was respected for his wisdom and courtesy. At the end of six years the wife died, and the burgher, left alone with his son, began to look round for an honourable marriage for the latter. Now there were in the country three knights who were brothers, who were descended of high families both by father and mother, and who were distinguished in arms :—

Mèe n'avoient point d'eritagé	But they had no inheritance left
Que tout n'eussent mis en gage,	Which they had not put all in pawn,
Terres et bois et tenemenz,	Lands, and woods, and tenements,
Por siurre les tornoiemenz.	In order to follow the tournaments.
Bien avoit sor lor tenéure	There was upon their fief quite
Quatre vingt livres à usure,	Eighty livres at usury,
Qui moult les destraint et escille.	Which much afflicted and impoverished them.

Barbazan, Fabliaux, vol. iv. p. 475.

But the oldest of the knights, who was a widower, had a fair daughter, who had inherited from her mother a house in Paris, near the residence of the burgher in question, and the knights fixed upon his son as a husband for her, with a view merely to his father's wealth. The match was soon arranged, but the burgher was persuaded to pass the whole of his property over to his son, on the understanding that he was to live with him as one of the family. The sequel of the story is intended to show the folly of a father giving his property to his children before his death. The lady was proud and haughty, treated her father-in-law with disdain, tyrannized over her husband, and after a short time forced him to turn his father out of the house. This incident, under different forms, was rather a popular story in the Middle Ages.*

* In one of the versions told in Latin in my *Selection of Latin Stories*, p. 28, the deserted father makes his reappearance with a chest, and is reinstated in his place in the household, in the belief that it is filled with treasure, and he is in consequence cherished till his death, when, on opening the chest, it is found to contain nothing but a beetle, or mallet, with the following inscription in English rhyme, which became proverbial :—

Wyht suyle a betel bo he smyten,	With such a beetle bo ho smitten,
That al the werld hyt mote wyten,	That all the world it may know,
That gyfht his sone al his thing,	Who gives his son all his property,
And golt hym self a beggyn.	And goes himself a begging.

We might be led to suppose that such treatment of parents by their children was not uncommon in the Middle Ages.

It was, however, more frequently with the agriculturist, the villain, who sometimes became possessed of landed property, that the impoverished knight sought these unequal marriages for his daughters. In such cases the match was never a happy one ; it was always contrary to the inclinations of the lady, and often forced upon her, and she was justified in disliking her husband, and proving unfaithful to him. On the other hand, the husband, who had been led into the marriage by vanity and ambition, and was jealous and suspicious, was unkind to his wife, and even beat her. In the fabliau of the *Vilain Mire*, there was a rich " villain," who was so miserly that, in spite of his riches, he still continued to follow his plough. He was unmarried. In the same country there was an aged knight, a widower, with a beautiful and courteous daughter, but, as he was poor, nobody offered to marry her. So the friends of the villain addressed themselves to the knight, and he consented, and the damoiselle yielded to her father's will, and was married to him. The villain soon repented of what he had done, became jealous of his wife, and ill-treated her. The manner in which she revenged herself is identical with the story of Molière's *Médecin malgré lui*. The elegant little poem of *La Chatelaine de Saint Gille*, printed in Barbazan (Fabliaux, vol. iii., p. 369), tells of a young damsel, daughter of a châtelain, whose lover is the son of a count, but who is forced by her father into a marriage with a rich villain. In this case the damsel's grief is told with much force, and she does not conceal her feelings from the priest.

" Maugré moi voir je l'averai :	" Against my will truly I shall have him ;
Mès jà foi ne li porterai,	But I will not engage my faith to him,
Sire prestres, bien le sachiez.''	Sir priest, be well assured of it."
" Il ne me chaut que vous faciez,''	" I care not what you do,"
Dist li prestres, " Je vous espouse."	Said the priest, " I espouse you.''

But the marriage was hardly concluded, when the lover made his appearance, seized upon the bride in the villain's hall, and carried her away on his palfrey. I might easily multiply examples of these unsuitable marriages between members of the aristocratic and of the unaristocratic classes.

In fact, the separation between them, however it might be broken into in practice from time to time, became wider than ever in theory. The lady of the castle could not bear to think that the fair bourgeoise wore a dress like her own, or of the same materials, or adorned with similar jewelry. For a long time, in accordance with these prejudices, the dress of the burgher women, however high their family might stand in riches or in municipal rank, continued to be plain and simple, and perhaps nearly uniform. Such was the case with Aelis, the wife of Jean Sarrazin, of Paris, mentioned above, the simplicity of whose costume, no doubt that of the bourgeoise of her time, was seen in her monumental effigy in the abbey of St. Victor. She died in 1293. In spite of the high political position of her father, and the high municipal functions of her husband, she wears the costume of her class; no fur, no gold or silver tissue, appear on the materials of her garments, and the only ornament on her costume is the clasp of her mantle, which is formed of a small gold chain, at the two ends of which are two precious stones mounted in gold. We have—or rather had—another example of a lady of municipal rank in the effigy of Hermessende de Ballegny, the wife of René de la Porte, a bourgeoise of Senlis, who died in 1284. This effigy was once to be seen in the cloister of the abbey of Chaalis. She was clad in a long robe, the train of which she held up under her left arm. A mantle lined with fur descended to her feet. Her head was enveloped in a flat veil, from which issued two fillets. She had long-rounded shoes.

The earlier illuminated manuscripts furnish us with few figures which can be identified as representing individuals of the burgher class. Those here given of a woman and her child are taken from a French manuscript of the closing years of the thirteenth century, preserved in Paris, and evidently represent persons of the better class of municipal society.

A WOMAN OF THE BURGHER CLASS.

The lady wears a plain tunic, or robe descending to the feet, and a headdress of an equally simple character. The second of our cuts is taken from an English source, the manuscript now so well known as Queen Mary's Psalter (MS. Reg. 2 B. VII.) which belongs to the beginning of the four-

34

teenth century. In the original it forms part of a group representing the relatives of Thomas Becket, when driven into exile by King Henry II.,

RELATIVES OF THOMAS BECKET.

making their way on foot towards the sea. Becket's family, as it is well known, were citizens of London, and the English costume of the class as shown here, is identical, or very nearly identical, with that of the bourgeoisie of France, as represented in the last cut. However, at this period, it had for some time been found more and more difficult to restrain the increasing desire of the women of the towns to imitate the extravagance in dress of the lady of the castle. This is sufficiently strongly indicated in the literature of France, but we have not the materials to trace it with equal distinctness in England. The young wife of the carpenter, in Chaucer's *Milleres Tale*, is described as one of the more coquettish of her class, and the poet's description of her costume is well known.

> Fair was tho yonge wyf, and therwithal
> As eny wesil hir body gent (*elegant*) and smal.
> A seynt (*girdle*) sche wered, barred (*striped*) al of silk;
> In barmcloth (*apron*) eek as whit as morne mylk
> Upon hir lendes (*loins*), ful of many a gore (*pleat*).
> Whit was hir smok, and browdid (*embroidered*) al byfore,
> And eek byhynde on hir coler aboute,
> Of cole-blak silk, withinne and eek withoute.
> The tapes of hir white voluper (*kerchief*)
> Weren of the same sute of hire coler;
> Hir filet brood (*broad*) of silk y-set ful heye.
> 　　*　　*　　*　　*　　*
> And by hir gurdil hyng (*hung*) a purs of lethir.
> 　　　　　　　　*Chaucer, Cant. T.,* l. 3233.

No doubt the popular literature of the feudal period would furnish materials for a much more elaborate description of the costume of the bourgeoise at different dates, but the figures here given will be sufficient for the present. Our third cut is taken from a manuscript of the fourteenth century in the British Museum (MS. Reg. 20, C. VII., fol. 32), and forms part of a group of burghers walking in the street.

In the cut on the next page we sink a little lower in the scale, and introduce an example or two of what may be taken to be the populace of the mediæval town, given by Lonandre from an illuminated manuscript of the *Moralité du Jeu des Echecs*, in the Royal Library at Brussels. The colours of the costumes are here rather bright and varied. The woman to the left, who carries her infant in swaddling-clothes, as was then the custom, wears a red robe, or gown, and has, like the carpenter's wife in Chaucer, a white apron. Her head-dress is white; and the envelope of the baby is white with blue swathes. The female on the right has a grey dress, and a green head-covering, and her stockings are yellow, and her boots grey.

Of the social life and character of the women of the higher and more

A SCENE IN THE STREET.

educated class of the bourgeoisie, the details we possess are not abundant, but a general idea may be formed from a perusal of the *Ménagier de Paris,* which I have so often quoted. For our knowledge of Womankind among the mass of the population of the town we must look to the fabliaux and popular tales, to the farces, and to the popular literature generally, and there we shall find it pictured pretty fully, and it must be confessed in not very amiable colours. The generality of the burgher women are represented as ill-educated, coarse in language and manners, and violent in temper. They tyrannize over their husbands, and beat them, and are often beaten in their turn. They loved gadding about. This is perhaps easily understood, when we consider that town life, as far as the male sex was concerned, was very much out-of-doors, and that the women were left to themselves, and therefore sought society among themselves, and, as they had not this at home, they sought some common place of meeting. This place was the tavern, which, in the mediæval town, was, there can be no doubt, the great place of

A GROUP OF THE POPULACE.

resort for both sexes. An early satirical writer, quoted from a manuscript in private hands by M. Jubinal, telling of the tricks employed by the taverners to cheat their customers, says that thus they enrich themselves :—

Quant les dames de la cité,	When the dames of the city,
Ainz q'au moustier ou au marchée,	Before going to church or to market,
Vers la taverne au matinée	Towards the tavern in the morning,
Venent trotant le petit pas.	Come trotting along quickly.

The love of the bourgeoise for the tavern is continually alluded to by the early popular writers. In one of the French black-letter farces of the fifteenth century, a joker of the time is introduced, boasting of the wonderful inventions be has made, and among them is a method to make women hold their tongues ; this is, by giving them plenty to drink.

> Baillez-leur à boire,
> Car je croy, tandis qu'ilz bevrent,
> Que alors point ilz ne parlerent.
> *Farce Nouvelle de Jenin Landore.*

These farces were first made to enliven the dull mysteries, or religious plays, with which the mediæval clergy sought to edify their congregations on certain occasions. When the hearers appeared to be too much wearied with the religious piece, or when it was judged probable that they might be, one of those farces was introduced between the scenes, the subject usually taken from vulgar life. Thus in the middle of the religions play of the Life of St. Fiacre, printed by Jubinal from a manuscript of the fifteenth century, a farce is introduced—*cy est interposé une farsse,* according to the stage direction in the manuscript,—the subject of which is a scene of popular life, the characters being men of the country instead of the town, but in this particular characteristic their manners appear not to have differed. A scuffle has taken place between a yeoman, a sergeant, or bailiff, and a brigand, in which the sergeant's arm is broken. The wives of the bailiff and yeoman meet in another scene, and the latter tells the former of her husband's mishap, at which she expresses her joy, inasmuch as he had beaten her severely the night before, and she hopes he may be disabled from doing it again. The yeoman's wife then proposes to adjourn to a tavern :—

Ma suer, je scay une taverne,	Sister, I know a tavern,
Où il a un moult ay friant,	Where there is a wine so dainty,
Qu'à touz corps fait le cuer riant	That to all bodies it sets the heart laughing
Qui en avalle.	Who drinks of it.

Accordingly, they proceed to the tavern, and address themselves to the hostess :—

Tavernière, si Diex vous voie,	Hostess, God's blessing to you,
En i. lieu privé nous metez,	Put us in a private room,
Puis à boire nous aportez.	And then bring us to drink.

So the women are shown into a private apartment, and are served with wine; and here they enter into a rather free conversation on the characters of their husbands, not much to the advantage of the latter. Says the wife of the bailiff:—

Vous buvrés tout premièrement,	You shall drink first of all,
Commère, vous estes l'ainée.	Gossip, you are the elder.
Aussi m'avez aportée	Moreover you have brought
La nouvelle premièrement	The news first
De mon mary qui malement	Of my husband, how he is
Est atourné; j'en ay grant feste,	In evil plight; I am in great joy,
Je vouldroie qu'eust la teste	I wish he had his head
Parmy brisiée.	Entirely broken.

However, it turns out that the bailiff's hurt was not so great as had been supposed; and the drinking-room was not so secret; for the women are alarmed soon after by seeing their husbands approach the tavern. They arrive, find their wives, and beat them, and, as their wives are very ready at defending themselves, the farce ends in a general scuffle. Such was burgher life in one of its lower phases.

There was another establishment peculiar to the mediæval towns which formed a favourite resort to the townswomen. All the Roman towns of any importance had their public baths, their thermæ, for which the popular name at the close of the Roman period appears to have been *stuphæ*, or some word nearly resembling it. The baths continued in the towns through the Middle Ages, and the same popular name was adopted both into the Romane languages and into the Teutonic. They were called in Italian *stufe*, in Provençal *estubas*, and in French *estuves*, or, in a later orthography, *étuves;* in our own Anglo-Saxon, the word had taken the name of *stofa*, and in the German dialect of the Middle Ages, that of *stobe* or *stove*. In English, the word took the form of *styves*, or *stuwes*, modernized into *stews.** The women of the mediæval towns appear to have spent much of their time in these estuves. They met there as at a party of amusement, and often clubbed together provisions to make a "bancquet," much in the manner of the fashionable pic-nics of the days of our George III. The earlier French popular literature introduces us to the scenes which occurred on these occasions, but they are so coarse and disreputable that I will not venture to describe any of them here. In the manner in which they were conducted, these establishments offered so many facilities to discreditable intrigues, that they became known as houses of ill-fame. They continued to exist in France until rather a later period; in London, they were suppressed by King Henry VIII. in 1546. The name is now only known in a bad sense. In principle they were, of

---

* It may be well to state, that from this word are derived the English word *stew*, and *stove*, and the modern French word *étuve* (a stove).

course, the representatives of the modern Turkish bath, and came originally from the same source.

The tone of society in the towns, as revealed by these scenes in the estuves, was extremely gross, and the language the women use, and the subjects of which they talk, would not bear repetition at the present day. This was, no doubt, less the case with the higher class of the bourgeoise, though, in the *Ménagier de Paris*, the women of this class are expressly warned against the use of obscene words and expressions, as though they were not uncommon. Morality, too, appears to have been at a low ebb, and the burgher women are represented as engaged continually in low intrigues, and as too often faithless to their husbands. Various circumstances conduced to this state of things. The women of the towns, and of the common class in the country, were left much to themselves, and were perhaps on that account more exposed to corruption. But the literature of the feudal age, its tales and fabliaux, its satires, as well as the more serious records of social history, unite in destroying any doubt which might remain on our minds that the Romish priesthood, deprived of the privilege of marriage, were the great corruptors of female morality. This was chiefly the case outside the walls of the feudal castle. The clergy within—the chaplains of the feudal chieftain—were too widely separated in social level from the ladies of the household, and too close under the observation of the lord and his knights and esquires, to be very dangerous. It was the parish priesthood especially, who mixed with their parishioners on a footing of equality, and, in fact, belonged generally, by blood, to the same class, who, armed with what I cannot but consider as the demoralizing system of auricular confession, were the great underminers of the social morals of the Middle Ages. In the popular stories of the time, every woman almost has a priest, or a "clerc," or a monk, for her lover, and not a few of the stories turn upon the alliance or rivalry of clergy and laity in the same pursuit. Moreover, a very considerable portion of the clergy, down to a very late period, so far set the regulations of the Church at defiance, that they lived with concubines, who were acknowledged by the parishioners as their wives, and were commonly spoken of as the "priestesses," who were considered as holding rather a high position in the popular society, and whose children were proud of their descent. The wife of Chaucer's Millar of Trumpington was daughter of the parson of the town—

> A wyf he hadde, come of noble kyn;
> The parsoun (*parson*) of the toun hir fader was.
>
> *Chaucer, Cant. T.*, l. 3940.

and it is added immediately afterwards,—

> And sche was proud and pert as is a pye (*a magpie*).
> *   *   *   *
> Ther durste no wight (*creature*) clepe (*call*) hir but *madame*;
> Was noon so hardy walkyng by the weye
> That with her dorste rage or elles pleye.

The priests' wives, or priestesses (*prêtresses*), formed quite a class in mediæval society, although they were not acknowledged by the Church.

The fabliaux, or stories in verse, and the fables, celebrate largely the manners of the villain and of the burgher class, and we find in them many anecdotes of the quarrelsome temper and obstinacy of the women, which seems to have been proverbial. Two of these stories are told in their shortest form in the fables of Marie of France. According to the first, a villain, that is a peasant, had a very contradictory wife. One day they went to walk together in the meadows, when the villain said to his wife, that he never saw a meadow so evenly mowed. "No," said the wife, curtly, "it is not mowed, but sheared." "I tell you," said the villain, "it was cut with the scythe." The wife persisted in contradicting him, till, in great anger, he threw her down, and cut off her tongue. "Now," said he, "was it mowed, or cut with the shears?" The woman, who could answer no longer with her tongue, held up her hand, and imitated with her fingers the movement of a pair of shears. This is, in perhaps its earliest form, a story often repeated by the mediæval story-tellers. Marie's other fable is as follows:—There was a villain who had a very quarrelsome and ill-disposed wife. One day he had work to do in the field, and his men asked for provisions, which they said would enable them to do their work better. The villain, who was afraid of his wife, sent the men to her, and, by his instructions, they said that her husband had refused to give them anything to eat and drink, and that therefore they had come to her. She was but too ready to contradict her husband, so she told them to go to their work, and promised to follow them with provisions, and she carried out her promise liberally and without delay. When, however, she saw that the good man was glad of what she had done, she was angry with him, and in their dispute she continued retiring before him till she fell into a deep and rapid river which ran behind her. The men, who hurried to save her, were naturally going down the stream to intercept her as she was carried down by its current, but the husband called to them that they were going wrong, that if they wished to find her they must go contrary to the stream, for it was the way in which she had been in the habit of going all her life. So the men went up the stream, and the woman was drowned.

The stories and satires generally describe the wife of the burgher as ill-tempered and quarrelsome, and as living more or less at discord with her husband, and she often beats him and tyrannizes over him. They are usually jealous of each other. The woman's work is spinning, which was equally the case among the inhabitants of the country and of the town; for this seems to have been looked upon as the natural occupation of Womankind. In the fabliau of Barat and Haimet, belonging apparently to the thirteenth century, a robber in the country entering one day the house of a man who was absent in the wood, finds his wife at home spinning.

Sa fame ont trovée filant.

The women assembled together at their work, just as they did in the étuves or baths, brought their provisions and made pic-nics, and thus often spent their long evenings, gossiping over their work, talking of the doings of their husbands, telling scandalous stories of their neighbours, and discussing miscellaneous subjects connected with their superstitions and popular prejudices. The conversation supposed to have taken place on one of these occasions was formed in the middle of the fifteenth century into that most curious of early popular books, *Les Evangiles des Quenouilles*, The Gospels of the Distaffs.*

The illuminations of the manuscripts furnish us with few illustrations of the social life of the yeomanry or of the peasantry during the period I am now describing. It appears to have been less known to, or to have been regarded more contemptuously by, the mediæval artists than that of the other classes. The accompanying cut is taken from a manuscript of the *Dance of Death* of the fifteenth century, in the Imperial Library in Paris. It represents a country labourer and a village woman of the fifteenth century. The female has a grey dress, with a brown apron, and she has red sleeves over those of the dress. Her head-covering is white. She carries a basket, which appears to contain bottles, on her head, just as it would be carried by many a woman of the peasantry at the present day, and she carries another basket on her arm. The illuminator probably intended to represent her coming from, or going to, market. Her companion has a puce coat, with pink lining and blue breeches, and his hat is orange and blue. His stockings are pink, and his sleeves red. Our next cut is taken from a

---

* A very nice edition of this book has been published in Paris in the *Bibliothèque Elzevirienne*, and may be had at a moderate price.

manuscript in the British Museum (MS. Harl., No. 2278, fol. 75, 1ᵒ), also of
the fifteenth century, but executed in England, and containing Lydgate's
metrical history of the life and miracles of St. Edmund the Martyr. It is
intended to illustrate one of the miracles performed by the saint, and represents a countryman and his wife, who were the subject of it, sitting
together in their cottage. To judge by the elegance displayed in the small
house and its furniture, we may suppose the couple to be intended for a
respectable yeoman and his wife. Their dresses are both white.

VILLAGERS OF THE FIFTEENTH CENTURY.

Whoever would form a true notion of the condition and manners of the
rural population during the Middle Ages, must read the *Propos Rustiques,
Baliverneries, Contes, et Discours d'Eutrapel,* of Noel du Fail. They form a
charming picture of rustic life, composed by a gentleman of Britanny
towards the middle of the sixteenth century; but they no doubt represent
social life as it had existed in the country, with very little change, through
the feudal period. The peasant was not ill at ease; he was neither hard
worked nor starved, nor oppressed in a manner which would be personally

painful, and, with religious feasts and holidays, he was indulged with frequent occasions for festivity. As the peasantry were in an entirely servile condition, attached to the ground on which they were born, they must have been more or less rude and uncultivated in their manners and character. One class, however, the shepherds and shepherdesses, are described as an

A YEOMAN AND HIS WIFE.

exception to this. Pastoral life would seem to have had the effect of softening down the character of those engaged in it, and they appear to us as passing their days in quiet happiness, occupied in weaving chaplets of flowers and leaves for each other's heads, the shepherd making love to his shepherdess, and the latter testifying to her attachment for her swain.

It is a curious fact that almost all ages, and almost all countries, have agreed in clothing the pastoral life in poetic form and sentiment. How this feeling arose, it is difficult to explain, but we know that it was eminently the case among the Greeks and Romans. This pastoral sentiment appears to have been carried into the mediæval literature of Western Europe through the poetry of the Provençals, of which it seems to have formed a part in the earliest ages of its history. We find pastoral poets among the small number of trobadors who lived before the middle of the twelfth century, and they belong evidently to a class which had existed long before. But feudalism introduced into this pastoral poetry a new and very characteristic element. The type of the mediæval shepherd and shepherdess is Robin and Marion. The latter is seen during much of her time seated alone, making a chaplet for her Robin or for herself, or engaged in some other rustic occupation, and watching her flocks. Then comes a knight, a chatelain, perhaps some great baron, riding over the land. He considers the shepherd maiden as his right, addresses himself to her, and seeks to overcome her virtue by persuasion or by force. Sometimes she yields easily, and perhaps he carries her away. At other times she resists, or at least is overcome only by degrees, or by personal violence. Or sometimes her Robin, with a sufficient number of his companions, comes to the rescue, and the intruder is obliged to relinquish his prey. It is the knight himself who always, in the Pastoral (called in the Langue d'oil a *Pastourelle*, in the Langue-d'oc, or Provençal, a *Pastoreta*), relates the adventure, whether it were to his advantage or not. As poetical compositions, these feudal pastorals are extremely elegant and graceful. A certain number of them are preserved, two or three in Provençal, and they therefore belong to the south of France, but the greater proportion are composed in the language of the north. These belong to the thirteenth century. The following Pastourelle, by Jehans Erars, will serve as an example :—

Pastourelle.	*Pastoral.*
L'autre ier chevauchai mon chemin,	The other day I was riding on my way,
Dejouste un ruissel	Beside a stream
Truis pastore soz un pin	I found a shepherdess under a pine
Novel.	Of young growth.
D'un ramissel	Of a branch
Ot fait chapel,	She had made a chaplet,
Et cote et chaperon ot	And she had a cote and chaperon
D'un burel ;	Of a coarse cloth ;
Frestel,	A flute and
Chalemel ot,	Pipe she had,
Si notoit	And played,
Et chantoit	And sang

Bien et bel,
Souvent regrete un pastorel,
Car sole gardoit son aignel.
Je m'arestai soz l'ombre d'un fraisnel,
Lez un boschel lassai mon poutrel ;
Sa vois, qui retentist el boschel,
De s'amor m'esprent,
Car le cors a gent,
Le vis clere et bel.

"Lasse !" fait-ele en souspirant ;
"De duel morrai ;
Robins ne m'aime de néant ;
Or maudirai
Le tans de Mai,
Et maudirai
Et foille et flor et glai.
Mal trai,
Si m'esmai ;
Por coi nem'aime Robins, je ne sai ;
Je l'aim de cuer vrai ;
Jà por biauté ne l' laisserai,
Jamais autrui m'amor n'otroierai,
Trop ai le cuer vrai ;
Mès je chanterai :
'Amé l'ai,
Et s'il ne m'aime je l' lairai,
Certes, je l' harrai.
Lasse ! qu'ai-je dit? voir, non ferai.'"

Quant je l'oi si dementer,
Adonc li dis : "Lessiez ester
Cel pastorel ;
Chaitis est, et sera toz dis,
Jamais n'aurois de lui soulaz tant com soit
    vis."
Tant dis et pramis
Qu'entre mes bras doucement la saisis,
Sor l'erbe verdoiant la mis,
Les ex li baisai et puis le vis ;
Lors me sambla que fus en Paradis.
De li fui espris,
S'en pris et repris,
    Puis li dis :
"N'aurez pis."
Ele jete un ris,
Si dit : "Mes amis
Serez mais toz dis."

Well and fair.
Often she regrets her shepherd,
For she kept alone her lamb.
I halted under the shade of an ash,
By a grove I left my steed ;
Her voice, which resounds in the grove,
Smites me with her love,
For she has an elegant body,
A face bright and fair.

"Alas !" says she, sighing,
"I shall die of grief ;
Robin does not love me at all ;
Now I shall curse
The season of May,
And I shall curse
Both leaf and flower and glai (the iris).
I am in a bad way,
And I am dismayed ;
Why Robin does not love me, I know not ;
I love him with true heart ;
Not for beauty will I leave him,
I will never grant my love to another.
I have a heart too true ;
But I will sing :
'Loved him I have,
And if he loves not me I will leave him ;
Truly, I will hate him.
Alas ! what have I said? truly, I will not do it.'"

When I heard her lament so,
Then I said to her : "Let be
That shepherd ;
He is a wretch, and will be ever,
Thou wilt never have solace from him as long
    as he lives."
I said and promised so much
That I seized her gently within my arms,
And seated her on the green grass,
I kissed her eyes and then her face ;
Then it seemed to me that I was in Paradise.
With her I was enchanted,
Enamoured more and more,
    Then I said to her :
"You will have no worse."
She uttered a laugh,
And said, "My love
You shall be for ever more."

Adam de la Halle, a writer also of the thirteenth century, and a native of

Arras, has left us a sort of dramatic pastoral, *The Play of Robin and Marion* (*li Gieus de Robin et de Marion*), which gives quite a charming picture of pastoral life in this poetic point of view. At the opening of the scene, Marion sits meditating on her love for Robin, and on the dresses and girdle he had brought for her, when a knight, returning from a tournament, rides up and pays his addresses somewhat rudely. She resists, tells him that she loves nobody but Robin, and he leaves her. Then Robin arrives, with an offering of apples, and she tells him of the behaviour of the knight. They sit down, eat bread and cheese and apples, and talk about their provisions. Robin asks her for her chapelet, and she produces it, and places it on his head with her own hand, after which they play. Robin then leaves her, to seek one or two of his companions as help against the knight should he return, and to fetch the tambour and the *musette au grand bourdon*. He finds Gautier and Baudon, and tells them about the knight, and they agree to assist in punishing him if he should come again, and they then seek another shepherdess, Peronelle, to make one of their party. Meanwhile the knight again makes his appearance, and makes another attempt upon Marion. His hawk flies from his fist, and they are disturbed by hearing Robin coming, and playing his silver flageolet, upon which Marion exclaims,—

> J'oi Robin flageoler
> Au flagol d'argent.

As Marion resists resolutely, the knight goes away again, meets Robin, finds that he has killed his hawk, beats him, and attempts to carry away Marion by force. Robin displays little courage, but he calls to Gautier and Baudon to come and rescue her, and she resists so obstinately, that the knight abandons her before they arrive. Robin then takes her in his arms, and she complains of his kissing her before strangers, so that modesty did exist among shepherdesses,—

> Esgarde de cest sosterel!   Look at this little fool!
> Qui me baise devant la gent.   Who kisses me before people.

Baudon tells her that they are his kinsmen, and that she need be under no restraint. Peronelle and Huart now arrive, and are welcomed. The whole party next consult on some amusement, and they agree to play at " Kings and Queens," one of the popular games of that period. They choose Baudon for king, and Peronelle places her straw hat on his head for a crown. It is, in fact, a game of questions, in the course of which Robin is condemned to embrace his Marion, and the following description of the maiden's coyness,

and the somewhat grotesque compliment paid to her by her lover open a
new scene :—

LI ROIS.	THE KING.
Va, s'acole dont Marion Si douchement que il li plaise.	Go, let him then kiss Marion So gently that it may please her.
MARIONS.	MARION.
Auvar dou sot, s'il ne me baise!	Away with the fool, if he is not kissing me!
ROBINS.	ROBIN.
Certes, non fac.	Indeed, I am not doing it.
MARIONS.	MARION.
Vous en mentés, Encore i pert-il, esgardés! Je cuit que mors m'ou visage.	There you lie. He is at it again, look! I believe that he has bitten me on the face.
ROBINS.	ROBIN.
Je cuidai tenir j. froumage, Si te senti-je tenre et mole! Vien avant, seur, et si m'acole l'ar pais faisant.	I thought I was holding a cheese, I felt thee so tender and soft! Come forward, sister, and kiss me To make peace.

It must be borne in mind that the cheese seems to have been the
favourite food of the rustic population of France. The questions go on till
Peronelle is enjoined to tell—

Le plus grant joie c'ainc éusses D'amours, en quel lieu que tu fusses.	The greatest joy that thou ever haddest Of love, in whatever place thou wast.

She replies without hesitation,—

Sire, volentiers le dirai. Par foi! chou est quant mes amis, Qui en moi cuer et cors a mis, Tient a moi as caus compaignie, Lés mes brebis, sans vilenie, Plusieurs fois, mieuu et souvent.	Sire, willingly I will tell it. By my faith! it is when my lover, Who has given me his heart and body, Keeps me company in the fields, By my sheep, without falsity, Several times, delicately and often.

After this, Marion is ordered to tell how greatly she loves Robin, and she
replies—

MARION.	MARION.
Par foi! je n'en mentirai jà. Je l'aim, sire, d'amour si vraie Que je n'aim tant brebis que j'aie, Nis cheli qui a aiguelé.	By my faith! I will not lie at all. I love him, sire, with love so true As I love no sheep I possess, Not even the one which has lambed.

BAUDONS.	BAUDON (*the King*).
Par le saint Dieu! c'est bien amé;	By God's saint! that is well loved;
Je vœil qu'il soit de tous séu.	I will that it be known by all.

The game is broken up by the news that the wolf is carrying off one of

THE SHEPHERDESS.

Marion's sheep. More love-making follows, and Robin is advised to take Marion, while Peronelle is put to choose between Gautier, Baudon, and Huart. Then they propose to eat together, club their provisions, have a pic-nic on the grass, and converse over it. Robin brings news of another shepherdess, named Mehalès.

Warnet, tu ne ses? Mehalès
Est hui agulé de no prestre.

Garnier, don't you know? Mehalès
Has to-day borne a child by our priest.

Mehalès appears to have been Garnier's love, and they console him ; and the play of Adam de la Halle ends with a dance.

These belong all to the thirteenth century. Towards the close of the fourteenth, the poetess Christine de Pisan composed a little poem on the shepherdess, one of those pieces so much in favour during the thirteenth, fourteenth, and fifteenth centuries, called a dit, *Le Dit de la Pastoure.* The shepherdess is introduced telling the story of her earlier years passed in rustic simplicity attending to her flock. There she sat under an oak, singing, and occupying herself in spinning and other woman's work. There the other shepherdesses assembled, each led by her favourite shepherd, one of whom would bring a flageolet, another a tabor, and another some other instrument of rustic music. Not one of them was so poor but she was rich in a lover.

N'il n'y avoit si povrete,
Qui ne fust riche d'ami.

She then tells how chance brought a gentle knight who loved and married her, and she talks of their affection with much of tender sentiment. I am not aware that this little poem has ever been printed, but a finely-illuminated manuscript of the works of Christine, written for presentation to the queen of France early in the fifteenth century, and now preserved in the British Museum (MS. Harl., No. 1431, fol. 223), contains a copy of it, accompanied by a picture of the shepherdess attending her sheep, of which we give a copy in the accompanying cut (page 280). She appears to be either making a *chapelet* or embroidering a *ceinturette*, as it is called in the poem.

En chantant à haulte alaine,
Ceinturetes je faisoie.

Our next cut represents a dance of shepherds and shepherdesses, taken from a manuscript *Livre d'Heures* of the fifteenth century, preserved in the Bibliothèque Imperiale in Paris (No. 1173, Lat.), said to have been executed in Flanders. In the original it forms part of the scene of the Annunciation,

36

and represents a group of shepherds and shepherdesses engaged in a carole, or dance, round a tree. The damsel to the left, with the chaplet on her head, is evidently the belle of the party.

A DANCE OF SHEPHERDS.

CHAPTER XVIII.

LITERATURE AMONG THE WOMEN OF THE FEUDAL PERIOD—MARIE DE FRANCE AND CHRISTINE DE PISAN.

It was a question debated at times during the feudal period, whether a knowledge of letters was good for the female sex or not. Some of the censorious part of the clergy, indeed, seem to have held that this knowledge was only an additional element of evil in the hands of Womankind, and would have proscribed it altogether, but their opinion does not appear to have been very generally accepted. We can trace from a rather early period the love of the ladies of the feudal ages for reading. One of the beauties of a lady described in an English song of the thirteenth century, printed in my *Specimens of Lyric Poetry*, is "a merry mouth to talk, with lovely red lips able to read Romance." That is, I presume, to read the French or Anglo-Norman in which books in England were then written.

> Heo hath a mury mouht to mele,
> With lefly rede lippes lele
> Romaunz forte rede.
> *Specimens of Lyric Poetry*, p. 34.

In the romance of *Flamenca*, written in a dialect which is half Provençal, there is a fine passage on this subject. "A rich man," says the damoiselle Alis to her lady Flamenca, "who is not a little instructed in letters, loses much of his value, and the lady who is somewhat instructed in letters, is only the more valued for it,"—

> E trop ne val meins totz vix hom,
> Si non sap letras ques a com;
> E dona es trop melz cubida
> S'es de letras un panc garnida.
> *Roman de Flamenca*, ed. Paul Meyer, l. 4812.

For indeed, you, Madame, tell me, if you had not known as much as you know, how would you have passed over these two years, during which you have suffered such cruel torments? You would have been dead with grief! But, however great were your sadness, it disappeared when you read a little." "Friend," said Flamenca, pressing her in her arms, "you speak wisely. For no repose is pleasant to a man who is ignorant of letters; and you will ever see that persons who are learned, regret that they are not more so." We have reasons for believing that generally in the knightly household the ladies were the most learned part of the family. Learning to read or write was not considered to form a necessary part of a gentleman's education until a comparatively late period; his instruction was in arms, and in the active pursuits of life. In the families of lesser rank, the female children were more frequently sent for education into a convent, where reading and writing, and some degree of learning, would be taught as a matter of course. As they grew up they formed at home the more knowing part of the household.

There is no reason why woman, when instructed, should not seek distinction in literary composition as well as the other sex, and we have already seen that this was the case at an early period of the Middle Ages. At all periods, indeed, when we can trace a literature, we find women shining in it. The Provençal poets, the trobadors, count among their ranks a number of poetesses, many of them of high rank, and all belonging to the twelfth century. Such were the countess of Provence, the countess of Dié, Clair d' Anduze, Adelaïde de Porcairgues, and the dame Capelloza. These sang their loves for their favourites of the male sex, just as the latter sang to the praise of the ladies. These Provençal poetesses all belong to the latter half of the twelfth century. In the century following we find poetesses in the North, who rivalled the Southerners. Among these comes the name of a duchess of Lorraine, whose identity is rather uncertain, and has been the subject of various conjectures. The little that remains of her writings, all songs, show that she was well read in the literature of her age. In the opening of one, she says, " People ask me often why I no longer compose songs as formerly; but the affliction of my heart ought to be visible to everybody. I would cease to live; and my vow would be to imitate Dido, who, for Æneas, gave herself to death." From the sequel it would appear that she had been deserted by a lover whose advances she had withstood. It appears evident from the passage I have quoted, that the fair Duchess of Lorraine had, if I may use the phrase, lived a life of poetry. There is preserved another very touching song by a lady whose lover apparently had gone to the crusade, and whose family sought to force her into a marriage with another in his absence. It has been printed by Paulin Paris, in the twenty-third volume of the *Histoire Literaire de la France*. It is ascribed in one of the manuscripts to the dame de la Fayel.

But the thirteenth century had a poetess whose reputation was substantially more durable than any of these. Her name was Marie. As she was always known by the name of Marie de France, there can be little doubt that she was by birth a Frenchwoman, but we have no information as to what part of France she belonged, though it was probably Normandy, which in her time was separated from the crown of England. The feelings of relationship between the two countries still, however, existed, and many of the families which considered themselves no less English than Norman, left the latter country to settle in England. Perhaps some feelings of this kind influenced the position of Marie, for she certainly lived in the latter country, and she acknowledges as her patron and protector a king Henry, who can be no other than our King Henry III. And she speaks of another of her powerful friends under the title of the Count William, who has been identified, with apparent reason, as the valiant William Longue-épée, earl of Salisbury. Marie, as a poetess, differs entirely from those I have just enumerated; she was a poetess of her age, and wrote for its edification and benefit, as she knew it. Her first work, as far as we know, was written at least to please the king, to whom it was dedicated; it was a collection of love tales professing to be derived from Breton legend, in that sentiment which had been made popular by the publication of the romances of the Round Table, and which had received the name of Lais. In the prologue to her collection she gives rather a curious account of herself, and of the motives which led her to become an authoress.. With her consciousness of her talent as a composer, she considered it her duty to employ it in these literary compositions. For, she says,—

Ki Deus ad doné en science	When God has given any one in knowledge
Jo parler la bone eloquence,	To speak true eloquence,
Ne s'en deit taisir ne celer;	He ought not to be silent or conceal it;
Ainz se deit volunters mustrer.	But he ought voluntarily to show himself.
Quant uns granz biens est mult oiz,	When a great good is much heard,
Dunc à per-mesmes est-il fluriz;	Then by its own movement it is blossomed;
E quant loez est de plusurs.	And when it is praised by many,
Dunc ad espandues ses flurs.	Then it has spread its blossoms.

Marie had been well instructed in school learning, for she quotes Priscian in support of her statements. She tells us that at first, with the sentiments derived from the study of the philosophers, it was her design to translate some book from Latin into French, but that she was deterred by the reflection, that many others had done this, and that the field was already occupied. Then she determined to reduce into French verse the Breton lais which she had so often heard, and publish them in the collective form in which she now presented them to the king. The success of these lais appears to have been great, as we learn from another source.

There lived in this same thirteenth century, and, as it would appear, contemporary with Marie, an Anglo-Norman poet named Denis Piramus, who in his earlier life had employed his muse on gayer subjects, but turned it afterwards to the composition of saints' legends in verse, some of which are preserved in a manuscript in the British Museum (MS. Cotton. Domitian XI.) In the beginning of one of these, the life of St. Edmund, Denis talks of the poetry of his time, and thus speaks of Marie and of her lais :—

E dame Marie autresi,	And dame Marie similarly,
Ki en ryme fist e basti,	Who made and formed in rhyme,
E compensa les vers de lays,	And compiled the verses of lays,
Ke ne sunt pas de tut verais;	Which are not at all true;
E si en est ele mult loée,	And yet she is much praised for them,
E la ryme par tut amée;	And the rhyme is everywhere loved;
Kar mult l'ayment si l'unt mult cher	For much love it and hold it very dear
Cunt, barun, e chivaler,	Earls, barons, and knights,
E si enayment mult l'escrit,	And they love very much the writing,
E lire le funt, si unt delit,	And cause it to be read, and have pleasure,
E si les funt soveut retreire.	And they cause them to be often recited.
Les lays soleient as dames pleire,	The lays usually please the ladies,
De joye les oyent e de gré,	They listen to them joyfully and willingly,
Qu'il sunt sulum lur volenté.	For they are in accordance with their liking.

Life of St. Edmund, MS. Cotton. Domit. XI. fol. 1.

We are not sure that Marie had not her enemies and detractors. Denis is speaking in some degree against her lais as frivolous compositions, which too often took the place of pious subjects; and Marie herself seems to intimate that some of the trouvères, or poets, of her time were jealous of her. In the opening lines of the *Lai de Gugemer,* she expresses her anxiety to compose well and successfully, and speaks of the feelings of envy and jealousy which influence some as though from personal experience.

Celui deivent la gent loer	People ought to praise him
Ki en bien fait de sei parler.	Who causes himself to be talked of in good.
Mais quant oent en un païs	But when they hear in a country
Humme u femme de grant pris,	Of a man or woman of great worth,

Cil ki do sun bien unt envie	They who are envious of his good
Suvent en dient vileinie,	Often speak basely of him,
Sun pris li volent abeisier.	Seek to detract from his merit.
Par ceo conmencent le mestier	In this manner they follow the example
Del malveis chien, coart, felun,	Of the bad dog, cowardly, wicked,
Ki mort la gent par traïsun.	Which bites people treacherously.
Ne l'voil mie pur ceo laissier.	I will not flinch on that account.
Si jangleur u si losengier	If mockers or if revilers
Le me volent à mal turner,	Will turn my doing to reproach,
Ceo est lur dreit de mesparler.	It is their quality to rail.

There is only one copy of Marie's Lais preserved, in a manuscript in the British Museum, which contains a dozen lais, and one or two others, conjectured to be hers, have been added in the edition edited in France by M. de Roquefort. It is different with another work of Marie's, which must, therefore, in its time have been far more popular. This work is a collection of fables, compiled also in Anglo-Norman verse, of which there are three manuscripts in the British Museum, and I have heard of at least eight in the Paris collection. The poetess professes, in the conclusion of the book, to have translated this book of fables out of English into French, which would show at once that she wrote for the aristocratic class of society, for the love of the valiant Earl William, and, that there might be no doubt as to the name of the translator, she informs us that it was Marie, and that she was a native of France.

Au finement de cest escrit	At the conclusion of this writing
K'en Romanz ai turné e dit,	Which I have turned into French and said,
Me numerai par remembraunce;	I will name myself for remembrance,
Marie ai num, si sui de Fraunce.	My name is Marie, and I am of France.
• • • •	• • • •
Pur amur le cumte Willaume,	For the love of earl William,
Le plus vaillant de cest royaume,	The most worthy of this kingdom,
M'entremis de cest livre feire,	I undertook to make this book,
E de l'Angleiz en Roman treire.	And to translate it from English into French.

From some expressions in the prologue to this book, we might suppose that Marie thought the subject hardly worthy of her, but she excuses herself by the greatness of the baron at whose request she undertook it.

Meiz ne purquant cil m'en semunt	But nevertheless he calls me to do it
Ki flourz est de chevalerie.	Who is the flower of chivalry,
D'anseignemeuz, de curteisie;	Of intelligence, of courtesy;
E quant tex hum m'en ad requise,	And when such a man has requested me to do it,
Ne voil lessier en nul guise	I will not fail on any account
Que n'i mette traveil e peine.	To put into it labour and pains.

The general opinion appears now to be that the earl Wiiliam, who was
Marie's patron, was no other than the celebrated William Longue-épée, earl
of Salisbury, the son of Henry II. by fair Rosamond. The heroic Longue-
épée, the court of Henry II., at which poetry flourished, Rosamond, a lady
poetess patronized by her son, plunge us into the midst of the romance of
history. William Longue-épée died in 1226.

Marie was essentially the poetess of feudal society. Just two centuries
after her time, there appeared another poetess, whose character and talents
marked the transition to another period of social history.

In the middle of the fourteenth century there flourished at Venice an
eminent physician named from the city of his birth Thomas de Pisan, who
united with his own profession a knowledge of some of those sciences forbidden by the Church, which were then so much sought after. Charles V.,
who at that time occupied the throne of France, heard of his fame, and
invited him to Paris, where he appointed him astrologer to the king and one
of his council, and loaded him with favours. Thomas de Pisan was introduced to the king in the month of December, 1368, with his wife and a
daughter named Christine. The latter was then five years of age, and
already remarkable for her great intelligence. Her father gave her a very
finished, we may say, a learned education, for she was evidently well
acquainted with Latin. Her personal accomplishments, combined with her
father's high favour at court, rendered the young Christine de Pisan a good
match, and she married while still young a gentleman of Picardie, named
Etienne Castel. Two years after the marriage, in 1370, Charles VI. died,
and Thomas de Pisan, deserted by the court, did not long outlive him. We
know little of the earlier period of the literary life of Christine de Pisan, but
in 1396 she was already well known by her poetry, for when the Earl of
Salisbury returned to England after attending the marriage of Richard II.
with the daughter of Charles VI. in that year, he brought with him a volume
of the poems of Christine de Pisan, which he had obtained in Paris. In
1402 her husband was carried away by the fearful pestilence which desolated
France in that year, and, through various circumstances, she was left with
children to educate and poor relatives to support, in all six persons dependent
entirely upon her literary labours. It was then that, as the resource most
accordant with her own inclinations, she devoted herself entirely to literary
labours; and it has been remarked that she was probably the first woman
who, in Western Europe, sought to live by her pen.

There was, no doubt, something great in the character of Christine de
Pisan, even as we see it through her own writings, and her own account of

herself, a singular combination of energy and trust in herself, with delicacy of sentiment. Her's was literally a life of work, yet she never seems to have flinched from it, or to have complained of it. She possessed a facility of style which extended equally to prose and verse. Her power of working seems to have been almost unlimited, and she tells us herself in 1405, that she had already composed fifteen principal works, without reckoning her smaller and more playful writings, that is, the poems of various kinds composed in her youth, which altogether, she says, "filled seventy quires of a large volume." * A quire (*cahier*), consisted of four leaves of vellum, or paper. I must add, that she appears at this time to have been not only an authoress, but to have taken upon herself the occupation of scribe, and to have made copies of her own writings. Her literary industry was a subject of admiration among the princes and nobles of her day; and she was induced to present copies of her works to different members of the royal family, and to other distinguished personages. Some of these presentation copies still remain, and more than one of them is illustrated with beautiful illuminations, in some of which Christine herself is represented either as writing or as presenting her book. One of these manuscripts is preserved in the Library of the British Museum (MS. Harl. No. 4431), a large handsome volume on vellum, richly illuminated, containing no less than thirty articles, some of which consists of a considerable number of separate pieces of poetry. This manuscript appears to have been written in 1404, for presentation to Isabelle of Bavaria, the queen of Charles VI., and it begins with a prologue to the queen, at the head of which is an exquisite illumination representing Christine in the act of presenting it. We give a copy of this illumination in its colours in the accompanying plate; and from the care with which it is executed in the original, we have every reason to suppose that the figures of Christine and the queen were intended to be portraits. It is probably the first portrait of a poetess of our Western regions that we possess. Another of her important works Christine dedicated to Charles VI. himself.

The poverty of Christine, and her courageous efforts to support her family, as well as her literary merits, seem at this time to have been well known. The volume of her poems brought to England by the Earl of Salisbury appears to have excited considerable interest, and Henry of Lancaster, now on the throne of England, invited her to seek a home in our

---

* Quinze ouvrages principaux, sans compter les autres particuliers petits dictiez, lesquels tous ensemble contiennent soixante-dix cahiers de grant volume.

island. Another prince, whose influence might be supposed to have had more weight with one whose family was identified with Italy, gave her a similar invitation. This was Galeas Visconti, Duke of Milan, whose daughter was married to the Duke of Orleans, brother of Charles VI., a name so intimately connected with the history of France at this period. But Christine had become a French woman, her children were French, and she had identified herself entirely with her adopted country. She was proof against both invitations.

Amid the troubles which now fell heavily upon France, Christine laid aside her taste for composing ballads and lays and rondeaux, and assumed a higher roll. She had, as described in a former chapter, presented herself as the champion of her sex and of public morals against the attacks of the *Roman de la Rose*, and the licentious spirit which was daily gaining ground. In the autumn of 1405, when civil war appeared inevitable, Christine entered into politics with all her energy, and presented herself as the champion of peace. She had still preserved some credit with the queen, Isabelle of Bavaria, and she addressed to her an expostulatory letter, entitled, "The Weeping Request of Loyal Frenchmen" (*La Plourable Requeste des Loyaux François*). It would perhaps be not assuming too much, if we suppose that a document so well timed and so well written had some influence on the minds of men already inclined to listen to conciliatory councils. A few days after its appearance was concluded the peace of Vincennes. But the reconciliation was insincere, and very few years passed before civil war threatened the land once more. Christine again appeared as a political writer, and she uttered her feelings of sadness on the political prospects under the title of her *Lamentation*. Then came the wars with England, and affairs went worse and worse, till at length Christine abandoned the world, and retired to a nunnery. There she remained eleven years, until her feelings of patriotism were again roused by the appearance of the Maid of Orleans, and she composed in her praise a poem, a copy of which was discovered by M. Jubinal among the manuscripts of the Library of Berne, and published by him in 1838. This was the year 1429, when Christine de Pisan was in her sixty-seventh year. How long Christine lived after the publication of this poem appears to be unknown.

CHAPTER XIX.

THE TRANSITION FROM FEUDALISM—THE BEGINNING OF THE SIXTEENTH CENTURY—LOUIS XII. AND HENRY VIII.

WE are now at the close of the Middle Ages, and have arrived at a new period of transition, the result of which was the formation of modern society. From without, a new element has come in to contribute to the general agitation in the revival of classical feeling, and historical and antiquarian writers seem agreed in giving to this period the title of the Renaissance.

At the beginning of the fifteenth century, feudalism itself may be considered to have perished, though its outward forms not only remained, but were much exaggerated in their character. The chivalrous spirit was gone, but the ostentation and extravagant display, the pride, the selfishness, the licence, the ferocity, which had entered so largely into it, were there still. Indeed, they now were taken as feudalism itself. This was especially remarkable in France, which was always looked upon as the centre of feudalism. The effect of feudalism was, as it has been more than once remarked in the present volume, to give a uniformity of character, at least outwardly, to the different peoples who entered into it, and we have had occasion to remark more than once how much this character prevailed throughout feudal society. In fact, there was one great model of social manners, which was France, and this feeling was so strong that it has left a certain impression down to modern times. The change began to take place very rapidly under Philippe de Valois, whose reign presented a series of events calculated to destroy the feudal unity. Feudalism in its military spirit perished on the field of Créci (1346). Philippe left his country, devastated by war, nearly reduced to poverty, and wasted by one of the most fearful pestilences that had yet visited it, to a prodigal and reckless successor, in King Jean, who only increased the number of its disasters. Jean offered himself as the champion of feudalism, and in the belief that he was restoring it, he only hastened its fall. The last spark of the chivalry of feudalism appears to have expired in the ranks of the free companies. Jean himself died a prisoner in England, and left France to a king, Charles V., who possessed those qualities which procured him the title of Charles the Wise. He did much towards restoring his country, but not towards bringing back feudalism; but he was followed by a weak-minded and extravagant prince, under whom the kingdom was abandoned to extravagant licentiousness on the part of the court and the nobility, and to turbulence on all sides, all which ended in the king's madness. Thus opened the fifteenth century in France.

The first quarter of the fifteenth century was in France a period of extreme misery. It was a period of civil war and of invasion from abroad; of open and reckless debauchery and extravagance, in which the country was impoverished and industry ruined, and all social movement was at a stand. The good qualities of Womankind were neither valued nor respected, nor even protected, but, on the contrary, they were universally exposed to contempt and outrage. During the whole of this period a continuous succession of famines added to the general distress.

It was during the period of which we have taken this rapid glance that the change in the forms and character of the dress of both sexes began to be frequent. It commenced with the reign of Philippe de Valois, when new forms and new ornaments were given to the female costume, and richer materials were continually introduced. The spirit of extravagance, moreover, spread itself through all classes; and, in spite of sumptuary laws, the commons sought to rival the aristocracy. Neither did the disasters of the reign of Jean, nor the austere simplicity of Charles V., do anything to arrest the evil which, under Charles VI., became greater than ever. Towards the middle of the fifteenth century, however, the country began to recover itself, and great efforts were made to revive trade and industry. The display of rich as well as elegant costumes increased everywhere. Workmen were brought from Italy and the East, and materials of a much richer and more expensive description were now manufactured in France. That country began to have its own factories of cloth of gold, of silks, of brocade, of damask, and of grogram; and cotton, too, was now brought into use in the manufacture of cloth. The use of silk became every day more general among the commonalty.

It will be well to give a rapid glance over the changes in the general character of costume in France during these ages of turbulence, and during the period which immediately followed. Under Charles VI., the robes and the houppelande were the principal articles of female dress, answering to the older tunic and outer tunic. The houppelande was common to both sexes; but the men's houppelande was closed behind, and that of the women before. The women's dress was generally loose and spreading, and they affected excessively long trains. Under Charles VII., the modifications in the female costume were chiefly imported from Italy. The ladies sought more and more to show the forms of their bodies, and they wore a close-fitting corsage, and petticoats and dress shortened so as to show the feet and lower part of the legs. At this time the customs of painting, and of dyeing the hair, prevailed more generally than before. Louis XI. sought to repress the extravagance and love of display which had exercised so fatal an influence over his kingdom, and he not only discouraged them in others, but he himself set the example of simplicity in his dress. This, indeed, was carried to an excess, and it is said that even in personal conference with sovereigns who came dressed in rich stuffs covered with gold and precious gems, Louis was seen in an old doublet of gray fustian, and a shabby felt hat. Towards the latter end of his reign, however, he appears to have affected more elegance of attire, and his successor, Charles VIII., returned to the old taste for extravagance. The close dresses appear to have been only partially adopted, and the spreading dress was still worn, so that, at the same time, some appeared in dresses which fitted so tight as to show the form of the body and limbs minutely, while some went to the other extreme and wore them unreasonably wide and flowing. But at the close of the century the close-fitting dress gained the mastery, and has influenced more or less the form of the dress from that time to the present. The more zealous of the clergy, in their sermons, were indefatigable in their declamations against the old extravagance, and against the old costume. The long trains, or tails, as they called them, especially provoked their indignation. One of the best known of them, Oliver Maillard, preaching in Paris against this fashion, towards the end of the fifteenth century, said, "And you, my ladies, who are painted, who carry your tail lifted up, and you, gentlemen, who suffer your daughters to wear tails, do you believe then that people go into paradise with such dresses?" *

The general character of the costume became more refined in the reign

---

* Et vous, mesdames les fardées, qui portez la queue troussée, et vous, messieurs qui souffrez que vos filles portent des queues, croyez-vous donc qu'on entre en Paradis avec une pareille toilette.

of Louis XII., who ascended the throne of France in 1498. Our cut represents that monarch with his first queen, Anne of Britany, and their daughter the Princess Claude. It is given by Willemin, from a large illuminated manuscript of a translation into French of Petrarch's Latin treatise

LOUIS XII AND ANNE OF BRITANY.

De remediis utriusque fortunæ, executed at Rouen in 1503, and now preserved in the Imperial Library at Paris. It will be seen at a glance that we have here in both figures costumes entirely different from those which we have contemplated during the feudal period. The king wears a gown of yellow damask, his sleeves are black, lined with dark fur, and he has violet stockings. His hat is black. Anne is dressed in the costume which she herself introduced into the court of France. She wears on her head the small flat hood, *à la mode de Bretagne,* which was called the *cape.Bretonne.* Her robe is black, with very spacious sleeves, lined with brown fur, of the fashion which was termed *à la grand' gorre,* which we may, perhaps, translate, of the first style. Her robe is hollowed square on the breast, and ungirt, or merely furnished with a loose girdle resting on the hips. The whole of the costume represents strictly the beginning of the sixteenth century. Still, at this period, it appears that even a queen did not think it beneath her dignity to nurse her child. The Princess Claude was at this time about three years of age.

In our next cut, we see Anne of Britany again, attended by the ladies of her court. Jean Desmaretz was one of the literary men of the day, who is not unknown to fame. He wrote a book on the victory of Louis XII. over the Genoese in 1507, a copy of which he is here represented as presenting to the queen. Our cut is taken from an illumination in the identical manuscript of this book which the queen thus received from its author, and which is now preserved in the Imperial Library in Paris. Her cape Bretonne is here adorned with pearls, and she wears a sort of girdle which was called a *Cordelière,* because it resembled that of the Cordeliers, or Franciscan friars.

As I have already stated, the feudal system was broken down, and the different nationalities which had composed it were separated and scattered, to follow their own fortunes, form their own national sentiments and character, and, as far as circumstances led them, assume their own costume. The struggle between the old and the new, under which feudalism expired, differed more or less in each of these nationalities, according to the characters of the peoples. In France, vanity and the love of display were the national characters, and the aristocracy there were proud, and excessively extravagant and licentious. There was no respectable middle class between them and the populace to hold them in check, for the action of the burghers hardly extended beyond their own towns, and their strength was chiefly expended in the defence of their own walls, or of their own municipal privileges, and that strength was exhausted in the spoliations and massacres of the civil wars of the fifteenth century. Thus the only two rival powers in France were the crown and the aristocracy, and the personal imbecility and folly of the kings during this period gave the easy mastery to the nobles. But these weakened and demoralized themselves by their own licence and

extravagance, and they were not united, but displayed a continual tendency
to separate and act against one another. They seemed to be actuated in
their relations to one another by no other motive than individual selfishness.

JEAN DESMARETZ PRESENTING HIS BOOK TO ANNE OF BRITANY.

They hung to the wasted shadows of feudalism, and talked loudly of
chivalry, but they only meant by it wild, exaggerated extravagance, which
left them exhausted. It was a sentiment displayed in great feasts and tourna-

ments, in which one of the great nobles would spend at once the collective amount of his income for several years. To supply this, he was obliged to borrow and plunder, in which the king and the nobles followed exactly the same course; thus both they and the people who depended upon them became hopelessly impoverished. Although eventually, after a long period of social debasement, the country recovered itself, a national character was left upon society in France, which endured to a very late period. In those melancholy times, as it has been remarked, every one seemed to be trying to prove who could ruin himself first. The court which, in this respect, rivalled most closely that of France, or perhaps, exceeded it, was that of Burgundy. The prodigality of Duke Philippe was so extraordinary, that, though he was by his own territory the richest prince in Europe, besides the immense sums he had realized by plundering the treasury of France, when he died in 1404, he left a debt so vast that all the goods he possessed were quite insufficient to pay it. As was customary in such cases, his duchess, with the due formalities, and in the presence of a notary, placed upon the coffin of her husband her girdle with the gipcière, or purse, and the keys attached to it, a ceremony by which she was understood to surrender his goods, said to be of inestimable value, to his creditors.

The case was otherwise in England, where the struggle with feudalism had been of a different character. Here the crown had not been overcome by the aristocracy, and, on the other hand, from the earliest times, the English barons had always possessed a greater amount of public spirit and of popular sympathies than was ever shown by their brethren in France. Society was different in our country, and from a rather early period there was gradually forming a middle class of landed proprietors—perhaps we may call it a lesser aristocracy—which was becoming more and more independent, and which was finally represented by the country gentleman. In that interesting monument of our old English society, the *Paston Letters,* we contemplate the English gentleman as he existed and lived in the fifteenth century, and we are struck with the bold, straightforward honesty of his character, no less than with the intelligence, purity, and good sense of his wife and daughters. They were the women of the manor-house, who were to take the place of the women of the castle. The independent power of the English gentleman, as a class, was not yet very great, for his position placed him still, more or less, a dependent on his feudal superior. The great mass of the land in England was then possessed in very large portions by two classes of landlords,—the old feudal barons and the monastic orders. Feudalism at this time no longer existed, except in some of its forms, but the landed

38

property, and, of course, the influence, of most of the great nobles was immense, and when, in the vicissitudes of the civil wars, or for any act of treason or rebellion, it was confiscated, it was, in most cases, only to be regranted to another individual of the same class. But another and far

ENGLISH LADIES OF THE END OF THE FIFTEENTH CENTURY.

greater confiscation was approaching, which I cannot but look upon as one which conferred suddenly a greater benefit on our English society than any other event we know. Henry VIII. dissolved the monasteries, and seized into the hands of the crown the whole of their possessions, the total amount of which had become enormous. Instead of giving back all these lands to the great barons from whom they had been originally taken, Henry distributed them largely among the middle class of landed proprietors, and thus raised them as a balance to the power of the great barons, securing at the same time the safety of the crown and the tranquillity of the country. Feudalism had now entirely disappeared in England, and it had not, as in France, left a broad noxious shadow behind it.

To these different processes of formation, no doubt, we owe the difference of tone and character which distinguished French from English society after the fall of feudalism. In the earlier ages of feudalism the difference was, probably, not so apparent, but the feudal barons in England never, except in particular and individual cases, ran into the same licence and extravagance as in France. One of the influences of feudalism on society may, perhaps, still be traced. It has been remarked on a former occasion, that, under feudalism in its flourishing period, the outward forms of society were nearly uniform through all the countries which belonged to it. France was the acknowledged centre of feudalism, and was looked to as the model to the rest for its forms and institutions; and there can be no doubt that, at a distance from the centre—in England, for example—every form was considered more perfect the nearer it resembled the model. English men and English women of the feudal class sought the fashions of their furniture, of their dress, from France, and this feeling was continued long after feudalism had lost its power. We seek our fashions in France at the present day, and we no doubt did the same at the end of the fifteenth century. MM. Lacroix and Seré, in their great work, *Le Moyen Age et la Renaissance*, have given a plate of figures of this period, which they profess to have taken from English sources, and of which I give three in the accompanying cut. Though their costume can hardly be said to be uniform, yet they exhibit a general similarity in character which is evidently copied from the French : the same close-fitting bodies of the robe, and the same wide sleeves. Our next cut is taken from a painting by Holbein, on the wall of the privy chamber in the palace of Whitehall, and forms, in the original, part of a picture, representing on one side Henry VIII. and his father, Henry VII., and on the other their two queens, Jane Seymour, to whom the former was newly married at the time when this picture was painted, and Elizabeth of York. We may, therefore, consider these dresses as representing the highest perfection of female fashion in England in those reigns, and we recognize them at once as copied from the French costume of the reign of Louis XII., as represented in our two former cuts.

At this period there can be no doubt that, through a variety of circumstances, Western Europe had greatly increased in wealth and material
prosperity.   The riches of America had begun to pour in as a new element
to promote the movement.   It has been remarked that the sixteenth century
opened with a great expansion in art, which had become more and more

QUEENS OF HENRY VII. AND HENRY VIII.

secularized, and was sought eagerly by all classes of society.   The taste for
show and luxury increased and spread, and there was more display of
ornament, not only among the superior classes of society, but among the
wealthier bourgeoisie.   The richness and variety of the materials of dress
exceeded those of the previous periods, and were in much more general use.

Much of these richer materials were supplied from Italy.　We are told that

A BURGHER'S WIFE AND A TRADER'S.

the average value of silk stockings imported annually from Italy into

France amounted to no less a sum than 800,000 *écus;* and the Italians carried off the wools of Languedoc, Provence, and Dauphiné, to sell them back transformed into stuffs of the most delicate workmanship. The employment of embroidery and of cloths of gold and silver had become extravagant beyond measure, and extended to all classes of society; for, in defiance of the sumptuary laws and edicts, which were very numerous in that age, people of all ranks wore what they liked. These sumptuary edicts were nevertheless continued with vigour through the whole century, and even into the next. One of the latter of these edicts, issued by Henri IV., is rather curiously worded:—"We prohibit," he says, "all inhabitants of this kingdom to wear either gold or silver on their clothes, except prostitutes and thieves, in whom we do not take interest enough to trouble ourselves about their conduct."*

There is in the Imperial Library in Paris a very curious copy of that singular idea of the close of the Middle Ages—the "Dance of Death"— painted at the end of the fifteenth century, and picturing with great care the dress and appearance of the different classes and ranks of society at that time. From this manuscript Louandre has given two figures, which are reproduced in our cut on the last page. The one to our left is given as a *bourgeoise,* or wife of a respectable burgher, and the other as a tradeswoman (*marchande*). Their dresses are sufficiently elegant, and are evidently copied from those of the superior classes. The head-covering, or cape, is in both cases black. The bourgeoise has a pink robe, with yellow sleeves lined with red. The dress of the marchande is blue, with white sleeves, also lined with red, and she has puce-coloured petticoats underneath.

Among the populace we can hardly expect to find much change in costume, for their dresses were made individually to last during a period which would witness many changes in fashion among the superior class. The English poet Skelton, writing at the time of which we are now speaking, says of his heroine, Elynour Rummyng,—

> Her huke (*cloake*) of Lyncole grene,
> It had ben bers, I wene,
> More than fourty yere;
> And so doth it apere

---

* Nous faisons défense à tous habitants de ce royaume de porter ni or ni argent sur les habits, excepté aux filles de joie et aux filous, à qui nous ne prenons pas assez d'intérêt pour nous inquiéter de leur conduit.

For the grene bare thredes
Loke lyke sere (*dry*) wedes,
Wyddered lyke hay,
The woll worne away.
Skelton's Poetical Works, ed. Dyce, vol. i., p. 97.

And so with the cloak, in a well-known old ballad, printed in Percy's Reliques,—

My cloake it was a verry good cloake,
Itt hath been alwayes true to the weare,
But now it is not worth a groat;
I have had it four and forty yeere.

Our cut is taken from a painting of the time, now preserved in the private apartments of Windsor Castle, representing that celebrated interview

WOMEN OF THE PEOPLE.

between King Henry VIII. of England and François I. of France, in the month of June, 1520, between Guines and Ardres, which was known as the meeting of the Champ du Drap d'Or. The whole picture has been engraved by the Society of Antiquaries. I give here a few of the female figures, who are seated in the foreground, drinking. As the painting is the work of an English artist, we may no doubt consider these as English women belonging to the populace. It may be remarked that the same kind of bowls, or dishes, for drinking, are seen in a contemporary picture of the battle of Carbery Hill, where the friends of Mary, queen of Scotland, were defeated, a painting also engraved by the Society of Antiquaries.

CHAPTER XX.

THE SOCIAL MOVEMENT OF THE SIXTEENTH CENTURY IN FRANCE—THE FEMALE COSTUME.

DURING the sixteenth century the tone of society in France was gradually passing through a great change. To this change many causes had been for a long period contributing. All that remained of the Middle Ages was the spirit of pride and ostentation, of extravagant display and of costly enjoyment, already mentioned, which had been increasing during the fifteenth century. The expenses of a man of any mark in the world, and especially of those who claimed a place at court or in fashionable society, were usually much greater than his income. The extravagance of the dress of either sex, was something we can hardly now conceive; and it was said proverbially that the nobleman, and often the gentleman too, carried all his income on his back. This state of things lasted through the whole century, and into that which followed. The reader will call to mind the story of his own troubles at the beginning of the latter period told by the Maréchal de Bassompierre in his *Mémoires*. He was engaged to a ball at Court, and one article only of his dress consisted of a coat of cloth of gold, ornamented with palm-branches, and laden with pearls to the weight of at least fifty pounds. The cost of this dress was estimated at fourteen thousand écus, of which seven hundred were reckoned for the making. When he applied to his tailor, the latter required earnest-money to the amount of four thousand écus, before he would begin the work. This, too, was a very large sum of money in those days, and Bassompierre knew not how to obtain it. But in the midst of this difficulty, the Maréchal was invited to sup with the Duke d'Epernon, and after supper, as was then usual in high society, the evening was spent in gambling, and they played high. Fortune took compassion on the Maréchal, and though he possessed no more than seven hundred écus when he began,

39

before the evening was over he had increased them to five thousand. Next morning he paid the earnest money for his dress, and fortune continued to favour him during several following days; before the evening of the court ball, Bassompierre had won seventeen thousand écus, which enabled him to pay the whole of his dress, including a magnificent sword enriched with diamonds. Such was fashionable life in France early in the seventeenth century, after the recklessness of the sixteenth century had been already greatly curbed by the policy of Henri IV.

The anecdote just related depicts a state of society in which morality must have stood very low. Men of rank, fortune, and personal distinction, who after squandering away their income in extravagance, could depend upon gambling to supply their wants, would have little hesitation in supplying themselves with money in almost any other way, and we unfortunately find, in studying the social history of the time, that this was too generally the case. In fact, since the end of the fourteenth century, or in other words, since the fall of feudalism, the life of the aristocracy in France had been one simply of selfishness, and their ambition that of obtaining money for self-gratification in one form or other. Places and dignities were sought as so many means of enabling those who obtained them to share in the money of the public. The crown itself was valued by its holder chiefly for the same reason, and because it gave a power of extortion and compulsion. The first idea of a noble or of a gentleman, when he wanted money, was to borrow, but there was soon a limit to borrowing, and nearly all the representatives of the old feudalism were overwhelmed with debts. The salaries derived from public honours and places were soon wasted. Wars were attractive, because they were looked upon as equivalent to plunder, or at least they withdrew the gentleman from a life at home which led only to ruin, to one in which he lived in an equal state of excitement, and mostly at the expense of others. The soldier was almost always engaged at home or abroad. And society was not at all improved, for the time, by the exchange of the old feudal wars for civil wars, in which brother fought against brother, and son against father, although it was, no doubt, a part of the long ordeal through which society had to pass in its way to a healthier state of things. Cheating or robbing was, under a variety of forms, a legitimate manner of obtaining money, when it was wanting. It was under this state of things, that nearly all the old feudal houses perished by their own incapacity to live, or fell down gradually from their rank and position in society through their want of the means to support it.

In this state of things the character of woman suffered equally with, if not more than, that of the other sex. She was liable in a greater degree to the same temptations and to the same impulses, and gave in in a greater degree to the same extravagances. Woman, too, wanted money, and she learnt from the other sex to value money more than other things, even than virtue itself. In the court of France, in the houses of the nobility generally, and indeed almost everywhere, Womankind was not respected, nor did woman respect herself. The State, indeed, was governed by vanity, by the love of luxury and extravagance, by the eagerness for self-indulgence, and by the absence of any respect for true dignity. Any attempts at reform coming from high quarters, were generally harsh and unconciliating, and therefore not lasting. In such times, a single reformer, however high his position, unless endowed with qualities which are seldom attached to humanity, is not often successful. France entered upon the sixteenth century burdened with all the social evils of the fifteenth, and with new dangers before her. For in the midst of the ruin of the old society, religion as well as social order had become embroiled, and the Church had run herself into as much danger as the State. Troubles of another origin were coming upon the land, which also were destined to exert an important influence in the formation of modern society.

This intense and almost reckless want of money had, it is true, been met by new means of supplying it. America had made Europe acquainted with its resources of gold and diamonds, and power was beginning to change hands from the aristocracy to the great mercantile interests. The gentry sought to recover their strength by joining in commerce, which contributed further to break down the barrier between the aristocracy and what were now becoming the middle classes. These middle classes were becoming the rich classes, and were therefore rising in power, while public sentiment was of little avail for good, and society was falling into a condition in which there was, so to say, no rule, but everything seemed as though governed by impulse. Whoever raised a banner was sure to obtain followers, whatever the motive; and in the religious wars which desolated France during the latter half of this sixteenth century, the soldiers of the Huguenot armies were not all Huguenots by conviction, but only sought in their ranks a cause to fight for. Hence their triumph was itself but partial, and brought with it no great improvement in public morals. Bassompierre, spoken of above, was a Huguenot general, and the court of Henri IV. was not celebrated for morality.

If, indeed, woman's character were not high in France during the sixteenth century, the history of the times sufficiently explains the reasons.

Facts like the following show us how far the sex had been taught to throw aside all those qualities which naturally belong to it. After the conspiracy of Amboise in 1560, when the prisoners were taken out daily by dozens to be executed, we are assured that the Guises reserved the principal prisoners for the purpose, by their torments, of affording amusement to the ladies of the court after dinner, who then, with the king and his brothers, placed themselves in the windows of the castle of Amboise, in which the court was then residing, while the victims were brought into the courtyard of the palace, a few every day, and put to death in the most barbarous manner in view of the ladies. We are told further, that the chancellor, Olivier, a man with more gentleness in his character, was so horrified by the atrocities committed on this occasion, that he took to his bed, and died before the end of the month. Such were some of the qualities which seem to have prevailed more or less among Womankind in France at the commencement of the great troubles of the latter half of the sixteenth century. Among the aristocratic classes, especially among those which were naturally taken for imitation, virtue had long been at a discount, and vice reigned without any control. The character of the ladies of the latter half of the century of which I am speaking, and of many of those of the earlier half also, may be studied in the pages of Branthôme and in the Journal of Pierre de l'Estoile. We see them there displaying their immoralities almost to the open day. The civil war of 1580 was ascribed almost entirely to the maids of honour of Queen Marguerite of Navarre and the young beauties of the court, who, in their feeling of hostility against the king of France, Henri III., distributed their last favours almost indiscriminately to all who would join in the insurrection against him, to such a degree that it was popularly called "the war of the lovers." This character of licence had become so strongly imprinted on the French character, that it remained more or less attached to it until comparatively recent times. It was only in the Hôtel de Rambouillet, and among les Précieuses, that woman herself began to raise herself to oppose the evil.

In this sixteenth century in France, the whole face of social life had been changed. The old feudal castles, heavy fortresses, with few conveniences, and ill furnished, had been abandoned, and exchanged for extensive and elegant châteaux or mansions, filled with furniture and ornaments of the most expensive description. The walls within were covered with rich pictorial tapestries. Everything, in fact, told of unbounded luxury and of the love of outward display. Extravagance in expenditure was visible everywhere, but especially in the great centres of population, among the higher aristocracy, and in the superior grades in the Church, while the sentiments of the olden time and some degree of moderation were found only among the bourgeoisie of the lesser towns, and among the poor nobility of the country. The whole social system had in fact assumed quite a new aspect.

It was indeed an age of innovations and of dissatisfaction with the ages which had preceded it. In the earlier part of it, this sort of scorn for the past was embodied in the satirical caricature of Rabelais. It was under its influence that what was old was now everywhere giving place to that which was new. Even the literature of that age composed for the lower bourgeoisie and for the yeomanry and peasantry teems with reminiscences, often accompanied with regret, of the different state of things which existed when that generation was young. Among the innovations of this age may be mentioned one which appears to have originated in France. The carosse, or fashionable carriage. It evidently came into use slowly, for it appears that the carosse was still so rare in the time of François I., that the court itself only possessed two. Like the older char, it remained long open to the air, and those who occupied it were only protected by curtains. The idea of supplying it with glass is said to have originated with the Maréchal de Bassompierre in the reign of Louis XIII.

Of the various forms in which the extravagance of that age showed itself, that of dress is perhaps the most easily described; for costume becomes now a picture of the social character of the time. The fashions in dress, indeed, were never carried to greater extravagance than during this century, and, as the ordinary materials of dress itself could hardly go beyond certain limits in cost, this was increased to any extent by covering them with jewelry. This was the case with the men quite as much as with the other sex, as in the dress of the Maréchal de Bassompierre, already mentioned. The pride of rank, and of social position, was, too, we may perhaps say, greater than ever, and there seems to have been quite a morbid anxiety to place limitations on the distinctive articles of dress allowed to be worn by individuals of each different class. The sumptuary laws became far more numerous and more various during this period than at any previous time, and they were subject to so many changes that the sixteenth century might furnish quite a history of the forbidding and not forbidding of particular articles of dress to this person or another. But so much difficulty was found in enforcing any of these injunctions, that, except within the immediate range of the court, they seem to have been but imperfectly carried into effect, and many circumstances combined to throw the costume of people in France into great confusion. We learn from the registrary of the Hôtel de

Ville of Paris, that it was a complaint in 1558 that the priests dressed like laymen and the merchants like nobles, while women appeared in the dress of men, and men almost in that of women; this extravagance began to be a little sobered down when we enter upon the seventeenth century.

The pride of dress appears at this time to have been spreading widely among the bourgeoisie; and this not only formed the excuse for the multiplication of sumptuary laws, but it provoked the frequent attacks of the satirical writers of the day. Some of these furnish us with curious sketches of contemporary dress and manners. Thus, towards the beginning of the century, when, during the Italian wars, the court of France was for several years established at Lyons, and a sort of rivalry arose between that city and Paris, there appeared a short piece in verse, purporting to be an attempt by the women of Lyons to reform those of the capital, who were especially charged with pride and extravagance. We learn from this poem that the women still continued to paint—

> Vous vous fardez pour avoir plus beau taint.

The women at that time, like the men, wore low shoes, held on by a band over the instep. They are accused of imitating the Italian women in everything, of adopting strange fashions, and of indulging largely in pride and vanity, till they became by their extravagance the ruin of their husbands.

> —Pour vostre gravité
> On vous nomme de Paris les poupées,
> Painctes, fardées, de grace mancipées;
> Enveloppées de folle vanité.

The dames de Paris—for now the Parisians had taken possession of the title of dame—are made to reply in terms equally severe and sarcastic.* Another poem of about the same date bears the title of an attempt to correct the superfluity of dress among the Parisian dames, and to teach them honest government (*sur le faict de la reformation de la superfluité des habitz des dames de Paris, et comment elles se doivent honnestement gouverner*).† In this very curious production the good lady of Paris is warned against wearing a collar or necklace of gold—

> Premièrement ne porteras
> Carcans dorez ne jazerans.

She was advised to cut off the tail of her robe, and not turn it up to show,

---

* These pieces are printed by M. de Montaiglon, in his *Anciennes Poésies Françaises*, tom. viii., pp. 244, 253.　　　　　　　　　　　† Ibid., p. 290.

as an article of pride, the rich lining underneath. She is warned especially against perfumes of all kinds, though she may use on occasion lavender or souchet (the *cyperus longus* of Linnæus). Lavender had now taken the place of the older saffron, and appears to have become the favourite perfume, though we still trace the saffron as a perfume among the less refined classes of society.

> Tout le parfum contemneras,
> Car il est par trop acointant;
> Et neantmoins sentir pourras
> Lavande et souchet, dont est tant.

One or two other aromatics are alluded to. The city lady was to abhor the vertugalle, and she was only to wear slit robes in two cases—first, when she folding her washed linen; and secondly, when she was killing her pigs, two or three days before Advent:—

> Le premier est quand tu plieras
> Ta lessive, et plus le suyvant
> Sera quand les pourceaux tueras
> Deux ou trois jours d'avant l'Advent.

She was to ride on the croop of the horse behind her husband; and, when she visited the farm, she was to sit on the shaft of the waggon, beside the waggoner, with her chambermaid behind her; but she was to keep her eye upon him, to prevent his making love to the maid. The woman riding on the pillion behind her husband, or her male conductor, had now become the fashion. In the course of this little poem, we have a tolerably minute description of the dress of the Parisian dames of this period. Another piece, printed by M. de Montaiglon, and directed against the wives of the bourgeoisie, bears the title of *Les Presomptions des Femmes.* From it we learn that a simple burgher's wife would wear "rubies, and diamonds, and jewels."

> Une simple bourgeoise aura
> Rubis, diamants, et joyaux.

The position of literature had been considerably changed by the introduction of printing, and popular satire was no longer published in the baronial hall, but it was spread among the middle classes of society; and it was naturally aimed at the class which was to read it. Moreover we have, at the period to which these satires refer, fewer pictures to furnish us with examples than at the periods which either preceded or followed it. The cut we give here represents a group of nobles, and is taken from the painted glass in the windows of the church of Notre Dame de Brou, in France, which was executed in the earlier part of the sixteenth century. The dress of the lady is much more simple than we have been accustomed to see it in the fifteenth century. The next cut is taken from a picture by Jost Ammon, and is understood to represent two French ladies of the same century, but

FRENCH NOBLES, EARLY IN THE SIXTEENTH CENTURY.

somewhat later. It will be seen at once that the whole character of the costume is changed.

Among the higher classes, and among those who aped gentility, the Italian fashions chiefly influenced the dress of both sexes, which still was far from wanting in elegance. The waist was fitted to the body in front, so as to give its form to it. The sleeves were fitted tight at the wrist, and

LADIES OF THE SIXTEENTH CENTURY.

the jupe was wide and flowing. After the arrival in France of Catharine de Medicis, the most extravagant exaggerations were introduced into every part of the dress. Amongst the most remarkable of these was the wide-flowing gown, stiffly formed, called the *vertugalle*. Some of the jokers of the time pretended that the name was a mere corruption of *vertu-gardien*, *i.e.*, the protector of virtue, though they seem to have acknowledged that it did not contribute greatly to this purpose. The vertugalle—or, as we called it in England, the fardingale—appears to have been derived originally from Spain, under the name of the vasquine, or basquine. People compared the general shape of the dress at this time, with some justice, to that of an hour-glass, or of two bells joined together at the extremities. The sleeves were formed of rolls, very large at the shoulder, and diminishing as they des-

MADAME DE SAUVE.

cended to the wrist, so as to present an object anything but graceful. The head emerged from a vast ruff, or frill, supported by wires, which gave it the form of a fan. It was called a *fraise*. In the reign of Henri IV., it was made to rise behind, more than a foot above the head. People of rank only were now allowed to wear trains, or tails, to their dresses, but these were extravagantly long, and proportioned to the degree of nobility of the wearer. They were usually from five to seven yards long, and of course a maid or a page followed the wearer to lift them up. The tail of the robe of Elizabeth of Austria, when she entered Paris in 1574, was twenty yards long, and was, in fact, the longest example known. It has been

A LADY IN FULL DRESS.

remarked that all the ridiculous fashions which have been witnessed from the seventeenth century to the present day are found under other names in the costume of the ladies of the sixteenth century.

Our next cut is taken from a portrait in the Library of St. Geneviève, in Paris. The lady it represents was the daughter of Jacques de Beaune,

Baron de Semblauçay, and was placed, when very young, in the household of Catharine de Medicis. This daughter of the Baron de Semblançay yielded herself readily to all the intrigues of the licentious court of that queen; but this, in those days, in France, was no hindrance to marriage, and, about the year 1570, she married Simon, Baron de Sauve, who had been made Secretary of State in 1567. Her married life was no better than that which had preceded it, for she openly gave her husband, for rivals, all the lords of the court who pleased her, and her conduct was considered excusable, and brought her no discredit. Such was Womankind at the court of France in the sixteenth century. Her first husband died in 1617, and she married another, with whom she is said to have been less faithful than ever. Madame de Sauve was a woman of celebrity in her time. Her portrait gives us a good example of one form of the ruff, as well as of the head-dress.

During this period, the variety of women's coiffures was very great, and they were generally elegant. Sometimes they raised the hair above the head in a sort of pyramid. At others, they smoothed it down in flat bands on the forehead, and collected the locks in a tuft behind, or let them fall loose on the shoulders. Sometimes they curled them. Towards the end of the sixteenth century, hair-powder came into common use. Pierre de l'Etoile speaks in his Journal of seeing nuns walking about the streets of Paris with their hair curled and powdered.

Our cut on the last page represents a lady of the time of Henri IV. Her dress, which is black upon a white petticoat, with its sleeves, represents the general forms of that time. She has earrings and necklace of gold, and her hair is bound by a band of pearls.

The fan was looked upon as indispensable, and was often of costly materials, and richly ornamented. The form of fan seen in our picture belongs to the earlier part of the seventeenth century, and was derived from Italy. The fan of the sixteenth century was of a round form, usually composed of feathers, and had often rather a long handle. The fan given by the queen of Navarre to Marguerite of Lorraine, the queen of Henri III., was made of mother-of-pearl, covered with rich gems, and was valued at twelve hundred écus of gold. Masks were greatly in vogue during the whole of this period, but especially during the reign of Henri III., arising, no doubt, from the general licence of manners. They were commonly called *loups*. They were generally made of black velvet, lined in the inside with white satin. In the inside was a little chain, with a pearl at the end, which, when the lady had the fan upon her face, she held tight between her lips, to keep it in its place and prevent its falling.

I have said that the practice of painting was still in general use. In the seventeenth century a new fashion came in, of ornamenting the face with spots or patches, which were call *mouches*, or flies. They were considered to add so much to the beauty of those who wore them, and to make such a decided impression on the hearts of the other sex, that people gave them the

A LADY OF FASHION.

name of *assassins*. The readers of La Fontaine's Fables will remember how he makes the fly say :—

> Je rehausse d'un teint la blancheur naturelle ;
> Et la dernière main que met à sa beauté
> Une femme allant en conquête,
> C'est un ajustement des mouches emprunté.

The general costume of the ladies under Louis XIII. differed little from that of the previous reign, but under Louis XIV. it was entirely changed. The vertugalle, the stiff formal body, the ruff, the puff sleeves, had all disappeared, and the dress altogether became more free and more easy. The

shoulders and breast were left uncovered, and the great outcry of the
moralists was now against what they called the indecent exposure of the
person.   Our cut on the preceding page represents a lady of this period, and
will best exhibit the change.   Her dress, as will be seen, is covered with
ornament.   She has a necklace of pearls round her neck; a double row of
large pearls are suspended over her breast; and she has a band of pearls
over the head.

A satirical poet, somewhat later in the century, describing the freedom
of manners which then prevailed, gives a glance back on the stiffness of the
dress of the days of Catharine de Medicis and Henri IV., and tells how the

A BEDROOM PARTY, IN THE AGE OF LOUIS XIII.

wide skirt had been abolished, the ruff had been suppressed, and the great
black dress banished.   The robes of ceremony—the dress robe—in the
paintings of this age, whether in France or England, are usually black, or of
a very dark colour, which was perhaps designed partly to show off to
advantage the jewelry with which the dress was then often profusely adorned.
"Now," this poet says, " the loosest dress gives her a freedom of which our

mothers had no experience." "Girded with a great vertugalle, they were not at their ease, for the stiff collar, the clasp, the lace (*i. e.*, tight stays), and the ruff, and the high-heeled shoes, caused them thousands of troubles."

Le corps de jupe est aboli,
La collerette est supprimée;
Le grand habit noir est banni;
La robe la plus négligée
La met dans une liberté
Dont nos mères n'ont point tâté.

Ceintes d'un grand vertugadin,
Elles n'estoient pas à leur aise;
Le collet monté de Quintin,
L'agrafe, le lacet, la fraise,
Et les souliers à pont-levis,
Leur causoient mille et mille ennuys.

A French artist of the earlier half of the seventeenth century, Abraham Bosse, has left us some engravings which furnish excellent illustrations of the manners of the reign of Louis XIII. The one we give here represents the female costume of the day very distinctly. It was the custom at that time for a woman, after childbirth, to keep her own room for some time in a sort of state, and receive her friends of the female sex. A scene of this kind is here represented, taken from a print by Abraham Bosse, bearing the date of 1631.

CHAPTER XXI.

HOW ENGLISHWOMEN LOOKED IN THE DAYS OF QUEEN ELIZABETH.

IN the reign of Queen Elizabeth, the painters and engravers employed in England were mostly Flemings or Dutchmen, who made their residence here. One of the former was Lucas de Heere, a talented painter, born at Ghent in 1534, who resided a part of his life in our island, and returned to die at his native town in 1584. He is stated to have been employed in 1570 to paint a gallery for the Lord High Admiral, Edward, Earl of Lincoln, in which he was to represent in compartments the habits of different nations; and Horace Walpole, to whose *Anecdotes of Painting* we owe this information, tells us that, when he came to the Englishman, instead of representing him in a well-known costume, he painted a naked man, with cloth of different kinds lying by him, and a pair of shears in his hand, in doubt as to what form of costume he should adopt, intending it for a satire upon the fickleness of fashions for which the English were then rather celebrated. The satire, though somewhat severe, was not an original thought with Lucas de Heere. Almost thirty years before, an English physician, well-known as a popular writer of his age, Andrew Borde, published a book entitled, *The first Boke of the Introduction of Knowlege*, treating upon the different peoples of the earth and their languages, in the first of which he speaks of the "naturall disposicion of an Englyshman." The cut accompanying it represents exactly the same idea as that here ascribed to Lucas de Heere, in evidence of which I give a copy of it. It is followed by verses, the first six of which read as follows:—

I am an Englyshe man, and naked I stand here,
Musyng in my mynd what rayment I shal were;
For now I wyll were thys, and now I wyl were that;
Now I wyl were I cannot tel what.
All new fashyons be pleasaunt to me;
I wyll have them, whether I thryve or thee.

The satire conveyed in these verses was severe; but it was not applicable to Englishmen alone, for it was much the same in France, where individuals appear to have borrowed the details of their costume from whatever foreign peoples they chose, and we hear of one who would wear a *pourpoint à la Suisse*, of another who would wear a *pourpoint à l'Allemande*, a third a *pourpoint à l'Espagnole*, and so on to any extent. We seem to have derived this excessive love of variety from France, although in the earlier half of the sixteenth century, and in the reign of Elizabeth, there was a

AN ENGLISHMAN IN DISTRESS.

decided tendency in England to imitate the dress of the Spaniards, and that of the Low Countries. It is worthy of remark that, in both countries, France and England, this love of variety in finery is still spoken of as being more conspicuous in the men than in the other sex; and this has always been the case at periods of which vanity in dress formed the especial characteristic. There is something almost grotesque in the male dress of the reign of Queen Elizabeth, more so even than in that of the ladies.

If we look at an Englishwoman of that age, we see plainly that the

41

Middle Ages have passed away, with all that their dresses presented of ease, elegance, and grace. The costume of the Elizabethan ladies was stiff and very formal; the more so as they were more elevated in rank and fashion, increasing, indeed, in this respect, up to royalty itself, and they were certainly not graceful. In our cut, we have a group of ladies and gentlemen

COURTIERS OF THE REIGN OF ELIZABETH.

of Elizabeth's court, taken from a contemporary painting representing the queen's visit to Hunsdon House in 1572, which was engraved by Vertue, and published by the Royal Society of Antiquaries in the last century. The lady in front, dressed in white, is believed to represent Lady Hunsdon herself. It will be seen at a glance that there is a general resemblance in character between the garments of the two sexes; both wore the tight close vest, which was called the doublet, and which, in the character of a somewhat looser vest of the same description which was sometimes worn over the doublet, was called a jerkin, or jacket. This doublet, as will be seen, differs little in the two sexes. It descended to the girdle, and there joined, in the men, the hose, and in ladies, the farthingale. The hose represented the breeches of a later period; but at this time they were stuffed out with different materials to an enormous width, as shown to some extent in our cut, and they were made of costly materials, often purple or scarlet. These wide-stuffed hose were commonly known by the name of trunk-hose; they were usually stuffed either with wool, or hair, or often with bran. Among the stories told of these hose by the satirists of the time, is one of a fashionable gallant, who wore hose of large dimensions; a nail of the chair on which he sat tore a hole in his hose, whereby, when he rose to bow to the ladies, the bran poured out as from a mill. A cry was raised against this fashion as carrying away the supply of hair from other more useful purposes, and making it rare and expensive, even to the destruction of the tails and manes of horses; and there is an English satirical song of the reign of Elizabeth, entitled, *A lamentable complaint of the pore countrymen againste great hose, for the loss of their cattelles tails.* The hose were sometimes embroidered, and richly ornamented in other ways.

It was, as it always has been, the custom in England, perhaps a tradition of feudal times when France was considered as presenting the type of every feudal fashion, to take our fashions in dress from France. The farthingales, or vardingales, of the ladies, represented of course the French *vertugalle;* they joined the doublet at the girdle, like the hose, and were stuffed out, not with bran, but with hoops. In fact they represented the hooped petticoats of the last century, and our more modern crinolines. They appear often to have been expanded to a very great width. From the hose, in the male sex, descended the stocking, called more usually in Elizabeth's time, the nether-stocks, which also were made of rich material, and were much ornamented, and had ornamental and even jewelled garters, as was the case also with the ladies, though their stockings and garters were not like those of the men, always exposed to view. To the dress of the ladies, at this period, belongs another article of dress, the petticoat. This garment—which appears by its name to have been a *petite cote*—originally belonged to the other sex, and thus occurs not unfrequently during the fifteenth century. In the *Promptorium Parvulorum,* an English-Latin Dictionary of that period, it is explained by *tunicula,* a little tunic, and in a record of the same period, we have mention of a "petticote of lynen cloth, withoughtt slyves," so that it appears

to have been an outer garment, perhaps having some relation to the kirtle.
Its real character even during Elizabeth's reign, is not very clear, but it is
spoken of as made of silk, and as rather an expensive article of dress. A
short Scottish poem of this period, by a well-known poet, Sir Richard
Maitland of Lethington, entitled a *Satire on the Town Ladyes*, speaks of a
wylie coit or *wylecot*, richly embroidered and sewed with lace, as being under
the gown of the ladies, and above their hose and stockings, for he remarks
of them, that—

> Sumtyme thay will beir up (*raise up*) their gown,
> To schaw thair wylecot hingeand (*hanging*) down;
> And sumtyme bayth (*both*) they will upbeir,
> To schaw thair hois (*hose*) of blak or broun;
> And all for newfangilness of geir.

This "wylecote" must have been an under garment, and the modern
petticoat is no doubt to be dated from this period. "Newfangleness" was
the word now introduced to signify the rage for new fashions which had
seized upon people in general, and, as stated above, was displayed more
strongly by the male than by the female sex. I have alluded above to the
readiness with which the English especially were accused of borrowing new
fashions from all the nations around. A satirical writer, of the reign of
Elizabeth, named Samuel Rowlands, in a volume of Epigrams, printed in
1600, tells us that the doublet was borrowed from France, and the hose from
Germany. He speaks of "a most accomplished cavalier"—

> Walking the streets his humours to disclose,
> In the French doublet and the German hose;
> The muffes, cloake, Spanish hat, Toledo blade,
> Italian ruffe, a shoe right Flemish made.

Connected with the doublet I have to speak of another article in modern
dress, the boddice or stays. There can be no doubt that the practice of
bracing into a slender form the upper part of the female body by means
of laces, as in our stays, existed in the twelfth century, as we have satirical
allusions to it in the illuminations of that period, when it appears to have
been one of the "newfangled" fashions of the period, but as we have no
allusion to it afterwards, nor anything in the costume of the illuminations of manuscripts down to the sixteenth century which would lead us to
suspect it, we are inclined to suppose that it was a fashion soon laid aside;
but the form given to the body in the dress of the reign of Elizabeth
betrays at once the presence of a contrivance of this kind. In fact
they are alluded to by the popular satirical writers of the day, one of

whom, who wrote in 1596, Stephen Gosson, describes the stays of that
time as—

> These privie coats, by art made strong
> With bones, with paste, with such like ware,
> Wherby ther back and sides grow long,
> And now they harnest gallants are :
> Were they for use against the foe,
> Our dames for Amazons might go.

It is from this period, no doubt, that we derive our modern stays; but at
that time they were in use equally with both sexes.

Above the doublet came the ruff, which surrounded the neck, and which
also was common to both sexes. According to Rowlands, as quoted above,
the ruff was derived from Italy. It was often of extravagant dimensions,
and was stiffened by what appears to have been then a newly invented
article, starch. The ruff was often fringed with lace, and otherwise ornamented.

Much labour and cost, as may be supposed, were expended in dressing
and adorning the lady's head. The hair was curled and twisted into a
variety of forms, and was further bedecked with gems, and with stars,
and other ornaments of gold and silver. It was frequently dyed of the
colour which suited each person's particular taste, and the fashion now
became general of employing false hair, to increase the bulk of that which
the lady possessed of her own. Perriwigs were also introduced at this
period, and another new custom, of which we now hear for the first time,
was that of wearing ear-rings, which is said to have prevailed more among
the gentlemen, the gay gallants, than among the ladies. The latter, perhaps,
hesitated in submitting their ears to be pierced. Above the head-dress was
worn a hat, which varied very much in shape, but generally presented little
elegance of form. Beaver hats were now introduced, but they appear to
have been rather rare and expensive. The introduction of two other articles
belonging to the toilette, may be ascribed to this period, and must not be
forgotten. The first was the fan. The fan of the Elizabethan age was
usually made of feathers, like the fans still in use in the east, from whence it
was probably derived. The handle was often very richly ornamented, and
set with precious stones, and even with diamonds. As, according to a
custom also derived from France, the lady who made any claim to dress in
fashion was never without her fan, it was usually suspended to the girdle by
a chain. A satirist of the day, Stephen Gosson, already quoted, approves of
the fan if employed in the right time of the year, when it was useful for
driving away flies, and for cooling the skin.

But seeing they are still in hand,
   In house, in field, in church, in street;
In summer, winter, water, land,
   In cold, in heat, in dry, in weet;—
I judge they are for wives such tools
As babies are in plays for fools.

Another article usually carried by the fine lady was the mask, a fashion which was also imported from France. Ben Jonson calls them "French masks." The English mask of the Elizabethan age only covered the upper part of the face.

These details of the costume of our English ladies of the reign of Elizabeth will perhaps be better understood by the accompanying figures. The first represents Queen Elizabeth herself in her state dress. Her doublet, as will be seen, is buttoned down the breast to the waist, where it joins the spreading farthingale. Her hair is here curled, and surmounted by the crown. The other is understood to represent the Countess of Derby, and is taken from a photograph of the original portrait in the South Kensington Museum. Her ladyship's ruffe is plainer in character than that of the queen, and her hair is surmounted by a small hat, much in the style of those worn by ladies of the present day.

QUEEN ELIZABETH.

Our coloured plate represents a lady of the Lytton family of the Elizabethan age, Anne, wife of Sir Rowland Lytton of Knebworth. The lady Anne Lytton, was a daughter of Oliver, Lord St. John of Bletso, and was the fifth in descent from Margaret Beaufort, duchess of Somerset, and may be considered as representing in an especial degree the English country aristocracy of the reign of Elizabeth. Our plate is copied, by Lord Lytton's permission, from the

La Pinchera by Marcus Gheeraerts

original contemporary portrait still preserved at Knebworth. Her dress resembles closely, even to the little hat, that of the countess of Derby given below.

Since the Middle Ages had expired, a new agent of progress had come into the world. This was the art of printing. The printing-press which William Caxton set up in the Almonry of Westminster Abbey forms the true division between the old world and the new in our island. Not that the books which followed for some years after this invention was brought in had any great social interest; but, gradually the new voice made itself heard, and there can be no doubt that at the time of which we are now speaking, the press had already become the great moving power in social and political progress. In our country, the example of our neighbours, and especially of France, had brought in a great amount of pride, and extravagance, and other social evils, which threatened society itself, but there was rising up against this a very decided and powerful resistance, in which became united a variety of principles and sentiments which finally made themselves heard under the name of Puritanism. Their weapon was the press, and

THE COUNTESS OF DERBY.

through it they showed themselves first in the form of satire, as well as of remonstrance and declamation. The number of satirists upon contemporary manners and feelings during the Elizabethan age, when they first became active, is quite remarkable. I have already quoted more than one, but I will now introduce the most remarkable of them all, for the manner in which he takes up and criticises the dress of his fair countrywomen. Philip Stubbes was a violent and fearless Puritan; he appears to have been a Londoner, but he was apparently educated in Cambridge, and his name is connected with that and the sister university. Stubbes, like many of the popular reformers of his times, was a fierce, but often rather a coarse, satirist. Among his books, one especially, entitled *The Anatomie of Abuses,* and published in 1585, attacks the contemporary fashions in dress, and throws great light upon many of its details. He begins by repeating against our countrymen the same accusation of an inordinate love of new fashions, which, as we have seen at the beginning of the present chapter, had been made more than half a century before. "Hereby," he says, "it appeareth that no people in the world are so curious in new fangles as they bee." After reviewing with considerable severity the failings of the gentlemen in this respect, Stubbes proceeds to the ladies, and quarrels first with their faces. "The women," he says, "many of them, use to colour their faces with certaine oyles, liquors, unguentes, and waters made to that end, whereby they thinke their beautie is greatly decored;" which painted faces, he assures us, are the devil's nets to entangle poor souls. "Then followeth the trimming and tricking of their heades, in laying out their haire to the shewe, which of force must be curled, frisled, and crisped, laid out (a world to see), on wreathes and borders, from one eare to another. And least it should fall down, it is underpropped with forks, wiers, and I cannot tell what, like grim sterne monsters, rather than chaste Christian matrones. Then on the edges of their boulstered hair (for it standeth crested rounde about their frontiers, and hanging over their faces like *pendices* or tailes, with glasse windowes on every side), there is laid great wreaths of golde and silver, curiously wrought and cunningly applied to the temples of their heades. And for fear of lacking anythinge to set forthe their pride withall, at their haire, thus wreathed and creasted, are hanged bugles (I dare not say bables), ouches, ringes, gold, silver, glasses, and suche other childishe gewgawes besides." Moreover, "if curling and laying out of their owne naturall haire were all, it were the less matter; but thei are not simplie content with their owne haire, but buye other haire, either of horses, mares, or any other straunge beasts, dyeing it of what colour they list themselves. And if there be any poore woman that hath faire haire, these nice dames will not rest till they have bought it. Or if any children have faire haire, they will entice them into a secret place, and for a penie or two they will cut of their haire; as I heard that one did of late, who, meeting a little childe with very faire haire, inveigled her into a house, promised her a penie, and so cutte off her haire. And this they were in the same order, as you have heard, as though it were their own naturall growing." And then, not content with this, "on toppes of these stately turrets (I meane their goodly heades), stand their other capitall ornaments, as French hood, hatte, caype, kercher, and such like, whereof some be of velvet, some of taffatie, some (but few) of wooll, some of this fashion, some of that, and some of this colour, some of that, according to the variable phantasies of their serpentine mindes. And to such excesse it is growne, as every artificer's wife (almost) will not sticke to goe in her hat of velvet every day, every merchant's wife and meane gentlewoman in her French hood, and every poore cottager's daughter in her taffatie hat, or els of wooll at least, well lined with silke, velvet, or taffatie; but howe they come by this (so they have it) they care not." "They have also other ornamentes besides these to furnishe forthe their ingeniouse heades, which they call (as I remember) cawles, made netwise to the ende, as I thinke, that the clothe of golde, clothe of silver, or els tinsel, may the better appeare, and shew itselfe in the bravest manner; so that a man that seeth them (their heades glisten and shine in such sorte) would thinke them to have golde heades. And some weare lattice cappes with three hornes, three corners, I should say like the forked cappes of popishe priestes, with their perriwinkles, chitterlings, and the like apishe toyes of infinite varietie." And there was something even still worse than all this: "Another sort of dissolute minions and wanton simpronians (for I can terme them no better), are so farre bewitched as they are not ashamed to make holes in their eares, whereat they hang ringes, and other jewels of gold and precious stones. But what this signifieth in them, I will holde my peace, for the thing itself speaketh sufficiently."

The ruffs next fall under the censure of worthy Philip Stubbes, and with the new "liquor" named starch he is especially offended. "The women there use great ruffes and neckerchers, of holland, laune, camericke, and such clothe, as the greatest thread shall not be so big as the least haire that is; and lest they should fall downe, they are smeared and starched with the devil's liquor—I mean starche; after that dried with great diligence, streaked, patted, and rubbed very nicely, and so applied to their goodly necks, and withal underpropped with supportasses, the stately arches of pride. Beyond all this, they have a further fetche, nothing inferior to the rest, as, namely, three or foure degrees of minor ruffes, placed *gradatim*, one beneath another, and all under the mayster devil-ruffe; the skirtes then of these great ruffes are long and wide, every way pleated, and crested full curiously, God wot. Then, last of all, they are either clogged with gold, silver, or silk lace of stately price, wrought all over with needle-worke, or

42

speckeled and sparkeled here and there with the sunne, the mone, the starres, and many other antiques strange to beholde. Some are wrought with open worke down to the midst of the ruffe and further; some with close worke, some with purled lace so cloied, and other gewgawes so pestered, as the ruffe is the least parte of itself. Sometimes they are pinned upp to their eares, and sometimes they are suffered to hange over theyr shoulders, like windmill sailes fluttering in the winde. And thus every one pleaseth her selfe in her foolish devices."

Next come the gowns, or, in other words, the farthingales. "Their gownes," Stubbes tells us, "be no less famous than the rest, for some are of silke, some of velvet, some of grograine, some of taffatie, some of scarlet, and some of fine clothe of x., xx., or xl. shillinges of a yarde. But if the whole gowne be not silke or velvet, then the same shall be layed with lace, two or three fingers broade, all over the gowne, or els the most parte; or if not so (as lace is not fine enough sometimes), then it must be garded with great gardes of velvet, every gard fower or sixe fingers broad at the least, and edged with costly lace; and as these gownes be of divers and sondry colours, so are they of divers fashions, chaunging with the moone—for some be of the new fashion, some of the olde, some of thys fashion, and some of that, some with sleeves hanging down to their skirtes, trailing on the ground, and cast over their shoulders like cowe tailes. Some have sleeves much shorter, cut up the arme, and poincted with silke ribbons very gallantly tied with true-love knottes (for so they call them). Some have capes reachyng down to the middest of their backes, faced with velvet, or els with some fine-wrought silke taffatie, at the least, and fringed about very bravely; and (to shut up all in a worde) some are pleated and rinsled downe the backe wonderfully, with more knackes than I can declare. Then have they petticoates of the beste clothe that can be bought, and of the fayrest dye that can be made. And sometimes they are not of clothe neither, that is thought to base, but of scarlet, grograine, taffatie, silke, and such like, fringed about the skirtes with silke fringe, of chaungeable colour. But whiche is more vayne, of whatsoever their petticoates be, yet must they have kirtles (for so they call them), either of silke, velvette, grograine, taffatie, sassen, or scarlet, bordered with gardes, lace, fringe, and I cannot tell what besides; so that, when they have all these goodly robes upon them, women seeme to be the smallest part of themselves."

Lastly, let us look to their stockings and shoes. We know that in Elizabeth's reign came into fashion high-heeled shoes, and shoes over which the wearers slipped sometimes what on that account were called slippers, or pantouffles. "Their netherbockes and stockings," Stubbes continues, "in like manner, are either of silk, jeansey, worsted, crewell, or, at least, of as fine yearne, thread, or clothe, as is possible to be hadde; yea, they are not ashamed to weare hose of all kinde of chaungeable colours, as green, red, white, russet, tawny, and els what. . . . . Then these delicate hosen must be cunningly knit, and curiously indented in every point with quirkes, clockes, open seame, and every thing els accordingly—whereto they have cooked shoes, pinsnets, pantoffles, and slippers; some of blacke velvet, some of white, some of Spanishe leather, and some of Englishe, stitched with silke, and embrodered with golde and silver all over the foot, with other gewgawes innumerable; all which if I should endeavour myself to expresse, I might with like facilitie number the sands of the sea, the starres in the skie, or the grasse upon the earth, so infinite and innumerable be their abuses." So far Master Philip Stubbes.

CHAPTER XXII.

CONTINUATION OF THE ELIZABETHAN AGE TO THAT OF CHARLES I.

THE social history of the reign of James I. was but a continuation of that of the Elizabethan period—we might say Elizabethan debased, in most senses of the word. The love of vanity and display which characterized the former remained undiminished; but the highmindedness, the feelings of honour and probity, the respect for the higher qualities of Womankind, were very much diminished under the influence of the rather loose morality of the Scottish court. Scandals like that of the Earl of Somerset and the Countess of Essex, in which Womankind made no respectable figure, were too characteristic of James's reign. But it is the object of the present chapter to trace outward forms, rather than the moral sentiments of the age.

Among the new fashions brought in from France was the *carosse*, or *carriage*, which was called in our English a *carroch*, or a *coach*. We have seen in a former chapter examples of the ponderous waggon-shaped carriages, drawn by a team of lumbering horses, which were allotted to the ladies during the Middle Ages, and were still in use till late in the fifteenth century. New forms brought in new names, and the ladies were no longer carried, as hitherto fore, in cars or chars, but in *coaches* and *carroches*. Nares, I know not on what authority, states that coaches are said to have been first brought into England in 1564, by William Boonen, a Dutchman, who became coachman to Queen Elizabeth. The *Nomenclator* (Junius, by Higins) interprets the Latin *pilentum* by "a stately waggon for ladies and gentlewomen : a coch." Thus we see the idea of the word waggon still lingering in men's minds. The *Nomenclator* was printed in 1585, and, as the name does not occur in that book, we are justified in believing that the carroche was not known in England at that time. Both, as well as the names, *coche* and *carrosse* in French, *coccio* and *carróccia*, or *carrozza*, in Italian, were, no doubt, derived from Italy through France. Cotgrave, in 1632, explains *carosse* as "caroach, or great coach;" and Ben Jonson, as quoted by Nares, speaks of "the *great caroch*," with "six horses, and the two coachmen." The Italian word is no doubt derived from *carro*, a car or char, reminding us again of the bulky ladies' carriage of the Middle Ages. It was doubtless larger than the coach, and John Cooke, in his play of *Green's Tu Quoque*, printed in 1614, speaks of the coach as being then considered more appropriate to the country, and the carroche for London.

> Nay, for a need, out of his easy nature,
> May'st draw him to the keeping of a *coach*
> For country, and *carroch* for London.

In a contemporary painting, of which an engraving was made in the last century by Vertue, Queen Elizabeth is represented in her state carriage

A LADIES' CARRIAGE IN ELIZABETH'S TIME.

in front of Nonsuch House in Surrey, and among her crowd of attendants is another carriage, of much less pretentious character, filled with ladies. The latter is represented in our cut. As at the time it was drawn the caroche appears not yet to have come into fashion, and as it has only two horses— not six, like Ben Jonson's "great caroch"—we may probably consider this as a coach of the Elizabethan period. The name of *coach* has lasted to our own times; the carroche appears to have gone out of fashion in the course of a few years, and we hear no more of it. But the satirists of the reign of James I. complain of the extravagance displayed by the ladies in their coaches and carroches.

Extravagance in every object of luxury had, indeed, been increasing since the reign of Henry VIII., and only experienced a check on the overthrow of royalty itself. This was especially shown in the great increase of domestic furniture, both in quantity and in its richness and value. Pageantry, and tilts, and tournaments, the last empty shadows of feudalism, were also carried on with greater extravagance and display than ever, though they began to decline rapidly during the reign of James. With these were held up all the forms at least, if not much of the real spirit, of the ancient chivalry. In the tragedy of *Gorboduc*, written in the reign of Elizabeth, a "noble prince" is reminded how often, in these tournaments, he had been seen "mounted on his fierce and trampling steede"—

> Shining in armour, bright before the tilte,
> And with thy mistress' sleeve tyed on thy helme,
> There charge thy staffe, to please thy ladie's eye,
> That bow'd the headpiece of thy friendly foe.

The tournaments always ended in banquets and dancing, and pageantry of all kinds, which involved an extravagant expenditure of money. It was the old practice, which we have already seen carried on to such a fatal extent on the continent, of the princes and nobles reducing themselves to poverty by their mad passion for display. It was in one of these tournaments that James met with his favourite, Robert Carr, afterwards Earl of Somerset.

During the reign of Queen Elizabeth the fashions in dress went through continual changes; in fact, they were almost always on the change, and two dresses of the same date often bore little resemblance to each other. At one time the extravagance of the farthingale costume seemed to be passing away; but towards the end of Elizabeth's reign farthingale and hose became more prominent than ever, and they were continued, with hardly any change, into the reign of James I. The extravagance in dress of this reign was often made a subject of satire by contemporary writers. The following description of the labours of dressing a fine woman, though it has been given more than once by writers on this subject, will bear repeating; it is taken from a play entitled *Lingua*, printed in 1607, and it may be premised that half-a-dozen maids are employed in the process. "There is such a doing," we are told, "with their looking-glasses, pinning, unpinning, setting, unsetting, formings, and conformings; painting blue veins and bloomy cheeks; such a stir with sticks, and combs, cascanets, dressings, purls, falls, squares, busks, boddices, scarfs, necklaces, carcanets, rabatoes, tires, fanns, palisadoes, puffs, ruffs, cuffs, muffs, pusles, fusles, partlets, frislets, bandlets, fillets, croslets, pendulets, annulets, amulets, bracelets, and so many lets, that yet she's scarce dressed to the girdle; and now there is such calling for fardingales, kirtles, busk-points, shoe-ties, etc., that seven pedlars' shops, nay, all Stourbridge fair, will scarcely furnish her. A ship is sooner rigged by far than a gentlewoman made ready." The joke about the *lets* was not new. John Heywood, at the beginning of Elizabeth's

THE EARL AND COUNTESS OF SOMERSET.

reign, in an interlude entitled *The Four P's,* two of the P's being a pedlar and a pardoner, makes the latter ask why—

> Women, after their uprising,
> Bee so long in their appareling?

To which the pedlar replies—

> Forsooth, women have many lets,
> And they be masked in many nets,
> As frontlets, fillets, partlets, and bracelets,
> And then their bonets, and their poynets.

It would appear that between this time and the beginning of the reign of James I., the number of lets or hindrances had considerably increased.

The costume of a fine gentleman and lady of the reign of our first king of the house of Stuart is well displayed in the pictures, copied in our cut from a print of the time, of the too notorious characters, the Earl and Countess of Somerset. The lady wears a cap of rich lace, of the fashion well known as a favourite with Mary Stuart, ornamented by a valuable jewel placed in the middle of the forehead. Two rows of necklaces surround her neck, one with pendents. Her ruff, which is of point lace, differs from those in the preceding reign in not being supported by props, but stiffened with starch. The countess's farthingale is of enormous size, exceeding in this and its ungraceful stiffness the same article of dress as it was worn in the days of Elizabeth. A peculiarity of this dress, too, is presented in the long pendents attached to the sleeves. The earl's doublet, it will be remarked, is equally tight-laced with that of his lady, and his richly-embroidered trunk-hose are quite as conspicuous as those of the preceding reign. Two other articles of the male dress are especially characteristic of the period: the garters, which presents the form of a sash tied in a bow, and the large roses on the shoes. Ben Jonson, in his comedy, *The Devil is an Ass*, speaks of " Garters and roses, fourscore pound a pair." Roland, one of the writers of satirical verse of that time, calls the laced doublet a "monkey-waiste." The dressing of the lady's head was, during all this period, a very long and laborious process, and in the reign of James, as in that of Elizabeth, the use of false hair, curling it, and painting the face, were largely indulged in. The dramatist Massinger, in his *City Madam*, speaking of the change which took place in the city dame after her husband was knighted, says:—

> The reverend hood cast off, your borrow'd hair
> Powdered and curled, was by your dresser's art
> Form'd like a coronet, haug'd with diamonds
> And richest orient pearls.

The principal characteristics of the costume I have been describing did not outlive the reign of James. In that of his son and successor there were no more farthingales, trunk-hose, laced doublets, or ruffs. The laced doublet or stays, was retained only by the fair sex, and the farthingale made its reappearance at times under such names as hoop-petticoats in the last century, and crinolines in our own time. The two accompanying figures are selected from Hollar's collection of pictures of Englishwomen, as they dressed and looked in the year 1645, entitled *Ornatus Muliebris Anglicanus*, and may be considered as fair examples of the ladies of the reign of Charles

GENTLEWOMAN OF THE REIGN OF
CHARLES I.

LADY OF QUALITY IN THE REIGN OF
CHARLES I.

I. The first represents an ordinary gentlewoman, the lady of one of those old manor-houses which are still scattered over many parts of our island ; the second is a lady of quality of the same date. We are surprised at the contrast offered by these figures to those we have been describing in the reigns of Elizabeth and James I., and especially at the character of plainness seen in that of the gentlewoman. This plainness, or we may say soberness, was general during the period at which we are now arrived, as may be seen in the numerous engravings by Hollar. The hair of the second lady is combed back over the forehead, and is allowed to flow freely in curls at the sides. The ruff and the farthingale have entirely disappeared, and the doublet only, or body, of the Elizabethan dress, less tightly laced, remains.

One custom of the Elizabethan period is retained by both these figures: that of carrying a fan of feathers, which in both cases appears to be hung to the waist. Masks, too, still continued to be worn by women of fashion, though perhaps not quite so generally as in the Elizabethan period. They covered the upper half of the face, leaving the mouth free. They continued in use down to the last century, as did also very generally, among women of fashion, the custom of painting the face. But at the close of Charles's reign, just on the eve of the Commonwealth, the ladies adopted a still more ridiculous fashion, that of covering the face with patches or spots. It, also, as we have seen, was borrowed from France. A popular satirist of the year 1650 tells us that "Our ladies have lately entertained a vaine custom of spotting their faces, after the affectation of a mole, to set off their beauty, such as Venus had." But they were not content with this simple molecular form, for the patches were cut into suns, and moons, and stars, and a variety of other shapes. One lady is represented with a patch on her forehead representing a coach and four horses. But great periods of transition, as this was, are usually marked by ridiculous excess in outward fashions. Such was the case in the beginning of feudalism, and so it was when feudalism passed into another state of things. So it was, too, in the great revolution in France at the close of the last century. Absurd, stiff, and exaggerated as the costume of the sixteenth century—that is, the period which followed the breaking-up and extinction of feudalism—may appear to us, it is in it that we shall find all the elements of the various forms of modern dress.

I have already pointed out how, during these periods of change and revolution, dress is one of the most important landmarks of the course of social history, a faithful picture of the age in which it appeared. The contrast just remarked between the costume of the ladies of the reign of Charles I. and that of his predecessor, marks, no doubt, a similar change in social character and sentiments, the result of a sudden reaction. This dress is the costume immortalized in the pictures of Vandyke. It no doubt originated in Charles's reign, but, as will be seen by comparison with examples of the costume in France at the same period, it also was derived from France. During the earlier part of the reign of Charles I., the taste in dress appears to have been very unsettled, and to have been never long fixed in one direction. It was a period of transition on a small scale. A dramatic pastoral, entitled *Rhodon and Iris*, printed in 1631, and quoted in the writers on the history of costume, describes very curiously this character of uncertainty. This rhymester tells us of the fashionable lady of the period:—

> But in her tyres so new-fangled is she,
> That which doth with her humour now agree,
> To-morrow she dislikes.

At one moment, he tells us, she insists upon the neatness of a loose body; ere an hour be gone, she prefers a strait gown as more graceful. Now she calls for a "boisterous" farthingale; she changes, and will have her garments fall to her hips. Sometimes she praises a long wide sleeve, and at others the contrary. Similarly with the "pavement-sweeping" train, which sometimes she adopts, while at other times she goes to the contrary extreme.

> Now she commends a shallow bande, so small
> That it may seem scarce any bande at all;
> But soon to a new fancy doth she reele,
> And calls for one as big as a coach-wheele.

Thus, sometimes she appears with a coronet on her head, at others a waving plume; sometimes in a hat, and sometimes dressed in her hair; and exhibits, within a short period, a continual transition from one style of costume to another.

This uncertainty had all disappeared at the date of the engraving given above, which had become the permanent type of elegant and fashionable costume. There was, however, at the same time, in progress beneath this a more violent and still more powerful reaction. This was the spirit called Puritanism, a spirit which had been long breeding, and the triumph of which had been hastened by the extravagance and vanity with which it was placed in antagonism. The Puritans, or Commonwealth men, prided themselves chiefly on the plainness and modesty of their apparel, in the midst of which the women only retained a small number of the articles of the old dress, such as the high-crowned hat, the hood, etc. Under the Protectorate, this harshness of character was becoming gradually softened down.

It was hardly consistent with human nature, that a state of constraint like that introduced and enforced by the Puritans could last long. The change which followed was sudden and decisive. With the restoration of the family of the Stuarts, in the person of Charles II., came a new influx of French manners and French sentiments, in which Womankind shone forth with new brilliancy. There had been no great interruption in the progress of fashion in France, as in England, and people seemed to come back suddenly to the costume which they had abandoned during the Commonwealth, but with far less of elegance and good taste. This was especially the case at the beginning of the reign, when the ladies seem still to have felt some difficulty in shaking off the rigidity of the previous period, and their costume presents a certain degree of stiffness.

In the latter part of the reign of Charles II., the costume of the ladies displayed a far greater amount of ease and elegance than at any other period since the days of Charles I. The wild and extravagant licence of the earlier years of this reign was beginning to subside, and the character of the nation was itself going through a change. With the final expulsion of the Stuarts everything was altered, and at the close of the century the ladies present themselves to our view in dresses as awkward and stiff as those of the days of Elizabeth. We now come successively upon the days of the lofty commodes of the ladies' head-dresses of the reign of William and Mary, the hoop-petticoats of that of George I., and the various extravagances of costume of the latter half of the last century. But enough has been said to show how, during these later periods, the changes in the costume of the female sex continue to mark, with sufficient distinctness, the contemporary variations in the character of society and in the national sentiment. But gradually this effect becomes less and less sensible, and the changes in fashion become more frequent, and more constantly the result of caprice. During the Middle Ages and the feudal period, as we have seen, any decided changes of this description occurred at sufficiently long intervals; they were gradual, and do not strike us as possessing any general historical meaning. In modern times, changes in fashion have become matters of course, occurring yearly, and even more than yearly, and they no longer possess any significance whatever.

THE END.

P. BENTLEY AND CO., PRINTERS, SHOE LANE, FLEET STREET, LONDON.

www.ingramcontent.com/pod-product-compliance
Lightning Source LLC
Chambersburg PA
CBHW030858270326
41929CB00008B/473